Thomas Erskine May

The Constitutional History of England

Vol. 3

Thomas Erskine May

The Constitutional History of England
Vol. 3

ISBN/EAN: 9783337338138

Printed in Europe, USA, Canada, Australia, Japan

Cover: Foto ©ninafisch / pixelio.de

More available books at **www.hansebooks.com**

THE

CONSTITUTIONAL HISTORY

OF ENGLAND

SINCE THE ACCESSION OF GEORGE THE THIRD

1760–1860

BY

SIR THOMAS ERSKINE MAY, K.C.B. D.C.L.

WITH A NEW SUPPLEMENTARY CHAPTER, 1861–71

Fifth Edition

IN THREE VOLUMES
VOL. III.

LONDON
LONGMANS, GREEN, AND CO.
1875

All rights reserved

CONTENTS

OF

THE THIRD VOLUME.

CHAPTER XI.

LIBERTY OF THE SUBJECT.

	PAGE
Liberty of the subject the earliest of political rights	1
General warrants, 1763	2
Arrest of Wilkes and the printers	3
Actions brought by them	4
Search-warrant for papers: case of Entinck v. Carrington	7
General warrants condemned by the courts, and in Parliament	9
Early cases of the suspension of the Habeas Corpus Act	10
Habeas Corpus Act suspended, 1794	12
Act of Indemnity, 1801	15
Habeas Corpus Act suspended, 1817	16
Bill of Indemnity	17
Suspension of the Habeas Corpus Act in Ireland	19
Impressment for the army	20
Impressment for the navy	21
Revenue laws	25
Imprisonment of Crown debtors	ib.
Imprisonment for contempt of court	26
Arrest on mesne process	29
Imprisonment for debt	31
Relief to insolvent debtors	33
Slavery in England: the Negro case, 1771	35
Negroes in Scotland	37

	PAGE
Slavery of colliers and salters in Scotland	38
Abolition of colonial slavery	39
Employment of spies and informers	ib.
Relations of the executive with informers	42
Opening letters at the Post-office	44
Petition of Mazzini and others, 1844	46
Protection of foreigners in England	49
Alien Acts	50
The Naturalisation Act, 1844	53
Right of asylum never impaired	54
Napoleon's demands refused, 1802	ib.
Principles on which aliens are protected	56
The Orsini conspiracy, 1858	57
The Conspiracy to Murder Bill	58
Extradition treaties	59

CHAPTER XII.

THE CHURCH AND RELIGIOUS LIBERTY.

Relations of the Church to political history	60
The Reformation	61
Toleration formerly unknown	62
Civil disabilities imposed by Elizabeth	63
Doctrinal moderation of the Reformation	64
Rigorous enforcement of conformity	65
Close relations of the Reformed Church with the State	67
The Reformation in Scotland	68
The Reformation in Ireland	70
The Church policy of James I.	71
The Church and religion under Charles I. and the Commonwealth	73
Persecution of Nonconformists under Charles II.	75
The Catholics also repressed	77
The Toleration Act of William III.	78
Catholics under William III.	79
The Church policy of Anne and Geo. I. and II.	81
State of the Church and religion on the accession of Geo. III.	82
Influence of Wesley and Whitefield	85
Relaxation of the penal code commenced	88
General character of the penal code	89

	PAGE
Subscription to the Thirty-nine Articles	91
Relief granted to dissenting ministers and schoolmasters, 1779	93
Prevalent opinions concerning Catholics	94
The Catholic Relief Act of 1778	96
The Protestant riots	97
Motions for the repeal of the Corporation and Test Acts, 1787–1790	100
The Catholic Relief Bill, 1791	106
Effect of the Test Act in Scotland	108
Restraints on Scotch Episcopalians repealed	ib.
Mr. Fox's bill for repeal of laws affecting Unitarians, 1792	109
Relief granted to the Irish Catholics, 1792–93	110
And to the Scotch Catholics	111
Claims of relief to Quakers	112
Union with Ireland in connection with Catholic disabilities	115
Concessions forbidden by Geo. III.	118
The Catholic question in abeyance	119
Motions on the Catholic claims in 1805	120
The Whig ministry of 1806 and the Catholic question	124
The Army and Navy Service Bill	126
Anti-Catholic sentiments of the Portland ministry	129
Catholic agitation, 1808–11	130

CHAPTER XIII.

THE CHURCH AND RELIGIOUS LIBERTY, CONTINUED.

The regency in connection with religious liberty	133
Freedom of worship to Catholic soldiers	134
Dissenters relieved from oaths imposed by the Toleration Act	135
The Catholic question in 1812	136
And in 1813	140
Relief of Catholic officers in army and navy, 1813 and 1817	143
Catholic claims, 1815–22	144
Roman Catholic Peers Bill, 1822	147
Position of the Catholic question in 1823	149
Bills for amendment of the marriage laws affecting Roman Catholics and dissenters	151
Agitation in Ireland, 1823–25	154
The Irish franchise, 1825	155
The Wellington ministry	156

viii   *Contents of the Third Volume.*

	PAGE
Repeal of the Corporation and Test Acts, 1828	157
The Catholic claims in 1828	161
The Clare election	163
Necessity of Catholic relief acknowledged by the ministry	164
The king consents to the measure	166
Mr. Peel loses his seat at Oxford	168
The Catholic Relief Act, 1829	ib.
Elective franchise in Ireland	172
Mr. O'Connell and the Clare election	174
Catholic emancipation too long deferred	175
Quakers and others admitted to the Commons on affirmation	177
Jewish disabilities	178
Mr. Grant's motions for relief to the Jews	179
Jews admitted to corporations	182
Baron L. N. de Rothschild returned for London	183
Claims to be sworn	ib.
Case of Mr. Alderman Salomons	184
Attempt to admit Jews by a declaration, 1857	185
The Jewish Relief Act, 1858	186

CHAPTER XIV.

THE CHURCH AND RELIGIOUS LIBERTY, CONTINUED.

Marriage laws affecting Roman Catholics and dissenters	188
Dissenters' Marriage Bills, 1834-35	190
Register of births, marriages, and deaths	192
Dissenters' Marriage Act, 1836	ib.
Dissenters' burials	193
Admission of dissenters to universities	195
Dissenters' Chapels Act	199
Final repeal of penalties on religious worship	200
The law of church rates	201
Earlier schemes for settling the church-rate question	203
The first Braintree case	205
The second Braintree case	ib.
Bills for the abolition of church rates, and present position of the question	207
State of the Church of England towards the latter part of the last century	209
Effect of sudden increase to population	211

Contents of the Third Volume.

	PAGE
Causes adverse to the clergy in presence of dissent	212
The regeneration of the Church	214
Church building and extension	215
Ecclesiastical revenues	216
Tithe commutation in England	218
Progress of dissent	222
Statistics of places of worship	223
Relations of the Church to dissent	224
And to Parliament	226
The Papal aggression, 1850	227
The Ecclesiastical Titles Bill, 1851	232
Schisms in the Church of England	235
The patronage question	236
The Veto Act, 1834	240
The Auchterarder and Strathbogie cases	242
The General Assembly address the Queen	248
And petition Parliament	250
The secession	251
The Free Church of Scotland	252
The Patronage Act, 1843	253
Religious disunion in Scotland	254
The Church in Ireland	255
Resistance to payment of tithes	256
The Church Temporalities (Ireland) Act, 1833	260
The appropriation question	261
The Irish Church commission	263
Sir Robert Peel's ministry overthrown on the appropriation question, 1835	266
Revenues and statistics of the Irish Church	268
Abandonment of the appropriation question	ib.
Commutation of tithes in Ireland	269
National education in Ireland	270
Maynooth College	ib.
The Queen's Colleges	273

CHAPTER XV.

LOCAL GOVERNMENT.

	PAGE
Local government the basis of constitutional freedom	275
The parish and the vestry	276
History of English corporations	278
Loss of popular rights	279
Abuses of close corporations	280
Monopoly of electoral rights	282
The Municipal Corporations Act, 1835	283
Corporation of the City of London	286
Reform of corporate abuses in Scotland	287
Corporations in Ireland	290
Their abuses: total exclusion of Catholics	291
The Corporations (Ireland) Bills, 1835–39	292
The Irish Corporations Act, 1840	295
Local Improvement and Police Acts	296
Courts of Quarter Sessions	297
Distinctive character of counties and towns	298

CHAPTER XVI.

IRELAND BEFORE THE UNION.

Progress of liberty in Ireland	299
The Irish Parliament before the Union	ib.
The executive government	302
Protestant ascendency	303
Subordination of the Irish Parliament to the Government and Parliament of England	304
Commercial restrictions	305
New era opened under George III.	306
The Irish Parliament asserts its independence	307
Condition of the people	309
Partial removal of commercial restrictions, 1778–79	310
The rise of the volunteers	311
They demand legislative independence, 1780	313
The convention of Dungannon	314
Legislative and judicial independence granted, 1782	316
Difficulties of Irish independence	317

Contents of the Third Volume. xi

	PAGE
Agitation for Parliamentary Reform	319
Mr. Pitt's commercial measures, 1785	320
Liberal measures of 1792-93	322
The United Irishmen, 1791	ib.
Feuds between Protestants and Catholics	324
The rebellion of 1798	325
The Union concerted	327
Means by which it was accomplished	330
Results of the Union	333
And of the Catholic Relief Act and Parliamentary Reform	335
Freedom and equality of Ireland	ib.

CHAPTER XVII.

BRITISH COLONIES AND DEPENDENCIES.

The rights and liberties of English colonists	338
Ordinary form of colonial constitutions	339
Supremacy of England over the colonies	340
Commercial restrictions imposed by England	341
Arguments on taxation of colonies for imperial purposes	343
The American Stamp Act, 1765	347
Mr. Townshend's colonial taxes, 1767	350
Repealed, except the tea duties	351
The attack on the tea ships at Boston	352
Boston Port Act, 1774	353
Constitution of Massachusetts suspended	ib.
Revolt of the American colonies	355
Crown colonies	356
Canada and other North American colonies	357
Australian colonies	358
Transportation	359
Colonial administration after the American war	360
Colonial patronage	361
Effects of free trade upon the political relation of England and her colonies	363
Contumacy of Jamaica repressed, 1838	364
Insurrection in Canada: union of the two provinces	365
Responsible government introduced into Canada and other colonies	366

Contents of the Third Volume.

	PAGE
Conflicting interests of England and the colonies	369
Colonial democracy	ib.
Military defence of the colonies	375
Administration of dependencies unfitted for self-government	376
India under the East India Company	377
Mr. Fox's India Bill, 1783	378
Mr. Pitt's India Bill, 1784	381
Later measures	382
India transferred to the Crown, 1858	383
Subsequent Indian administration	ib.
Freedom and good government of the British Empire	384

CHAPTER XVIII.

PROGRESS OF GENERAL LEGISLATION.

Improved spirit of modern legislation	385
Revision of official emoluments	386
Defects and abuses in the law	387
Law reforms already effected	389
The spirit and temper of the judges	391
Merciless character of the criminal code	393
Its revision	396
Other amendments of the criminal law	398
Improvement of prisons and prison discipline	401
Reformatories	403
Establishment of police in England	404
The old and the new poor laws in England	405
In Scotland and Ireland	408
Care and protection of lunatics	409
Protection to women and children in factories and mines	411
Measures for the improvement of the working classes	ib.
Popular education	412
Former commercial policy	415
Free trade	417
Modern financial policy: its value to the community	418
Increase of national expenditure since 1850	420
Democracy discouraged and content promoted by good government	421
Pressure of legislation since the Reform Act	422
Foreign relations of England affected by her freedom	424
Conclusion	ib.

Contents of the Third Volume. xiii

SUPPLEMENTARY CHAPTER.

1861–1871.

	PAGE
Constitutional changes, 1760–1860	425
Political tranquillity under Lord Palmerston	426
Attempts to disturb the franchises of 1832	428
Dissolution of Parliament, 1865	429
Mr. Gladstone rejected by University of Oxford	ib.
Death of Lord Palmerston	ib.
Succeeded by Earl Russell	ib.
Revival of parliamentary reform	430
Considerations adverse to its settlement	ib.
Earl Russell's Reform Bill	431
'The Cave'	ib.
Earl Grosvenor's amendment	432
Bills for the franchise and redistribution of seats united	ib.
Continued opposition to the bill	ib.
Resignation of ministers	433
Earl of Derby premier, 1866	ib.
Popular agitation	ib.
Hyde Park riots, 23rd July, 1866	434
Impulse given to reform	ib.
Position of ministers in regard to reform	435
Introduction of the question, 1867	ib.
Mr. Disraeli's resolutions	436
Earl of Derby's Reform Bill	ib.
Its securities and compensations	ib.
Its ultimate form	437
Meeting in Hyde Park, 6th May, 1867	439
Boundaries of boroughs and counties	ib.
Earl of Derby succeeded by Mr. Disraeli	440
The Scotch Reform Act, 1868	ib.
Election Petitions and Corrupt Practices Act, 1868	441
Constitutional importance of these measures	ib.
Irish Church Question, 1868	443
Mr. Gladstone's resolutions	444
His Suspensory Bill	ib.
The dissolution of 1868	445
Its decisive results	446

	PAGE
Conflicting interests of England and the colonies	369
Colonial democracy	ib.
Military defence of the colonies	375
Administration of dependencies unfitted for self-government	376
India under the East India Company	377
Mr. Fox's India Bill, 1783	378
Mr. Pitt's India Bill, 1784	381
Later measures	382
India transferred to the Crown, 1858	383
Subsequent Indian administration	ib.
Freedom and good government of the British Empire	384

CHAPTER XVIII.

PROGRESS OF GENERAL LEGISLATION.

Improved spirit of modern legislation	385
Revision of official emoluments	386
Defects and abuses in the law	387
Law reforms already effected	389
The spirit and temper of the judges	391
Merciless character of the criminal code	393
Its revision	396
Other amendments of the criminal law	398
Improvement of prisons and prison discipline	401
Reformatories	403
Establishment of police in England	404
The old and the new poor laws in England	405
In Scotland and Ireland	408
Care and protection of lunatics	409
Protection to women and children in factories and mines	411
Measures for the improvement of the working classes	ib.
Popular education	412
Former commercial policy	415
Free trade	417
Modern financial policy: its value to the community	418
Increase of national expenditure since 1850	420
Democracy discouraged and content promoted by good government	421
Pressure of legislation since the Reform Act	422
Foreign relations of England affected by her freedom	424
Conclusion	ib.

Contents of the Third Volume. xiii

SUPPLEMENTARY CHAPTER.

1861–1871.

	PAGE
Constitutional changes, 1760–1860	425
Political tranquillity under Lord Palmerston	426
Attempts to disturb the franchises of 1832	428
Dissolution of Parliament, 1865	429
Mr. Gladstone rejected by University of Oxford	ib.
Death of Lord Palmerston	ib.
Succeeded by Earl Russell	ib.
Revival of parliamentary reform	430
Considerations adverse to its settlement	ib.
Earl Russell's Reform Bill	431
'The Cave'	ib.
Earl Grosvenor's amendment	432
Bills for the franchise and redistribution of seats united	ib.
Continued opposition to the bill	ib.
Resignation of ministers	433
Earl of Derby premier, 1866	ib.
Popular agitation	ib.
Hyde Park riots, 23rd July, 1866	434
Impulse given to reform	ib.
Position of ministers in regard to reform	435
Introduction of the question, 1867	ib.
Mr. Disraeli's resolutions	436
Earl of Derby's Reform Bill	ib.
Its securities and compensations	ib.
Its ultimate form	437
Meeting in Hyde Park, 6th May, 1867	439
Boundaries of boroughs and counties	ib.
Earl of Derby succeeded by Mr. Disraeli	440
The Scotch Reform Act, 1868	ib.
Election Petitions and Corrupt Practices Act, 1868	441
Constitutional importance of these measures	ib.
Irish Church Question, 1868	443
Mr. Gladstone's resolutions	444
His Suspensory Bill	ib.
The dissolution of 1868	445
Its decisive results	446

Contents of the Third Volume.

	PAGE
Resignation of ministers	446
Mr. Gladstone's administration	447
The Irish Church Bill, 1869	ib.
The Irish land bill, 1870	448
Settlement of the church-rate controversy	ib.
University Tests	449
Ecclesiastical Titles Act, 1871	451
Endowed Schools Act, 1869	ib.
Education (Scotland) bill, 1869	ib.
Elementary Education Act, 1870	452
The Ballot	453

CHAPTER XI.

LIBERTY OF THE SUBJECT SECURED BEFORE POLITICAL PRIVILEGES:—GENERAL WARRANTS:—SUSPENSION OF HABEAS CORPUS ACT:—IMPRESSMENT:—REVENUE LAWS AS AFFECTING CIVIL LIBERTY:—COMMITMENTS FOR CONTEMPT:—ARRESTS AND IMPRISONMENT FOR DEBT:—LAST RELICS OF SLAVERY:—SPIES AND INFORMERS:—OPENING LETTERS:—PROTECTION OF FOREIGNERS:—EXTRADITION TREATIES.

DURING the last hundred years, every institution has been popularised,—every public liberty extended. Long before this period, however, Englishmen had enjoyed personal liberty, as their birthright. More prized than any other civil right, and more jealously guarded,—it had been secured earlier than those political privileges, of which we have been tracing the development. The franchises of Magna Charta had been firmly established in the seventeenth century. The Star Chamber had fallen: the power of arbitrary imprisonment had been wrested from the crown and privy council: liberty had been guarded by the Habeas Corpus Act: judges redeemed from dependence and corruption; and juries from intimidation and servile compliance. The landmarks of civil liberty were fixed: but relics of old abuses were yet to be swept away; and traditions of times less favourable to freedom to be forgotten. Much remained to be done for the consolidation of rights

Liberty of the subject assured earlier than political privileges.

already recognised; and we may trace progress, not less remarkable than that which has characterised the history of our political liberties.

Among the remnants of a jurisprudence which had favoured prerogative at the expense of liberty, was that of the arrest of persons under general warrants, without previous evidence of their guilt, or identification of their persons. This practice survived the Revolution, and was continued without question, on the ground of usage, until the reign of George III., when it received its death-blow from the boldness of Wilkes, and the wisdom of Lord Camden. This question was brought to an issue by No. 45 of the 'North Briton,' already so often mentioned. There was the libel, but who was the libeller? Ministers knew not, nor waited to inquire, after the accustomed forms of law: but forthwith Lord Halifax, one of the secretaries of state, issued a warrant, directing four messengers, taking with them a constable, to search for the authors, printers, and publishers; and to apprehend and seize them, together with their papers, and bring them in safe custody before him. No one having been charged, or even suspected,—no evidence of crime having been offered,—no one was named in this dread instrument. The offence only was pointed at,—not the offender. The magistrate, who should have sought proofs of crime, deputed this office to his messengers. Armed with their roving commission, they set forth in quest of unknown offenders; and unable to take evidence, listened to rumours, idle tales, and curious guesses. They held in their hands the liberty of every man, whom they were pleased to suspect. Nor were they triflers in their work. In three days, they arrested no less than forty-nine persons on suspicion,—many as innocent as Lord Halifax himself. Among the number was Dryden Leach, a printer, whom they took from his bed at night. They seized his papers; and even apprehended his journeymen and servants. He had printed one number of the 'North Briton,' and was then reprinting some other numbers: but as he happened not to have printed No. 45, he was released, without being brought before Lord Halifax. They succeeded, however, in arresting Kearsley, the publisher, and Balfe the printer, of the obnoxious number, with all their workmen. From them it was discovered that Wilkes was the culprit of whom they were in search: but the evidence was not on oath; and the messengers received verbal directions to apprehend Wilkes, under the general warrant. Wilkes, far keener than the crown lawyers, not seeing his own name there, declared it 'a ridiculous warrant against the whole English nation,' and refused to obey it. But after being in custody of the messengers for some hours, in his own house, he was taken away in a chair, to appear before the secretaries of state. No sooner had he been removed, than the messengers, returning to his house, proceeded to ransack his drawers; and carried off all his private papers, including even his will and pocket-book. When brought into the presence of Lord Halifax and Lord Egremont, questions were put to Wilkes, which he refused to answer: where-

Arrest of Wilkes.

upon he was committed, close prisoner, to the Tower, —denied the use of pen and paper, and interdicted from receiving the visits of his friends, or even of his professional advisers. From this imprisonment, however, he was shortly released, on a writ of *habeas corpus*, by reason of his privilege, as a member of the House of Commons.[1]

April 30th, 1763.

May 2nd, 1763.

Wilkes and the printers, supported by Lord Temple's liberality, soon questioned the legality of the general warrant. First, several journeymen printers brought actions against the messengers. On the first trial, Lord Chief Justice Pratt, —not allowing bad precedents to set aside the sound principles of English law,—held that the general warrant was illegal: that it was illegally executed; and that the messengers were not indemnified by statute. The journeymen recovered 300*l.* damages; and the other plaintiffs also obtained verdicts. In all these cases, however, bills of exceptions were tendered and allowed.

Actions against the messengers, July 6th, 1763.

Mr. Wilkes himself brought an action against Mr. Wood, under-secretary of state, who had personally superintended the execution of the warrant. At this trial it was proved that Mr. Wood and the messengers, after Wilkes' removal in custody, had taken entire possession of his house, refusing admission to his friends; had sent for a blacksmith, who opened the drawers of his bureau; and having taken out the papers, had carried them away in a sack; without taking any list

Wilkes' action against Wood, Dec. 6th, 1763.

---

[1] Almon's Corr. of Wilkes, i. 95–124; iii. 196–210, &c.

or inventory. All his private manuscripts were seized, and his pocket-book filled up the mouth of the sack.[1] Lord Halifax was examined, and admitted that the warrant had been made out, three days before he had received evidence that Wilkes was the author of the 'North Briton.' Lord Chief Justice Pratt thus spoke of the warrant:—'The defendant claimed a right, under precedents, to force persons' houses, break open escritoires, and seize their papers, upon a general warrant, where no inventory is made of the things thus taken away, and where no offenders' names are specified in the warrant, and therefore a discretionary power given to messengers to search wherever their suspicions may chance to fall. If such a power is truly invested in a secretary of state, and he can delegate this power, it certainly may affect the person and property of every man in this kingdom, and is totally subversive of the liberty of the subject.' The jury found a verdict for the plaintiff, with 1000*l.* damages.[2]

Four days after Wilkes had obtained his verdict against Mr. Wood, Dryden Leach, the printer, gained another verdict, with 400*l.* damages, against the messengers. A bill of exceptions, however, was tendered and received in this, as in other cases, and came on for hearing before the Court of King's Bench, in 1756. After much argument, and the citing of precedents showing the practice of the secretary of state's office ever since

Leach v. Money, Dec. 10th, 1763.

---

[1] So stated by Lord Camden in Entinck *v.* Carrington.
[2] Lofft's Reports, St. Tr., xix. 1153.

the Revolution, Lord Mansfield pronounced the warrant illegal, saying, 'It is not fit that the judging of the information should be left to the discretion of the officer. The magistrate should judge and give certain directions to the officer.' The other three judges agreed that the warrant was illegal and bad, believing that 'no degree of antiquity can give sanction to an usage bad in itself.'[1] The judgment was therefore affirmed.

Wilkes had also brought actions for false imprisonment against both the secretaries of state. Lord Egremont's death put an end to the action against him; and Lord Halifax, by pleading privilege, and interposing other delays unworthy of his position and character, contrived to put off his appearance until after Wilkes had been outlawed,—when he appeared and pleaded the outlawry. But at length, in 1769, no further postponement could be contrived,—the action was tried, and Wilkes obtained no less than 4000*l.* damages.[2] Not only in this action, but throughout the proceedings in which persons aggrieved by the general warrant had sought redress, the government offered an obstinate and vexatious resistance. The defendants were harassed by every obstacle which the law permitted, and subjected to ruinous costs.[3] The ex-

Wilkes and Lord Halifax.

---

[1] Burrow's Rep., iii. 1742; St. Tr., xix. 1001; Sir W. Blackstone's Rep., 555.
[2] Wilson's Rep., ii. 256; Almon's Correspondence of Wilkes, iv. 13; Adolph. Hist., i. 136, *n.*; St. Tr., xix. 1406.
[3] On a motion for a new trial in one of these numerous cases on the ground of excessive damages, Ch. Justice Pratt said: 'They heard the king's counsel, and saw the solicitor of the treasury endeavouring to support and maintain the legality of the warrant in a tyrannical and severe manner.'—*St. Tr.*, xix. 1405.

penses which government itself incurred in these various actions were said to have amounted to 100,000*l*.[1]

The liberty of the subject was further assured, at this period, by another remarkable judgment of Lord Camden. In November, 1762, the Earl of Halifax, as secretary of state, had issued a warrant directing certain messengers, taking a constable to their assistance, to search for John Entinck, Clerk, the author, or one concerned in the writing, of several numbers of the 'Monitor, or British Freeholder,' and to seize him, 'together with his books and papers,' and to bring them in safe custody before the secretary of state. In execution of this warrant, the messengers apprehended Mr. Entinck in his house, and seized the books and papers in his bureau, writing-desk, and drawers. This case differed from that of Wilkes, as the warrant specified the name of the person against whom it was directed. In respect of the person, it was not a general warrant: but as regards the papers, it was a general search-warrant,—not specifying any particular papers to be seized, but giving authority to the messengers to take all his books and papers, according to their discretion.

Search-warrant for papers: Entinck v. Carrington, 1765.

Mr. Entinck brought an action of trespass against the messengers for the seizure of his papers,[2] upon which the jury found a special verdict with 300*l*. damages. This special verdict was twice learnedly argued before the Court of Common Pleas, where at

[1] Almon's Corr. of Wilkes.
[2] Entinck *v.* Carrington, St. Tr., xix. 1030.

length, in 1765, Lord Camden pronounced an elaborate judgment. He even doubted the right of the secretary of state to commit persons at all, except for high treason: but in deference to prior decisions[1] the court felt bound to acknowledge the right. The main question, however, was the legality of a search-warrant for papers. 'If this point should be determined in favour of the jurisdiction,' said Lord Camden, 'the secret cabinets and bureaus of every subject in this kingdom will be thrown open to the search and inspection of a messenger, whenever the secretary of state shall think fit to charge, or even suspect, a person to be the author, printer, or publisher of a seditious libel.' 'This power, so assumed by the secretary of state, is an execution upon all the party's papers in the first instance. His house is rifled, his most valuable papers are taken out of his possession, before the paper, for which he is charged, is found to be criminal by any competent jurisdiction, and before he is convicted either of writing, publishing, or being concerned in the paper.' It had been found by the special verdict that many such warrants had been issued since the Revolution: but he wholly denied their legality. He referred the origin of the practice to the Star Chamber, which in pursuit of libels had given search-warrants to their messenger of the press,—a practice which, after the abolition of the Star Chamber, had been revived and authorised by the Licensing Act of Charles II. in the person of the

[1] Queen *v.* Derby, Fort., 140, and R. *v.* Earbury, 2 Barnadist, 293, 346.

secretary of state. And he conjectured that this practice had been continued after the expiration of that act,—a conjecture shared by Lord Mansfield and the Court of King's Bench.[1] With the unanimous concurrence of the other judges of his court, this eminent magistrate now finally condemned this dangerous and unconstitutional practice.

Meanwhile, the legality of a general warrant had been repeatedly discussed in Parliament.[2] Several motions were offered, in different forms, for declaring it unlawful. While trials were still pending, there were obvious objections to any proceeding by which the judgment of the courts would be anticipated: but in debate, such a warrant found few supporters. Those who were unwilling to condemn it by a vote of the House, had little to say in its defence. Even the attorney and solicitor-general did not venture to pronounce it legal. But whatever their opinion, the competency of the House to decide any matter of law was contemptuously denied. Sir Fletcher Norton, the attorney-general, even went so far as to declare that 'he should regard a resolution of the members of the House of Commons no more than the oaths of so many drunken porters in Covent Garden,'—a sentiment as unconstitutional as it was insolent. Mr. Pitt affirmed 'that there was not a man to be found of sufficient profligacy to defend this warrant upon the principle of legality.'

General warrants discussed in Parliament.

---

[1] Leach v. Money and others, Burrow's Rep., iii. 1692, 1767; Sir W. Blackstone's Rep., 555. The same view was also adopted by Blackstone, *Comm.*, iv. 336, *n*. (Kerr's Ed., 1862.)

[2] Jan. 19th, Feb. 3rd, 6th, 13th, 14th, and 17th, 1764; Parl. Hist., xv. 1393-1418 Jan. 29th, 1765; *Ibid.*, xvi. 6.

In 1766, the Court of King's Bench had condemned the warrant, and the objections to a declaratory resolution were therefore removed; the Court of Common Pleas had pronounced a search-warrant for papers to be illegal; and lastly, the more liberal administration of the Marquess of Rockingham had succeeded to that of Mr. Grenville. Accordingly, resolutions were now agreed to, condemning general warrants, whether for the seizure of persons or papers, as illegal; and declaring them, if executed against a member, to be a breach of privilege.[1]

Resolutions of the Commons, April 22nd, 1766.

A bill was introduced to carry into effect these resolutions, and passed by the House of Commons: but was not agreed to by the Lords.[2] A declaratory act was, however, no longer necessary. The illegality of general warrants had been judicially determined, and the judgment of the courts confirmed by the House of Commons, and approved as well by popular opinion, as by the first statesmen of the time. The cause of public liberty had been vindicated, and was henceforth secure.

Declaratory bill, April 29th, 1766.

The writ of Habeas Corpus is unquestionably the first security of civil liberty. It brings to light the cause of every imprisonment, approves its lawfulness, or liberates the prisoner. It exacts obedience from the highest courts: Parliament itself submits to its authority.[3] No right is more justly valued. It protects the subject from

Suspension of Habeas Corpus Act.

---

[1] Parl. Hist., xvi. 209.   [2] *Ibid.*, 210.
[3] May's Law and Usage of Parliament, p. 75 (6th Ed.).

unfounded suspicions, from the aggressions of power, and from abuses in the administration of justice.[1] Yet this protective law, which gives every man security and confidence, in times of tranquillity, has been suspended, again and again, in periods of public danger or apprehension. Rarely, however, has this been suffered without jealousy, hesitation, and remonstrance; and whenever the perils of the state have been held sufficient to warrant this sacrifice of personal liberty, no minister or magistrate has been suffered to tamper with the law, at his discretion. Parliament alone, convinced of the exigency of each occasion, has suspended, for a time, the rights of individuals, in the interests of the state.

The first years after the Revolution were full of danger. A dethroned king, aided by foreign enemies, and a powerful body of English adherents, was threatening the new settlement of the crown with war and treason. Hence the liberties of Englishmen, so recently assured, were several times made to yield to the exigencies of the state. Again, on occasions of no less peril,—the rebellion of 1715, the Jacobite conspiracy of 1722, and the invasion of the realm by the Pretender in 1745,—the Habeas Corpus Act was suspended.[2] Henceforth, for nearly half a century, the law remained inviolate. During the

Cases from the Revolution to 1794.

---

[1] Blackstone's Comm. (Kerr), iii. 138–147, &c.
[2] Parl. Hist., viii. 27–39; xiii. 671. In 1745 it was stated by the solicitor-general that the act had been suspended nine times since the Revolution; and in 1794 Mr. Secretary Dundas made a similar statement.—*Parl. Hist.*, xxx. 539.

American war, indeed, it had been necessary to empower the king to secure persons suspected of high treason, committed in North America, or on the high seas, or of the crime of piracy:[1] but it was not until 1794 that the civil liberties of Englishmen, at home, were again to be suspended. The dangers and alarms of that dark period have already been recounted.[2] Ministers, believing the state to be threatened by traitorous conspiracies, once more sought power to countermine treason by powers beyond the law.

Relying upon the report of a secret committee, Mr. Pitt moved for a bill to empower His Majesty to secure and detain persons suspected of conspiring against his person and government.

Habeas Corpus Suspension Act, 1794. May 16th.

He justified this measure on the ground, that whatever the temporary danger of placing such power in the hands of the government, it was far less than the danger with which the constitution and society were threatened. If ministers abused the power entrusted to them, they would be responsible for its abuse. It was vigorously opposed by Mr. Fox, Mr. Grey, Mr. Sheridan, and a small body of adherents. They denied the disaffection imputed to the people, ridiculed the revelations of the committee, and declared that no such dangers threatened the state as would justify the surrender of the chief safeguard of personal freedom. This measure would give ministers absolute power over every individual in the kingdom. It would em-

---

[1] In 1777, act 17 Geo. III. c. 9.   [2] *Supra*, Vol. Il. p. 302.

power them to arrest, on suspicion, any man whose opinions were obnoxious to them,—the advocates of reform,—even the members of the parliamentary opposition. Who would be safe, when conspiracies were everywhere suspected, and constitutional objects and language believed to be the mere cloak of sedition? Let every man charged with treason be brought to justice; in the words of Sheridan, 'where there was guilt, let the broad axe fall;' but why surrender the liberties of the innocent?

Yet thirty-nine members only could be found to oppose the introduction of the bill.[1] Ministers, representing its immediate urgency, endeavoured to pass it at once through all its stages. The opposition, unable to resist its progress by numbers, endeavoured to arrest its passing for a time, in order to appeal to the judgment of the country: but all their efforts were vain. With free institutions, the people were now governed according to the principles of despotism. The will of their rulers was supreme, and not to be questioned. After eleven divisions, the bill was pressed forward as far as the report, on the same night; and the galleries being closed, the arguments urged against it were merely addressed to a determined and taciturn majority. On the following day, the bill was read a third time and sent up to the Lords, by whom, after some sharp debates, it was speedily passed.[2]

The strongest opponents of the measure, while denying its present necessity, admitted that when

[1] Ayes, 201; Noes, 39.   [2] Parl. Hist., xxxi. 497, 521, 525.

danger is imminent, the liberty of the subject must be sacrificed to the paramount interests of the state. Ringleaders must be seized, outrages anticipated, plots disconcerted, and the dark haunts of conspiracy filled with distrust and terror. And terrible indeed was the power now entrusted to the executive. Though termed a suspension of the Habeas Corpus Act, it was, in truth, a suspension of Magna Charta,[1] and of the cardinal principles of the common law. Every man had hitherto been free from imprisonment until charged with crime, by information upon oath; and entitled to a speedy trial and the judgment of his peers. But any subject could now be arrested on suspicion of treasonable practices, without specific charge or proof of guilt: his accusers were unknown; and in vain might he demand public accusation and trial. Spies and treacherous accomplices, however circumstantial in their narratives to secretaries of state and law officers, shrank from the witness-box; and their victims rotted in gaol. Whatever the judgment, temper, and good faith of the executive, such a power was arbitrary, and could scarcely fail to be abused.[2] Whatever the dangers by which it was justified,—never did the subject so much need the protection of the laws, as when government and society were filled with suspicion and alarm.

Grounds and character of the measure.

[1] 'Nullus liber homo capiatur aut imprisonetur, nisi per legale judicium parium suorum.' . . . . 'Nulli negabimus, nulli differemus justiciam.'
[2] Blackstone says: 'It has happened in England during temporary suspensions of the statute, that persons apprehended upon suspicion have suffered a long imprisonment, merely because they were forgotten.'—*Comm.*, iii. (Kerr), 146.

Notwithstanding the failure of the state prosecutions, and the discredit cast upon the evidence of a traitorous conspiracy, on which the Suspension Act had been expressly founded, ministers declined to surrender the invidious power with which they had been entrusted. Strenuous resistance was offered by the opposition to the continuance of the act: but it was renewed again and again, so long as the public apprehensions continued. From 1798 to 1800, the increased malignity and violence of English democrats, and their complicity with Irish treason, repelled further objections to this exceptional law.[1] *Its continuance; 1794–1800.*

At length, at the end of 1801, the act being no longer defensible on grounds of public danger, was suffered to expire, after a continuous operation of eight years.[2] But before its operation had ceased, a bill was introduced to indemnify all persons who since the 1st of February, 1793, had acted in the apprehension of persons suspected of high treason. A measure designed to protect the ministers and their agents from responsibility, on account of acts extending over a period of eight years, was not suffered to pass without strenuous opposition.[3] When extraordinary powers had first been sought, it was said that minis- *Habeas Corpus Suspension Act expired 1801.*

---

[1] In 1798 there were only seven votes against its renewal. In 1800 it was opposed by twelve in the Commons, and by three in the Lords. It was then stated that twenty-nine persons had been imprisoned, some for more than two years, without being brought to trial.—*Parl. Hist.*, xxxiv. 1484.

[2] The act 41 Geo. III. c. 26, expired six weeks after the commencement of the next session, which commenced on the 29th of Oct., in the same year.

[3] *Parl. Hist.*, xxxv. 1507–1549.

ters would be responsible for their proper exercise; and now every act of authority, every neglect or abuse, was to be buried in oblivion. It was stated in debate that some persons had suffered imprisonment for three years, and one for six, without being brought to trial;[1] and Lord Thurlow could 'not resist the impulse to deem men innocent until tried and convicted.' The measure was defended, however, on the ground that persons accused of abuses would be unable to defend themselves, without disclosing secrets dangerous to the lives of individuals, and to the state. Unless the bill were passed, those channels of information would be stopped, on which government relied for guarding the public peace.[2] When all the accustomed forms of law had been departed from, the justification of the executive would indeed have been difficult: but evil times had passed, and a veil was drawn over them. If dangerous powers had been misused, they were covered by an amnesty. It were better to withhold such powers, than to scrutinise their exercise too curiously; and were any further argument needed against the suspension of the law, it would be found in the reasons urged for indemnity.

Suspension of Habeas Corpus Act, 1817. For several years, the ordinary law of arrest was free from further invasion. But on the first appearance of popular discontents and combinations, the government resorted to the same ready expedient for strengthening the hands of the executive, at the expense of public liberty. The suspension of the Habeas Corpus Act

[1] Parl. Hist., xxxv. 1517. [2] Ibid., 1510.

formed part of Lord Sidmouth's repressive measures in 1817,[1] when it was far less defensible than in 1794. At the first period, the French Revolution was still raging: its consequences no man could foresee; and a deadly war had broken out with the revolutionary government of France. Here, at least, there may have been grounds for extraordinary precautions. But in 1817, France was again settled under the Bourbons: the revolution had worn itself out: Europe was again at peace; and the state was threatened with no danger but domestic discontent and turbulence.

Again did ministers, having received powers to apprehend and detain in custody persons suspected of treasonable practices,—and, having imprisoned many men without bringing them to trial,—seek indemnity for all concerned in the exercise of these powers, and in the suppression of tumultuous assemblies.[2] Magistrates had seized papers and arms, and interfered with meetings, under circumstances not warranted even by the exceptional powers entrusted to them: but having acted in good faith for the repression of tumults and sedition, they claimed protection. This bill was not passed without a spirited resistance. The executive had not been idle in the exercise of its extraordinary powers. Ninety-six persons had been arrested on suspicion. Of these, forty-four were taken by warrant of the secretary of state; four by warrant of the privy council: the remainder on the

Bill of Indemnity, 1817.

---

[1] *Supra*, Vol. II. p. 373.
[2] Hans. Deb., 1st Ser., xxxv. 491, 551, 643, 708, 795, &c.; 57 Geo. III. c. 55; repealed by 58 Geo. III. c. 1.

warrants of magistrates. Not one of those arrested on the warrant of the secretary of state had been brought to trial. The four arrested on the warrant of the privy council were tried and acquitted.[1] Prisoners had been moved from prison to prison in chains; and after long, painful, and even solitary imprisonment, discharged on their recognisances, without trial.[2]

Numerous petitions were presented, complaining of cruelties and hardships; and though falsehood and exaggeration characterised many of their statements, the justice of inquiry was insisted on, before a general indemnity was agreed to. 'They were called upon,' said Mr. Lambton, 'to throw an impenetrable veil over all the acts of tyranny and oppression that had been committed under the Suspension Act. They were required to stifle the voice of just complaint,—to disregard the numerous petitions that had been presented, arraigning the conduct of ministers, detailing acts of cruelty unparalleled in the annals of the Bastile, and demanding full and open investigation.'[3] But on behalf of government, it appeared that in no instance had warrants of detention been issued, except on information upon oath;[4] and the attorney-general declared that none of the prisoners had been

Petitions complaining of ill-usage.

---

[1] Lords' Report on the state of the country. In ten other cases the parties had escaped. Hans. Deb., 1st Ser., xxxvii. 573; Sir M. W. Ridley, March 9th, 1818; *Ibid.*, 901.

[2] Petitions of Benbow, Drummond, Bagguley, Leach, Scholes, Ogden, and others—Hans. Deb., 1st Ser., xxxvii. 438, 441, 453, 461, 519.

[3] March 9th, 1818; Hans. Deb., 1st Ser., xxxvii. 891.

[4] Lords' Rep. on State of the Nation, Hans. Deb., 1st Ser., xxxvii. 574.

deprived of liberty for a single hour, on the evidence of informers alone, which was never acted on, unless corroborated by other undoubted testimony.[1]

Indemnity was granted for the past: but the discussions which it provoked, disclosed, more forcibly than ever, the hazard of permitting the even course of the law to be interrupted. *Habeas Corpus Act since respected.* They were not without their warning. Even Lord Sidmouth was afterwards satisfied with the rigorous provisions of the Six Acts; and, while stifling public discussion, did not venture to propose another forfeiture of personal liberty. And happily, since his time, ministers, animated by a higher spirit of statesmanship, have known how to maintain the authority of the law, in England, without the aid of abnormal powers.

In Ireland, a less settled state of society,—agrarian outrages,—feuds envenomed by many deeds of blood,—and dangerous conspiracies, have too often called for sacrifices of liberty. *Suspension of Habeas Corpus Act in Ireland.* Before the Union, a bloody rebellion demanded this security; and since that period, the Habeas Corpus Act was suspended on no less than six occasions prior to 1860.[2] The last Suspension Act, in 1848, was rendered necessary by an imminent rebellion, openly organised and threatened: when the people were arming, and their leaders inciting

---

[1] Feb. 17th, 1818, Hans. Deb., 1st Ser., xxxvii. 499, 881, 953, &c.
[2] It was suspended in 1800, at the very time of the Union; from 1802 till 1805; from 1807 till 1810; in 1814; and from 1822 till 1824; subsequently to 1860, it was suspended, in 1866; and this suspension was twice continued until March 1869. Again, in 1871, it was suspended in Westmeath, and parts of adjacent counties.

them to massacre and plunder.[1] Other measures in restraint of crime and outrage have also pressed upon the constitutional liberties of the Irish people. But let us hope that the rapid advancement of that country in wealth and industry, in enlightenment and social improvement, may henceforth entitle its spirited and generous people to the enjoyment of the same confidence as their English brethren.

But perhaps the greatest anomaly in our laws,— the most signal exception to personal freedom,—is to be found in the custom of impressment, for the land and sea service. There is nothing incompatible with freedom, in a conscription or forced levy of men, for the defence of the country. It may be submitted to, in the freest republic, like the payment of taxes. The services of every subject may be required, in such form as the state determines. But impressment is the arbitrary and capricious seizure of individuals, from among the general body of citizens. It differs from conscription, as a particular confiscation differs from a general tax.

Impressment.

The impressment of soldiers for the wars was formerly exercised as part of the royal prerogative: but among the services rendered to liberty by the Long Parliament, in its earlier councils, this custom was condemned, 'except in case of necessity of the sudden coming in of strange enemies into the kingdom, or except' in the case of persons 'otherwise bound by the tenure of their lands or possessions.'[2] The prerogative was discontinued: but during the exigencies of war, the temptation of

Impressment for the army.

---

[1] Hans Deb., 3rd Ser., c. 696–755.   [2] 16 Charles I. c. 28.

impressment was too strong to be resisted by Parliament. The class on whom it fell, however, found little sympathy from society. They were rogues and vagabonds, who were held to be better employed in defence of their country, than in plunder and mendicancy.[1] During the American war, impressment was permitted in the case of all idle and disorderly persons, not following any lawful trade, or having some substance sufficient for their maintenance.[2] Such men were seized upon, without compunction, and hurried to the war. It was a dangerous license, repugnant to the free spirit of our laws; and, in later times, the state has trusted to bounties and the recruiting sergeant, and not to impressment, —for strengthening its land forces.

But for manning the navy in time of war, the impressment of seamen has been recognised by the common law, and by many statutes.[3] *Impressment for the navy.* The hardships and cruelties of the system were notorious.[4] No violation of natural liberty could be more gross. Free men were forced into a painful and dangerous service, not only against their will, but often by fraud and violence. Entrapped in taverns, or torn from their homes by armed press-gangs, in the dead of night, they were hurried on board ship, to die of wounds or pestilence. Impressment was restricted by law to seamen, who

[1] Parl. Hist., xv. 547.
[2] 19 Geo. III. c. 10; Parl. Hist., xx. 114.
[3] Sir M. Foster's Rep., 154; Stat. 2 Rich. II. c. 4; 2 & 3 Phil. and Mary, c. 16, &c.; 5 & 6 Will. IV. c. 24; Barrington on the Statutes, 334; Blackstone, i. 425 (Kerr); Stephen's Comm., ii. 576; Parl. Hist., vi. 518.
[4] Parl. Hist., xv. 544, xix. 81, &c.

being most needed for the fleet, chiefly suffered from the violence of the press-gangs. They were taken on the coast, or seized on board merchant-ships, like criminals: ships at sea were rifled of their crews, and left without sufficient hands to take them safely into port. Nay, we even find soldiers employed to assist the press-gangs: villages invested by a regular force; sentries standing with fixed bayonets; and churches surrounded, during divine service, to seize seamen for the fleet.[1]

Press-gangs. The lawless press-gangs were no respecters of persons. In vain did apprentices and landsmen claim exemption. They were skulking sailors in disguise, or would make good seamen, at the first scent of salt-water; and were carried off to the sea-ports. Press-gangs were the terror of citizens and apprentices in London, of labourers in villages, and of artisans in the remotest inland towns. Their approach was dreaded like the invasion of a foreign enemy. To escape their swoop, men forsook their trades and families and fled,—or armed themselves for resistance. Their deeds have been recounted in history, in fiction, and in song. Outrages were of course deplored: but the navy was the pride of England, and everyone agreed that it must be recruited. In vain were other means suggested for manning the fleet,—higher wages, limited service, and increased pensions. Such schemes were doubtful expedients: the navy could not be hazarded: press-gangs must still go forth and execute their

[1] Dec. 2nd, 1755, Parl. Hist., xv. 549.

rough commission, or England would be lost. And so impressment prospered.[1]

So constant were the draughts of seamen for the American war, that in 1779 the customary exemptions from impressment were withdrawn. *Retrospective Act, 1779.* Men following callings under the protection of various statutes were suddenly kidnapped, by the authority of Parliament, and sent to the fleet; and this invasion of their rights was effected in the ruffianly spirit of the press-gang. A bill proposed late at night, in a thin house, and without notice,—avowedly in order to surprise its victims,—was made retrospective in its operation. Even before it was proposed to Parliament, orders had been given for a vigorous impressment, without any regard to the existing law. Every illegal act was to be made lawful; and men who had been seized in violation of statutes, were deprived of the protection of a writ of *habeas corpus*.[2] Early in the next exhausting war, the state, unable to spare its rogues and vagabonds for the army, allowed them *Enlistment Act, 1795.* to be impressed, with smugglers and others of doubtful means and industry, for the service of the fleet. The select body of electors were exempt: but all other men out of work were lawful prize.

---

[1] See debate on Mr. Luttrell's motion, March 11th, 1777; Parl. Hist., xix. 81. On the 22nd Nov., 1770, Lord Chatham said: 'I am myself clearly convinced, and I believe every man who knows anything of the English navy will acknowledge, that, without impressing, it is impossible to equip a respectable fleet within the time in which such armaments are usually wanted.'—*Parl. Hist.*, xvi. 1101.

[2] June 23rd, 1779. Speech of the attorney-general Wedderburn; Parl. Hist., xx. 962; 29 Geo. III. c. 75.

Their service was without limit: they might be slaves for life.[1]

Throughout the war, these sacrifices of liberty were exacted for the public safety. But when the land was once more blessed with peace, it was asked if they would be endured again. The evils of impressment were repeatedly discussed in Parliament, and schemes of voluntary enlistment proposed by Mr. Hume[2] and others.[3] Ministers and Parliament were no less alive to the dangerous principles on which recruiting for the navy had hitherto been conducted; and devised new expedients more consistent with the national defences of a free country. Higher wages, larger bounties, shorter periods of service, and a reserve volunteer force,[4]—such have been the means by which the navy has been strengthened and popularised. During the Russian war great fleets were manned for the Baltic and the Mediterranean by volunteers. Impressment,—not yet formally renounced by law,—has been condemned by the general sentiment of the country;[5] and we may hope that modern statesmanship has, at length, provided for the efficiency of the fleet, by measures consistent with the liberty of the subject.

Enlistment since the peace.

[1] 35 Geo. III. c. 34.
[2] June 10th, 1824; Hans. Deb., 2nd Ser., xi. 1171; June 9th, 1825; *Ibid.*, xiii. 1097.
[3] Mr. Buckingham, Aug. 15th, 1833; March 4th, 1834; Hans. Deb., 3rd Ser., xx. 691; xxi. 1061; Earl of Durham, March 3rd, 1834; *Ibid.*, xxi. 992; Capt. Harris, May 23rd, 1850; *Ibid.*, cxi. 279.
[4] 5 & 6 Will. IV. c. 24; Hans. Deb., 3rd Ser., xxvi. 1120; xcii. 10, 729; 16 & 17 Vict. c. 69; 17 and 18 Vict. c. 18.
[5] The able commission on manning the navy, in 1859, reported 'the evidence of the witnesses, with scarcely an exception, shows that the system of naval impressment, as practised in former wars, could not now be successfully enforced.'—p. xi.

The personal liberty of British subjects has further suffered from rigours and abuses of the law. The supervision necessary for the collection of taxes,—and especially of the excise, —has been frequently observed upon, as a restraint upon the natural freedom of the subject. The visits of revenue officers, throughout the processes of manufacture,—the summary procedure by which penalties are enforced,—and the encouragement given to informers, have been among the most popular arguments against duties of excise.[1] The repeal of many of these duties, under an improved fiscal policy, has contributed as well to the liberties of the people, as to their material welfare.

Revenue Laws.

But restraints and vexations were not the worst incident of the revenue laws. An onerous and complicated system of taxation involved numerous breaches of the law. Many were punished with fines, which, if not paid, were followed by imprisonment. It was right that the law should be vindicated: but while other offences escaped with limited terms of imprisonment, the luckless debtors of the crown, if too poor to pay their fees and costs, might suffer imprisonment for life.[2] Even when the legislature at length took pity upon other debtors, this class of prisoners were excepted from its merciful care.[3] But they have since shared in the milder policy of our laws; and

Crown debtors.

---

[1] Adam Smith, speaking of 'the frequent visits and odious examination of the tax-gatherers,' says: 'Dealers have no respite from the continual visits and examination of the excise efficers.'—*Book* v. c. 2.—Blackstone says: 'The rigour, and arbitrary proceedings of excise laws, seem hardly compatible with the temper of a free nation.' —*Comm.*, i. 308 (Kerr's ed.).

[2] Hans. Deb., 2nd Ser., viii. 808.   [3] 53 Geo. III. c. 102, § 51.

have received ample indulgence from the Treasury and the Court of Exchequer.[1]

While Parliament continued to wield its power of commitment capriciously and vindictively,—not in vindication of its own just authority, but for the punishment of libels, and other offences cognisable by the law,—it was scarcely less dangerous than those arbitrary acts of prerogative which the law had already condemned, as repugnant to liberty. Its abuses, however, survived but for a few years after the accession of George III.[2]

Vindictive exercise of privileges by Parliament, another encroachment upon liberty.

But another power, of like character, continued to impose—and still occasionally permits—the most cruel restraints upon personal liberty. A court of equity can only enforce obedience to its authority, by imprisonment. If obedience be refused, commitment for contempt must follow. The authority of the court would otherwise be defied, and its jurisdiction rendered nugatory. But out of this necessary judicial process, grew up gross abuses and oppression. Ordinary offences are purged by certain terms of imprisonment; men suffer punishment and are free again. And, on this principle, persons committed for disrespect or other contempt to the court itself, were released after a reasonable time, upon their apology and submission.[3] But no such mercy was shown to those who failed to obey the decrees of the court, in any suit. Their

Commitments for contempt.

---

[1] 7 Geo. IV. c. 57, § 74; 1 & 2 Vict. c. 110, § 103, 104.
[2] *Supra*, Chap. VII.; and see Townsend's Mem. of the House of Commons, *passim*.
[3] Hans. Deb., 2nd Ser., viii. 808.

imprisonment was indefinite, if not perpetual. Their contempt was only to be purged by obedience, —perhaps wholly beyond their power. For such prisoners there was no relief but death. Some persisted in their contempt from obstinacy, sullenness, and litigious hate: but many suffered for no offence but ignorance and poverty. Humble suitors, dragged into court by richer litigants, were sometimes too poor to obtain professional advice, or even to procure copies of the bills filed against them. Lord Eldon himself, to his honour be it said, had charitably assisted such men to put in answers in his own court.[1] Others, again, unable to pay money and costs decreed against them, suffered imprisonment for life. This latter class, however, at length became entitled to relief as insolvent debtors.[2] But the complaints of other wretched men, to whom the law brought no relief, were often heard. In 1817, Mr. Bennet, in presenting a petition from one of these prisoners, thus stated his own experience: 'Last year,' he said, 'Thomas Williams had been in confinement for thirty-one years by an order of the Court of Chancery. He had visited him in his wretched house of bondage, where he had found him sinking under all the miseries that can afflict humanity, and on the following day he died. At this time,' he added, 'there were in the same prison with the petitioner, a woman who had been in confinement twenty-eight years, and two other persons

---

[1] Hans. Deb., 2nd Ser., xiv. 1178.
[2] 49 Geo. III. c. 6; 53 Geo. III. c. 102, § 47; Hans. Deb., 2nd Ser., xiv. 1178.

who had been there seventeen years.'[1] In the next year, Mr. Bennet presented another petition from prisoners confined for contempt of court, complaining that nothing had been done to relieve them, though they had followed all the instructions of their lawyers. The petitioners had witnessed the death of six persons, in the same condition as themselves, one of whom had been confined four, another eighteen, and another thirty-four years.[2]

April 22nd, 1818.

In 1820, Lord Althorp presented another petition; and among the petitioners was a woman, eighty-one years old, who had been imprisoned for thirty-one years.[3] In the eight years preceding 1820, twenty prisoners had died while under confinement for contempt, some of whom had been in prison for upwards of thirty years.[4] Even so late as 1856, Lord St. Leonards presented a petition, complaining of continued hardships upon prisoners for contempt; and a statement of the Lord Chancellor revealed the difficulty and painfulness of such cases. 'A man who had been confined in the early days of Lord Eldon's Chancellorship for refusing to disclose certain facts, remained in prison, obstinately declining to make any statement upon the subject, until his death a few months ago.'[5]

Aug. 31st, 1820.

---

[1] 6th May, 1817; Hans. Deb., 1st Ser., xxxvi. 158. Mr. Bennet had made a statement on the same subject in 1816; *Ibid.*, xxxiv. 1099.

[2] Hans. Deb., 1st Ser., xxxviii. 284.

[3] Hans. Deb., 2nd Ser., i. 693.

[4] *Ibid.*, xiv. 1178; Mr. Hume's Return, Parl. Paper, 1820 (302).

[5] Hans. Deb., 3rd Ser., cxlii. 1570. In another recent case, a lad

Doubtless the peculiar jurisdiction of courts of equity has caused this extraordinary rigour in the punishment of contempts: but justice and a respect for personal liberty alike require that punishment should be meted out according to the gravity of the offence. The Court of Queen's Bench upholds its dignity by commitments for a fixed period; and may not the Court of Chancery be content with the like punishment for disobedience, however gross and culpable?

Every restraint on public liberty hitherto noticed has been permitted either to the executive government, in the interests of the state, or to courts of justice, in the exercise of a necessary jurisdiction. Individual rights have been held subordinate to the public good; and on that ground, even questionable practices admitted of justification. But the law further permitted, and society long tolerated, the most grievous and wanton restraints, imposed by one subject upon another, for which no such justification is to be found. The law of debtor and creditor, until a comparatively recent period, was a scandal to a civilised country. For the smallest claim, any man was liable to be arrested, on mesne process, before legal proof of the debt. He might be torn from his family, like a malefactor,—at any time of day or night,—and detained until bail was given; and in default of bail, imprisoned until the debt was paid. Many of these arrests were wanton and vexatious; and writs were issued with a

---

was committed for refusing to discontinue his addresses to a ward of the court, and died in prison.

facility and looseness which placed the liberty of every man,—suddenly and without notice,—at the mercy of anyone who claimed payment of a debt. A debtor, however honest and solvent, was liable to arrest. The demand might even be false and fraudulent: but the pretended creditor, on making oath of the debt, was armed with this terrible process of the law.[1] The wretched defendant might lie in prison for several months before his cause was heard; when, even if the action was discontinued, or the debt disproved, he could not obtain his discharge without further proceedings, often too costly for a poor debtor, already deprived of his livelihood by imprisonment. No longer even a debtor,—he could not shake off his bonds.

Slowly and with reluctance, did Parliament address itself to the correction of this monstrous abuse. In the reign of George I. arrests on mesne process, issuing out of the superior courts, were limited to sums exceeding 10*l*.:[2] but it was not until 1779, that the same limit was imposed on the process of inferior jurisdictions.[3] This sum was afterwards raised to 15*l*., and in 1827 to 20*l*. In that year 1,100 persons were confined, in the prisons of the metropolis alone, on mesne process.[4]

The total abolition of arrests on mesne process was frequently advocated, but it was not until 1838 that it was at length accomplished. Provision was

---

[1] An executor might even obtain an arrest on swearing to his belief of a debt. Report, 1792, Com. Journ., xlvii. 640.
[2] 12 Geo. I. c. 29.   [3] 19 Geo. III. c. 70.
[4] Hans. Deb., 2nd Ser., xvii. 386. The number in England amounted to 3,662.

made for securing absconding debtors: but the old process for the recovery of debt, in ordinary cases, which had wrought so many acts of oppression, was abolished. While this vindictive remedy was denied, the creditor's lands were, for the first time, allowed to be taken in satisfaction of a debt;[1] and extended facilities were afterwards afforded for the recovery of small claims, by the establishment of county courts.[2]

The law of arrest was reckless of liberty: the law of execution for debt was one of savage barbarity. A creditor is entitled to every protection and remedy, which the law can reasonably give. All the debtor's property should be his; and frauds by which he has been wronged should be punished as criminal. But the remedies of English law against the property of a debtor were strangely inadequate,—its main security being the body of the debtor. This became the property of the creditor, until the debt was paid. The ancients allowed a creditor to seize his debtor, and hold him in slavery. It was a cruel practice, condemned by the most enlightened lawgivers:[3] but it was more rational and humane than the law of England. By servitude a man might work out his debt: by imprisonment, restitution was made impossible. A man was torn from his trade and industry, and

Imprisonment for debt.

---

[1] 1 & 2 Vict. c. 110.   [2] 9 & 10 Vict. c. 95.
[3] Solon renounced it, finding examples amongst the Egyptians.— *Plutarch's Life of Solon; Diod. Sic.*, lib. i. part 2, ch. 3; *Montesquieu*, livr. xii. ch. 21. It was abolished in Rome, A.D. 428, when the true principle was thus defined—'Bona debitoris, non corpus obnoxium esset.'—*Livy*, lib. 8; *Montesquieu*, livr. xx. ch. 14.

buried in a dungeon: the debtor perished, but the creditor was unpaid. The penalty of an unpaid debt, however small, was imprisonment for life. A trader within the operation of the bankrupt laws might obtain his discharge, on giving up all his property: but for an insolvent debtor there was no possibility of relief, but charity or the rare indulgence of his creditor. His body being the property of his creditor, the law could not interfere. He might become insane, or dangerously sick: but the court was unable to give him liberty. We read with horror of a woman dying in the Devon County Gaol, after an imprisonment of forty-five years, for a debt of 19*l*.[1]

While the law thus trifled with the liberty of debtors, it took no thought of their wretched fate, after the prison-door had closed upon them. The traditions of the debtors' prison are but too familiar to us all. The horrors of the Fleet and the Marshalsea were laid bare in 1729. The poor debtors were found crowded together on the 'common side,'—covered with filth and vermin, and suffered to die, without pity, of hunger and gaol fever. Nor did they suffer from neglect alone. They had committed no crime: yet were they at the mercy of brutal gaolers, who loaded them with irons, and racked them with tortures.[2] No attempt was made to distinguish the fraudulent from the unfortunate debtor. The rich rogue,—able, but unwilling to pay his debts,—might riot in luxury and

Debtors' prisons.

---

[1] Rep. of 1792, Com. Journ., xlvii. 647.
[2] Com. Journ., xxi. 274, 376, 513.

debauchery, while his poor, unlucky fellow-prisoner was left to starve and rot on the 'common side.'[1]

The worst iniquities of prison life were abated by the active benevolence of John Howard; and poor debtors found some protection, in common with felons, from the brutality of gaolers. But otherwise their sufferings were without mitigation. The law had made no provision for supplying indigent prisoners with necessary food, bed-clothes, or other covering;[2] and it was proved, in 1792, that many died of actual want, being without the commonest necessaries of life.[3]

The first systematic relief was given to insolvent debtors, by the benevolence of the Thatched House Society, in 1772. In twenty years this noble body released from prison 12,590 honest and unfortunate debtors; and so trifling were the debts for which these prisoners had suffered confinement, that their freedom was obtained at an expense of forty-five shillings a head. Many were discharged merely on payment of the gaol fees, for which alone they were detained in prison: others on payment of costs, the original debts having long since been discharged.[4]

The Thatched-house Society, 1772.

---

[1] Rep. 1792, Com. Journ., xlvii. 652; Vicar of Wakefield, ch. xxv.-xxviii.

[2] Report, 1792, Com. Journ., xlvii. 641. The only exception was under the act 32 Geo. II. c. 28, of very partial operation, under which the detaining creditor was forced to allow the debtor 4d. a day; and such was the cold cruelty of creditors, that many a debtor confined for sums under 20s., was detained at their expense, which soon exceeded the amount of the debt.—*Ibid.*, 644, 650. This allowance was raised to 3s. 6d. a week by 37 Geo. III. c. 85.

[3] *Ibid.*, 651.

[4] Report, 1792, Com. Journ., xlvii. 648.

VOL. III. D

<small>Exposure of abuses, 1792 and 1815.</small> The monstrous evils and abuses of imprisonment for debt, and the sufferings of prisoners, were fully exposed, in an able report to the House of Commons drawn by Mr. Grey in 1792.[1] But for several years, these evils received little correction. In 1815 the prisons were still over-crowded, and their wretched inmates left without allowance of food, fuel, bedding, or medical attendance. Complaints were still heard of their perishing of cold and hunger.[2]

<small>Insolvent Debtors' Act, 1813.</small> Special acts had been passed, from time to time, since the reign of Anne,[3] for the relief of insolvents: but they were of temporary and partial operation. Overcrowded prisons had been sometimes thinned: but the rigours and abuses of the laws affecting debtors were unchanged; and thousands of insolvents still languished in prison. In 1760, a remedial measure of more general operation was passed: but was soon afterwards repealed.[4] Provision was also made for the release of poor debtors in certain cases:[5] but it was not until 1813 that insolvents were placed under the jurisdiction of a court, and entitled to seek their discharge on rendering a true account of all their debts and property.[6] A distinction was at length recognised between poverty and crime. This

---

[1] Com. Journ., xlvii. 640.

[2] 7th March, 1815, Hans. Deb., 1st Ser., xxx. 39; Commons' Report on King's Bench, Fleet, and Marshalsea Prisons, 1815. The King's Bench, calculated to hold 220 prisoners, had 600; the Fleet, estimated to hold 200, had 769.

[3] 1 Anne, st. i. c. 25.

[4] 1 Geo. III. c. 17; Adolph. Hist., i. 17, *n*.

[5] 32 Geo. II. c. 28; 33 Geo. III. c. 5.

[6] 53 Geo. III. c. 102; Hans. Deb., 1st Ser., xxvi. 301, &c.

great remedial law restored liberty to crowds of wretched debtors. In the next thirteen years upwards of 50,000 were set free.[1] Thirty years later, its beneficent principles were further extended, when debtors were not only released from confinement, but able to claim protection to their liberty, on giving up all their goods.[2] And at length, in 1861, the law attained its fullest development, in the liberal measure of Sir R. Bethell: when fraudulent debt was dealt with as a crime, and imprisonment of common debtors was repudiated.[3] Nor did the enlightened charity of the legislature rest here. Debtors already in confinement were not left to seek their liberation: but were set free by the officers of the Court of Bankruptcy.[4] Some had grown familiar with their prison walls, and having lost all fellowship with the outer world, clung to their miserable cells, as to a home.[5] They were led forth gently, and restored to a life that had become strange to them; and their untenanted dungeons were condemned to destruction.

Later measures of relief to debtors.

The free soil of England has, for ages, been relieved from the reproach of slavery. The ancient condition of villenage expired about the commencement of the seventeenth century;[6] and no other form of slavery was recognised

The negro case, 1771.

---

[1] Mr. Hume's Return, 1827 (430).
[2] Protection Acts, 5 & 6 Vict. c. 96; 7 & 8 Vict. c. 96.
[3] Bankruptcy Act, 24 & 25 Vict. c. 134, § 221.
[4] *Ibid.*, § 98–105.
[5] In January, 1862, John Miller was removed from the Queen's Bench Prison, having been there since 1814.—*Times*, Jan. 23rd, 1862.
[6] Noy, 27. Hargrave's Argument in Negro Case, St. Tr., xx. 40;

by our laws. In the colonies, however, it was legalised by statute;[1] and it was long before the rights of a colonial slave, in the mother country, were ascertained. Lord Holt, indeed, had pronounced an opinion that, 'as soon as a negro comes into England, he becomes free;' and Mr. Justice Powell had affirmed that 'the law takes no notice of a negro.'[2] But these just opinions were not confirmed by express adjudication until the celebrated case of James Sommersett in 1771. This negro having been brought to England by his owner, Mr. Stewart, left that gentleman's service, and refused to return to it. Mr. Stewart had him seized and placed in irons, on board a ship then lying in the Thames, and about to sail for Jamaica,—where he intended to sell his mutinous slave. But while the negro was still lying on board, he was brought before the Court of King's Bench by *habeas corpus*. The question was now fully discussed, more particularly in a most learned and able argument by Mr. Hargrave; and at length, in June 1772, Lord Mansfield pronounced the opinion of the Court, that slavery in England was illegal, and that the negro must be set free.[3]

It was a righteous judgment: but scarcely worthy of the extravagant commendation bestowed upon it, at that time and since. This boasted law, as declared by Lord Mansfield, was already recog-

Smith's Commonwealth, book 2, ch. 10; Barrington on the Statutes, 2nd ed. p. 232.
[1] 10 Will. III. c. 26; 5 Geo. II. c. 7; 32 Geo. II. c. 31.
[2] Smith *v.* Browne and Cowper, 2 Salk. 666.
[3] Case of James Sommersett, St. Tr., xx. 1; Lofft's Rep., 1.

nised in France, Holland, and some other European countries; and as yet England had shown no symptoms of compassion for the negro beyond her own shores.[1]

In Scotland, negro slaves continued to be sold as chattels, until late in the last century.[2] It was not until 1756, that the lawfulness of negro slavery was questioned. In that year, however, a negro who had been brought to Scotland, claimed his liberty of his master, Robert Sheddan, who had put him on board ship to return to Virginia. But before his claim could be decided, the poor negro died.[3] But for this sad incident, a Scotch court would first have had the credit of setting the negro free on British soil. Four years after the case of Sommersett, the law of Scotland was settled. Mr. Wedderburn had brought with him to Scotland, as his personal servant, a negro named Knight, who continued several years in his service, and married in that country. But, at length, he claimed his freedom. The sheriff being appealed to, held 'that the state of slavery is not recognised by the laws of this kingdom.' The case being brought before the Court of Session, it was adjudged that the master had no right to the negro's service, nor to send him out of the country without his consent.[4]

Negroes in Scotland.

[1] Hargrave's Argument, St. Tr., xx. 62.
[2] Chambers' Domestic Annals of Scotland, iii. 453. On the 2nd May, 1722, an advertisement appeared in the Edinburgh Evening Courant, announcing that a stolen negro had been found, who would be sold to pay expenses, unless claimed within two weeks.—*Ibid.*
[3] See Dictionary of Decisions, *tit.* Slave, iii. 14545.
[4] *Ibid.*, p. 14549.

The negro in Scotland was now assured of freedom: but, startling as it may sound, the slavery of native Scotchmen continued to be recognised, in that country, to the very end of last century. The colliers and salters were unquestionably slaves. They were bound to continue their service during their lives, were fixed to their places of employment, and sold with the works to which they belonged. So completely did the law of Scotland regard them as a distinct class, not entitled to the same liberties as their fellow-subjects, that they were excepted from the Scotch Habeas Corpus Act of 1701. Nor had their slavery the excuse of being a remnant of the ancient feudal state of villenage, which had expired before coal-mines were yet worked in Scotland. But being paid high wages, and having peculiar skill, their employers had originally contrived to bind them to serve for a term of years, or for life; and such service at length became a recognised custom.[1] In 1775 their condition attracted the notice of the legislature, and an act was passed for their relief.[2] Its preamble stated that 'many colliers and salters are in a state of slavery and bondage;' and that their emancipation 'would remove the reproach of allowing such a state of servitude to exist in a free country.' But so deeply rooted was this hateful custom, that Parliament did not venture to condemn it as illegal. It was provided that colliers

Colliers and salters, in Scotland.

---

[1] Forb. Inst., part 1, b. 2, t. 3; Macdonal. Inst., i. 63; Cockburn's Mem., 76.
[2] 15 Geo. III. c. 28.

and salters commencing work after the 1st of July, 1775, should not become slaves; and that those already in a state of slavery might obtain their freedom in seven years, if under twenty-one years of age; in ten years, if under thirty-five. To avail themselves of this enfranchisement, however, they were obliged to obtain a decree of the Sheriff's Court; and these poor ignorant slaves, generally in debt to their masters, were rarely in a condition to press their claims to freedom. Hence the act was practically inoperative. But at length, in 1799, their freedom was absolutely established by law.[1]

The last vestige of slavery was now effaced from the soil of Britain: but not until the land had been resounding for years with outcries against the African slave trade. Seven years later that odious traffic was condemned; and at length colonial slavery itself,—so long encouraged and protected by the legislature,—gave way before the enlightened philanthropy of another generation. *Slave trade and colonial slavery.*

Next in importance to personal freedom is immunity from suspicions, and jealous observation. Men may be without restraints upon their liberty: they may pass to and fro at pleasure: but if their steps are tracked by spies and informers, their words noted down for crimination, their associates watched as conspirators,—who shall say that they are free? Nothing is more revolting to Englishmen than the espionage which forms part of the administrative system of continental despotisms. It haunts men like an evil genius, chills *Spies and informers.*

[1] 39 Geo. III. c. 56.

their gaiety, restrains their wit, casts a shadow over their friendships, and blights their domestic hearth. The freedom of a country may be measured by its immunity from this baleful agency.[1] Rulers who distrust their own people, must govern in a spirit of absolutism; and suspected subjects will be ever sensible of their bondage.

Our own countrymen have been comparatively exempt from this hateful interference with their moral freedom. Yet we find many traces of a system repugnant to the liberal policy of our laws. In 1764, we see spies following Wilkes everywhere, dogging his steps like shadows, and reporting every movement of himself and his friends to the secretaries of state. Nothing was too insignificant for the curiosity of these exalted magistrates. Every visit he paid or received throughout the day was noted: the persons he chanced to encounter in the streets were not overlooked: it was known where he dined, or went to church, and at what hour he returned home at night.[2]

Spies in 1764.

In the state trials of 1794, we discover spies and informers in the witness-box, who had been active members of political societies, sharing their councils, and encouraging, if not prompting, their criminal extravagance.[3] And throughout that period

In 1794.

---

[1] Montesquieu speaks of informers as 'un genre d'hommes funeste.'—Liv. vi. ch. 8. And of spies, he says: 'Faut-il des espions dans la monarchie? ce n'est pas la pratique ordinaire des bons princes.'—Liv. xii. ch. 23. And again: 'L'espionage seroit peut-être tolérable s'il pouvoit être exercé par d'honnêtes gens: mais l'infamie nécessaire de la personne peut faire juger de l'infamie de la chose.'—*Ibid.*

[2] Grenville Papers, ii. 155.   [3] St. Tr., xxiv. 722, 800, 806.

of dread and suspicion, society was everywhere infested with espionage.[1]

Again, in 1817, government spies were deeply compromised in the turbulence and sedition of that period. Castle, a spy of infamous character, having uttered the most seditious language, and incited the people to arm, proved in the witness-box the very crimes he had himself prompted and encouraged.[2] Another spy, named Oliver, proceeded into the disturbed districts, in the character of a London delegate, and remained for many weeks amongst the deluded operatives, everywhere instigating them to rise and arm. He encouraged them with hopes that in the event of a rising, they would be assisted by 150,000 men in the metropolis; and thrusting himself into their society, he concealed the craft of the spy, under the disguise of a traitorous conspirator.[3] Before he undertook this shameful mission, he was in communication with Lord Sidmouth; and throughout his mischievous progress was corresponding with the government or its agents. Lord Sidmouth himself is above the suspicion of having connived at the use of covert incitements to treason. The spies whom he employed had sought him out and offered their services in the detection of crime; and, being responsible for the public peace, he had thought it

Spies in 1817.

---

[1] *Supra*, Vol. II. p. 304, *et seq.*; Wilberforce's Life, iv. 369; Cartwright's Life, i. 209; Currie's Life, i. 172; Holcroft's Mem., ii. 190; Stephens' Life of Horne Tooke, ii. 118.

[2] St. Tr., xxxii. 214, 284, *et seq.*; Earl Grey, June 16th, 1817; Hans. Deb., 1st Ser., xxxvi. 102.

[3] Bamford's Life of a Radical, i. 77, 158; Mr. Ponsonby's Statement, June 23rd, 1817; Hans. Deb., 1st Ser., xxxvi. 1114.

necessary to secure information of the intended movements of dangerous bodies of men.[1] But Oliver's activity was so conspicuous as seriously to compromise the government. Immediately after the outbreak in Derbyshire, his conduct was indignantly reprobated in both Houses;[2] and after the outrages, in which he had been an accomplice, had been judicially investigated, his proceedings received a still more merciless exposure in Parliament.[3] There is little doubt that Oliver did more to disturb the public peace by his malign influence, than to protect it, by timely information to the government. The agent was mischievous, and his principals could not wholly escape the blame of his misdeeds. Their base instrument, in his coarse zeal for his employers, brought discredit upon the means they had taken, in good faith, for preventing disorders. To the severity of repressive measures, and a rigorous administration of the law, was added the reproach of a secret alliance between the executive and a wretch who had at once tempted and betrayed his unhappy victims.

Relations of the executive with informers.

The relations between the government and its informers are of extreme delicacy. Not to profit by timely information were a crime: but to retain in government pay, and to reward spies and informers, who consort with con-

---

[1] Lord Sidmouth's Life, iii. 185.
[2] 16th and 23rd June, 1817; Hans. Deb., 1st Ser., xxxvi. 1016, 1111.
[3] St. Tr., xxxii. 755, *et seq.*; 11th Feb., 1818; Hans. Deb., xxxvii. 338; Speeches of Lord Milton, Mr. Bennet; Feb. 19th, and March 5th: (Lords), *Ibid.*, 522, 802.

spirators as their sworn accomplices, and encourage while they betray them in their crimes, is a practice for which no plea can be offered. No government, indeed, can be supposed to have expressly instructed its spies to instigate the perpetration of crime: but to be unsuspected, every spy must be zealous in the cause which he pretends to have espoused; and his zeal in a criminal enterprise is a direct encouragement of crime. So odious is the character of a spy, that his ignominy is shared by his employers, against whom public feeling has never failed to pronounce itself, in proportion to the infamy of the agent, and the complicity of those whom he served.

Three years later, the conduct of a spy named Edwards, in connection with the Cato Street Conspiracy, attracted unusual obloquy. *The spy Edwards, 1820.* For months he had been at once an active conspirator and the paid agent of the government; prompting crimes, and betraying his accomplices. Thistlewood had long been planning the assassination of the ministers; and Edwards had urged him to attempt that monstrous crime, the consummation of which his treachery prevented. He had himself suggested other crimes, no less atrocious. He had counselled a murderous outrage upon the House of Commons; and had distributed hand grenades among his wretched associates, in order to tempt them to deeds of violence.[1] The conspirators were

---

[1] Ann. Reg., 1820, p. 30; Hans. Deb., 2nd Ser., i. 54, 242; Lord Sidmouth's Life, iii. 216; Edinb. Rev., xxxiii. 211; St. Tr., xxxiii. 749, 754, 987, 1004, 1435.

justly hung: the devilish spy was hidden and rewarded. Infamy so great and criminal in a spy had never yet been exposed: but the frightfulness of the crime which his information had prevented, and the desperate character of the men who had plotted it, saved ministers from much of the odium that had attached to their connection with Oliver. They had saved themselves from assassination; and could they be blamed for having discovered and prevented the bloody design? The crime had been plotted in darkness and secrecy, and countermined by the cunning and treachery of an accomplice. That it had not been consummated, was due to the very agency which hostile critics sought to condemn. But if ministers escaped censure, the iniquity of the spy-system was illustrated in its most revolting aspects.

Again, in 1833, complaint was made that the police had been concerned in equivocal practices, too much resembling the treachery of spies: but a parliamentary inquiry elicited little more than the misconduct of a single policeman, who was dismissed from the force.[1] And the organisation of a well-qualified body of detective police has at once facilitated the prevention and discovery of crime, and averted the worst evils incident to the employment of spies.

Detective police.

Akin to the use of spies, to watch and betray the acts of men, is the intrusion of government into the confidence of private letters, en-

Opening letters.

---

[1] Petition of F. Young and others; Commons' Rep. 1833; Hans. Deb., 3rd Ser., xviii. 1359; xx. 404, 834.

trusted to the Post-office. The state having assumed a monopoly in the transmission of letters on behalf of the people, its agents could not pry into their secrets without a flagrant breach of trust, which scarcely any necessity could justify. For the detection of crimes dangerous to the state, or society, a power of opening letters was, indeed, reserved to the secretary of state. But for many years, ministers or their subordinate officers appear to have had no scruples in obtaining information, through the Post-office, not only of plots and conspiracies, but of the opinions and projects of their political opponents. Curiosity more often prompted this vexatious intrusion than motives of public policy.

The political correspondence of the reign of George III. affords conclusive evidence that the practice of opening the letters of public men at the Post-office, was known to be general. We find statesmen of all parties alluding to the practice, without reserve or hesitation, and entrusting their letters to private hands whenever their communications were confidential.[1]

---

[1] From a great number of examples, the following may be selected:—

Lord Hardwicke, writing in 1762 to Lord Rockingham of the Duke of Devonshire's spirited letter to the Duke of Newcastle, said: 'Which his grace judged very rightly in sending by the common post, and trusting to their curiosity.'—*Rockingham Mem.*, i. 157.

Mr. Hans Stanley, writing to Mr. Grenville, Oct. 14th, 1765, says: 'Though this letter contains nothing of consequence, I chuse to send it by a private hand, observing that all my correspondence is opened in a very awkward and bungling manner, which I intimate in case you should chuse to write anything which you would not have publick.'—*Grenville Papers*, iii. 99. Again, Mr. Whately, writing to Mr. Grenville, June 4th, 1768, says: 'I may have some things to say which I would not tell the postmaster, and for that reason have chosen this manner of conveyance.'—*Ibid.*, iv. 299.

Traces of this discreditable practice, so far as it ministered to idle or malignant curiosity, have disappeared since the early part of the present century. From that period, the general correspondence of the country, through the Post-office, has been inviolable. But for purposes of police and diplomacy,—to thwart conspiracies at home, or hostile combinations abroad,—the secretary of state has continued, until our own time, to issue warrants for opening the letters of persons suspected of crimes, or of designs injurious to the state. This power, sanctioned by long usage, and by many statutes, had been continually exercised for two centuries. But it had passed without observation until 1844, when a petition was presented to the House of Commons from four persons,—of whom the notorious Joseph Mazzini was one,—complaining that their letters had been detained at the Post-office, broken open, and read. Sir James Graham, the secretary of state, denied that the

<small>*Petition of Mazzini and others, June 14th, 1844.*</small>

Lord Temple, writing to Mr. Beresford, Oct. 23rd, 1783, says: 'The shameful liberties taken with my letters, both sent and received (for even the speaker's letter to me had been opened) make me cautious on politics.'—*Beresford Correspondence*, i. 243.

Mr. Pitt, writing to Lady Chatham, Nov. 11th, 1783, said: 'I am afraid it will not be easy for me, by the post, to be anything else than a fashionable correspondent, for I believe the fashion which prevails, of opening almost every letter that is sent, makes it almost impossible to write anything worth reading.'—*Lord Stanhope's Life of Pitt*, i. 136.

Lord Melville, writing to Mr. Pitt, April 3rd, 1804, said: 'I shall continue to address you through Alexander Hope's conveyance, as I remember our friend Bathurst very strongly hinted to me last year, to beware of the Post-office, when you and I had occasion to correspond on critical points, or in critical times.'—*Ibid.*, iv. 145; see also Currie's Life, ii. 160; Stephens' Mem. of Horne Tooke, ii. 118; Court and Cab. of George III., iii. 265, &c.

letters of three of these persons had been opened: but avowed that the letters of one of them had been detained and opened by his warrant, issued under the authority of a statute.[1] Never had any avowal, from a minister, encountered so general a tumult of disapprobation. Even Lord Sidmouth's spy-system had escaped more lightly. The public were ignorant of the law, though renewed seven years before,[2] —and wholly unconscious of the practice which it sanctioned. Having believed in the security of the Post-office, they now dreaded the betrayal of all secrecy and confidence. A general system of espionage being suspected, was condemned with just indignation.

Five-and-twenty years earlier, a minister,—secure of a parliamentary majority, — having haughtily defended his own conduct, would have been content to refuse further inquiry, and brave public opinion. And in this instance, inquiry was at first successfully resisted:[3] but a few days later, Sir James Graham adopted a course, at once significant of the times, and of his own confidence in the integrity and good faith with which he had discharged a hateful duty. He proposed the appointment of a secret committee, to investigate the law in regard to the opening of letters, and the mode in which it had been exercised.[4] A similar

Parliamentary inquiries.

---

[1] Hans. Deb., 3rd Ser., lxxv. 892.
[2] Post-office Act, 1837, 1 Vict. c. 33, s. 25.
[3] June 24th, 1844; Mr. Duncombe's motion for a committee—Ayes, 162; Noes, 206.—*Hans. Deb.*, 3rd Ser., lxxv. 1264.
[4] July 2nd, as an amendment to another motion of Mr. Duncombe; Hans. Deb., 3rd Ser., lxxvi. 212.

committee was also appointed in the House of Lords.[1] These committees were constituted of the most eminent and impartial men to be found in Parliament; and their inquiries, while eliciting startling revelations as to the practice, entirely vindicated the personal conduct of Sir James Graham. It appeared that foreign letters had, in early times, been constantly searched to detect correspondence with Rome, and other foreign powers: that by orders of both Houses, during the Long Parliament, foreign mails had been searched; and that Cromwell's Postage Act expressly authorised the opening of letters, in order 'to discover and prevent dangerous and wicked designs against the peace and welfare of the commonwealth.' Charles II. had interdicted, by proclamation, the opening of any letters, except by warrant from the secretary of state. By an act of the 9th Anne, the secretary of state first received statutory power to issue warrants for the opening of letters; and this authority had been continued by several later statutes for the regulation of the Post-office. In 1783, a similar power had been entrusted to the Lord Lieutenant of Ireland.[2] In 1722, several letters of Bishop Atterbury having been opened, copies were produced in evidence against him, on the bill of pains and penalties. During the rebellion of 1745, and at other periods of public danger, letters had been extensively opened. Nor were warrants restricted to the detection of crimes or practices dangerous to the state. They had been constantly issued for the discovery of forgery and

[1] Hans. Deb., 3rd Ser., lxxvi. 296.   [2] 23 & 24 Geo. III. c. 17.

other offences, on the application of the parties concerned in the apprehension of offenders. Since the commencement of this century, they had not exceeded an annual average of eight. They had been issued by successive secretaries of state, of every party, and except in periods of unusual disturbance, in about the same annual numbers. The public and private correspondence of the country, both foreign and domestic, practically enjoyed complete security. A power so rarely exercised could not have materially advanced the ends of justice. At the same time, if it were wholly withdrawn, the Post-office would become the privileged medium of criminal correspondence. No amendment of the law was recommended; and the secretary of state retains his accustomed authority.[1] But no one can doubt that, if used at all, it will be reserved for extreme occasions, when the safety of the state demands the utmost vigilance of its guardians.

Nothing has served so much to raise, in other states, the estimation of British liberty, as the protection which our laws afford to foreigners. Our earlier history, indeed, discloses many popular jealousies of strangers settling in this country. But to foreign merchants special consideration was shown by Magna Charta; and whatever the policy of the state, or the feelings of the people, at later periods, aliens have generally enjoyed the same personal liberty as British subjects, and complete protection from the jealousies and

Protection of foreigners.

---

[1] Reports of Secret Committees of Lords and Commons; and see Torrens' Life of Sir J. Graham, ii. 285–349.

vengeance of foreign powers. It has been a proud distinction for England to afford an inviolable asylum to men of every rank and condition, seeking refuge on her shores, from persecution and danger in their own lands. England was a sanctuary to the Flemish refugees driven forth by the cruelties of Alva; to the Protestant refugees who fled from the persecutions of Louis XIV.; and to the Catholic nobles and priests who sought refuge from the bloody guillotine of revolutionary France. All exiles from their own country—whether they fled from despotism or democracy,—whether they were kings discrowned, or humble citizens in danger,—have looked to England as their home. Such refugees were safe from the dangers which they had escaped. No solicitation or menace from their own government could disturb their right of asylum; and they were equally free from molestation by the municipal laws of England. The crown indeed had claimed the right of ordering aliens to withdraw from the realm: but this prerogative had not been exercised since the reign of Elizabeth.[1] From that period,—through civil wars and revolutions, a disputed succession, and treasonable plots against the state, no foreigners had been disturbed. If guilty of crimes, they were punished: but otherwise enjoyed the full protection of the law.

It was not until 1793, that a departure from this generous policy was deemed necessary, in the interests of the state. The revolution in France had driven hosts of political refugees to

Alien Act, 1793.

[1] Viz., in 1571, 1574, and 1575.

our shores.[1] They were pitied, and would be welcome. But among the foreigners claiming our hospitality, Jacobin emissaries were suspected of conspiring, with democratic associations in England, to overthrow the government. To guard against the machinations of such men, ministers sought extraordinary powers for the supervision of aliens, and, if necessary, for their removal from the realm. Whether this latter power may be exercised by the crown, or had fallen into desuetude, became a subject of controversy: but however that might be, the provisions of the Alien Bill, now proposed, far exceeded the limits of any ancient prerogative. An account was to be taken of all foreigners arriving at the several ports, who were to bring no arms or ammunition: they were not to travel without passports: the secretary of state might remove any suspected alien out of the realm; and all aliens might be directed to reside in such districts as were deemed necessary for public security, where they would be registered, and required to give up their arms. Such restraints upon foreigners were novel, and wholly inconsistent with the free and liberal spirit with which they had been hitherto entertained. Marked with extreme jealousy and rigour, they could only be justified by the extraordinary exigency of the times. They were, indeed, equivalent to a suspension of the Habeas Corpus Act, and demanded proofs of public danger no less conclusive. In opposition to the measure, it was said

[1] In Dec. 1792, it appeared that 8,000 had emigrated to England.—*Parl. Hist.*, xxx. 147.

that there was no evidence of the presence of dangerous aliens: that discretionary power to be entrusted to the executive might be abused; and that it formed part of the policy of ministers to foment the public apprehensions. But the right of the state, on sufficient grounds, to take such precautions, could not be disputed.[1] The bill was to continue in force for one year only,[2] and was passed without difficulty.

So urgent was deemed the danger of free intercourse with the continent at this period, that even British subjects were made liable to unprecedented restraints, by the Traitorous Correspondence Bill.[3]

Traitorous Correspondence Bill, 1793.

The Alien Bill was renewed from time to time; and throughout the year foreigners continued under strict surveillance. When peace was at length restored, government relaxed the more stringent provisions of the war alien bills; and proposed measures better suited to a time of peace. This was done in 1802, and again in 1814. But, in 1816, when public tranquillity prevailed throughout Europe, the propriety of continuing such measures, even in a modified form, was strenuously contested.[4]

Alien Bill renewed.

Again, in 1818, opposition no less resolute was offered to the renewal of the Alien Bill. Ministers were urged to revert to the liberal policy of former times, and not to insist fur-

Alien Bill, 1818,

---

[1] Parl. Hist., xxx. 155-238.
[2] 33 Geo. III. c. 4.
[3] Parl. Hist., xxx. 582, 928.
[4] Hans. Deb., 1st Ser., xxxiv. 430, 617.

ther upon jealous restrictions and invidious powers. The hardships which foreigners might suffer from sudden banishment were especially dwelt upon. Men who had made England their home,—bound to it by domestic ties and affections, and carrying on trade under protection of its laws,—were liable, without proof of crime, on secret information, and by a clandestine procedure, to one of the gravest punishments.[1] This power, however, was rarely exercised, and in a few years was surrendered.[2] During the political convulsions of the continent in 1848, the executive again received authority, for a limited time, to remove any foreigners who might be dangerous to the peace of the country:[3] but it was not put in force in a single instance.[4] The law has still required the registration of aliens:[5] but its execution has fallen more and more into disuse. The confidence of our policy, and the prodigious intercourse developed by facilities of communication and the demands of commerce, have practically restored to foreigners that entire freedom which they enjoyed before the French Revolution.

The improved feeling of Parliament in regard to foreigners was marked in 1844 by Mr. Hutt's wise and liberal measure for the naturalisation of aliens.[6] Confidence succeeded to jealousy; and the legislature, instead of devising

Naturalisation Act, 1844.

---

[1] Hans. Deb., 1st Ser., xxxviii. 521, 735, 811, &c.; 58 Geo. III. c. 96.
[2] In 1826: 5 Geo. IV. c. 37; Hans. Deb., 2nd Ser., x. 1376.
[3] 11 & 12 Vict. c. 20.   [4] Parl. Return, 1850 (688).
[5] 7 Geo. IV. c. 54; 6 & 7 Will. IV. c. 11.
[6] 7 & 8 Vict. c. 66; 10 & 11 Vict. c. 83.

impediments and restraints, offered welcome and citizenship.

<small>Right of asylum never impaired.</small> While the law had provided for the removal of aliens, it was for the safety of England,— not for the satisfaction of other states. The right of asylum was as inviolable as ever. It was not for foreign governments to dictate to England the conditions on which aliens under her protection should be treated. Of this principle, the events of 1802 offered a remarkable illustration.

<small>Napoleon's demands in 1802.</small> During the short peace succeeding the treaty of Amiens, Napoleon, First Consul of the French Republic, demanded that our government should 'remove out of the British dominions all the French princes and their adherents, together with the bishops and other individuals, whose political principles and conduct must necessarily occasion great jealousy to the French Government.'[1]

To this demand Lord Hawkesbury replied, his Majesty 'certainly expects that all foreigners who may reside within his dominions should not only hold a conduct conformable to the laws of the country, but should abstain from all acts which may be hostile to the government of any country, with which his Majesty may be at peace. As long, however, as they conduct themselves according to these principles, his Majesty would feel it inconsistent with his dignity, with his honour, and with the common laws of hospitality, to deprive them of

---

[1] Mr. Merry to Lord Hawkesbury, June 4th, 1802; Parl. Hist., xxx. 1263.

that protection which individuals, resident in his dominions, can only forfeit by their own misconduct.'[1]

Still more decidedly were these demands reiterated. It was demanded, 1st. That more effectual measures should be adopted for the suppression of seditious publications. 2nd. That certain persons named should be sent out of Jersey. 3rd. 'That the former bishops of Arras and St. Pol de Leon, and all those who, like them, under the pretext of religion, seek to raise disturbances in the interior of France, shall likewise be sent away.' 4th. That Georges and his adherents shall be transported to Canada. 5th. That the princes of the House of Bourbon be recommended to repair to Warsaw, the residence of the head of their family. 6th. That French emigrants, wearing orders and decorations of the ancient government of France, should be required to leave England. These demands assumed to be based upon a construction of the recent treaty of Amiens; and effect was expected to be given to them, under the provisions of the Alien Act.[2]

These representations were frankly and boldly met. For the repression of seditious writings, our government would entertain no measure but an appeal to the courts of law.[3] To apply the Alien Act in aid of the law of libel, and to send foreign writers out of the country,

Reply of the English Government.

[1] Lord Hawkesbury to Mr. Merry, 10th June, 1802.
[2] M. Otto to Lord Hawkesbury, Aug. 17th, 1802.
[3] See *supra*, Vol. II. p. 332.

because they were obnoxious, not to our own government, but to another, was not to be listened to.

The removal of other French emigrants, and especially of the princes of the House of Bourbon, was refused, and every argument and precedent adduced in support of the demand refuted.[1] The emigrants in Jersey had already removed, of their own accord; and the bishops would be required to leave England if it could be proved that they had been distributing papers on the coast of France, in order to disturb the government: but sufficient proof of this charge must be given. As regards M. Georges, who had been concerned in circulating papers hostile to the government in France, his Majesty agreed to remove him from our European dominions. The king refused to withdraw the rights of hospitality from the French princes, unless it could be proved that they were attempting to disturb the peace between the two countries. He also declined to adopt the harsh measures which had been demanded against refugees who continued to wear French decorations.[2]

The ground here taken has been since maintained.

Principles on which foreigners are protected. It is not enough that the presence or acts of a foreigner may be displeasing to a foreign power. If that rule were accepted, where would be the right of asylum? The refugee would be followed by the vengeance of his own government, and driven forth from the home he had chosen, in a free country. On this point,

---

[1] Mr. Merry to Lord Hawkesbury, June 17th, 1802.
[2] Lord Hawkesbury to Mr. Merry, Aug. 28th, 1802.

Englishmen have been chivalrously sensitive. Having undertaken to protect the stranger, they have resented any menace to him, as an insult to themselves. Disaffection to the rulers of his own country is natural to a refugee: his banishment attests it. Poles hated Russia: Hungarians and Italians were hostile to Austria: French Royalists spurned the republic and the first empire: Charles X. and Louis Napoleon were disaffected to Louis-Philippe, King of the French: legitimists and Orleanists alike abhorred the French republic of 1848, and the revived empire of 1852. But all were safe under the broad shield of England. Every political sentiment, every discussion short of libel, enjoyed freedom. Every act not prohibited by law,—however distasteful to other states,—was entitled to protection. Nay more: large numbers of refugees, obnoxious to their own rulers, were maintained by the liberality of the English government.

This generosity has sometimes been abused by aliens, who, under cover of our laws, have plotted against friendly states. There are acts, indeed, which the laws could only have tolerated by an oversight; and in this category was that of conspiracy to assassinate the sovereign of a friendly state. The horrible conspiracy of Orsini, in 1858, had been plotted in England. Not countermined by espionage, nor checked by jealous restraints on personal liberty, it had been matured in safety; and its more overt acts had afterwards escaped the vigilance of the police in France. The crime was

The Orsini conspiracy, 1858.

execrated: but how could its secret conception have been prevented? So far our laws were blameless. The government of France, however, in the excitement of recent danger, angrily remonstrated against the alleged impunity of assassins in this country.[1] Englishmen repudiated, with just indignation, any tolerance of murder. Yet on one point were our laws at fault. Orsini's desperate crime was unexampled; planned in England, it had been executed beyond the limits of British jurisdiction; it was doubtful if his confederates could be brought to justice; and certain that they would escape without adequate punishment. Ministers, believing it due, no less to France than to the vindication of our own laws, that this anomaly should be corrected, proposed a measure, with that object, to Parliament. But the Commons, resenting imputations upon this country, which had not yet been repelled; and jealous of the apparent dictation of France, under which they were called upon to legislate, refused to entertain the bill.[2] A powerful ministry was struck down; and a rupture hazarded with the Emperor of the French. Yet to the measure itself, apart from the circumstances under which it was offered, no valid objection could be raised; and three years later, its provisions were silently admitted to a place in our revised criminal laws.[3]

Conspiracy to Murder Bill, Feb. 8th, 1858.

A just protection of political refugees is not incom-

[1] Despatch of Count Walewski, Jan. 20th, 1858.
[2] Mr. Milner Gibson's amendment on second reading.—*Hans. Deb.*, 3rd Ser., cxlviii. 1742, &c.
[3] 24 & 25 Vict. c. 100, § 4.

patible with the surrender of criminals. All nations have a common interest in the punishment of heinous crimes; and upon this principle, England entered into extradition treaties with France, and the United States of America, for mutually delivering up to justice persons charged with murder, piracy, arson, or forgery, committed within the jurisdiction of either of the contracting states.[1] England offers no asylum to such criminals; and her own jurisdiction has been vastly extended over offenders escaping from justice. It is a wise policy,—conducive to the comity of civilised nations.

Extradition treaties.

---

[1] Treaty with France, 1843, confirmed by 6 & 7 Vict. c. 75; treaty with United States, 1842, confirmed by 6 & 7 Vict. c. 76. Provisions to the same effect had been comprised in the treaty of Amiens; and also in a treaty with the United States in 1794.—*Phillimore, Int. Law*, i. 427; Hans. Deb., 3rd Ser., lxx. 1325; lxxi. 564. In 1862, after the period of this history, the like arrangement was made with Denmark; 25 & 26 Vict. c. 70. In 1864, a similar treaty was entered into with Prussia, but not confirmed by Parliament; Hans. Deb., 25th and 27th July. See also 'The Extradition Act,' 1870.'

CHAPTER XII.

RELATIONS OF THE CHURCH TO POLITICAL HISTORY:—LEADING INCIDENTS AND CONSEQUENCES OF THE REFORMATION IN ENGLAND, SCOTLAND, AND IRELAND:—EXACTION OF CONFORMITY WITH THE STATE CHURCH:—SKETCH OF THE PENAL CODE AGAINST ROMAN CATHOLICS AND NONCONFORMISTS:—STATE OF THE CHURCH AND OTHER RELIGIOUS BODIES ON THE ACCESSION OF GEORGE III.:—GENERAL RELAXATION OF THE PENAL CODE:—HISTORY OF CATHOLIC CLAIMS PRIOR TO THE REGENCY.

Relations of the church to political history. IN the sixteenth century, the history of the church is the history of England. In the seventeenth century, the relations of the church to the state and society, contributed, with political causes, to convulse the kingdom with civil wars and revolutions. And in later and more settled times, they formed no inconsiderable part of the political annals of the country. The struggles, the controversies, the polity, and the laws of one age, are the inheritance of another. Henry VIII. and Elizabeth bequeathed to their successors ecclesiastical strifes which have disturbed every subsequent reign; and, after three centuries, the results of the Reformation have not yet been fully developed.

The church before the Reformation. A brief review of the leading incidents and consequences of that momentous event will serve to elucidate the later history of the church and other religious bodies, in their relations to the state.

For centuries, the Catholic church had been at

once the church of the state, and the church of the people. All the subjects of the crown acknowledged her authority, accepted her doctrines, participated in her offices, and worshipped at her consecrated shrines. In her relations to the state she approached the ideal of Hooker, wherein the church and the commonwealth were identified: no one being a member of the one, who was not also a member of the other.[1] But under the shadow of this majestic unity grew ignorance, errors, superstition, imperious authority and pretensions, excessive wealth, and scandalous corruption. Freedom of thought was proscribed. To doubt the infallible judgment of the church was heresy,—a mortal sin, for which the atonement was recantation or death. From the time of Wickliffe to the Reformation, heresies and schisms were rife:[2] the authority of the church and the influence of her clergy were gradually impaired; and at length, she was overpowered by the ecclesiastical revolution of Henry VIII. With her supremacy, perished the semblance of religious union in England.

So vast a change as the Reformation, in the religious faith and habitudes of a people, could not have been effected, at any time, without wide and permanent dissensions. When men were first invited to think, it was not probable that they

The Reformation.

---

[1] Book viii., [2] Keble's Ed. iii. 411. Bishop Gardiner had already expressed the same theory: 'the realm and the church consist of the same persons; and as the king is the head of the realm, he must, therefore, be head of the church.'—*Gilpin*, ii. 29.—See also *Gladstone's State and Church*, 4th Ed., i. 9-31.

[2] Warner, i. 527; Kennet's Hist., i. 265; Collier's Eccl. Hist., i. 579; Echard's Hist., 159; Burnet's Hist. of the Reformation, i. 27.

should think alike. But the time and circumstances of the Reformation were such as to aggravate theological schisms, and to embitter the contentions of religious parties. It was an age in which power was wielded with a rough hand; and the reform of the church was accompanied with plunder and persecution. The confiscation of church property envenomed the religious antipathies of the Catholic clergy: the cruel and capricious rigour with which every communion was, in turn, oppressed, estranged and divided the laity. The changes of faith and policy, —sometimes progressive, sometimes reactionary,— which marked the long and painful throes of the Reformation, from its inception under Henry VIII. to its final consummation under Elizabeth, left no party without its wrongs and sufferings.

Toleration and liberty of conscience were unknown. Catholics and Protestants alike recognised the duty of the state to uphold truth and repress error. In this conviction, reforming prelates concurred with popes and Roman divines. The Reformed church, owing her very life to the right of private judgment, assumed the same authority, in matters of doctrine, as the church of Rome, which pretended to infallibility. Not to accept the doctrines or ceremonies of the state church, for the time being, was a crime; and conformity with the new faith as with the old, was enforced by the dungeon, the scaffold, the gibbet, and the torch.[1]

Toleration unknown.

[1] 'A prince being God's deputy, ought to punish impieties against God,' said Archbishop Cranmer to Edward VI.—*Burnet's Hist.*, i. 111.

The Reformation.

The Reformed church being at length established under Elizabeth, the policy of her reign demands especial notice. Finding her fair realm distracted by the religious convulsions of the last three reigns, she insisted upon absolute unity. She exacted a strait conformity of doctrine and observance, denied liberty of conscience to all her subjects, and attached civil disabilities to dissent from the state church. By the first act of her reign,[1] the oath of supremacy was required to be taken as a qualification for every ecclesiastical benefice, or civil office under the crown. The act of uniformity[2] enforced, with severe penalties, conformity with the ritual of the established church, and attendance upon its services. A few years later, the oath of supremacy was, for the first time, required to be taken by every member of the House of Commons.[3]

Policy of Elizabeth.

Civil disabilities.

The Catholics were not only hostile to the state church, but disaffected to the queen herself. They contested her right to the crown; and despairing of the restoration of the ancient faith, or even of toleration, during her life, they plotted against her throne. Hence the Catholic religion was associated with treason; and the measures adopted for its repression were designed as well for the safety of the state, as for the discouragement of an obnoxious faith.[4]

The Catholic faith associated with treason.

To punish popish recusants, penalties for non-

---

[1] 1 Eliz. c. 1.   [2] 2 Eliz. c. 2.   [3] 5 Eliz. c. 1.
[4] 13 Eliz. c. 2; Burnet's Hist., ii. 354; Short's Hist. of the Church, 273.

attendance upon the services of the church were multiplied,[1] and enforced with merciless rigour.[2] The Catholic religion was utterly proscribed: its priests were banished, or hiding as traitors:[3] its adherents constrained to attend the services of a church which they spurned as schismatic and heretical.

Popish recusants.

While Catholics were thus proscribed, the ritual and polity of the Reformed church were narrowing the foundations of the Protestant establishment. The doctrinal modifications of the Roman creed were cautious and moderate. The new ritual, founded on that of the Catholic church,[4] was simple, eloquent, and devotional. The patent errors and superstitions of Rome were renounced: but otherwise her doctrines and ceremonies were respected. The extreme tenets of Rome, on the one side, and of Geneva on the other, were avoided. The design of Reformers was to restore the primitive church,[5] rather than to settle controversies already arising among Protestants.[6] Such moderation,—due rather to the predilections of Lutheran Reformers, and the leaning of some of them to the Roman faith, than to a profound policy,

Doctrinal moderation of the Reformation.

---

[1] 23 Eliz. c. 1; 29 Eliz. c. 6; 33 Eliz. c. 2; 35 Eliz. c. 1; Strype's Life of Whitgift, 95; Collier's Eccl. Hist., ii. 637; Warner, ii. 287; Kennet's Hist., ii. 497.

[2] Lingard, note *u*, viii. 356; Dodd's Church Hist., iii. 75; and Butler's Hist. Mem. of the Catholics, i. 230.

[3] 27 Eliz. c. 2.

[4] Cardwell's Hist. of the Book of Common Prayer.

[5] Bishop Jewell's Apology, ch. vii. Div. 3, c. x. Div. 1, &c.; Short's Hist. of the Church, 238; Mant's Notes to Articles.

[6] Lawrence's Bampton Lectures, 237; Short's Hist., 199; Froude's Hist., vii. 79.

—was calculated to secure a wide conformity. The respect shown to the ritual, and many of the observances of the Church of Rome, made the change of religion less abrupt and violent to the great body of the people. But extreme parties were not to be reconciled. The more faithful Catholics refused to renounce the supremacy of the Pope, and other cherished doctrines and traditions of their church. Neither conciliated by concessions, nor coerced by intimidation, they remained true to the ancient faith.

On the other hand, these very concessions to Romanism repelled the Calvinistic Reformers, who spurned every vestige of the Roman ritual, and repudiated the form of church government, which, with the exception of the Papal supremacy, was maintained in its ancient integrity. They condemned every ceremony of the church of Rome as idolatrous and superstitious;[1] they abhorred episcopacy, and favoured the Presbyterian form of government in the church. Toleration might have softened the asperities of theological controversy, until time had reconciled many of the differences springing from the Reformation. A few enlightened statesmen would gladly have practised it;[2] but the imperious temper of the queen,[3] and the bigoted zeal of her *The Puritans.*

Rigorous enforcement of conformity.

---

[1] In matters of ceremonial they objected to the wearing of the surplice, the sign of the cross and the office of sponsors in baptism; the use of the ring in the marriage ceremony, kneeling at the sacrament, the bowing at the name of Jesus, and music in the services of the church. They also objected to the ordination of priests without a call by their flocks.—Heylyn's Hist. of the Presbyterians, 259.

[2] Strype's Life of Whitgift, i. 431.

[3] Elizabeth's policy may be described in her own words: 'She would suppress the papistical religion, that it should not grow; but

ruling churchmen, would not suffer the least liberty of conscience. Not even waiting for outward signs of departure from the standard of the church, they jealously enforced subscription to the articles of religion; and addressed searching interrogatories to the clergy, in order to extort confessions of doubt or nonconformity.[1] Even the oath of supremacy, designed to discover Catholics, was also a stumbling-block to many Puritans. The former denied the queen's supremacy, because they still owned that of the Pope; many of the latter hesitated to acknowledge it, as irreconcilable with their own church polity. One party were known to be disloyal: the other were faithful subjects of the crown. But conformity with the reformed ritual, and attendance upon the services of the church, were enforced against both, with indiscriminating rigour.[2] In aiming at unity, the church fostered dissent.

The early Puritans had no desire to separate from the national church: but were deprived of their benefices, and cast forth by persecution. They sought further to reform her polity and ceremonies, upon the Calvinistic model; and claimed greater latitude in their own conformity. They objected to clerical vestments, and other forms, rather than to matters of faith and doctrine; and were

Growth of nonconformity.

would root out puritanism, and the favourers thereof.'—*Strype's Eccl. Annals*, iv. 242.

[1] Strype's Eccl. Annals, iii. 81; Strype's Life of Whitgift, iii. 106; Fuller's Church Hist., ix. 156; Sparrow, 123.

[2] Burnet's Hist. of the Reformation, iii. 587; Short's Hist. of the Church, 306; Strype's Eccl. Annals, iv. 93, *et seq.*; Strype's Parker, 155, 225; Strype's Grindal, 99; Froude's Hist., ii. 134.

slow to form a distinct communion. They met secretly for prayer and worship, hoping that truth and pure religion would ultimately prevail in the church, according to their cherished principles, as Protestantism had prevailed over the errors of Rome. The ideal of the Presbyterians was a national church, to which they clung through all their sufferings: but they were driven out, with stripes, from the church of England. The Independents, claiming self-government for each congregation, repelling an ecclesiastical polity, and renouncing all connection with the state, naturally favoured secession from the establishment. Separation and isolation were the very foundation of their creed;[1] and before the death of Elizabeth they had spread themselves widely through the country, being chiefly known as Brownists.[2] Protestant nonconformity had taken root in the land; and its growth was momentous to the future destinies of church and state.

While the Reformed church lost from her fold considerable numbers of the people, her connection with the state was far more intimate than that of the church of Rome. There was no longer a divided authority. The crown was supreme in church and state alike. The Reformed church was the creation of Parliament: her polity and ritual, and even her doctrines, were prescribed by statutes. She could lay no claim

Close connection of the Reformed church with the state,

---

[1] Heylyn's Hist. of the Presbyterians, lib. vi.-x.; Neal's Hist. of the Puritans, i. ch. iv. &c.; Bogue and Bennett's Hist. of Dissenters, Intr. 58-65; i. 109-140; Price's Hist. of Nonconformity; Conder's View of all Religions.

[2] The act 35 Eliz. c. 1, was passed to suppress them.

to ecclesiastical independence. Convocation was restrained from exercising any of its functions without the king's licence.[1] No canons had force without his assent; and even the subsidies granted by the clergy, in convocation, were henceforward confirmed by Parliament. Bishops, dignitaries and clergy looked up to the crown, as the only source of power within the realm. Laymen administered justice in the ecclesiastical courts; and expounded the doctrines of the church. Lay patronage placed the greater part of the benefices at the disposal of the crown, the barons, and the landowners. The constitution of the church was identified with that of the state; and their union was political as well as religious. The church leaned to the government, rather than to the people; and, on her side, became a powerful auxiliary in maintaining the ascendency of the crown, and the aristocracy. The union of ecclesiastical supremacy with prerogatives, already excessive, dangerously enlarged the power of the crown over the civil and religious liberties of the people. Authority had too strong a fulcrum; and threatened the realm with absolute subjection: but the wrongs of Puritans produced a spirit of resistance, which eventually won for Englishmen a surer freedom.

Meanwhile, the Reformation had taken a different course in Scotland. The Calvinists had triumphed. They had overthrown episcopacy, and established a Presbyterian church, upon

Reformation in Scotland.

[1] 25 Hen. VIII. c. 19; Froude's Hist., ii. 193-198, 325, iv. 479.

their own cherished model.¹ Their creed and polity suited the tastes of the people, and were accepted with enthusiasm. The Catholic faith was renounced everywhere but in some parts of the Highlands; and the Reformed establishment at once assumed the comprehensive character of a national church. But while supported by the people, it was in constant antagonism to the state. Its rulers repudiated the supremacy of the crown:² resisted the jurisdiction of the civil courts;³ and set up pretensions to spiritual authority and independence, not unworthy of the church they had lately overthrown.⁴ They would not suffer temporal power to intrude upon the spiritual church of Christ.⁵

The constitution of the Scottish church was republican: her power at once spiritual and popular. Instead of being governed by *The church of Scotland.*

---

¹ 1560–1592.—The events of this period are amply illustrated in Spottiswood's Hist. of the Church of Scotland; M'Crie's Lives of Knox and Melville; Knox's Hist. of the Reformation; Robertson's Hist. of Scotland; Tytler's Hist. of Scotland; Cook's Hist. of the Reformation in Scotland; Cunningham's Church Hist., i. 351; Row's Hist. of the Kirk of Scotland; Stephen's Hist. of the Church of Scotland; Buckle's Hist., ii. ch. 3; Froude's Hist., vii. 116, 269.

² In the Book of Polity, it is laid down that 'the power ecclesiastical flows immediately from God and the Mediator Jesus Christ, and is spiritual, not having a temporal head on earth, but only Christ, the only spiritual governor and head of his kirk.'

³ Cunningham's Church Hist., 535; Calderwood's Hist., v. 457–460, 475; Spottiswood's Hist., iii. 21; Tytler's Hist., vii. 326; Buchanan's Ten Years' Conflict, i. 73–81.

⁴ Mr. Cunningham, comparing the churches of Rome and Scotland, says: 'With both there has been the same union and energy of action, the same assumption of spiritual supremacy, the same defiance of law courts, parliaments, and kings.'—*Pref. to Church Hist. of Scotland.*

⁵ 'When the church was Roman, it was the duty of the magistrate to reform it. When the church was Protestant, it was impiety in the magistrate to touch it.'—*Cunningham's Church Hist.*, i. 537.

courtly prelates and an impotent convocation, she was represented by the general assembly,—an ecclesiastical Parliament of wide jurisdiction, little controlled by the civil power. The leaders of that assembly were bold and earnest men, with high notions of ecclesiastical authority, a democratic temper, and habitual reliance upon popular support. A church so constituted was, indeed, endowed and acknowledged by the state: but was more likely to withstand the power of the crown and aristocracy, than to uphold it.

The formal connection of the church with the state was, nevertheless, maintained with scarcely less strictness than in England. The new establishment was the work of the legislature; the Protestant religion was originally adopted; the church's confession of faith ratified; and the entire Presbyterian polity established by statute.[1] And further, the crown was represented in her assembly, by the Lord High Commissioner.

Her connection with the state.

The Reformation had also been extended to Ireland: but in a manner the most extraordinary and exceptional. In England and Scotland, the clergy and people had unquestionably been predisposed to changes in the Catholic church; and the reforms effected were more or less the expression of the national will. But in Ireland, the Reformation was forced upon an unyielding priesthood and a half-conquered people. The priests were driven from their churches and homes, by

Reformation in Ireland.

---

[1] Scots Acts, 1560; 1567, c. 4, 6, 7, 1592, c. 116; *Ibid.*, 1690, c. 5, 23.

ministers of the new faith,—generally Englishmen or strangers,—who were ignorant of the language of their flocks, and indifferent to their conversion or teaching. Conformity was exacted in obedience to the law, and under severe penalties: not sought by appeals to the reason and conscience of a subject race. Who can wonder that the Reformation never took root in Ireland? It was accepted by the majority of the English colonists: but many who abjured the Catholic faith, declined to join the new establishment, and founded Presbyterian communions of their own. The Reformation added a new element of discord between the colonists and the natives: embittered the chronic discontents against the government; and founded a foreign church, with few communicants, in the midst of a hostile and rebellious people. It was a state church: but, in no sense, the church of the nation.[1]

Such having been the results of the Reformation, the accession of James united the three crowns of these realms; and what were his relations to the church? In England, he was the head of a state church, environed by formidable bodies of Catholics and Puritans. In Scotland, a Presbyterian church had been founded upon the model approved by English Puritans. In Ireland, he was the head of a church maintained by the sword. This incongruous heritage, unwisely used, brought ruin on his royal house. Reared

The three churches under James I.

---

[1] Leland's Hist., ii. 165, 224, &c.; Lanigan's Eccl. Hist., iv. 207, &c.; Mant's Hist. of the Church of Ireland, i. ch. 2, 3, 4; Goldwin Smith's Irish History and Irish Character, 83, 88, 92, 100.

among a Presbyterian people, he vexed the English Puritans with a more rigorous conformity; and spurning the religion of his own countrymen, forced upon them a hated episcopacy, the supremacy of the crown, and observances repugnant to their creed. No less intolerant of his own mother's church, he hastened to aggravate the penalties against Popish recusants. Such was his rancour that he denied them the right of educating their children in the Catholic faith.[1] The laws against them were also enforced with renewed severity.[2] The monstrous plot of Guy Fawkes naturally incensed Parliament and the people against the whole body of Catholics, whose religion was still associated with imminent danger to the state; and again were treason and Popery scourged with the same rod. Further penalties were imposed on Popish recusants, not attending the services and sacraments of the church; and a new oath of allegiance was devised to test their loyalty.[3] In Ireland, Catholic priests were banished by proclamation; and the laws rigorously enforced against the laity who absented themselves from Protestant worship. The king's only claim upon the favour of the Puritans was his persecution of Papists; and this he suddenly renounced. In compliance with engagements entered into with foreign powers, he began openly to tolerate the Catholics; and granted a pardon to all who had incurred the penalties of recusancy. The breach was ever widening between the Puritans and the

---

[1] 1 Jac. I. c. 4.   [2] Lingard's Hist., ix. 41, 55.
[3] 3 Jac. I. c. 4, 5.

throne; and while the monarch was asserting the divine right of kings, his bishops were exalting prelacy, and bringing the Reformed church nearer to the Romish model.

Charles continued to extend an indulgence to Catholics, at once offensive to the Puritan party, and in violation of laws which his prerogative could not rightfully suspend. Even the toleration of the Stuarts, like their rigour, was beyond the law. The prerogatives and supremacy of the crown were alike abused. Favouring absolutism in the state, and domination in the church, Charles found congenial instruments of tyranny in the Star Chamber and High Commission,—in Strafford and in Laud. In England he oppressed Puritans: in Scotland he introduced a high church liturgy, which provoked rebellion. Arbitrary rule in church and state completed the alienation of the Puritan party; and their enmity was fatal. The church was overthrown; and a republican commonwealth established on the ruins of the monarchy. The polity of the Reformation was riven, as by a thunderbolt. *Relations of Charles I. with Catholics and Puritans.*

The Commonwealth was generally favourable to religious liberty. The intolerance of Presbyterians, indeed, was fanatical.[1] In the words of Milton, 'new Presbyter was but *Religion under the Commonwealth.*

---

[1] Life of Baxter, 103. Their clergy in London protested against toleration to the Westminster Assembly, Dec. 18th, 1645, saying, 'we cannot dissemble how we detest and abhor this much endeavoured toleration.'—*Price's Hist. of Nonconformity*, ii. 329. Edwards, a Presbyterian minister, denounced toleration as 'the grand design of the devil,' and 'the most ready, compendious, and sure way to destroy all religion,'—' all the devils in hell and their instruments being at work to promote it.'—*Gangræna*, part i. 58.

old Priest,—writ large.' Had they been suffered to exercise uncontrolled dominion, they would have rivalled Laud himself in persecution. But Cromwell guaranteed freedom of worship to all except Papists and Prelatists; declaring 'that none be compelled to conform to the public religion by penalties or otherwise.'[1] Such was his policy, as a statesman and an Independent.[2] He extended toleration even to the Jews.[3] Yet was he sometimes led, by political causes, to put his iron heel upon the bishops and clergy of the Church of England, upon Roman Catholics, and even upon Presbyterians.[4] The church party and Roman Catholics had fought for the king in the civil war; and the hands of churchmen and Puritans were red with each others' blood. To religious rancour was added the vengeance of enemies on the battle-field.

Before the king's fall, he had been forced to restore the Presbyterian polity to Scotland;[5] and the Covenanters, in a furious spirit of fanaticism, avenged upon Episcopalians the wrongs which their cause had suffered in the last two reigns.

Presbyterians in Scotland.

---

[1] Whitelock's Mem., 499, 576, 614; Neal's Hist. of the Puritans, iv. 28, 138, 338, &c.

[2] Hume affirms, somewhat too broadly, that 'of all the Christian sects this was the first which during its prosperity as well as its adversity, always adopted the principles of toleration.'—Hist., v. 168. See also Neal's Hist. of the Puritans, ii. 98; iv. 144; Collier, 829; Hallam's Const. Hist., i. 621; Short's Hist., 425; Brook's Hist. of Religious Liberty, i. 504, 513–528.

[3] Bate's Elen., part ii. 211.

[4] Lord Clarendon's Hist., vii. 253, 254; Baxter's Life, i. 64; Kennet's Hist., iii. 206; Neal's Hist. of the Puritans, iv. 39, 122, 138, 144; Hume's Hist., v. 368; Butler's Rom. Cath., ii. 407; Parr's Life of Archbishop Usher; Rushworth, vii. 308, &c.

[5] In 1641.

Every age brought new discords; and religious differences commingled with civil strifes.

After the Restoration, Roundheads could expect no mercy from Cavaliers and churchmen. They were spurned as dissenters and republicans. While in the ascendant, their gloomy fanaticism and joyless discipline had outraged the natural sentiments and taste of the people; and there was now a strong reaction against them. And first the church herself was to be purged of Puritans. Their consciences were tried by a new Act of Uniformity, which drove forth two thousand of her clergy, and further recruited the ranks of Protestant nonconformists.[1] This measure, fruitful of future danger to the church, was followed by a rigorous code of laws, proscribing freedom of worship, and multiplying civil disabilities, as penalties for dissent.

Puritans under Charles II.

By the Corporation Act, none could be elected to a corporate office who had not taken the sacrament within the year.[2] By another Act, no one could serve as a vestryman, unless he made a declaration against taking up arms and the covenant, and engaged to conform to the Liturgy.[3] The Five Mile Act prohibited any nonconformist minister from coming within five miles of a corporate town; and all nonconformists, whether lay or clerical, from teaching in any public or private school.[4] The monstrous Conventicle Act punished

Oppressive laws of this reign.

---

[1] 13 & 14 Car. II. c. 4. Calamy's Nonconformist's Memorial, Intr. 31, &c.; Baxter's Life and Times, by Calamy, i. 181.
[2] 13 Car. II. stat. 2, c. 1.   [3] 15 Car. II. c. 5.
[4] 13 & 14 Car. II. c. 4.

attendance at meetings of more than five persons, in any house, for religious worship, with imprisonment and transportation.[1] This, again, was succeeded by a new test, by which the clergy were required to swear that it was not lawful, on any pretence whatever, to take up arms against the king.[2] This test, conceived in the spirit of the high church, touched the consciences of none but the Calvinistic clergy, many of whom refused to take it, and further swelled the ranks of dissent.

While the foundations of the church were narrowed by such laws as these, nonconformists were pursued by incessant persecutions. Eight thousand Protestants are said to have been imprisoned, besides great numbers of Catholics.[3] Fifteen hundred Quakers were confined: of whom three hundred and fifty died in prison.[4] During this reign, indeed, several attempts were made to effect a reconciliation between the church and nonconformists:[5] but the irreconcilable differences of the two parties, the unyielding disposition of churchmen, and the impracticable temper of nonconformists, forbad the success of any scheme of comprehension.

Persecution of nonconformists.

Attempts at comprehension.

[1] 16 Car. II. c. 4, continued and amended by 22 Car. II. c. 1.
[2] 17 Car. II. c. 2.
[3] Delaune's Plea for Nonconformists, preface; Short's Hist., 559. Oldmixon goes so far as to estimate the total number who suffered on account of their religion, during this reign, at 60,000!—History of the Stuarts, 715.
[4] Neal's Hist. of the Puritans, v. 17.
[5] The Savoy Conference, 1661; Baxter's Life and Times, i. 139; Burnet's Own Time, i. 309; Collier's Church Hist., ii. 879; Perry's Hist., ii. 317. In 1669; Baxter's Life, iii. 23; Burnet's Own Time, i. 439; Scheme of Tillotson and Stillingfleet, 1674; Burnet's Life of Tillotson, 42.

Nonconformists having been discouraged at the beginning of this reign, Catholics provoked repression at the end. In 1673, Parliament, impelled by apprehension for the Protestant religion and civil liberties of the people, passed the celebrated Test Act.[1] Designed to exclude Roman Catholic ministers from the king's councils, its provisions yet embraced Protestant nonconformists. That body, for the sake of averting a danger common to all Protestants, joined the church in supporting a measure fraught with evil to themselves. They were, indeed, promised further indulgence in the exercise of their religion, and even an exemption from the Test Act itself: but the church party, having secured them in its toils, was in no haste to release them.[2] *The Catholics under Charles II.*

The Church of Scotland fared worse than the English nonconformists, after the Restoration. Episcopacy was restored: the king's supremacy reasserted: the entire polity of the church overthrown;[3] while the wrongs of Episcopalians, under the Commonwealth, were avenged, with barbarous cruelty, upon Presbyterians.[4] *Church of Scotland after Restoration.*

The Protestant faith and civil liberties of the people being threatened by James II., all classes of Protestants combined to expel him from his throne. Again the noncon- *Union of church and dissenters against James II.*

---

[1] 25 Car. II. c. 2.
[2] Kennet's Hist., iii. 294; Burnet's Own Time, i. 348, 516.
[3] Scots Acts, 1661, c. 11; 1669, c. 1; 1681, c. 6; Wodrow's Church Hist., i. 190.
[4] Wodrow's Church Hist., i. 57, 236, 390, &c.; Burnet's Own Time, i. 365, ii. 416, &c.; Crookshank's Hist., i. 154, 204, &c.; Buckle's Hist., ii. 281-292; Cunningham's Church Hist., ii. ch. i.-vi.

formists united with the church, to resist a common danger. They were not even conciliated by his declarations of liberty of conscience and indulgence, in which they perceived a stretch of prerogative, and a dangerous leaning towards the Catholic faith, under the guise of religious freedom. The revolution was not less Protestant than political; and Catholics were thrust further than ever beyond the pale of the constitution.

The recent services of dissenters to the church and the Protestant cause were rewarded by the Toleration Act.[1] This celebrated measure repealed none of the statutes exacting conformity with the Church of England: but exempted all persons from penalties, on taking the oaths of allegiance and supremacy, and subscribing a declaration against transubstantiation. It relieved dissenting ministers from the restrictions imposed by the Act of Uniformity and the Conventicle Act, upon the administration of the sacrament and preaching in meetings: but required them to subscribe the thirty-nine articles, with some exceptions.[2] The dissenting chapels were to be registered; and their congregations protected from any molestation. A still easier indulgence was given to the Quakers: but toleration was withheld from Roman Catholics and Unitarians, who found no favour either with the church or nonconformists.

The Toleration Act.

The Toleration Act, whatever its shortcomings,

---

[1] 1 Will. & Mar. c. 8; confirmed by 10 Anne, c. 2; Bogue and Bennett's Hist. of Dissenters, i. 187-204.
[2] All except three and part of a fourth. See *infra*, p. 93.

was at least the first recognition of the right of public worship, beyond the pale of the state church. It was the great charter of dissent. Far from granting religious liberty, it yet gave indulgence and security from persecution. *Right of public worship conceded.*

The age was not ripe for wider principles of toleration. Catholics and Unitarians were soon afterwards pursued with severer penalties;[1] and in 1700, the intolerant spirit of Parliament was displayed by an Act,—no less factious than bigoted,—which cannot be read without astonishment. It offered a reward of 100*l.* for the discovery of any Catholic priest performing the offices of his church: it incapacitated every Roman Catholic from inheriting or purchasing land, unless he abjured his religion upon oath; and on his refusal, it vested his property, during his life, in his next of kin, being a Protestant. He was even prohibited from sending his children abroad, to be educated in his own faith.[2] And while his religion was thus proscribed, his civil rights were further restrained by the oath of abjuration.[3] *Further measures against Unitarians and Catholics.*

Again the policy of comprehension was favoured by William III.: but it was too late. The church was far too strong to be willing to sacrifice her own convictions to the scruples of nonconformists. Nor was she forgetful of her own wrongs under the Commonwealth, or *Scheme of comprehension under William III.*

---

[1] 1 Will. & M. c. 9, 15, 26; 9 & 10 Will. III. c. 32.
[2] 11 & 12 Will. III. c. 4; Burnet's Own Time, iv. 409; Butler's Hist. Mem. of the Catholics, iii. 134–138, 279; Burke's Speech at Bristol, 1780, Works, iii. 385.
[3] 13 Will. III. c. 6.

insensible to the sufferings of Episcopalians in Scotland. On the other side, the nonconformists, confirmed in their repugnance to the doctrines and ceremonies of the church, by the persecutions of a hundred and fifty years, were not to be tempted by small concessions to their consciences, or by the doubtful prospects of perferment, in an establishment from which they could expect little favour.[1]

To the Church of Scotland the Revolution brought freedom and favour. The king's supremacy was finally renounced; Episcopacy, against which she had vainly struggled for a hundred years, for ever abolished; her confession of faith recognised by statute; and the Presbyterian polity confirmed.[2] But William III., in restoring the privileges of the church, endeavoured to impress upon her rulers his own moderation and tolerant spirit. Fearing the persecution of Episcopalians at their hands, he wrote thus nobly and wisely to the General Assembly: 'We expect that your management shall be such that we may have no reason to repent what we have done. We never could be of the mind that violence was suited to the advancing of true religion: nor do we intend that our authority shall ever be a tool to the irregular passions of any party.'[3] And not many years afterwards, when Presbyterian Scotland was united to Episcopalian England, the rights of her church, in worship, disci-

Church of Scotland after the Revolution.

---

[1] D'Oyley's Life of Sancroft, 327, 520; Burnet's Own Time, ii. 1033, &c.; Kennet's Hist., iii. 483, 551, *et seq.*; Macaulay's Hist., iii. 89, 468—495; Bogue and Bennett's Hist., i. 207.

[2] Scots Acts, 1689, c. 2; 1690, c. 5; 1692, c. 117.

[3] Macaulay's Hist., iii. 708.

pline, and government, were confirmed and declared unalterable.¹

To the Catholics of Ireland, the reign of William was made terrible by new rigours and oppression. They were in arms for the exiled king; and again was their faith the symbol of rebellion. Overcome by the sword, they were condemned to proscription and outlawry. *Catholics of Ireland under William III.*

It was long before Catholics were to enjoy indulgence. In 1711, a proclamation was published for enforcing the penal laws against them in England.² And in Ireland, the severities of former reigns were aggravated by Acts of Queen Anne.³ After the rebellion of 1715, Parliament endeavoured to strengthen the Protestant interest, by enforcing the laws against Papists.⁴ Again, in 1722, the estates of Roman Catholics and non-jurors were made to bear a special financial burden, not charged upon other property.⁵ And, lastly, the rebellion of 1745 called forth a proclamation, in the spirit of earlier times, offering a reward of 100*l.* for the discovery of Jesuits and popish priests, and calling upon magistrates to bring them to justice. *Catholics under Anne, Geo. I. and II.*

Much of the toleration which had been conceded to Protestant nonconformists at the Revolution, was again withdrawn during the four last years of Queen Anne. Having found their way into many offices, by taking the *Nonconformists under Anne, Geo. I. & II.*

---

[1] Act of Union, 5 Anne, c. 8; Scots Acts, 1705, c. 4; 1706, c. 7.
[2] Boyce's Reign of Queen Anne, 429, &c.
[3] 2 Anne, c. 3, 6; 8 Anne, c. 3.
[4] 1 Geo. I. c. 55.   [5] 9 Geo. I. c. 18; Parl. Hist., viii. 51, 353.

sacrament, an Act was passed, in 1711, against occasional conformity, by which dissenters were dispossessed of their employments, and more rigorously disqualified in future.[1] Again were nonconformists repelled, with contumely, from honourable fellowship with the state. Two years afterwards the Schism Bill was passed, prohibiting the exercise of the vocation of schoolmaster or private teacher, without a declaration of conformity, and a licence from a bishop.[2] Both these statutes, however, were repealed in the following reign.[3] With the reign of George II. a wider toleration was commenced, in another form. The time was not yet come for repealing the laws imposing civil disabilities upon dissenters: but annual Acts of Indemnity were passed, by which persons who had failed to qualify themselves for office, were protected.[4]

State of the church and religion on the accession of George III.

The reign of George III. opened under circumstances favourable to religious liberty. The intolerant spirit of the high church party had been broken since the death of Anne. The phrensies of Sacheverell and Atterbury had yielded to the liberal philosophy of Milton and Locke, of Jeremy Taylor, Hoadley, Warburton, and Montesquieu. The angry disputations of convocation were silenced. The church was at peace; and the state had ceased to distrust either Roman

---

[1] 10 Anne, c. 2; Burnet's Own Time, ii. 364, 585, &c.; Bogue and Bennett's Hist., i. 228, 262.

[2] 12 Anne, c. 7; Parl. Hist., vi. 1349; Bogue and Bennett's Hist., 268.

[3] 5 Geo. I. c. 4.

[4] The first of these Acts was in 1727; 1 Geo. II. c. 23. Hallam's Const. Hist., ii. 412.

Catholics or nonconformists. Never since the Reformation, had any monarch succeeded to the throne, at a period so free from religious discords and embarrassments. In former reigns, high churchmen had been tainted with Jacobite sympathies: now all parties vied in attachment and loyalty. Once more the church was wholly with the king: and added all her weight to the influence of the crown. Many English Catholics, crushed by persecution, and losing hopes of the restoration of their own faith, had gradually conformed to a church, already beginning to boast a certain antiquity,—enshrined in the ancient temples of their forefathers,—respecting their traditions,—allied to the state,—and enjoying the power, wealth, fashion, and popularity of a national establishment. Some of this body had been implicated in both the Jacobite rebellions: but their numbers had ceased to be formidable; and they were now universally well-disposed and loyal.[1] The dissenters had been uniformly attached to the House of Hanover; and, having ceased to be oppressed, quietly prospered, without offence to the church. The old nonconformist bodies,—the offspring of the Reformation, and the Act of Uniformity,—so far from making progress, had declined in numbers and activity, since the time of William III.[2] There had

---

[1] In 1767, there appear to have been no more than 67,916; and, in 1780, 69,376. They had 200 chapels.—Census, 1851: Report on Religious Worship, ci. In 1696, out of 2,599,786 freeholders in England and Wales, there had been 13,856 Catholics.—*Ibid.*, c. Dalrymple, book i. part ii. App.; Butler's Historical Mem. of the Catholics, iii. 162.

[2] Calamy's Life and Times, ii. 529; Lord Mahon's Hist., ii. 372; Bogue and Bennett's Hist., iii. 314–324. In 1696 it appeared that

been little religious zeal, either within or without the church. It was an age of spiritual indifference and lethargy.[1] With many noble exceptions, the clergy had been inert and apathetic. A benefice was regarded as an estate, to which was attached the performance of certain ecclesiastical duties. These once performed,—the service read, the weekly sermon preached, the child christened, the parishioner buried,—and the parson differed little from the squire. He was generally charitable, kindly, moral, and well educated—according to the standard of the age,—in all but theology.[2] But his spiritual calling sat lightly upon him. Zealous for church and king, and honestly hating dissenters, he was unconscious of a mission to spread the knowledge of the gospel among the people, to solve their doubts, to satisfy their spiritual longings, and to attach their religious sympathies to the church.[3] The nonconformist ministers, comfortably established among their flocks,

---

108,676 freeholders in England and Wales were nonconformists (Census Report, 1851, c.); but as dissent chiefly prevailed in the towns, this report must have fallen very far short of the total numbers.

[1] Bishop Gibson's Pastoral Letters, 2nd Ed., 1728, p. 2; Butler's advertisement to Analogy of Revealed Religion, 1736; Archbishop Secker's Eight Charges, 1738, p. 4; Southey's Life of Wesley, i. 324, &c.

[2] Bishop Burnet thus speaks of candidates for ordination:—'Those who have read some few books, yet never seem to have read the scriptures.' 'The case is not much better in many, who, having got into orders, come for instruction and cannot make it appear that they have read the scriptures, or any one good book, since they were ordained.'—*Pastoral Care*, 3rd Ed., 1713: Preface.

[3] 'A remiss, unthinking course of life, with little or no application to study, and the bare performing of that, which, if not done, would draw censures when complained of, without even pursuing the pastoral care in any suitable degree, is but too common, as well as too evident.'—*Ibid.* See also Intr. to last volume of Burnet's Hist.

and enjoying their modest temporalities, shared the spiritual ease of churchmen. They were ruffled by no sectarian zeal, or restless spirit of encroachment. Many even conformed to the Church of England. The age was not congenial to religious excitement and enthusiasm; a lull had succeeded to storms and agitations.

But this religious calm had lately been disturbed by Wesley and Whitefield, the apostles of modern dissent. These eminent men were both brought up as faithful disciples of the church, and admitted to holy orders. Not impelled to their extraordinary mission by any repugnance to her doctrines and discipline, they went forth to rouse the people from their religious apathy, and awaken them to a sense of sin. They penetrated the haunts of ignorance and vice; and braved ridicule, insults, and violence. They preached in the open air, to multitudes who had scarcely heard of the gospel. On the hill-side,—by ruins,—on the sea-shore, they appealed to the imagination as well as to the devotional sentiments of their hearers. They devoted their lives to the spiritual instruction of the middle and lower classes: preached to them everywhere: prayed with them: read the scriptures in public and private; and addressed them with familiar speech and homely illustration.[1] Wesley, still in communion with the

---

[1] 'I design plain truth for plain people; therefore, of set purpose I abstain from all nice and philosophical speculations, from all perplexed and intricate reasonings; and, as far as possible, from even the show of learning, unless in sometimes citing the original scriptures. I labour to avoid all words which are not easy to be understood,—all which are not used in common life, and in particular

church, and holding her in love and reverence, became the founder of a new sect.[1] He preached to reclaim men from sin: he addressed the neglected heathens of society, whom the church knew not: he laboured as a missionary, not as a sectarian. Schism grew out of his pious zeal: but his followers, like their revered founder, have seldom raised their voices, in the spirit of schismatics, against their parent church.[2] Whitefield, for a time the fellow-labourer of Wesley, surpassed that great man as a preacher; and moved the feelings and devotion of his hearers with the inspiration of a prophet: but, less gifted with powers of organisation and government, he left fewer monuments of his labours, as the founder of a religious sect.[3] Holding to the doctrine of absolute predestination, he became the leader of the Calvinistic Methodists, and Lady Huntingdon's connection.[4] The Methodists were regarded by churchmen as fanatical enthusiasts rather than dissenters; while their close relations with the church repelled the favour of other sects. They suffered

---

those kinds of technical terms that so frequently occur in bodies of divinity.'—*Wesley's Pref. to Sermons*, 1746.—In another place Wesley wrote: 'I dare no more write in a fine style, than wear a fine coat.'—*Pref. to 2nd Ser. of Sermons*, 1788.

[1] Rev. J. Wesley's Works, i. 185; ii. 515; vii. 422-3; viii. 111, 254, 269, 311; Southey's Life of Wesley, ch. xii., xx., &c.

[2] Wesley's Works, viii. 205, 321; Centenary of Wesleyan Methodism, 183; Lord Mahon's Hist., ii. 365-366. Wesley himself said: 'We are not seceders; nor do we bear any resemblance to them:' and after his sect had spread itself over the land, he continually preached in the churches of the establishment.

[3] Dr. Adam Clarke's Works, xiii. 257; Southey's Life of Wesley, ch. xxi.

[4] Wesley's Works, iii. 84; Philip's Life of Whitefield, 195, &c.; Southey's Life of Wesley, ch. xxv.; Life of Countess of Huntingdon, 8vo. 1840.

ridicule, but enjoyed toleration; and, labouring in a new field, attracted multitudes to their communion.[1]

The revival of the religious spirit by the Methodists gradually stimulated the older sects of nonconformists. Presbyterians, Independents, and Baptists, awakened by Wesley and Whitefield to a sense of the spiritual wants of the people, strove, with all their energies, to meet them. And large numbers, whose spiritual care had hitherto been neglected alike by the church and by nonconformists, were steadily swelling the ranks of dissent. The church caught the same spirit more slowly. She was not alive to the causes which were undermining her influence, and invading her proper domain,—the religious teaching of the people,—until chapels and meeting houses had been erected in half the parishes of England.[2]

Revival of dissent.

The church of Scotland, which in former reigns had often been a tissue with the civil power, had now fallen under the rule of the moderate party, and was as tractable as the church of England herself. She had ever been faithful to the Revolution settlement, by which her own privileges were assured; and, when free from persecution, had cast off much of her former puritanism. Her spirit had been tempered by learning, cultivation, society, and the gentle influences of the South, until she had become a stanch ally of the crown and aristocracy.[3]

Church of Scotland.

---

[1] Southey's Life of Wesley, ch. xxix.; Watson's Observations on Southey's Life, 138; Lord Mahon's Chapter on Methodism, Hist., ii. 354; Brook's Hist. of Relig. Lib., ii. 326–333.

[2] See *infra*, p. 222.

[3] Cunningham's Church Hist. of Scotland, ii. 491, 578, &c.

In Ireland, the Protestant church had made no progress since the days of Elizabeth. The mass of the population were still Catholics. The clergy of the state church, indifferent and supine, read the English liturgy in empty churches, while their parishioners attended mass in the Catholic chapels. Irish benefices afforded convenient patronage to the crown, and the great families. The Irish church was a good rallying point for Protestant ascendency; but instead of fulfilling the mission of a national establishment, it provoked religious animosity and civil dissensions. For the present, however, Protestant rule was absolute; and the subjection of the Catholics undisturbed.[1]

<small>Church of Ireland.</small>

Such being the state of the church, and other religious bodies, the gradual relaxation of the penal code was, at length, to be commenced. This code, the growth of more than two centuries, was wholly inconsistent with the policy of a free state. Liberty of thought and discussion was allowed to be a constitutional right: but freedom of conscience was interdicted. Religious unity was still assumed, while dissent was notorious. Conformity with the state church was held to be a duty, the neglect of which was punishable with penalties and disabilities. Freedom of worship and civil rights were denied to all but members of the church. This policy, originating in the doctrines

<small>Gradual relaxation of the penal code commenced.</small>

---

[1] Bishop Berkeley's Works, ii. 381; Wesley's Works, x. 209, &c.; Mant's Hist. of the Church of Ireland, ii. 288–294, 421–429, &c.; Lord Mahon's Hist. ii. 374.

of a church pretending to infallibility, and admitted into our laws in the plenitude of civil and ecclesiastical power, grew up amid rebellions and civil wars, in which religion became the badge of contending parties. Religious intolerance was its foundation: political expediency its occasional justification. Long after the state had ceased to be threatened by any religious sect, the same policy was maintained on a new ground,—the security of the established church.

The penal code, with all its anomalies and inconsistencies, admitted of a simple division. One part imposed restraints on religious worship: the other attached civil disabilities to faith and doctrine. *General character of the penal code.* The former was naturally the first to be reviewed. More repugnant to religious liberty, and more generally condemned by the enlightened thinkers of the age, it was not to be defended by those political considerations which were associated with the latter. Men, earnest in upholding securities to our Protestant constitution, revolted from the persecution of conscience. These two divisions, however, were so intermixed in the tangled web of legislation: principles had been so little observed in carrying out the capricious and impulsive policy of intolerance; and the temper of Parliament and the country was still so unsettled in regard to the doctrines of religious liberty, that the labour of revision proceeded with no more system than the original code. Now a penalty affecting religion was repealed; now a civil disability removed. Sometimes Catholics received indulgence; and sometimes a particular sect of nonconformists. First one grievance was redressed, and then another: but Parliament continued to shrink from the broad assertion of religious liberty, as the right of British subjects, and the policy of the state. Toleration and connivance at dissent, had already succeeded to active persecution: society had outgrown the law: but a century of strife and agitation had yet to pass, before the penal code was blotted out, and religious liberty established. We have now to follow this great cause through its lengthened annals, and to trace its halting and unsteady progress.

Early in this reign, the broad principles of toleration were judicially affirmed by the House of Lords. The city of London had perverted the Corporation Act into an instrument of extortion, by electing dissenters to the office of sheriff, and exacting fines when they refused to qualify. No less than 15,000*l.* had thus been levied before the dissenters resisted this imposition. The law had made them ineligible: then how could they be fined for not serving? The City Courts upheld the claims of the Corporation: but the dissenters appealed to the Court of Judges or commissioners' delegates, and obtained a judgment in their favour. In 1759, the Corporation brought the cause before the House of Lords, on a writ of error. The judges being consulted, only one could be found to support the claims of the Corporation; and the House of Lords unanimously affirmed the judgment of the Court below. In

[margin: Corporation of London and the Dissenters, Feb. 3rd, 1767.]

moving the judgment of the House, Lord Mansfield thus defined the legal rights of dissenters:—'It is now no crime,' he said, 'for a man to say he is a dissenter; nor is it any crime for him not to take the sacrament according to the rites of the Church of England: nay, the crime is if he does it, contrary to the dictates of his conscience.' And again:— 'The Toleration Act renders that which was illegal before, now legal; the dissenters' way of worship is permitted and allowed by this Act. It is not only exempted from punishment, but rendered innocent and lawful; it is established; it is put under the protection, and is not merely under the connivance, of the law.' And in condemning the laws to force conscience, he said:—'There is nothing certainly more unreasonable, more inconsistent with the rights of human nature, more contrary to the spirit and precepts of the Christian religion, more iniquitous and unjust, more impolitic, than persecution. It is against natural religion, revealed religion, and sound policy.'[1] In his views of toleration, the judge was in advance of the legislature.

Several years elapsed before Parliament was invited to consider matters affecting the church and dissenters. In 1772, Sir William Meredith presented a petition from several clergymen and others, complaining that subscription to the thirty-nine articles was required of the clergy, and at the universities. So

Subscription to 39 articles, Feb. 6th, 1772.

---

[1] Parl. Hist., xvi. 316.—Horace Walpole unjustly sneers at this speech as 'another Whig oration' of Lord Mansfield's.—*Mem.*, ii. 414. Lord Campbell's Chief Justices, ii. 512. Brook's Hist. of Relig. Lib., ii. 432.

far as this complaint concerned the clergy, it was a question of comprehension and church discipline: but subscription on matriculation affected the admission of dissenters to the University of Oxford; and subscription on taking the degrees of Doctor of Laws and Doctor of Medicine excluded dissenters from the practice of the civil law, as advocates, and the practice of medicine, as physicians. In debate this complaint was treated chiefly as a question affecting the discipline of the church and universities: but sentiments were expressed that marked a growing spirit of toleration. It being objected that if subscription were relaxed, sectaries might gain admission to the church, Sir G. Savile said finely, 'sectaries, Sir! had it not been for sectaries, this cause had been tried at Rome. Thank God, it is tried here.' The motion for bringing up the petition found no more than seventy-one supporters.[1] The University of Cambridge, however, made a concession to the complaints of these petitioners, by admitting bachelors of arts, on subscribing a declaration that they were *boná fide* members of the Church of England, instead of requiring their subscription to the thirty-nine articles.[2] Sir W. Meredith renewed the discussion in the two following years, but found little encouragement.[3]

In 1772, Sir H. Hoghton brought in a bill, with

---

[1] Ayes, 71; Noes, 217. Parl. Hist., xvii. 245; Clarke, iii. 261; Brook's Hist. of Relig. Lib., ii. 365. Walpole's Journal, i. 7.
[2] Hughes' Hist., ii. 56.
[3] Feb. 23rd, 1773; May 5th, 1774; Parl. Hist., xvii. 742, 1326; Fox's Mem., i. 92.

little opposition, for relieving dissenting ministers and schoolmasters from the subscription required by the Toleration Act.[1] Dissenters conceived it to be a just matter of complaint that the law should recognise such a test, after dissent had been acknowledged to be lawful. No longer satisfied with connivance at a breach of the law, they prayed for honourable immunity. Their representations were felt to be so reasonable by the Commons, that the bill was passed with little opposition. In the Lords it was warmly supported by Lord Chatham,[2] the Duke of Richmond, Lord Camden, and Lord Mansfield: but was lost on the second reading by a majority of seventy-three.[3]

Subscription of dissenting ministers and schoolmasters, April 3rd, 1772.

In the next year, Sir H. Hoghton introduced an amended measure, and passed it through all its stages, in the Commons, by large majorities. Arguments were still heard that connivance was all that dissenters could expect; in reply to which, Mr. Burke exclaimed, 'What, Sir, is liberty by connivance but a temporary relaxation of slavery?' In the Lords, the bill met with the same fate as in the previous year.[4]

Feb. 17th, 1773.

---

[1] The 34th, 35th, 36th, and part of the 20th articles had been excepted by the Toleration Act, as expressing the distinctive doctrines of the church.

[2] See outline of his speech, Chatham Corr., iv. 219.

[3] Contents, 29; Non-contents, 102. Parl. Hist., xvii. 431-446. Walpole's Journal, i. 93.

[4] *Ibid.*, 759-791. With reference to this bill Lord Chatham wrote: 'I hear, in the debate on the dissenters, the ministry avowed enslaving them, and to keep the cruel penal laws, like bloodhounds coupled up, to be let loose on the heels of these poor conscientious men, when government pleases; i.e. if they dare to dislike some ruinous measure, or to disobey orders at an election. Forty years ago, if any minister had avowed such a doctrine, the Tower! the

In 1779, however, Sir Henry Hoghton at length succeeded in passing his measure. Dissenters were enabled to preach and to act as schoolmasters, without subscribing any of the thirty-nine articles. No other subscription was proposed to be substituted: but, on the motion of Lord North, a declaration was required to be made, that the person taking it was a Christian and a Protestant dissenter; and that he took the scriptures for the rule of his faith and practice. Except upon the question of this declaration, the Bill passed through both Houses, with little opposition.[1]

Dissenting Ministers' Act, 1779.

In Ireland, a much greater advance was made, at this time, in the principles of toleration. An Act was passed admitting Protestants to civil and military offices who had not taken the sacrament,—a measure nearly fifty years in advance of the policy of the British Parliament.[2] It must, however, be confessed that the dissenters owed this concession less to an enlightened toleration of their religion, than to the necessity of uniting all classes of Protestants in the cause of Protestant ascendency.

Dissenters admitted to offices in Ireland, 1779.

At this period, the penal laws affecting Roman Catholics also came under review. By the government, the English Catholics were no longer regarded with political distrust. The memory of Jacobite troubles had nearly passed

Prevalent opinions concerning Catholics.

Tower! would have echoed round the benches of the House of Lords; but *fuit Ilium*, the whole constitution is a shadow.'—*Letter to Lord Shelburne*, April 14th, 1773; Chatham Corr., iv. 259.

[1] Parl. Hist., xx. 239, 306–322. See 19 Geo. III. c. 44; Clarke, iii. 269, 355; Brook's Hist. of Relig. Lib., ii. 369.

[2] 19 & 20 Geo. III. c. 6 (Ireland).

away; and the Catholics of this generation were not suspected of disloyalty. Inconsiderable in numbers, and in influence, they threatened no danger to church or state. Their religion, however, was still held in aversion by the great body of the people; and they received little favour from any political party. With the exception of Fox, Burke, and Sir G. Savile, few of the Whigs felt any sympathy for their grievances. The Whigs were a party strongly influenced by traditions and hereditary sympathies. In struggling for civil and religious liberty at the Revolution, they had been leagued with the Puritans against the Papists: in maintaining the House of Hanover and the Protestant succession, they had still been in alliance with the church and dissenters, and in opposition to Catholics. Toleration to the Catholics, therefore, formed no part of the traditional creed of the Whig party.[1] Still less indulgence was to be expected from the Tories, whose sympathies were wholly with the church. Believing penal laws to be necessary to her interests, they supported them, indifferently, against dissenters and Catholics. But the growing enlightenment of the time made the more reflecting statesmen, of all parties, revolt against some of the penal laws still in force against the Catholics. They had generally been suffered to sleep: but could, at any time, be revived by the bigotry of zealots, or the cupidity of relatives and informers. Several priests had been prosecuted for saying mass. Mr. Maloney, a priest,

---

[1] Fox's Mem., i. 176, 203-4; Rockingham Memoirs, i. 228; Macaulay's Hist., iv. 118.

having been informed against, was unavoidably condemned to perpetual imprisonment. The government were shocked at this startling illustration of the law; and the king being afraid to grant a pardon, they ventured, on their own responsibility, to give the unfortunate priest his liberty.[1] Another priest owed his acquittal to the ingenuity and tolerant spirit of Lord Mansfield.[2] In many cases, Roman Catholics had escaped the penalties of the law, by bribing informers not to enforce them.[3] Lord Camden had protected a Catholic lady from spoliation, under the law, by a private Act of Parliament.[4]

To avert such scandals as these, and to redeem the law from the reproach of intolerance, Sir George Savile, in 1778, proposed a measure of relief for English Catholics.

Roman Catholic Relief Act, 1778.

Its introduction was preceded by a loyal address to the king, signed by ten Catholic Lords and one hundred and sixty-three Commoners, giving assurance of their affection for His Majesty, and attachment to the civil constitution of the country; and expressing sentiments calculated to conciliate the favour of Parliament and ministers. When it was explained that the penalties, imposed in 1700, and now to be repealed, were the perpetual imprisonment of priests for officiating in the services of their church,—the forfeiture of the estates of Roman

---

[1] Lord Shelburne's Speech, May 25th, 1773; Parl. Hist., xix. 1145; Butler's Hist. Mem., iii. 276.
[2] Holl., 176; Lord Campbell's Chief Justices, ii. 514.
[3] Parl. Hist., xix. 1137–1145.
[4] Butler's Hist. Mem., iii. 284. Burke's Works, iii. 389.

Catholic heirs, educated abroad, in favour of the next Protestant heir,—and the prohibition to acquire land by purchase,[1]—the bill was allowed to be introduced without a dissentient voice; and was afterwards passed through both Houses, with general approbation.[2] Such was the change in the feelings of the legislature, since the beginning of the century!

But in its views of religious liberty, Parliament was far in advance of considerable classes of the people. The fanaticism of the puritans was not yet extinct. Any favour extended to Roman Catholics, however just and moderate, aroused its latent flames. This bill extended to England only. The laws of Scotland relating to Roman Catholics, having been passed before its union with England, required further consideration, and a different form of treatment. The lord advocate had, therefore, promised to introduce a similar measure, applicable to Scotland, in the ensuing session. But in the meantime, the violent fanatics of a country which had nothing to fear from Catholics, were alarmed at the projected measure. They had vainly endeavoured to oppose the English bill, and were now resolved that, at least, no relief should be granted to their own fellow-countrymen. They banded together in 'Protestant Associations;'[3] and by inflammatory language incited the people to dangerous outrages. In Edinburgh, the mob

Riots in Scotland, 1778.

[1] 11 & 12 Will. III. c. 4.
[2] Parl. Hist., xix. 1137-1145; 18 Geo. III. c. 60; Butler's Hist. Mem., iii. 286-297.
[3] *Supra*, Vol. II. p. 272.

VOL. III.   H

destroyed two Roman Catholic chapels, and several houses of reputed Papists. In Glasgow, there were no chapels to destroy: but the mob were able to show their zeal for religion, by sacking the factory of a Papist. The Roman Catholics trembled for their property and their lives. Few in numbers, they found little protection from Presbyterian magistrates; and were at the mercy of the rioters. Preferring indemnity for their losses, and immediate protection for their persons, to a prospective relief from penal statutes, they concurred with the government in the postponement of the contemplated measure, till a more favourable occasion.[1] In an admirable petition to the House of Commons, they described the outrages which had been committed against them, and expressed their loyalty and attachment to the constitution. While they readily forbore to press for a revision of the penal statutes, they claimed a present compensation for the damages inflicted upon their property. Such compensation was at once promised by the government.[2]

March 18th, 1779.

The success of the fanatical rioters in Scotland, who had accomplished an easy triumph over the Roman Catholics and the government, encouraged the anti-Catholic bigotry in England. If it was wrong to favour Papists in Scotland, the recent English Act was also an error, of which Parliament must now repent. The fanatics found a congenial leader in Lord George Gordon; and the

Riots in London, 1780.

---

[1] March 15th, 1779; Parl. Hist., xx. 280; Ann. Reg., 1780, p. 26.
[2] Parl. Hist., xx. 322.

metropolis of England soon exceeded the two first cities of the North in religious zeal, and outrage. London was in flames, and Parliament invested by the mob, because some penalties against Roman Catholics, condemned by sober men of all parties, had lately been repealed. The insensate cry of 'No Popery' resounded in the streets, in the midst of plunder, and the torches of incendiaries.[1]

Petitions praying for the repeal of the recent Act were met by resolutions of the House of Commons, vindicating its provisions from misrepresentation.[2] One unworthy concession, however, was made to the popular excitement. Sir George Savile, hitherto the foremost friend of toleration, consented to introduce a bill to restrain Papists from teaching the children of Protestants. It was speedily passed through the House of Commons.[3] In the House of Lords, however, the lord chancellor inserted an amendment limiting the bill to boarding-schools; and this limitation being afterwards opposed by the bishops, led to the loss of the bill.[4]

For several years, the grievances of Catholics were permitted to rest in oblivion: but the claims of Protestant dissenters to further toleration elicited ample discussion.

The grievances suffered by dissenters, under the

[1] See *supra*, Vol. II. p. 273.
[2] June 20th, 1780; Parl. Hist., xxi. 713.
[3] Parl. Hist., xxi. 726.
[4] *Ibid.*, 754–766. In this year (1780) the Earl of Surrey, eldest son of the Duke of Norfolk, and Sir Thomas Gascoigne, abjured the Roman Catholic faith, and were immediately returned to Parliament.—Lord Mahon's Hist., vii. 111.

Corporation and Test Acts, had not been urged upon Parliament since the days of Sir Robert Walpole:[1] but in 1787, the time seemed favourable for obtaining redress. In Mr. Pitt's struggle with the coalition, the dissenters having sided with the minister, and contributed to his electoral triumphs, expected a recognition of their services, at his hands.[2] Having distributed a printed case,[3] in which the history and claims of nonconformists were ably stated, they entrusted their cause to Mr. Beaufoy, who moved for a bill to repeal the Corporation and Test Acts. He showed how the patriotism of a nonconformist soldier might be rewarded with penalties and proscription; and how a public-spirited merchant would be excluded from municipal offices, in the city which his enterprise had enriched, unless he became an apostate from his faith. The annual indemnity acts proved the inutility of penal laws, while they failed effectually to protect dissenters. Members were admitted to both Houses of Parliament without any religious test: then why insist upon the orthodoxy of an exciseman? No danger to the state could be apprehended from the admission of dissenters to office. Who, since the Revolution, had been more faithful to the constitution and monarchy than they? Was there danger to the church? The church was in no danger from dis-

Corporation and Test Acts, 1787.

Mr. Beaufoy's motion, March 28th, 1787.

---

[1] Parl. Hist., ix. 1046.
[2] Tomline's Life of Pitt, ii. 254; Lord Stanhope's Life of Pitt, i. 337, &c.
[3] Case of the Protestant Dissenters, with reference to the Test and Corporation Acts.—Parl. Hist., xxvi. 780, *n*.

senters before the Test Act: the church of Scotland was in no danger where no Test Act had ever existed: the church of Ireland was in no danger now, though dissenters had for the last seven years been admitted to office in that country.[1] But danger was to be apprehended from oppressive laws which united different bodies of dissenters, otherwise hostile, in a common resentment to the church. Howard, the philanthropist, in serving his country, had braved the penalties of an outlaw, which any informer might enforce. Even members of the church of Scotland were disqualified for office in England. Belonging to the state church, they were treated as dissenters. In conclusion, he condemned the profanation of the holy sacrament itself: that rite should be administered to none unworthy to receive it; yet it had become the common test of fitness for secular employments. Such was the case presented in favour of dissenters. Mr. Beaufoy was not in the first rank of debaters, yet from the force of truth and a good cause, his admirable speech puts to shame the arguments with which the first statesmen of the day then ventured to oppose him.

Lord North regarded the Test Act as 'the great bulwark of the constitution, to which we owed the inestimable blessings of freedom, which we now happily enjoyed.' He contended that the exclusion of dissenters from office was still as necessary as when it was first imposed by the legislature; and denied that it involved the least contradiction to the principles of toleration. The state had allowed all

[1] *Supra*, Vol. III. p. 94.

persons to follow their own religion freely: but might decline to employ them unless they belonged to the established church.

Mr. Pitt was no friend to the penal laws: his statesmanship was superior to the narrow jealousies which favoured them.[1] On this occasion he had been disposed to support the claims of the dissenters: but yielding to the opinion of the bishops,[2] he was constrained to oppose the motion. His speech betrayed the embarrassment of his situation. His accustomed force and clearness forsook him. He drew distinctions between political and civil liberty; maintained the right of the state to distribute political power to whom it pleased; and dwelt upon the duty of upholding the established church. Mr. Fox supported the cause of the dissenters; and promised them success if they persevered in demanding the redress of their grievances. The motion was lost by a majority of seventy-eight.[3]

In 1789, Mr. Beaufoy renewed his motion: and to a recapitulation of his previous arguments, added some striking illustrations of the operation of the law. The incapacity of dissenters extended not only to government employments, but to the direction of the Bank of England, the East India Company, and other chartered companies. When the Pretender had marched to the very centre of England, the dissenters had

Corporation and Test Acts, May 8th, 1789.

---

[1] 'To the mind of Pitt the whole system of penal laws was utterly abhorrent.'—*Lord Stanhope's Life*, ii. 276.

[2] See Tomline's Life of Pitt, ii. 255; Lord Stanhope's Life of Pitt, i. 337; Life of Bishop Watson, written by himself, i. 261.

[3] Ayes, 98; Noes, 176. Parl. Hist., xxvi. 780–832.

taken up arms in defence of the king's government: but instead of earning rewards for their loyalty, they were obliged to shelter themselves from penalties, under the Act of Grace,—intended for the protection of rebels.

Mr. Fox supported the motion with all his ability. Men were to be tried, he said, not by their opinions, but by their actions. Yet the dissenters were discountenanced by the state,—not for their actions, which were good and loyal, but for their religious opinions, of which the state disapproved. No one could impute to them opinions or conduct dangerous to the state; and Parliament had practically admitted the injustice of the disqualifying laws, by passing annual acts of indemnity. To one remarkable observation, later times have given unexpected significance. He said: 'It would perhaps be contended that the repeal of the Corporation and Test Acts might enable the dissenters to obtain a majority. This he scarcely thought probable: but it appeared fully sufficient to answer, that if the majority of the people of England should ever be for the abolition of the established church, in such a case the abolition ought immediately to follow.'[1]

Mr. Pitt opposed the motion in a temperate speech. 'Allowing that there is no natural right to interfere with religious opinions,' he contended that 'when they are such as may produce a civil inconvenience, the government has a right to guard

---

[1] 'If the dissenters from the establishment become a majority of the people, the establishment itself ought to be altered or qualified.'—*Paley's Moral and Political Philosophy*, book vi. ch. x.

against the probability of the civil inconvenience being produced.' He admitted the improved intelligence and loyalty of Roman Catholics, whose opinions had formerly been dangerous to the state; and did justice to the character of the dissenters: while he justified the maintenance of disqualifying laws, as a precautionary measure, in the interests of the established church. The motion was lost by the small majority of twenty.[1]

Encouraged by so near an approach to success, the dissenters continued to press their claims; and at their earnest solicitation, Mr. Fox himself undertook to advocate their cause. In March 1790, he moved the consideration of the Test and Corporation Acts, in a committee of the whole House. He referred to the distinguished loyalty of the dissenters, in 1715 and 1745, when the high church party, who now opposed their claims, had been 'hostile to the reigning family, and active in exciting tumults, insurrections, and rebellions.' He urged the repeal of the test laws, with a view to allay the jealousies of dissenters against the church; and went so far as to affirm that 'if this barrier of partition were removed, the very name of dissenter would be no more.'

Corporation and Test Acts. Mr. Fox's motion, March 2nd, 1790.

Mr. Pitt's resistance to concession was now more decided than on any previous occasion. Again he maintained the distinction between religious toleration and the defensive policy of excluding from office those who were likely to prejudice the esta-

[1] Ayes, 102; Noes, 122. Parl. Hist., xxviii. 1–41. See Tomline's Life of Pitt, iii. 18.

blished church. No one had a right to demand public offices, which were distributed by the government for the benefit of the state; and which might properly be withheld from persons opposed to the constitution. The establishment would be endangered by the repeal of the test laws, as dissenters, honestly disapproving of the church, would use all legal means for its subversion.

Mr. Beaufoy replied to Mr. Pitt in a speech of singular force. If the test laws were to be maintained, he said, as part of a defensive policy, in deference to the fears of the church, the same fears might justify the exclusion of dissenters from Parliament,—their disqualification to vote at elections,—their right to possess property, or even their residence within the realm. If political fears were to be the measure of justice and public policy, what extremities might not be justified?

Mr. Burke, who on previous occasions had absented himself from the House when this question was discussed, and who even now confessed 'that he had not been able to satisfy himself altogether' on the subject, spoke with characteristic warmth against the motion. His main arguments were founded upon the hostility of the dissenters to the established church, of which he adduced evidence from the writings of Dr. Priestley and Dr. Price, and from two nonconformist catechisms. If such men had the power, they undoubtedly had the will to overthrow the church of England, as the church of France had just been overthrown. Mr. Fox, in reply, deplored the opposition of Mr. Burke, which he referred to its true cause,—a horror of the French Revolution,—which was no less fatal to the claims of dissenters, than to the general progress of a liberal policy. Mr. Fox's motion, which, in the previous year, had been lost by a narrow majority, was now defeated by a majority of nearly three to one.[1]

The further discussion of the test laws was not resumed for nearly forty years: but other questions affecting religious liberty were not overlooked. In 1791, Mr. Mitford brought in a bill for the relief of 'Protesting Catholic Dissenters,' —or Roman Catholics who protested against the pope's temporal authority, and his right to excommunicate kings and absolve subjects from their allegiance,—as well as the right alleged to be assumed by Roman Catholics, of not keeping faith with heretics. It was proposed to relieve such persons from the penal statutes, upon their taking an oath to this effect. The proposal was approved by all but Mr. Fox, who, in accepting the measure, contended that the relief should be extended generally to Roman Catholics. Mr. Pitt also avowed his wish that many of the penal statutes against the Catholics should be repealed.[2]

Catholic Relief Bill, 1791.

---

[1] 294 to 105. Parl. Hist., xxviii. 387–452; Lord Sidmouth's Life, i. 73; Tomline's Life of Pitt, iii. 99; Fox's Mem., ii. 361, 362. The subject gave rise, at this time, to much written controversy. Tracts by Bishops Sherlock and Hoadley were republished. One of the best pamphlets on the side of the dissenters was 'The Rights of Protestant Dissenters, by a Layman, 1789.' The Bishop of Oxford, writing to Mr. Peel in 1828, speaks of fourteen volumes on the subject, written in 1789 and 1790.—*Peel's Mem.*, i. 65.

[2] Parl. Hist., xxviii. 1262, 1364; Tomline's Life of Pitt, iii. 249; Lord Stanhope's Life of Pitt, ii. 100.

The bill was open to grave objections. It imputed to the Catholics as a body, opinions repudiated by the most enlightened professors of their faith. Mr. Pitt received an explicit assurance from several foreign universities that Catholics claimed for the pope no civil jurisdiction in England, nor any power to absolve British subjects from their allegiance; and that there was no tenet by which they were justified in not keeping faith with heretics.[1] Again, this proposed oath required Catholics to renounce doctrines in no sense affecting the state. In the House of Lords, these objections were forcibly urged by the Archbishop of Canterbury, and Dr. Horsley, bishop of St. David's; and to the credit of the episcopal bench, the latter succeeded in giving to the measure a more liberal and comprehensive character, according to the views of Mr. Fox. An oath was framed, not obnoxious to the general body of Catholics, the taking of which secured them complete freedom of worship and education; exempted their property from invidious regulations; opened to them the practice of the law in all its branches; and restored to peers their ancient privilege of intercourse with the king.[2]

In the debates upon the Test Act, the peculiarity of the law, as affecting members of the church of Scotland, had often been alluded to; and in 1791, a petition was presented from the

Test Act (Scotland), 1791.

---

[1] See his questions and the answers, Plowden's Hist., i. 199, App. No. 91; Butler's Hist. Mem., iv. 10.
[2] Parl. Hist., xxix. 113-115, 664; 31 Geo. III. c. 32; Butler's Hist. Mem., iv. 44, 52; Quarterly Rev., Oct. 1852, p. 555.

General Assembly, praying for relief. On the 10th of May, Sir Gilbert Elliot moved for a committee of the whole House upon the subject. To treat the member of an established church as a dissenter, was an anomaly too monstrous to be defended. Mr. Dundas admitted that, in order to qualify himself for office, he had communicated with the church of England,—a ceremony to which members of his church had no objection. It would have been whimsical indeed to contend that the Scotch were excluded from office by any law, as their undue share in the patronage of the state had been a popular subject of complaint and satire: but whether they enjoyed office by receiving the most solemn rites of a church of which they were not members, or by the operation of acts of indemnity, their position was equally anomalous. But as their case formed part of the general law affecting dissenters, which Parliament was in no humour to entertain, the motion was defeated by a large majority.[1]

April 18th, 1791.

In 1792, Scotch Episcopalians were relieved from restraints which had been provoked by the disaffection of the Episcopalian clergy in the reigns of Anne and George II. As they no longer professed allegiance to the Stuarts, or refused to pray for the reigning king, there was no pretext for these invidious laws; and they were repealed with the concurrence of all parties.[2]

Restraints on Scotch Episcopalians repealed.

In the same year Mr. Fox, despairing, for the

[1] Ayes, 62; Noes, 149. Parl. Hist., xxix. 488–510.
[2] Parl. Hist., xxix. 1372.

present, of any relaxation of the test laws, endeavoured to obtain the repeal of certain penal statutes affecting religious opinions. His bill proposed to repeal several Acts of this nature:[1] but his main object was to exempt the Unitarians, who had petitioned for relief, from the penalties specially affecting their particular persuasion. They did not pray for civil enfranchisement, but simply for religious freedom. In deprecating the prejudices excited against this sect, he said, 'Dr. South had traced their pedigree from wretch to wretch, back to the devil himself. These descendants of the devil were his clients.' He attributed the late riots at Birmingham, and the attack upon Dr. Priestley, to religious bigotry and persecution; and claimed for this unpopular sect, at least the same toleration as other dissenting bodies. Mr. Burke, in opposing the motion, made a fierce onslaught upon the Unitarians. They were hostile to the church, he said, and had combined to effect its ruin: they had adopted the doctrines of Paine; and approved of the revolutionary excesses of the French Jacobins. The Unitarians were boldly defended by Mr. William Smith,—a constant advocate of religious liberty, who, growing old and honoured in that cause, lived to be the Father of the House of Commons. Mr. Pitt declared his reprobation of the Unitarians, and opposed the motion, which was lost by a majority of seventy-nine.[2] Mr.

Penal statutes respecting religious opinions (Unitarians), May 11th, 1792.

---

[1] Viz. 9 & 10 Will. III. c. 32 (for suppressing blasphemy and profaneness); 1 Edw. VI. c. 1; 1 Mary, c. 3; 13 Eliz. c. 2.

[2] Ayes, 63; Noes, 142. Parl. Hist., xxix. 1372; Tomline's Life of Pitt, iii. 317.

Pitt and other statesmen, in withholding civil rights from dissenters, had been careful to admit their title to religious freedom: but this vote unequivocally declared that doctrines and opinions might justly be punished as an offence.

Meanwhile the perilous distractions of Ireland, and a formidable combination of the Catholic body, forced upon the attention of the government the wrongs of Irish Catholics. The great body of the Irish people were denied all the rights of citizens. Their public worship was still proscribed: their property, their social and domestic relations, and their civil liberties were under interdict: they were excluded from all offices civil and military, and even from the professions of law and medicine.[1] Already the penal code affecting the exercise of their religion had been partially relaxed:[2] but they still laboured under all the civil disqualifications which the jealousy of ages had imposed. Mr. Pitt not only condemned the injustice of such disabilities: but hoped by a policy of conciliation, to heal some of the unhappy feuds by which society was divided. Ireland could no longer be safely governed upon the exclusive principles of Protestant ascendency. Its people must not claim in vain the franchises of British subjects. And accordingly in 1792, some of the most galling dis-

Catholic relief, Ireland, 1792.

---

[1] Some restrictions had been added even in this reign. Butler's Hist. Mem., iii. 367, et seq.; 467–477, 484; O'Conor's Hist. of the Irish Catholics; Sydney Smith's Works, i. 269; Goldwin Smith's Irish Hist., &c., 124.

[2] Viz. in 1774, 1778, and 1782; 13 & 14 Geo. III. c. 35; 17 & 18 Geo. III. c. 49; 22 Geo. III. c. 24 (Irish); Parnell's Hist. of the Penal Laws, 84, &c.; Butler's Hist. Mem., iii. 486.

abilities were removed by the Irish Parliament. Catholics were admitted to the legal profession on taking the oath of allegiance, and allowed to become clerks to attorneys. Restrictions on the education of their children, and on their intermarriages with Protestants, were also removed.[1]

In the next year more important privileges were conceded. All remaining restraints on Catholic worship and education, and the disposition of property, were removed. Catholics were admitted to vote at elections, on taking the oaths of allegiance and abjuration: to all but the higher civil and military offices, and to the honours and emoluments of Dublin University. In the law they could not rise to the rank of king's counsel: nor in the army beyond the rank of colonel: nor in their own counties, could they aspire to the offices of sheriff and sub-sheriff:[2] their highest ambition was still curbed; but they received a wide enfranchisement, beyond their former hopes. *Catholic relief, Ireland, 1793.*

In this year tardy justice was also rendered to the Roman Catholics of Scotland. All excitement upon the subject having passed away, a bill was brought in and passed without opposition, to relieve them, like their English brethren, from many grievous penalties to which they were exposed. In proposing the measure, the *Catholic relief, Scotland, 1793.*

---

[1] 32 Geo. III. c. 21 (Irish); Debates (Ireland), xii. 39, &c.; Life of Grattan, ii. 53.

[2] 33 Geo. III. c. 21 (Irish); Debates of Irish Parliament, xiii. 199; Plowden's Hist., ii. 421; Adolphus' Hist., vi. 249-256; Lord Stanhope's Life of Pitt, ii. 277; Butler's Hist. Mem., iv. 62; Life of Grattan, iv. 87; Parnell's Hist. of the Penal Laws, 124.

lord advocate stated that the obnoxious statutes were not so obsolete as might be expected. At that very time a Roman Catholic gentleman was in danger of being stripped of his estate,—which had been in his family for at least a century and a half,—by a relation having no other claim to it, than that which he derived, as a Protestant, from the cruel provisions of the law.[1]

The Quakers next appealed to Parliament for relief. In 1796, they presented a petition describing their sufferings on account of religious scruples; and Mr. Sergeant Adair brought in a bill to facilitate the recovery of tithes from members of that sect, without subjecting them to imprisonment; and to allow them to be examined upon affirmation in criminal cases. The remedy proposed for the recovery of tithes had already been provided by statute, in demands not exceeding 10*l*.;[2] and the sole object of this part of the bill was to ensure the recovery of all tithes without requiring the consent of the Quakers themselves, to which they had so strong a religious scruple, that they preferred perpetual imprisonment. At that very time, seven of their brethren were lying in the gaol at York, without any prospect of relief. The bill was passed by the Commons, but was lost in the Lords, upon the representation of the Archbishop of Canterbury that it involved a question of right of very great importance, which there was not then time to consider.[3]

Quakers. April 21st, 1796.

---

[1] Parl. Hist., xxx. 766; 33 Geo. III. c. 44; Butler's Hist. Mem., iv. 103.

[2] 7 & 8 Will. III. c. 34; 1 Geo. I., st. 2, c. 6; Parl. Hist., ix. 1220.

[3] Parl. Hist., xxxii. 1022.

In the next session the bill was renewed,[1] when it encountered the resolute opposition of Sir William Scott.[2] 'The opinions held by the Quakers,' he said, 'were of such a nature as to affect the civil rights of property, and therefore he considered them as unworthy of legislative indulgence.' If one man had conscientious scruples against the payment of tithes to which his property was legally liable, another might object to the payment of rent as sinful, while a third might hold it irreligious to pay his debts. If the principle of indulgence were ever admitted, 'the sect of anti-tithe Christians would soon become the most numerous and flourishing in the kingdom.' He argued that the security of property in tithes would be diminished by the bill, and that 'the tithe-owner would become an owner, not of property, but of suits.' It was replied that the tithe-owner would be enabled by the bill to recover his demands by summary distress, instead of punishing the Quaker with useless imprisonment. The very remedy, indeed, was provided, which the law adopted for the recovery of rent. The bill was also opposed by the solicitor-general, Sir John Mitford, who denied that Quakers entertained any conscientious scruples at all, against the payment of tithes. The question for going into committee on the bill was decided by the casting vote of the speaker: but upon a subsequent day, the bill was lost by a majority of sixteen.[3]

Such had been the narrow jealousy of the state,

[1] Parl. Hist., xxxii. 1206.   [2] Afterwards Lord Stowell.
[3] Parl. Hist., xxxii. 1508.

that Roman Catholics and dissenters, however loyal and patriotic, were not permitted to share in the defence of their country. They could not be trusted with arms, lest they should turn them against their own countrymen. In 1797, Mr. Wilberforce endeavoured to redress a part of this wrong, by obtaining the admission of Roman Catholics to the militia. Supported by Mr. Pitt, he succeeded in passing his bill through the Commons. In the Lords, however, it was opposed by Bishop Horsley and other peers; and its provisions being extended to dissenters, its fate was sealed.[1]

Catholics and the militia.

The English ministers were still alive to the importance of a liberal and conciliatory policy, in the government of Ireland. In 1795, Lord Fitzwilliam accepted the office of lord-lieutenant, in order to carry out such a policy. He even conceived himself to have the authority of the cabinet to favour an extensive enfranchisement of Catholics: but having committed himself too deeply to that party, he was recalled.[2] There were, indeed, insurmountable difficulties in reconciling an extended toleration to Catholics, with Protestant ascendency in the Irish Parliament.

Lord Fitzwilliam's policy, 1795.

But the union of Catholic Ireland with Protestant

---

[1] Wilberforce's Life, ii. 222. The debates are not to be found in the Parliamentary History. 'No power in Europe, but yourselves, has ever thought, for these hundred years past, of asking whether a bayonet is Catholic, or Presbyterian, or Lutheran; but whether it is sharp and well-tempered.'—*Peter Plymley's Letters*; Sydney Smith's Works, iii. 63.

[2] Parl. Hist., xxxiv. 672, &c.; Plowden's Hist., ii. 467; Butler's Hist. Mem., iv. 65.

Great Britain, introduced new considerations of state policy. To admit Catholics to the Parliament of the United Kingdom would be a concession full of popularity to the people of Ireland, while their admission to a legislature comprising an overwhelming Protestant majority, would be free from danger to the established church, or to the Protestant character of Parliament. In such a union of the two countries, the two nations would also be embraced. In the discussions relating to the Union, the removal of Catholic disabilities, as one of its probable consequences, was frequently alluded to. Mr. Canning argued that the Union 'would satisfy the friends of the Protestant ascendency, without passing laws against the Catholics, and without maintaining those which are yet in force.'[1] And Mr. Pitt said: 'No man can say that in the present state of things, and while Ireland remains a separate kingdom, full concessions could be made to the Catholics, without endangering the state, and shaking the constitution of Ireland to its centre.' . . . . But 'when the conduct of the Catholics shall be such as to make it safe for the government to admit them to a participation of the privileges granted to those of the established religion, and when the temper of the times shall be favourable to such a measure, it is obvious that such a question may be agitated in a united Imperial Parliament, with much greater safety than it could be in a

Union with Ireland, in connection with Catholic disabilities.

Jan. 23rd, 1799.

Jan. 31st.

[1] Parl. Hist., xxxiv. 230; Lord Holland's Mem., i. 161.

separate legislature.'[1] He also hinted at the expediency of proposing some mode of relieving the poorer classes from the pressure of tithes, and for making a provision for the Catholic clergy, without affecting the security of the Protestant establishment.[2]

In securing the support of different parties in Ireland to the Union, the question of Catholic disabilities was one of great delicacy. Distinct promises, which might have secured the hearty support of the Catholics, would have alienated the Protestants,—by far the most powerful party,—and endangered the success of the whole measure. At the same time, there was hazard of the Catholics being gained over to oppose the Union, by expectations of relief from the Irish Parliament.[3] Lord Cornwallis, alive to these difficulties, appears to have met them with consummate address. Careful not to commit himself or the government to any specific engagements, he succeeded in encouraging the hopes of the Catholics, without alarming the Protestant party.[4] The sentiments of the govern-

The Irish executive and the Catholics.

[1] Parl. Hist., xxxiv. 272.
[2] Mr. Pitt and Lord Grenville agreed generally upon the Catholic claims. 'Previously to the Union with Ireland, it had never entered into the mind of the latter that there could be any further relaxation of the laws against Papists: but from that time he had been convinced that everything necessary for them might be granted without the slightest danger to the Protestant interest.'—Abstract of Lord Grenville's Letter to the Principal of Brazenose, 1810.—*Lord Colchester's Diary*, ii. 224.
[3] Cornwallis Corr., iii. 51.
[4] Jan. 2nd, 1799, he writes: 'I shall endeavour to give them (the Catholics) the most favourable impressions without holding out to them hopes of any relaxation on the part of government, and shall leave no effort untried to prevent an opposition to the Union being made the measure of that party.'—*Corr.*, iii. 29.

ment were known to be generally favourable to measures of relief: but Mr. Pitt had been forbidden by the king to offer any concessions whatever;[1] nor had he himself determined upon the measures which it would be advisable to propose.[2] He was, therefore, able to deny that he had given any pledge upon the subject, or that the Catholics conceived themselves to have received any such pledge:[3] but he admitted that they had formed strong expecta-

And again, Jan. 28th, 1799: 'I much doubt the policy of at present holding out to them any decided expectations: it might weaken us with the Protestants, and might not strengthen us with the Catholics, whilst they look to carry their question unconnected with Union.' —*Corr.*, iii. 55. See also *Ibid.*, 63, 149, 327, 344, 347.

[1] June 11th, 1798, the king writes to Mr. Pitt: 'Lord Cornwallis must clearly understand that no indulgence can be granted to the Catholics farther than has been, I am afraid unadvisedly, done in former sessions, and that he must by a steady conduct effect in future the union of that kingdom with this.—*Lord Stanhope's Life of Pitt*, iii. App. xvi.

Again, Jan. 24th, 1790, having seen in a letter from Lord Castlereagh 'an idea of an established stipend by the authority of government for the Catholic clergy of Ireland,' he wrote: 'I am certain any encouragement to such an idea must give real offence to the established church in Ireland, as well as to the true friends of our constitution; for it is certainly creating a second church establishment, which could not but be highly injurious.'—*Ibid.*, xviii.

[2] Mr. Pitt wrote to Lord Cornwallis, Nov. 17th, 1788: 'Mr. Elliot, when he brought me your letter, stated very strongly all the arguments which he thought might induce us to admit the Catholics to Parliament and office, but I confess he did not satisfy me of the practicability of such a measure at this time, or of the propriety of attempting it. With respect to a provision for the Catholic clergy, and some arrangement respecting tithes, I am happy to find an uniform opinion in favour of the proposal, among all the Irish I have seen.'—*Lord Stanhope's Life of Pitt*, iii. 161. See also Castlereagh Corr., i. 73; Lord Colchester's Mem., i. 250, 511.

'Lord Camden told me that being a member of Mr. Pitt's government in 1800, he knew that Mr. Pitt had never matured any plan for giving what is called emancipation to the Roman Catholics.'— *Lord Colchester's Diary*, iii. 326.

[3] March 25th, 1801; Parl. Hist., xxxv. 1124; and see Cornwallis Corr., iii. 343–350.

tions of remedial measures after the Union,—of which indeed there is abundant testimony.[1]

These expectations Mr. Pitt and his colleagues were prepared to satisfy. When the Union had been accomplished, they agreed that the altered relations of the two countries would allow them to do full justice to the Catholics, without any danger to the established church. They were of opinion that Catholics might now be safely admitted to office, and to the privilege of sitting in Parliament; and that dissenters should, at the same time, be relieved from civil disabilities. It was also designed to attach the Catholic clergy to the state, by making them dependent upon public funds for a part of their provision, and to induce them to submit to superintendence.[2] It was a measure of high and prescient statesmanship,—worthy of the genius of the great minister who had achieved the Union.

Concessions to Catholics proposed, after the Union.

But toleration, which had formerly been resisted by Parliament and the people, now encountered the invincible opposition of the king, who refused his assent to further measures of concession, as inconsistent with the obligations of his coronation oath. To his unfounded scruples were sacrificed the rights of millions, and the peace

Concessions forbidden by the king.

---

[1] Lord Liverpool's Mem., 128; Castlereagh Corr., iv. 11, 13, 34; Lord Stanhope's Life of Pitt, iii. 263, 281-288, &c., App., xxiii. *et seq.*; Lord Malmesbury's Corr., iv. 1, *et seq.*; Cornwallis' Corr., ii. 436; Butler's Hist. Mem., iv. 70; see also Edinb. Rev., Jan. 1858.

[2] Mr. Pitt's Letter to the King, Jan. 31st, 1801; Lord Sidmouth's Life, i. 289; Lord Cornwallis's Corr., iii. 325, 335, 344; Court and Cabinets of Geo. III., iii. 129. The Irish Catholic Bishops had consented to allow the crown a *veto* on their nomination.—Butler's Hist. Mem., iv. 112-134.

of Ireland. The measure was arrested at its inception. The minister fell; and in deference to the king's feelings, was constrained to renounce his own wise and liberal policy.[1]

But the question of Catholic disabilities, in connection with the government of Ireland, was too momentous to be set at rest by the religious scruples of the king, and the respectful forbearance of statesmen. In the rebellion of 1798, the savage hatred of Protestants and Catholics had aggravated the dangers of that critical period. Nor were the difficulties of administering the government overcome by the Union. The abortive rebellion of Robert Emmett, in 1803, again exposed the alarming condition of Ireland; and suggested that the social dislocation of that unhappy country needed a more statesmanlike treatment than that of Protestant ascendency and irritating disabilities. For the present, however, the general question was in abeyance, in Parliament. Mr. Pitt had been silenced by the king; and Mr. Addington's administration was avowedly anti-Catholic. Yet in 1803, Catholics obtained a further instalment of relief,—being exempted from certain penalties and disabilities, on taking the oath and subscribing the declaration prescribed by the Act of 1791.[2]

Critical condition of Ireland.

The Catholic question in abeyance.

In 1804, a serious agitation for Catholic relief commenced in Ireland: but as yet the cause was without hope. On Mr. Pitt's restoration to power, he was still restrained by his engagement to the king, from proposing any measure

Mr. Pitt, 1804-5.

[1] *Supra*, Vol. I. 92-97.   [2] 43 Geo. III. c. 30.

for the relief of Catholics himself; and was even obliged to resist their claims when advocated by others.[1] In 1805, the discussion of the general question was resumed in Parliament by Lord Grenville, who presented a petition from the Roman Catholics of Ireland, recounting the disabilities under which they still suffered.[2]

Catholic petition, March 25th, 1805.

On the 10th May, his lordship moved for a committee of the whole House to consider this petition. He urged that three-fourths of the people of Ireland were Roman Catholics, whose existence the state could not ignore. At the time of the Revolution they had been excluded from civil privileges, not on account of their religion, but for their political adhesion to the exiled sovereign. In the present reign they had received toleration in the exercise of their religion, power to acquire land, the enjoyment of the elective franchise, and the right to fill many offices from which they had previously been excluded. Whatever objections might have existed to the admission of Roman Catholics to the Parliament of Ireland, had been removed by the Union; as in the Parliament of the United Kingdom there was a vast preponderance of Protestants. This argument had been used by those who had promoted the Union. It had encouraged the hopes of the Roman Catholics; and now, for the first time since the Union, that body had appealed to Parliament. His lordship dwelt upon their loyalty, as frequently declared by the Irish Parliament, exone-

Lord Grenville's motion, May 10th, 1805.

---

[1] Lord Stanhope's Life of Pitt, iv. 297, 391.
[2] Hans. Deb., 1st Ser., iv. 97.

rated them from participation, as a body, in the Rebellion, combated the prejudice raised against them on account of the recent coronation of Napoleon by the pope, and illustrated the feelings which their exclusion from lawful objects of ambition naturally excited in their minds. He desired to unite all classes of the people in the common benefits and common interests of the state.

This speech, which ably presented the entire case of the Roman Catholics, opened a succession of debates, in which all the arguments relating to their claims were elicited.[1] As regards the high offices of state, it was urged by Lord Hawkesbury, that while the law excluded a Roman Catholic sovereign from the throne of his inheritance, it could scarcely be allowed that the councils of a Protestant king should be directed by Roman Catholics. Roman Catholics, it was argued, would not be fit persons to sit in Parliament, so long as they refused to take the oath of supremacy, which merely renounced foreign dominion and jurisdiction. In Ireland, their admission would increase the influence of the priesthood in elections, and array the property of the country on one side, and its religion and numbers on the other. The Duke of Cumberland opposed the prayer of the petition, as fatal to all the principles upon which the House of Hanover had been called to the throne. Every apprehension and prejudice which could be appealed to, in opposition to the claims of the Roman Catholics, was exerted in this debate. The pope, their master, was the slave and tool of

[1] Hans. Deb., 1st Ser., iv. 651-729, 742.

Napoleon. If entrusted with power, they would resist the payment of tithes, and overthrow the established church. Nay, Catholic families would reclaim their forfeited estates, which for five generations had been in the possession of Protestants, or had since been repurchased by Catholics. After two nights' debate, Lord Grenville's motion was negatived by a majority of 129.[1]

Mr. Fox also offered a similar motion to the Com-

<small>Mr. Fox's motion in the Commons, May 13th, 1805.</small>

mons, founded upon a petition addressed to that House. The people whose cause he was advocating, amounted, he said, to between a fourth and a fifth of the entire population of the United Kingdom. So large a portion of his fellow-subjects had been excluded from civil rights, not on account of their religion, but for political causes which no longer existed. Queen Elizabeth had not viewed them as loyal subjects of a Protestant Queen. The character and conduct of the Stuarts had made the people distrustful of the Catholics. At the time of the Revolution 'it was not a Catholic, but a Jacobite, you wished to restrain.' In Ireland, again, the restrictions upon Catholics were political and not religious. In the civil war which had raged there, the Catholics were the supporters of James, and as Jacobites were discouraged and restrained. The Test Act of Charles II. was passed because the sovereign himself was suspected; and Catholic officers were excluded, lest they should assist him in his endeavours to subvert the constitution. There was no fear, now, of a

---

[1] Contents, 49; Non-contents, 178. Hans. Deb., 1st Ser., iv. 843.

Protestant king being unduly influenced by Catholic ministers. The danger of admitting Catholics to Parliament was chimerical. Did any one believe that twenty Catholic members would be returned from the whole of Ireland?[1] In reply to this question, Dr. Duigenan asserted that Ireland would return upwards of eighty Catholic members, and the English boroughs twenty more,—thus forming a compact confederacy of 100 members, banded together for the subversion of all our institutions in church and state.

He was answered eloquently, and in a liberal spirit, by Mr. Grattan, in the first speech addressed by him to the Imperial Parliament. The general discussion, however, was not distinguished, on either side, by much novelty.

The speech of Mr. Pitt serves as a land-mark, denoting the position of the question at that time. He frankly admitted that he retained his opinion, formed at the time of the Union, that Catholics might be admitted to the united Parliament, 'under proper guards and conditions,' without 'any danger to the established church or the Protestant constitution.' But the circumstances which had then prevented him from proposing such a measure 'had made so deep, so lasting an impression upon his mind, that so long as those circumstances continued to operate, he should feel it a duty imposed upon him, not only not to bring forward, but not in any manner to be a party in bringing forward, or in agitating this question.' At the same time, he de-

[1] Hans. Deb., 1st Ser., iv. 834-854.

precated its agitation by others, under circumstances most unfavourable to its settlement. Such a measure would be generally repugnant to members of the established church,—to the nobility, gentry, and middle classes, both in England and Ireland,—assuredly to the House of Lords, which had just declared its opinion;[1] and, as he believed, to the great majority of the House of Commons. To urge forward a measure, in opposition to obstacles so insuperable, could not advance the cause; while it encouraged delusive hopes, and fostered religious and political animosities.[2]

Mr. Windham denied that the general sentiment was against such a measure; and scouted the advice that it should be postponed until there was a general concurrence in its favour. 'If no measure,' he said, 'is ever to pass in Parliament which has not the unanimous sense of the country in its favour, prejudice and passion may for ever triumph over reason and sound policy.' After a masterly reply by Mr. Fox, which closed a debate of two nights, the House proceeded to a division, when his motion was lost by a decisive majority of one hundred and twelve.[3]

The Whig ministry of 1806, and the Catholics.

The present temper of Parliament was obviously unfavourable to the Catholic cause. The hopes of the Catholics, however, were again raised by the death of Mr. Pitt, and the

[1] The debate had been adjourned till the day after the decision in the Lords.
[2] Hans. Deb., 1st Ser., iv. 1013.
[3] Ayes, 124; Noes, 236. Hans. Deb., 1st Ser., iv. 1060; Grattan's Life, v. 253-264.

formation of the Whig Ministry of 1806. The cabinet comprised Lord Grenville, Mr. Fox, and other statesmen who had advocated Catholic relief in 1801, and in the recent debates of 1805; and the Catholics of Ireland did not fail to press upon them the justice of renewing the consideration of their claims. This pressure was a serious embarrassment to ministers. After the events of 1801, they needed no warning of the difficulty of their position, which otherwise was far from secure. No measure satisfactory to the Catholics could be submitted to the king; and the bare mention of the subject was not without danger. They were too conscious not only of His Majesty's inflexible opinions, but of his repugnance to themselves. Mr. Fox perceived so clearly the impossibility of approaching the king, that he persuaded the Catholic leaders to forbear their claims for the present. They had recently been rejected, by large majorities, in both Houses; and to repeat them now, would merely embarrass their friends, and offer another easy triumph to their enemies.[1] But it is hard for the victims of wrong to appreciate the difficulties of statesmen; and the Catholics murmured at the apparent desertion of their friends. For a time they were pacified by the liberal administration of the Duke of Bedford in Ireland: but after Mr. Fox's death, and the dissolution of Parliament in 1806, they again became impatient.[2]

[1] Lord Sidmouth's Life, ii. 436; Ann. Reg., 1806, p. 25; Lord Holland's Mem. of the Whig Party, i. 213, *et seq.*; Butler's Hist. Mem., iv. 184–187.
[2] Butler's Hist. Mem., iv. 188; Grattan's Life, v. 282–296, 334.

At length Lord Grenville, hoping to avert further pressure on the general question, resolved to redress a grievance which pressed heavily in time of war, not upon Catholics only, but upon the public service. By the Irish Act of 1793, Catholics were allowed to hold any commission in the army in Ireland, up to the rank of colonel: but were excluded from the higher staff appointments of commander-in-chief, master-general of the ordnance, and general of the staff. As this Act had not been extended to Great Britain, a Catholic officer in the king's service, on leaving Ireland, became liable to the penalties of the English laws. To remove this obvious anomaly, the government at first proposed to assimilate the laws of both countries, by two clauses in the Mutiny Act; and to this proposal the king reluctantly gave his consent. On further consideration, however, this simple provision appeared inadequate. The Irish Act applied to Catholics only, as dissenters had been admitted, by a previous Act, to serve in civil and military offices; and it was confined to the army, as Ireland had no navy. The exceptions in the Irish Act were considered unnecessary; and it was further thought just to grant indulgence to soldiers in the exercise of their religion. As these questions arose, from time to time, ministers communicated to the king their correspondence with the lord-lieutenant, and explained the variations of their proposed measure from that of the Irish Act, with the grounds upon which they were recommended. Throughout these communications His Majesty did not conceal his general dislike and disapprobation of the measure: but was understood to give his reluctant assent to its introduction as a separate bill.[1]

In this form the bill was introduced by Lord Howick. He explained that when the Irish Act of 1793 had been passed, a similar measure had been promised for Great Britain. That promise was at length to be fulfilled: but as it would be unreasonable to confine the measure to Catholics, it was proposed to embrace dissenters in its provisions. The act of 1793 had applied to the army only: but it was then distinctly stated that the navy should be included in the Act of the British Parliament. If Catholics were admitted to one branch of the service, what possible objection could there be to their admission to the other? He did not propose, however, to continue the restrictions of the Irish Act, which disqualified a Catholic from the offices of commander-in-chief, master-general of the ordnance, or general on the staff. Such restrictions were at once unnecessary and injurious. The appointment to these high offices was vested in the crown, which would be under no obligation to appoint Roman Catholics; and it was an injury to the public service to exclude by law a man 'who might be called by the voice of the army and the people' to fill an office, for which he had proved his

Bill brought in by Lord Howick, March 5th, 1807.

---

[1] Explanations of Lord Grenville and Lord Howick, March 26th, 1807; Hans. Deb., 1st Ser., ix. 231, 261–279; Lord Castlereagh's Corr., iv. 374; Lord Sidmouth's Life, ii. 436; Lord Grenville's Letter, Feb. 10th, 1807; Court and Cabinets of Geo. III., iv. 117; Lord Holland's Mem., ii. 159–199, App. 270; Lord Malmesbury's Corr., iv. p. 365; Wilberforce's Life, iii. 306.

fitness by distinguished services. Lastly, he proposed to provide that all who should enter His Majesty's service should enjoy the 'free and unrestrained exercise of their religion, so far as it did not interfere with their military duties.'[1] Mr. Spencer Perceval sounded the note of alarm at these proposals, which, in his opinion, involved all the principles of complete emancipation. If military equality were conceded, how could civil equality be afterwards resisted? His apprehensions were shared by some other members: but the bill was allowed to be introduced without opposition.

Withdrawal of bill, and fall of ministers. Its further progress, however, was suddenly arrested by the king, who refused to admit Catholics to the staff, and to include dissenters in the provisions of the bill.[2] He declared that his previous assent had been given to the simple extension of the Irish Act to Great Britain; and he would agree to nothing more. Again a ministry fell under the difficulties of the Catholic question.[3] The embarrassments of ministers had undoubtedly been great. They had desired to maintain their own character and consistency, and to conciliate the Catholics, without shocking the well-known scruples of the king. Their scheme was just and moderate: it was open to no rational objection: but neither in the preparation of the measure itself, nor in their communications with the king, can they be acquitted of errors which were

---

[1] Hans. Deb., 1st Ser., ix. 2-7.   [2] Ibid., 149, 173.
[3] The constitutional questions involved in their removal from office have been related elsewhere; Vol. I. p. 105.

turned against themselves and the unlucky cause they had espoused.[1]

Again were the hopes of the Catholics wrecked, and with them the hopes of a liberal government in England. An anti-Catholic administration was formed under the Duke of Portland and Mr. Perceval; and cries of 'No Popery,' and 'Church and King,' were raised throughout the land.[2] Mr. Perceval in his address to the electors of Northampton, on vacating his seat, took credit for 'coming forward in the service of his sovereign, and endeavouring to stand by him at this important crisis, when he is making so firm and so necessary a stand for the religious establishment of the country.'[3] The Duke of Portland wrote to the University of Oxford, of which he was Chancellor, desiring them to petition against the Catholic Bill; and the Duke of Cumberland, Chancellor of the University of Dublin, sought petitions from that University. No pains were spared to arouse the fears and prejudices of Protestants. Thus Mr. Perceval averred that the measure recently withdrawn would not have 'stopped short till it had brought Roman Catholic bishops to the House of Lords.'[4] Such cries as these were re-echoed at the

Anti-Catholic sentiments of the new ministers.

---

[1] Hans. Deb., 1st Ser., ix. 231, 247, 261, 340, &c.; Lord Holland's Mem., ii. 160, et seq.; App. to vol. ii. 270; Lord Malmesbury's Corr., iv. 367, 379; Lord Sidmouth's Life, ii. 448–472; Bulwer's Life of Lord Palmerston, i. 62–76.

[2] Mr. Henry Erskine said to the Duchess of Gordon: 'It was much to be lamented that poor Lord George did not live in these times, when he would have stood a chance of being in the cabinet, instead of being in Newgate.'—*Romilly's Mem.*, ii. 193.

[3] Romilly's Mem., ii. 192.

[4] Hans. Deb., 1st Ser., ix. 315.

VOL. III.　　　　　K

elections. An ultra-Protestant Parliament was assembled; and the Catholic cause was hopeless.[1]

The Catholics of Ireland, however, did not suffer their claims to be forgotten: but by frequent petitions, and the earnest support of their friends, continued to keep alive the interest of the Catholic question, in the midst of more engrossing subjects. But discussions, however able, which were unfruitful of results, can claim no more than a passing notice. Petitions were fully discussed in both Houses in 1808.[2] And again, in 1810, Earl Grey presented two petitions from Roman Catholics in England, complaining that they were denied many privileges which were enjoyed by their Roman Catholic brethren in other parts of the empire. He stated that in Canada Roman Catholics were eligible to all offices, in common with their Protestant fellow-subjects. In Ireland, they were allowed to act as magistrates, to become members of lay corporations, to take degrees at Trinity College, to vote at elections, and to attain to every rank in the army except that of general of the staff. In England, they could not be included in the commission of the peace, nor become members of corporations, were debarred from taking degrees at the univer-

Roman Catholic petitions, 1808.

Catholic petitions presented by Earl Grey, Feb. 22nd, 1810.

---

[1] Lord Malmesbury says: 'The spirit of the whole country is with the king; and the idea of the church being in danger (perhaps not quite untrue), makes Lord Grenville and the Foxites most unpopular.'—*Corr.*, iv. 394.

[2] Lords' Debates, May 27th, 1808; Commons' Debates, May 25th, 1808; Hans. Deb., 1st Ser., xi. 1, 30, 489, 549–638, 643–694; Grattan's Life, v. 376.

sities, and could not legally hold any rank in the army.[1] The Roman Catholics of Ireland also presented petitions to the House of Commons through Mr. Grattan, in this session.[2] But his motion to refer them to a committee was defeated, after a debate of three nights, by a majority of one hundred and four.[3] {Mr. Grattan's motion, May 18th, 1810.}

In the same session, Lord Donoughmore moved to refer several petitions from the Roman Catholics of Ireland to a committee of the House of Lords. But as Lord Grenville had declined, with the concurrence of Lord Grey, to bring forward the Catholic claims, the question was not presented under favourable circumstances; and the motion was lost by a majority of eighty-six.[4] {Lord Donoughmore's motion, June 6th, 1810.}

One other demonstration was made during this session in support of the Catholic cause. Lord Grey, in his speech on the state of the nation, adverted to the continued postponement of concessions to the Catholics, as a source of danger and weakness to the state in the conduct of the war; and appealed to ministers to 'unite the hearts and hands of all classes of the people in defence of their common country.' An allusion to this question was also made in the address which he proposed to the crown.[5] {Earl Grey's motion on the state of the nation, June 13th, 1810.}

---

[1] Hans. Deb., 1st Ser., xv. 503.
[2] Feb. 27th, *ibid.*, 634.
[3] *Ibid.*, xvii. 17, 183, 235. Ayes, 109; Noes, 213. Grattan's Life, v. 410.
[4] Contents, 68; Non-contents, 154. Hans. Deb., 1st Ser., xvii. 353–440.
[5] Hans. Deb., 1st Ser., xvii. 3, 577.

Approach of the regency. In the autumn of this year, an event fraught with sadness to the nation, once more raised the hopes of the Catholics. The aged king was stricken with his last infirmity; and a new political era was opening, full of promise to their cause.

CHAPTER XIII.

HISTORY OF CATHOLIC CLAIMS FROM THE REGENCY:—MEASURES FOR THE RELIEF OF DISSENTERS:—MARRIAGES OF CATHOLICS AND DISSENTERS:—REPEAL OF THE CORPORATION AND TEST ACTS IN 1828: —PASSING OF THE CATHOLIC RELIEF ACT IN 1829:—ITS RESULTS: —QUAKERS, MORAVIANS, AND SEPARATISTS:—JEWISH DISABILITIES.

THE regency augured well for the commencement of a more liberal policy in church and state. The venerable monarch, whose sceptre was now wielded by a feebler hand, had twice trampled upon the petitions of his Catholic subjects; and, by his resolution and influence, had united against them ministers, Parliament, and people. It seemed no idle hope that Tory ministers would now be supplanted by statesmen earnest in the cause of civil and religious liberty, whose policy would no longer be thwarted by the influence of the crown. The prince himself, once zealous in the Catholic cause, had, indeed, been for some years inconstant,—if not untrue,—to it. His change of opinion, however, might be due to respect for his royal father, or the political embarrassments of the question. None could suspect him of cherishing intractable religious scruples.[1] Assuredly he would not reject the liberal counsels of the ministers of his

Hopes of the regency disappointed.

---

[1] Moore's Life of Sheridan, ii. 333; Lord Brougham's Statesmen, i. 186; Lord Holland's Mem., ii. 196.

choice. But these visions were soon to collapse and vanish, like bubbles in the air;[1] and the weary struggle was continued, with scarcely a change in its prospects.

<small>Freedom of worship to Roman Catholic soldiers.</small>

The first year of the regency, however, was marked by the consummation of one act of toleration. The Grenville ministry had failed to secure freedom of religious worship to Catholic soldiers by legislation:[2] but they had partially secured that object by a circular to commanding officers. Orders to the same effect had since been annually issued by the commander-in-chief. The articles of war, however, recognised no right in the soldier to absent himself from divine service; and in ignorance or neglect of these orders, soldiers had been punished for refusing to attend the services of the established church. To repress such an abuse, the commander-in-chief issued general orders, in January 1811; and Mr. Parnell afterwards proposed

<small>March 11th, 1811.</small>

a clause in the Mutiny Bill, to give legal effect to them. The clause was not agreed to: but, in the debate, no doubt was left that, by the regulations of the service, full toleration would henceforth be enjoyed by Catholic soldiers, in the exercise of their religion.[3]

<small>Protestant Dissenting Ministers' Bill, 1811.</small>

Another measure, affecting dissenters, was conceived in a somewhat different spirit. Lord Sidmouth complained of the facility with which dissenting ministers were able to obtain certificates, under the Act of 1779,[4] without

---

[1] Vol. I. 119.   [2] *Supra*, p. 128.
[3] Hans. Deb., 1st Ser., xix. 350.   [4] *Supra*, p. 94.

any proof of their fitness to preach, or of there being any congregation requiring their ministrations. Some had been admitted who could not even read and write, but were prepared to preach by inspiration. One of the abuses resulting from this facility was the exemption of so many preachers from serving on juries, and from other civil duties. To correct these evils, he proposed certain securities, of which the principal was a certificate of fitness from six reputable householders, of the same persuasion as the minister seeking a licence to preach.[1] His bill met with little favour. It was, at best, a trivial measure: but its policy was in the wrong direction. It ill becomes a state, which disowns any relations with dissenters, to intermeddle with their discipline. The dissenters rose up against the bill; and before the second reading, the House was overwhelmed with their petitions. The government discouraged it: the Archbishop of Canterbury counselled its withdrawal: the leading peers of the liberal party denounced it; and Lord Sidmouth, standing almost alone, was obliged to allow his ill-advised measure to be defeated, without a division.[2]

May 9th, 1811.

Lord Sidmouth's bill had not only alarmed the dissenters, but had raised legal doubts, which exposed them to further molestation.[3] And, in the next year, another bill was passed, with the grateful approval of the dissenters, by which they were relieved from the oaths

Protestant Dissenting Ministers' Bill, 1812.

---

[1] Hans. Deb., 1st Ser., xix. 1128–1140.
[2] *Ibid.*, xx. 233; Lord Sidmouth's Life, iii. 38–65; Brook's Hist. of Relig. Lib., ii. 386.
[3] Brook's Hist. of Relig. Lib., ii. 394.

and declaration required by the Toleration Act, and the Act of 1779, and from other vexatious restrictions.[1] And in the following year, Mr. W. Smith obtained for Unitarians that relief which, many years before, Mr. Fox had vainly sought from the legislature.[2]

Unitarians' relief, 1813.

Nothing distinguished the tedious annals of the Catholic question in 1811, but a motion, in one House, by Mr. Grattan, and, in the other, by Lord Donoughmore, which met with their accustomed fate.[3] But, in 1812, the aspect of the Catholic question was, in some degree, changed. The claims of the Catholics, always associated with the peace and good government of Ireland, were now brought forward, in the form of a motion, by Lord Fitzwilliam, for a committee on the state of Ireland; and were urged more on the ground of state policy than of justice. The debate was chiefly remarkable for a wise and statesmanlike speech of the Marquess Wellesley. The motion was lost by a majority of eighty-three.[4] A few days afterwards, a similar motion was made in the House of Commons, by Lord Morpeth. Mr. Canning opposed it in a masterly speech,—more encouraging to the cause than the support of most other men.

Catholic petitions, May 31st, June 18th, 1811.

Catholic question, 1812.

State of Ireland.

Jan. 31st.

Feb. 3rd.

---

[1] 52 Geo. III. c. 155; Hans. Deb., 1st Ser., xxiii. 994, 1105, 1247; Lord Sidmouth's Life, iii. 65; Brook's Hist. of Relig. Lib., ii. 394.

[2] 53 Geo. III. c. 160; Brook's Hist. of Relig. Lib., ii. 395.

[3] Ayes, 83; Noes, 146, in the Commons, Hans. Deb., 1st Ser., xx. 369–427. Contents, 62; Non-contents, 121, in the Lords. Hans. Deb., 1st Ser., xx. 645–685; Grattan's Life, v. 376.

[4] Hans. Deb., 1st Ser., xxi. 408–483. The House adjourned at half-past 6 in the morning.

Objecting to the motion in point of time alone, he urged every abstract argument in its favour; declared that the policy of enfranchisement must be progressive; and that since the obstacle caused by the king's conscientious scruples had been removed, it had become the duty of ministers to undertake the settlement of a question, vital to the interests of the empire.[1] The general tone of the discussion was also encouraging to the Catholic cause; and after two nights' debate, the motion was lost by a majority of ninety-four,—a number increased by the belief that the motion implied a censure upon the executive government of Ireland.[2]

Another aspect in the Catholic cause is also observable in this year. Not only were petitions from the Catholics of England and Ireland more numerous and imposing: but Protestant noblemen, gentlemen of landed property, clergy, commercial capitalists, officers in the army and navy, and the inhabitants of large towns, added their prayers to those of their Catholic fellow-countrymen.[3] Even the universities of Oxford and Cambridge, which presented petitions against the Catholic claims, were much divided in opinion; and minorities, considerable in academic rank, learning, and numbers, were ranged on the other side.[4]

Protestant sympathy.

Thus fortified, motions in support of the Catholic

---

[1] It was in this speech that he uttered his celebrated exclamation, 'repeal the Union! restore the Heptarchy!'
[2] Hans. Deb., 1st Ser., xxi. 494, 605. The House adjourned at half-past 5.
[3] Hans. Deb., 1st Ser., xxii. 452, 478, 482–706, &c.
[4] *Ibid.*, 462, 507; Grattan's Life, v. 467.

claims were renewed in both Houses; and being now free from any implication of censure upon the government, were offered under more favourable auspices. That of the Earl of Donoughmore, in the House of Lords, elicited from the Duke of Sussex an elaborate speech in favour of the Catholic claims, which His Royal Highness afterwards edited with many learned notes. Who that heard the arguments of Lord Wellesley and Lord Grenville, could have believed that the settlement of this great question was yet to be postponed for many years? Lord Grenville's warning was like a prophecy. 'I ask not,' he said, 'what in this case will be your ultimate decision. It is easily anticipated. We know, and it has been amply shown in former instances,—the cases of America and of Ireland have but too well proved it, —how precipitately necessity extorts what power has pertinaciously refused. We shall finally yield to these petitions. No man doubts it. Let us not delay the concession, until it can neither be graced by spontaneous kindness, nor limited by deliberative wisdom.' The motion was defeated by a majority of seventy-two.[1]

Lord Donoughmore's motion, April 21st, 1812.

Mr. Grattan proposed a similar motion in the House of Commons, in a speech more than usually earnest and impassioned. In this debate, Mr. Brougham raised his voice in support of the Catholic cause,—a voice ever on the side of freedom.[2] And now Mr. Canning supported

Mr. Grattan's motion, April 23rd, 1812.

---

[1] Contents, 102; Non-contents, 174. Hans. Deb., 1st Ser., xxii. 509-703. The House divided at 5 in the morning.

[2] Mr. Brougham had entered Parliament in 1810.

the motion, not only with his eloquence, but with his vote; and continued henceforth one of the foremost advocates of the Catholic claims. After two nights' debate, Mr. Grattan's motion was submitted to the vote of an unusual number of members, assembled by a call of the House, and lost by a majority of eighty-five.[1]

But this session promised more than the barren triumphs of debate. On the death of Mr. Perceval, the Marquess Wellesley being charged with the formation of a new administration, assumed, as the very basis of his negotiation, the final adjustment of the Catholic claims. The negotiation failed, indeed:[2] but the Marquess and his friends, encouraged by so unprecedented a concession from the throne, sought to pledge Parliament to the consideration of this question in the next session. First, Mr. Canning, in the House of Commons, gained an unexampled victory. For years past, every motion favourable to this cause had been opposed by large majorities: but now his motion for the consideration of the laws affecting His Majesty's Roman Catholic subjects in Great Britain and Ireland, was carried by the extraordinary majority of one hundred and twenty-nine.[3] *Mr. Canning's motion, June 22nd, 1812.*

Shortly after this most encouraging resolution, the Marquess Wellesley made a similar motion, in the House of Lords,[4] where the decision was scarcely less remarkable. The *Lord Wellesley's motion. July 1st, 1812.*

---

[1] Ayes, 215; Noes, 300. Hans. Deb., 1st Ser., xxii. 728, 860. The House adjourned at half-past 6 in the morning.
[2] *Supra*, Vol. I. 125.
[3] Ayes, 235; Noes, 129. Hans. Deb., 1st Ser. xxiii. 633–710.
[4] Hans. Deb., 1st Ser., xxiii. 711, 814.

lord chancellor had moved the previous question, and even upon that indefinite and evasive issue, the motion was only lost by a single vote.[1]

Another circumstance, apparently favourable to the cause, was also disclosed. The Earl of Liverpool's administration, instead of uniting their whole force against the Catholic cause, agreed that it should be an 'open question;' and this freedom of action, on the part of individual members of the government, was first exercised in these debates. The introduction of this new element into the contest, was a homage to the justice and reputation of the cause: but its promises were illusory. Had the statesmen who espoused the Catholic claims steadfastly refused to act with ministers who continued to oppose them, it may be doubted whether any competent ministry could much longer have been formed, upon a rigorous policy of exclusion. The influence of the crown and church might, for some time, have sustained such a ministry: but the inevitable conflict of principles would sooner have been precipitated.

The Catholic disabilities an open question in 1812.

Alarmed by the improved position of the Catholic question in Parliament, the clergy and strong Protestant party hastened to remonstrate against concession. The Catholics responded by a renewal of their reiterated appeals. In February 1813, Mr. Grattan, in pursuance of the resolution of the previous session, moved the immediate considera-

Catholic claims, 1812-13.

Mr. Grattan's motion, Feb. 25th, 1813.

[1] Non-contents, 126; Contents, 125. Hans. Deb., 1st Ser., xxiii. 814-868.

tion of the laws affecting the Roman Catholics, in a committee of the whole House. He was supported by Lord Castlereagh, and opposed by Mr. Peel. After four nights' debate, rich in maiden speeches, well suited to a theme which had too often tried the resources of more practised speakers, the motion was carried by a majority of forty [1]

In committee, Mr. Grattan proposed a resolution affirming that it was advisable to remove the civil and military disqualifications of the Catholics, with such exceptions as may be necessary for preserving the Protestant succession, the church of England and Ireland, and the church of Scotland. Mr. Speaker Abbot, free, for the first time, to speak upon this occasion, opposed the resolution. It was agreed to by a majority of sixty-seven.[2]

March 9th, 1813.

The bill founded upon this resolution provided for the admission of Catholics to either House of Parliament, on taking one oath, instead of the oaths of allegiance, abjuration and supremacy, and the declarations against transubstantiation and the invocation of saints. On taking this oath, and without receiving the sacrament, Catholics were also entitled to vote at elections, to hold any civil and military office under the crown, except that of lord-chancellor or lord-lieutenant of Ireland, and any lay corporate office. No Catholic was to advise the crown, in the disposal of church patronage.

Mr. Grattan's bill, 1813.

---

[1] Ayes, 264; Noes, 224. Hans. Deb., 1st Ser., xxiv. 747, 849, 879, 985.
[2] Ayes, 186; Noes, 119. Hans. Deb., 1st Ser., xxiv. 1194–1249.

Every person exercising spiritual functions in the church of Rome was required to take this oath, as well as another, by which he bound himself to approve of none but loyal bishops; and to limit his intercourse with the pope to matters purely ecclesiastical. It was further provided, that none but persons born in the United Kingdom, or of British parents, and resident therein, should be qualified for the episcopal office.[1]

After the second reading,[2] several amendments were introduced by consent,[3] mainly for the purpose of establishing a government control over the Roman Catholic bishops, and for regulating the relations of the Roman Catholic church with the see of Rome. These latter provisions were peculiarly distasteful to the Roman Catholic body, who resented the proposal as a surrender of the spiritual freedom of their church, in exchange for their own civil liberties.

Bill defeated, May 24th, 1813. The course of the bill, however,—thus far prosperous,—was soon brought to an abrupt termination. The indefatigable speaker, again released from his chair, moved, in the first clause, the omission of the words, 'to sit and vote in either House of Parliament;' and carried his amendment by a majority of four.[4] The bill having thus lost its principal provision, was

---

[1] Hans. Deb., 1st Ser., xxv. 1107; Peel's Mem., i. 354.
[2] Hans. Deb., 1st Ser., xxvi. 171; Ayes, 245; Noes, 203.
[3] The Bill as thus amended is printed in Hans. Deb., 1st Ser., xxvi. 271.
[4] *Ibid.*, 312–361; Ayes, 247; Noes, 251; Grattan's Life, v. 489–496.

immediately abandoned; and the Catholic question was nearly as far from a settlement as ever.[1]

This session, however, was not wholly unfruitful of benefit to the Catholic cause. The Duke of Norfolk succeeded in passing a bill, enabling Irish Roman Catholics to hold all such civil or military offices in England, as by the Act of 1793 they were entitled to hold in Ireland. It removed one of the obvious anomalies of the law, which had been admitted in 1807, even by the king himself.[2] *Roman Catholic Officers' Relief Bill, 1813.*

This measure was followed, in 1817, by the Military and Naval Officers' Oaths Bill, which virtually opened all ranks in the army and navy to Roman Catholics and Dissenters.[3] Introduced by Lord Melville simply as a measure of regulation, it escaped the animadversion of the Protestant party,—ever on the watch to prevent further concessions to Catholics. A measure, denounced in 1807 as a violation of the constitution and the king's coronation oath, was now agreed to with the acquiescence of all parties. The church was no longer in danger; 'no popery' was not even *Military and Naval Officers' Oaths Bill, 1817.*

---

[1] The speaker, elated by his victory, could not forbear the further satisfaction of alluding to the failure of the bill, in his speech to the Prince Regent, at the end of the session,—an act of indiscretion, if not disorder, which placed him in the awkward position of defending himself, in the chair, from a proposed vote of censure. From this embarrassment he was delivered by the kindness of his friends, and the good feeling of the House, rather than by the completeness of his own defence.—*Hans. Deb.*, 1st Ser., xxvi. 1224; *Ibid.*, xxvii. 465; Lord Colchester's Diary, ii. 453-458, 483-496; Romilly's Life, iii. 133.

[2] Hans. Deb., 1st Ser., xxvi. 639; 53 Geo. III. c. 128.

[3] 57 Geo. III. c. 92; Hans. Deb., 1st Ser., xxxvi. 1208; *Ibid.*, xl. 24; Butler's Hist. Mem., iv. 257.

whispered. 'It was some consolation for him to reflect,' said Earl Grey, 'that what was resisted, at one period, and in the hands of one man, as dangerous and disastrous, was adopted at another, and from a different quarter, as wise and salutary.'[1]

In 1815, the Roman Catholic body in Ireland being at issue with their parliamentary friends, upon the question of 'securities,' their cause languished and declined.[2] Nor in the two following years, did it meet with any signal successes.[3]

Catholic claims, 1815–1817.

In 1819, the general question of Catholic emancipation found no favour in either House;[4] and in vain Earl Grey submitted a modified measure of relief. He introduced a bill for abrogating the declarations against the doctrines of transubstantiation and the invocation of saints, required to be taken[5] by civil and military officers, and members of both Houses of Parliament.[6] This measure was offered on the ground that these declarations were simply tests of faith and doctrine, and independent of any question of foreign spiritual supremacy. It had been admitted, on all hands, that no one ought to be

Declaration against transubstantiation, May 25th, 1819.

---

[1] June 10th, 1819; Hans. Deb., 1st Ser., xl. 1042.

[2] May 18th and 30th; June 8th, 1815; Hans. Deb., 1st Ser., xxxi. 258, 474, 666.

[3] May 21st and June 21st, 1816; Hans. Deb., 1st Ser., xxxiv. 655, 1239; May 9th and 16th, 1817; *Ibid.*, xxxvi. 301, 600; Mr. Grattan's motion on May 21st, 1816, was the only one carried,—by a majority of 31.

[4] Commons, May 4th, Ayes, 241; Noes, 243. Hans. Deb., 1st Ser., xl. 6; Lords, May 17th, Contents, 106; Non-contents, 147. Hans. Deb., 1st Ser., xl. 386.

[5] By 25 Car. II. c. 2; and 30 Car. II. st. 2, c. 2.

[6] Hans. Deb., 1st Ser., xl. 748.

excluded from office merely on account of his religious belief,—and that nothing would warrant such exclusion, but political tenets connected with religion which were, at the same time, dangerous to the state. The oath of supremacy guarded against such tenets: but to stigmatise purely religious doctrines as 'idolatrous and superstitious,' was a relic of offensive legislation, contrary to the policy of later times. As a practical measure of relief the bill was wholly inoperative: but even this theoretical legislation,—this assertion of a principle without legal consequences,—was resisted, as fraught with danger to the constitution; and the second reading of the bill was accordingly denied by a majority of fifty-nine.[1]

The weary struggle for Catholic emancipation survived its foremost champion. In 1820, Mr. Grattan was about to resume his exertions in the cause, when death overtook him. His last words bespoke his earnest convictions and sincerity. 'I wished,' said he, 'to go to the House of Commons to testify with my last breath my opinions on the question of Catholic emancipation: but I cannot. The hand of death is upon me.' . . . . 'I wish the question to be settled, because I believe it to be essential to the permanent tranquillity and happiness of the country, which are, in fact, identified with it.' He also counselled the Catholics to keep aloof from the democratic agitations of that period.[2]

[1] Contents, 82; Non-contents, 141. Hans. Deb., 1st Ser., xl. 1034.
[2] Statement by Mr. Becher, June 14th, 1820; Hans. Deb., 2nd Ser., 1065; Life of Grattan by his Son, v. 541, 544, 549.

The mantle of Mr. Grattan descended upon a fellow-countryman of rare eloquence and ability,—Mr. Plunket, who had already distinguished himself in the same cause. His first efforts were of happy augury. In February 1821, in a speech replete with learning, argument, and eloquence, he introduced the familiar motion for a committee on the Roman Catholic oaths, which was carried by a majority of six.[1] His bill, founded upon the resolutions of this committee,[2] provided for the abrogation of the declarations against transubstantiation and the invocation of saints, and a legal interpretation of the oath of supremacy, in a sense not obnoxious to the consciences of Catholics. On the 16th of March the bill, after an animated debate, illustrated by one of Mr. Canning's happiest efforts, and generally characterised by moderation, was read a second time, by a majority of eleven.[3] In committee, provisions were introduced to regulate the relations of the Roman Catholic church with the state, and with the see of Rome.[4] And at length, on the 2nd of April, the bill was read a third time, and passed by a majority of nineteen.[5] The fate of this measure, thus far successful, was soon determined in the House of Lords. The Duke of York stood forth as its foremost opponent, saying that 'his opposition to the bill arose from principles which he had embraced ever since he had been able to judge for himself, and

Mr. Plunket's bill, Feb. 28th, 1821.

Rejected by the Lords, April 16th and 17th, 1821.

---

[1] Ayes, 227; Noes, 221. Hans. Deb., 2nd Ser., iv. 961.
[2] *Ibid.*, 1066. [3] *Ibid.*, 1269; Ayes, 254; Noes, 243.
[4] *Ibid.*, 1412–1489.
[5] Ayes, 216; Noes, 197. Hans. Deb., 2nd Ser., iv. 1523.

which he hoped he should cherish to the last day of his life.' After a debate of two days, the second reading of the bill was refused by a majority of thirty-nine.[1]

Before the next session, Ireland was nearly in a state of revolt; and the attention of Parliament was first occupied with urgent measures of repression,—an Insurrection Bill, and the suspension of the Habeas Corpus Act. The Catholic question was now presented in a modified and exceptional form. A general measure of relief having failed again and again, it occurred to Mr. Canning that there were special circumstances affecting the disqualification of Catholic peers, which made it advisable to single out their case for legislation. And accordingly, in a masterly speech,—at once learned, argumentative, and eloquent,—he moved for a bill to relieve Roman Catholic peers from their disability to sit and vote in the House of Lords. Peers had been specially exempted from taking Queen Elizabeth's oath of supremacy, because the queen was 'otherwise sufficiently assured of the faith and loyalty of the temporal lords of her high court of parliament.'[2] The Catholics of that order had, therefore, continued to exercise their right of sitting in the Upper House unquestioned, until the evil times of Titus Oates. The Act of 30 Charles II. was passed in the very paroxysm of excitement,

Disturbed state of Ireland, 1822.

Roman Catholic Peers Bill, 1822.

April 30th.

---

[1] Contents, 120; Non-contents, 159. Hans. Deb., 2nd Ser., v. 220, 279.
[2] 5 Eliz. c. 1, s. 17.

which marked that period. It had been chiefly directed against the Duke of York, who had escaped from its provisions; and was forced upon the Lords by the earnestness and menaces of the Commons. Eighteen Catholic peers had been excluded by it, of whom five were under arrest on charges of treason; and one, Lord Stafford, was attainted,—in the judgment of history and posterity, unjustly. 'It was passed under the same delusion, was forced through the House of Lords with the same impulse, as it were, which brought Lord Stafford to the block.' It was only intended as a temporary Act; and with that understanding was assented to by the king, as being 'thought fitting at that time.' Yet it had been suffered to continue ever since, and to deprive the innocent descendants of those peers of their right of inheritance. The Act of 1791 had already restored to Catholic peers their privilege of advising the crown, as hereditary councillors, of which the Act of Charles II. had also deprived them; and it was now sought to replace them in their seats in Parliament. In referring to the recent coronation, to which the Catholic peers had been invited, for the first time for upwards of 130 years, he pictured, in the most glowing eloquence, the contrast between their lofty position in that ceremony, and their humiliation in the senate, where 'he who headed the procession of the peers to-day, could not sit among them as their equal on the morrow.' Other Catholics might never be returned to Parliament: but the peer had the inherent hereditary right to sit with his peers; and yet was personally and invidiously excluded on account of his religion. Mr. Canning was opposed by Mr. Peel, in an able and temperate argument, and supported by the accustomed power and eloquence of Mr. Plunket. It was obvious that his success would carry the outworks,—if not the very citadel,—of the Catholic question; yet he obtained leave to bring in his bill by a majority of five.[1]

He carried the second reading by a majority of twelve;[2] after which he was permitted, by the liberality of Mr. Peel, to pass the bill through its other stages, without opposition.[3] But the Lords were still inexorable. Their stout Protestantism was not to be beguiled even by sympathy for their own order; and they refused a second reading to the bill, by a majority of forty-two.[4]

After so many disappointments, the Catholics were losing patience and temper. Their cause was supported by the most eminent members of the government; yet it was invariably defeated and lost. Neither argument nor numbers availed it. Mr. Canning was secretary of state for foreign affairs, and leader of the House of Commons; and Mr. Plunket attorney-general for Ireland. But it was felt that so long as Catholic emancipation continued to be an open question, there would be eloquent debates, and sometimes a promising division, but no substantial redress. In the House of Commons, one secretary of state was

Position of the Catholic question in 1823.

---

[1] Ayes, 249; Noes, 244. Hans. Deb., 2nd Ser., vii. 211.
[2] *Ibid.*, 475. [3] *Ibid.*, 673.
[4] *Ibid.*, 1216; Court and Cabinets of Geo. IV., i. 306.

opposed to the other; and in the House of Lords, the premier and the chancellor were the foremost opponents of every measure of relief. The majority of the cabinet, and the great body of the ministerial party, in both Houses, were adverse to the cause.

April 17th, 1823. This irritation burst forth on the presentation of petitions, before a motion of Mr. Plunket's. Sir Francis Burdett first gave expression to it. He deprecated 'the annual farce,' which trifled with the feelings of the people of Ireland. He would not assist at its performance. The Catholics would obtain no redress, until the government were united in opinion as to its necessity. An angry debate ensued, and a fierce passage of arms between Mr. Brougham and Mr. Canning. At length, Mr. Plunket rose to make his motion; when Sir Francis Burdett, accompanied by Mr. Hobhouse, Mr. Grey Bennet, and several other members of the opposition, left the House. Under these discouragements Mr. Plunket proceeded with his motion. At the conclusion of his speech, the House becoming impatient, refused to give any other members a fair hearing; and after several divisions, ultimately agreed, by a majority of upwards of two hundred, to an adjournment of the House.[1] This result, however unfavourable to the immediate issue of the Catholic question, was yet a significant warning that so important a measure could not much longer be discussed as an open question.

A smaller measure of relief was next tried in vain.

---

[1] Ayes, 313; Noes, 111. Hans. Deb., 2nd Ser., viii. 1070–1123.

Lord Nugent sought to extend to English Catholics the elective franchise, the commission of the peace, and other offices to which Catholics in Ireland were admissible, by the Act of 1793. Mr. Peel assented to the justice and moderation of this proposal.[1] The bill was afterwards divided into two,[2]—the one relating to the elective franchise,—and the other to the magistracy and corporate offices.[3] In this shape they were agreed to by the Commons, but both miscarried in the House of Lords.[4] In the following year, they were revived in the House of Lords by Lord Lansdowne, with no better success, though supported by five cabinet ministers.[5]

Lord Nugent's bill, May 28th, 1823.

Ineffectual attempts were also made, at this period, to amend the law of marriage, by which Catholics and dissenters were alike aggrieved. In 1819,[6] and again in 1822, Mr. William Smith presented the case of dissenters, and particularly of Unitarians. Prior to Lord Hardwicke's Marriage Act, dissenters were allowed to be married in their own places of worship: but under that Act the marriages of all but Jews and Quakers were required to be solemnised in church, by ministers of the establishment, and according to its ritual. At that time the Unitarians were a small sect; and had not a single

Marriage law amendment, 1819–1827.

Mr. W. Smith's bill, April 18th, 1822.

---

[1] Hans. Deb., 2nd Ser., ix. 573.
[2] Ibid., 1031. [3] Ibid., 1341.
[4] Ibid., 1476: Lord Colchester's Diary, iii. 292, 299.
[5] May 24th, 1824; Hans. Deb., 2nd Ser., xi. 817, 842; Lord Colchester's Diary, iii. 326.
[6] June 16th, 1819; Hans. Deb., 1st Ser., xl. 1200, 1503.

place of worship. Having since prospered and multiplied, they prayed that they might be married in their own way. They were contented, however, with the omission from the marriage service of passages relating to the Trinity; and Mr. Smith did not venture to propose a more rational and complete relief,—the marriage of dissenters in their own chapels.[1]

In 1823, the Marquess of Lansdowne proposed a more comprehensive measure, embracing Roman Catholics as well as dissenters, and permitting the solemnisation of their marriages in their own places of worship. The chancellor, boasting 'that he took as just a view of toleration as any noble Lord in that House could do,' yet protested against 'such mighty changes in the law of marriage.' The Archbishop of Canterbury regarded the measure in a more liberal spirit; and merely objected to any change in the church service, which had been suggested by Lord Liverpool. The second reading of the bill was refused by a majority of six.[2]

Lord Lansdowne's bill, June 12th, 1823.

In the following session, relief to Unitarians was again sought, in another form. Lord Lansdowne introduced a bill enabling Unitarians to be married in their own places of worship, after publications of bans in church, and payment of the church fees. This proposal received the support of the Archbishop of Canterbury, and the Bishop of London: but the chancellor, more sensitive in his orthodoxy, de-

Unitarian marriages.

Lord Lansdowne's bill, April 2nd, May 4th, 1824.

---

[1] Hans. Deb., 2nd Ser., vi. 1460.   [2] *Ibid.*, ix. 967.

nounced it as 'tending to dishonour and degrade the church of England.' To the Unitarians he gave just offence, by expressing a doubt whether they were not still liable to punishment, at common law, for denying the doctrine of the Trinity.[1] The bill passed the second reading by a small majority: but was afterwards lost on going into committee, by a majority of thirty-nine.[2]

Dr. Phillimore, with no better success, brought in another bill to permit the solemnisation of marriages between Catholics, by their own priests,—still retaining the publication of bans or licences, and the payment of fees to the Protestant clergyman. Such a change in the law was particularly desirable in the case of Catholics, on grounds distinct from toleration. In the poorer parishes, large numbers were married by their own priests: their marriages were illegal, and their children, being illegitimate, were chargeable on the parishes in which they were born.[3] This marriage law was even more repugnant to principles of toleration than the code of civil disabilities. It treated every British subject,—whatever his faith,—as a member of the Church of England,—ignored all religious differences; and imposed, with rigorous uniformity, upon all communions alike, the altar,

Roman Catholic marriages, April 13th, 1824.

---

[1] See also Rex v. Curl: Strange, 789; St. Tr., xvii. 154.

[2] Hans. Deb., 2nd Ser., xi. 75, 434; Twiss's Life of Eldon, ii. 512. Mr. C Wynn, writing to the Duke of Buckingham, May 6th, 1824, said, 'You will, I am sure, though you doubted the propriety of the Unitarian Marriage Act, regret the triumphant majority of the intolerant party, who boast of it as a display of their strength, and a proof how little any power in the country can cope with them.'—*Court and Cabinets of Geo. IV.*, ii. 72.

[3] Hans. Deb., 2nd Ser., xi. 408.

the ritual, the ceremonies, and the priesthood of the state. And under what penalties?—celibacy, or concubinage and sin!

Three years later, Mr. W. Smith renewed his measure, in a new form. It permitted Unitarian dissenters, after the publication of bans, to be married before a magistrate,—thus reviving the principle of a civil contract, which had existed before Lord Hardwicke's Act of 1752. This bill passed the Commons:[1] but failed in the Lords, by reason of the approaching prorogation.[2] And here the revision of the law of marriage was left to await a more favourable opportunity.[3]

Unitarian marriages, 1827.

In 1824, Lord Lansdowne vainly endeavoured to obtain for English Catholics the elective franchise, the right to serve as justices of the peace, and to hold offices in the revenue.[4]

Lord Lansdowne's Catholic relief bills, May 24th, 1824.

But in the same year Parliament agreed to one act of courtly acknowledgment to a distinguished Catholic peer. An Act was passed, not without opposition, to enable the Duke of Norfolk to execute his hereditary office of Earl Marshal, without taking the oath of supremacy, or subscribing the declarations against transubstantiation and the invocation of saints.[5]

Office of Earl Marshal, 1824.

Meanwhile, the repeated failures of the Catholic cause had aroused a dangerous spirit of discontent in Ireland. The Catholic leaders,

Agitation in Ireland, 1823–1825.

[1] Hans. Deb., 2nd Ser., xvii. 1343.
[2] *Ibid.*, 1407, 1426; Lord Colchester's Diary, iii. 520.
[3] *Infra*, p. 188.
[4] Hans. Deb., 2nd Ser., xi. 842; Twiss's Life of Eldon, ii. 518.
[5] Hans. Deb., 2nd Ser., xi. 1455, 1470, 1482; 5 Geo. IV. c. 109; Lord Colchester's Diary, iii. 326; Twiss's Life of Eldon, ii. 521.

despairing of success over majorities unconvinced and unyielding, were appealing to the excited passions of the people; and threatened to extort from the fears of Parliament what they had vainly sought from its justice. To secure the peace of Ireland, the legislature was called upon, in 1825, to dissolve the Catholic Association:[1] but it was too late to check the progress of the Catholic cause itself by measures of repression; and ministers disclaimed any such intention.

While this measure was still before Parliament, the discussion of the Catholic question was revived, on the motion of Sir Francis Burdett, with unusual spirit and effect. *Sir Francis Burdett's motion, Feb 28th, 1825.* After debates of extraordinary interest, in which many members avowed their conversion to the Catholic cause,[2] a bill was passed by the Commons, framing a new oath in lieu of the oath of supremacy, as a qualification for office; and regulating the intercourse of Roman Catholic subjects, in Ireland, with the see of Rome.[3] On reaching the House of Lords, however, this bill met the same fate as its predecessors; the second reading being refused by a majority of forty-eight.[4]

With a view to make the Catholic Relief Bill more acceptable, and at the same time to remove a great electoral abuse, Mr. Littleton had introduced a measure for regulating *Irish 40s. freeholders, 1825.*

---

[1] *Supra*, Vol. II. 371.
[2] February 28th, April 19th and 21st, May 10th, 1825.
[3] Hans. Deb., 2nd Ser., xii. 764, 1151; *Ibid.*, xiii. 21, 71, 486. The second reading was carried by a majority of 27, and the third reading by 21.
[4] May 17th. Contents, 130; Non-contents, 178. Hans. Deb., 2nd Ser., xiii. 662.

the elective franchise in Ireland. Respecting vested interests, he proposed to raise the qualification of 40s. freeholders; and to restrain the creation of fictitious voters, who were entirely in the power of their landlords. By some this bill was regarded as an obnoxious measure of disfranchisement: but being supported by several of the steadiest friends of Ireland, and of constitutional rights, its second reading was agreed to. When the Catholic Relief Bill, however, was lost in the House of Lords, this bill was at once abandoned.[1]

In April of this year, Lord Francis Leveson Gower carried a resolution, far more startling to the Protestant party than any measure of enfranchisement. He prevailed upon the Commons to declare the expediency of making provision for the secular Roman Catholic clergy, exercising religious functions in Ireland.[2] It was one of those capricious and inconsequent decisions, into which the Commons were occasionally drawn, in this protracted controversy, and was barren of results.

Lord F. Leveson Gower's motion, April 29th, 1825.

In 1827, the hopes of the Catholics, raised for a time by the accession of Mr. Canning to the head of affairs, were suddenly cast down by his untimely death.

Mr. Canning's death.

At the meeting of Parliament in 1828,[3] the Duke of Wellington's administration had been formed. Catholic emancipation was still an open question:[4] but the cabinet, repre-

The Duke of Wellington's administration.

---

[1] Hans. Deb., 2nd Ser., xiii. 126, 176, &c., 902.
[2] Ayes, 205; Noes, 162. *Ibid.*, 308.
[3] Lord Goderich's ministry had been formed and dissolved during the recess.   [4] Peel's Mem., i. 12, 16.

sented in one House by the Duke, and in the other by Mr. Peel, promised little for the cause of religious liberty. If compliance was not to be expected, still less was such a government likely to be coerced by fear. The great soldier at its head retained, for a time, the command of the army; and no minister knew so well as he how to encounter turbulence or revolt. In politics he had been associated with the old Tory school; and unbending firmness was characteristic of his temper and profession. Yet was this government on the very eve of accomplishing more for religious liberty than all the efforts of its champions had effected in half a century.

The dissenters were the first to assault the Duke's strong citadel. The question of the repeal of the Corporation and Test Acts had slumbered for nearly forty years,[1] when Lord John Russell worthily succeeded to the advocacy of a cause which had been illustrated by the genius of Mr. Fox. In moving for a committee to consider these Acts, he ably recapitulated their history, and advanced conclusive arguments for their repeal. The annual indemnity Acts, though offering no more than a partial relief to dissenters, left scarcely an argument against the repeal of laws which had been so long virtually suspended. It could not be contended that these laws were necessary for the security of the church; for they extended neither to Scotland nor to Ireland. Absurd were the number and variety of offices embraced by the Test Act; non-commissioned officers

Corporation and Test Acts, 1828.

Feb. 26th, 1828.

[1] *Supra*, p. 105.

as well as officers,—excisemen, tidewaiters, and even pedlars. The penalties incurred by these different classes of men were sufficiently alarming,—forfeiture of the office,—disqualification for any other,—incapacity to maintain a suit at law, to act as guardian or executor, or to inherit a legacy; and, lastly, a pecuniary penalty of 500*l.* Even if such penalties were never enforced, the law which imposed them was wholly indefensible. Nor was it forgotten again to condemn the profanation of the holy sacrament, by reducing it to a mere civil form, imposed upon persons who either renounced its sacred character, or might be spiritually unfit to receive it. Was it decent, it was asked,

> 'To make the symbols of atoning grace
> An office key, a pick-lock to a place?'[1]

Nor was this objection satisfactorily answered by citing Bishop Sherlock's version, that receiving the sacrament was not the qualification for office, but the evidence of qualification. The existing law was defended on the grounds so often repeated: that the state had a right to disqualify persons on the ground of their religious opinions, if it were deemed expedient: that there was an established church inseparable from the state, and entitled to its protection; and that the admission of dissenters would endanger the security of that church.

Mr. Peel,—always moderate in his opposition to measures for the extension of religious liberty,—acknowledged that the maintenance of the Corpora-

[1] Cowper's Expostulation, Works, i. p. 80 (Pickering).

tion and Test Acts was not necessary for the protection of the church; and opposed their repeal mainly on the ground that they were no practical grievance to the dissenters. After a judicious and temperate discussion on both sides, the motion was affirmed by a majority of forty-four.[1] The bill was afterwards brought in, and read a second time without discussion.[2]

The government, not being prepared to resign office in consequence of the adverse vote of the Commons, endeavoured to avoid a conflict between the two Houses. The majority had comprised many of their own supporters, and attached friends of the established church; and Mr. Peel undertook to communicate with the Archbishop of Canterbury and other prelates, in order to persuade them to act in concert with that party, and share in the grace of a necessary concession.[3] These enlightened churchmen met him with singular liberality, and agreed to the substitution of a declaration for the sacramental test.[4] Lord John Russell and his friends, though satisfied that no such declaration was necessary, accepted it as a pledge that this important measure should be allowed to pass, with the general acquiescence of all parties;[5] and the bill now proceeded through the House, without further opposition.[6]

Concurrence of the bishops.

In the House of Lords, the Archbishop of York, expressing the opinion of the primate as well as his

---

[1] Ayes, 237; Noes, 193. Hans. Deb., 2nd Ser., xviii. 676.
[2] Ibid., 816, 1137.   [3] Peel's Mem., i. 69, 79.
[4] Ibid., 70-98.
[5] Hans. Deb., 2nd Ser., xviii. 1180.   [6] Ibid., 1330.

own, 'felt bound, on every principle, to give his vote for the repeal of an Act which had, he feared, led, in too many instances, to the profanation of the most sacred ordinance of our religion.' 'Religious tests imposed for political purposes, must in themselves be always liable, more or less, to endanger religious sincerity.' His grace accepted the proposed declaration as a sufficient security for the church. The bill was also supported, in the same spirit, by the Bishops of Lincoln, Durham, and Chester.

The bill in the Lords, April 17th, 1828.

But there were lay peers more alive to the interests of the church than the bench of bishops. Lord Winchilsea foresaw dangers, which he endeavoured to avert by further securities; and Lord Eldon denounced the entire principle of the bill. He had little expected 'that such a bill as that proposed would ever have been received into their Lordships' House;' and rated those who had abandoned their opposition to its progress in the Commons. This stout champion of the church, however, found no supporters to the emphatic 'Not content,' with which he encountered the bill; and its second reading was affirmed without a division.[1]

In committee, the declaration was amended by the insertion of the words 'on the true faith of a Christian,' — an amendment which

April 21st and 24th.

---

[1] Hans. Deb., 2nd Ser., xviii. 1450. Lord Eldon, in his private correspondence, called it 'a most shameful bill,'—'as bad, as mischievous, and as revolutionary as the most captious dissenter could wish it to be.' And again: 'The administration have, to their shame be it said, got the archbishops and most of the bishops to support this revolutionary bill.'—*Twiss's Life of Lord Eldon*, iii. 37-45; Peel s Mem., i. 99.

pointedly excluded the Jews, and gave rise to further legislation, at a later period.[1] Some other amendments were also made. Lord Winchilsea endeavoured to exclude Unitarians; and Lord Eldon to substitute an oath for a declaration, and to provide more effectual securities against the admission of Catholics: but these and other amendments, inconsistent with the liberal design of the measure, were rejected, and the bill passed.[2] The Lords' amendments, though little approved by the Commons, were agreed to, in order to set this long-vexed question at rest, by an act of enlightened toleration. *April 28th. May 2nd.*

This measure was received with gratitude by dissenters; and the grace of the concession was enhanced by the liberality of the bishops, and the candour and moderation of the leading statesmen, who had originally opposed it. The liberal policy of Parliament was fully supported by public opinion, which had undergone a complete revulsion upon this question. 'Thirty years since,' said Alderman Wood, 'there were only two or three persons in the city of London favourable to the repeal: the other day, when the corporation met to petition for the repeal, only two hands were held up against the petition.' *The Act passed.*

The triumph of dissenters was of happy augury to the Catholic claims, which in a few days were again presented by Sir Francis Bur- *Catholic claims.*

---

[1] On the third reading Lord Holland desired to omit the words, but without success.
[2] Hans. Deb., 2nd Ser., xviii. 1571; xix. 39, 110, 156, 186.

dett. The preponderance of authority as well as argument, was undeniably in favour of the motion. Several conversions were avowed; and the younger members especially showed an increasing adhesion to the cause of religious liberty.[1] After a debate of three nights, in which the principal supporters of the measure expressed the greatest confidence in its speedy triumph, the motion was carried by a majority of six.[2] A resolution was agreed to, that it was expedient to consider the laws affecting Roman Catholics, with a view to a final and conciliatory adjustment. Resolutions of this kind had, on former occasions, preceded the introduction of bills which afterwards miscarried; but Sir Francis Burdett resolved to avoid the repetition of proceedings so tedious and abortive. This resolution was accordingly communicated to the Lords, at a conference.[3] The Marquess of Lansdowne invited their Lordships to concur in this resolution, in a most forcible speech; and was supported in the debate by the Dukes of Sussex and Gloucester, by Lord Goderich, the Marquess of Londonderry, Lord Plunket, the Marquess of Wellesley, and other peers. It was opposed by the Duke of Cumberland, the powerful Chancellor,—Lord Lyndhurst,—the ever-consistent Lord Eldon, the Duke of Wellington, and an overpowering number of speakers. After two nights' debate, the Lords refused to concur in this resolution, by a majority of forty-four.[4]

Sir Francis Burdett's motion, May 8th, 1828.

June 9th, 1828.

[1] Peel's Mem., i. 102.
[2] Ayes, 272; Noes, 266. Hans. Deb., 2nd Ser., xix. 375–675.
[3] Hans. Deb., 2nd Sér.. xix. 680, 767. [4] Ibid., 1133, 1214.

But while these proceedings seemed as illusory as those of former years, popular agitation was approaching a crisis in Ireland,[1] which convinced the leading members of the administration that concessions could no longer be safely withheld.[2] Soon after this discussion, an event of striking significance marked the power and determination of the Irish people. Mr. Vesey Fitzgerald having vacated his seat for the county of Clare, on accepting office, found his re-election contested by an opponent no less formidable than Mr. O'Connell. Under other circumstances, he could have confidently relied upon his personal popularity, his uniform support of the Catholic claims, his public services, and the property and influence which he enjoyed in his own county. But now all his pretensions were unavailing. The people were resolved that he should succumb to the champion of the Catholic cause; and, after scenes of excitement and turbulence which threatened a disturbance of the public peace, he was signally defeated.[3]

State of Ireland, 1828.

Clare election. June and July, 1828.

Perhaps no one circumstance contributed more than this election, to extort concessions from the government. It proved the dangerous power and organisation of the Roman Catholic party. A general election, while such

Doubtful fidelity of the Catholic soldiers in Ireland.

---

[1] *Supra*, Vol. II. 373.   [2] Peel's Mem., i. 129.
[3] Mr. Vesey Fitzgerald, writing to Sir R. Peel, July 5th, 1828, said: 'I have polled all the gentry and all the fifty-pound freeholders,—the gentry to a man.' . . . 'All the great interests broke down, and the desertion has been universal. Such a scene as we have had! such a tremendous prospect as it opens to us!' . . . 'The conduct of the priests has passed all that you could picture to yourself.'—*Peel's Mem.*, i. 113.

excitement prevailed, could not be contemplated without alarm.[1] If riots should occur, the executive were not even assured of the fidelity of Catholic soldiers, who had been worked upon by their priests. They could not be trusted against rioters of their own faith.[2] The Catholic Association, however, continued to be the chief embarrassment to the government. It had made Ireland ripe for rebellion. Its leaders had but to give the word: but, believing their success assured, they were content with threatening demonstrations.[3] Out of an infantry force of 30,000 men, no less than 25,500 were held in readiness to maintain the peace of Ireland.[4] Such was the crisis, that there seemed no alternative between martial law and the removal of the causes of discontent. Nothing but open rebellion would justify the one; and the Commons had, again and again, counselled the other.[5]

Catholic Association.

In the judgment of Mr. Peel, the settlement of the Catholic question had, at length, become a political necessity; and this conviction was shared by the Duke of Welling-

Necessity of Catholic relief acknowledged by ministers.

---

[1] Peel's Mem., i. 117–122, et seq.

'This business,' wrote Lord Eldon, 'must bring the Roman Catholic question, which has been so often discussed, to a crisis and a conclusion. The nature of that conclusion I do not think likely to be favourable to Protestantism.'—*Twiss's Life*, iii. 54.

[2] Lord Anglesey's Letters, July 20th, 26th, 1828; Peel's Mem., i. 127, 158, 164.

[3] Lord Anglesey's Letter, July 2nd, 1828; Peel's Mem., i. 147; Ibid., 207, 243–262; supra, Vol. II. 374.

[4] Peel's Mem., i. 293.

[5] In each of 'the five parliaments elected since 1807, with one exception, the House of Commons had come to a decision in favour of a consideration of the Catholic question;' and Mr. Peel had long been impressed with the great preponderance of talent and influence on that side.—*Peel's Mem.*, i. 146; Ibid., 61, 288, 289.

ton, the Marquess of Anglesey, and Lord Lyndhurst.[1] But how were ministers to undertake it? The statesmen who had favoured Catholic claims had withdrawn from the ministry; and Lord Anglesey had been removed from the government of Ireland.[2] It was reserved for the Protestant party in the cabinet to devise a measure which they had spent their lives in opposing. They would necessarily forfeit the confidence, and provoke the hostility, of their own political adherents; and could lay no claim to the gratitude or good will of the Catholics.

But another difficulty, even more formidable, presented itself,—a difficulty which, on former occasions, had alone sufficed to paralyse the efforts of ministers. The king evinced no less repugnance to the measure than his 'revered and excellent father' had displayed, nearly thirty years before;[3] and had declared his determination not to assent to Catholic emancipation.[4] *Repugnance of the king;*

The Duke of Wellington, emboldened by the success of Mr. Peel's former communications with the bishops, on the Sacramental Test, endeavoured to persuade them to support concessions to the Catholics. Their concurrence would secure *and of the bishops.*

[1] Peel's Mem., i. 180, 181, 188, 284.
[2] The circumstances of his removal were fully discussed in the House of Lords, May 4th, 1829.—*Hans. Deb.*, 2nd Ser., xx. 990.
[3] Peel's Mem., i. 274, 276. The king assured Lord Eldon that Mr. Canning had engaged that he would never allow his majesty 'to be troubled about the Roman Catholic question.'—*Peel's Mem.*, i. 275. But Sir R. Peel expresses his conviction that no such pledge had been given by Mr. Canning (*Ibid.*); and even Lord Eldon was satisfied that the king's statement was unfounded.'—*Twiss's Life of Eldon*, iii. 82.
[4] Lord Colchester's Diary, iii. 380, 473.

the co-operation of the church and the House of Lords, and influence the reluctant judgment of the king. But he found them resolutely opposed to his views; and the government were now alarmed, lest their opinions should confirm the objections of his majesty.

It was under these unpromising circumstances that, in January 1829, the time had arrived at which some definite course must be submitted to the king, in anticipation of the approaching session. It is not surprising that Mr. Peel should have thought such difficulties almost insuperable. 'There was the declared opinion of the king,—the declared opinion of the House of Lords, —the declared opinion of the church,—unfavourable to the measures we were about to propose;' and, as he afterwards added, 'a majority, probably, of the people of Great Britain was hostile to concession.'[1]

Embarrassment of ministers.

Mr. Peel, considering the peculiarity of his own position, had contemplated the necessity of retirement:[2] but viewing, with deep concern, the accumulating embarrassments of the government, he afterwards placed his services at the command of the Duke of Wellington.[3]

Proffered resignation of Mr. Peel.

At length, an elaborate memorandum by Mr. Peel having been submitted to the king, His Majesty gave audience to those members of his cabinet who had always opposed the Catholic claims; and then consented that the cabinet

The king consents to the measure.

---

[1] Peel's Mem., i. 278, 308.
[2] Letter of Duke of Wellington, Aug. 11th, 1828. Peel's Mem., i. 184.
[3] Letter, Jan. 12th, 1829. Peel's Mem., i. 283, 294, 295.

should submit their views on the state of Ireland, without pledging himself to concur in them, even if adopted unanimously.[1] A draft of the king's speech was accordingly prepared, referring to the state of Ireland, the necessity of restraining the Catholic Association, and of reviewing the Catholic disabilities. To this draft the king gave a 'reluctant consent;'[2] and it was, accordingly, delivered at the commencement of the session.

The government projected three measures, founded upon this speech,—the suppression of the Catholic Association, a Relief Bill, and a revision of the elective franchise in Ireland. *Government measures.*

The first measure submitted to Parliament was a bill for the suppression of dangerous associations or assemblies in Ireland. It met with general support. The opponents of emancipation complained that the suppression of the Association had been too long delayed. The friends of the Catholic claims, who would have condemned it separately, as a restraint upon public liberty, consented to it, as a necessary part of the measures for the relief of the Catholics, and the pacification of Ireland.[3] Hence the bill passed rapidly through both Houses.[4] But before it became law, the Catholic Association was dissolved. A measure of relief having been promised, its mission was accomplished.[5] *Associations Suppression Bill, Feb. 10th, 1829.*

When this bill had passed the Commons, Mr. Peel

---

[1] Peel's Mem., i. 297.   [2] *Ibid.*, 310.
[3] Hans. Deb., 2nd Ser., xx. 177.
[4] *Ibid.*, 280, 519, &c.
[5] On Feb. 24th, Lord Anglesey said it was 'defunct.'

accepted the Chiltern Hundreds, in order to give his constituents at Oxford an opportunity of expressing their opinion of his new policy. The Protestant feeling of the university was unequivocally pronounced. He was defeated by Sir Robert Inglis, and obliged to take refuge at Westbury.

Mr. Peel loses his election at Oxford.

The civil disabilities of the Catholics were about to be considered, on the 5th of March, when an unexpected obstacle arose. On the 3rd, the king commanded the attendance of the Duke of Wellington, the Lord Chancellor, and Mr. Peel on the following day. He then desired a more detailed explanation of the proposed measure. On finding that it was proposed to alter the oath of supremacy, his majesty refused his consent; and his three ministers at once tendered their resignation, which was accepted. Late the same evening, however, he desired them to withdraw their resignation, and gave his consent, in writing, to their proceeding with the proposed measure.[1]

Further difficulties with the king.

This last obstacle being removed, Mr. Peel opened his measure of Catholic emancipation to the House of Commons. In a speech of four hours, he explained the various circumstances, already described, which, in the opinion of the government, had made the emancipation of the Catholics a necessity. The measure itself was complete: it admitted Roman Catholics,—on taking

Catholic Relief Bill, March 5th, 1829.

---

[1] Peel's Mem., i. 343-349. The king gave Lord Eldon a different version of this interview, evidently to excuse himself from consenting to a measure of which his old councillor disapproved so strongly.—*Twiss's Life of Eldon*, iii. 83.

a new oath, instead of the oath of supremacy,—to both Houses of Parliament, to all corporate offices, to all judicial offices, except in the ecclesiastical courts; and to all civil and political offices, except those of regent, lord chancellor in England and Ireland, and lord-lieutenant of Ireland. Restraints, however, were imposed upon the interference of Roman Catholics in the dispensation of church patronage. The government renounced the idea of introducing any securities, as they were termed, in regard to the Roman Catholic church, and its relations to the state. When proposed at an earlier period, in deference to the fears of the opponents of emancipation,[1] they had offended Roman Catholics, without allaying the apprehensions of the Protestant party. But it was proposed to prevent the insignia of corporations from being taken to any place of religious worship except the established church,—to restrain Roman Catholic bishops from assuming the titles of existing sees,—to prevent the admission of Jesuits to this country, to ensure the registration of those already there, and to discourage the extension of monastic orders. After two nights' debate, Mr. Peel's motion for going into committee of the whole House was agreed to by a majority of one hundred and eighty-eight.[2] Such was the change which the sudden conversion of the government, and the pressure of circumstances, had effected in the opinions of Parliament. Meanwhile, the church and the Protestant party throughout the

[1] In 1813. *Supra*, p. 141.
[2] Ayes, 348; Noes, 160. Hans. Deb., 2nd Ser., 727-892.

country, were in the greatest alarm and excitement. They naturally resented the sudden desertion of their cause, by ministers in whom they had confided.[1] The press overflowed with their indignant remonstrances; and public meetings, addresses, and petitions gave tokens of their activity. Their petitions far outnumbered those of the advocates of the measure;[2] and the daily discussions upon their presentation, served to increase the public excitement. The higher intelligence of the country approved the wise and equitable policy of the government: but there can be little question, that the sentiments of a majority of the people of Great Britain were opposed to emancipation. Churchmen dreaded it, as dangerous to their church; and dissenters inherited from their Puritan forefathers a pious horror of Papists. But in Parliament, the union of the ministerial party with the accustomed supporters of the Catholic cause, easily overcame all opposition; and the bill was passed through its further stages, in the Commons, by large majorities.[3]

On the second reading of the bill, in the House of Lords, the Duke of Wellington justified the measure, irrespective of other considerations, by the necessity of averting a civil war, saying: 'If I could avoid, by any sacrifice whatever, even one month of civil war in the country to which I am attached, I would sacrifice my life in order to do it.' He added, that when the Irish re-

The bill in the Lords, April 2nd, 1829.

---

[1] *Supra*, Vol. II. 193. [2] See *supra*, Vol. II. 66.
[3] On the second reading—Ayes, 353; Noes, 173. Hans. Deb., 2nd Ser., xx. 1115–1290. On the third reading—Ayes, 320; Noes, 142. *Ibid.*, 1633.

bellion of 1798 had been suppressed, the Legislative Union had been proposed in the next year, mainly for the purpose of introducing this very measure of concession; and that had the civil war, which he had lately striven to avert, broken out, and been subdued,—still such a measure would have been insisted upon by one, if not by both Houses of Parliament.

The bill was opposed by the Archbishop of Canterbury,—Dr. Howley,—in a judicious speech, in which he pointed out the practical evils to which the church and the Protestant religion might be exposed, by the employment of Roman Catholics as ministers of the crown, especially in the office of secretary of state. It was also opposed in debate by the Archbishops of York and Armagh, the Bishops of Durham and London, and several lay peers. But of the Protestant party, Lord Eldon was still the leader. Surrounded by a converted senate,—severed from all his old colleagues,—deserted by the peers who had hitherto cheered and supported him,—he raised his voice against a measure which he had spent a long life in resisting. Standing almost alone among the statesmen of his age, there was a moral dignity in his isolation which commands our respect. The bill was supported by Mr. Peel's constant friend, the Bishop of Oxford, the Duke of Sussex, the Lord Chancellor, Lord Goderich, Earl Grey, Lord Plunket, and other peers. The second reading was affirmed by a majority of one hundred and five.[1]

[1] Contents, 217; Non-contents, 112. Hans. Deb., 2nd Ser., xxi. 42-394.

The bill passed through committee without a single amendment: and on the 10th of April the third reading was affirmed by a majority of one hundred and four.[1]

Meanwhile the king, whose formal assent was still to be given, was as strongly opposed to the measure as ever; and even discussed with Lord Eldon the possibility of preventing its further progress, or of refusing his assent. But neither the king nor his old minister could seriously have contemplated so hazardous an exercise of prerogative; and the Royal assent was accordingly given, without further remonstrance.[2] The time had passed, when the word of a king could overrule his ministers and Parliament.

The Royal assent.

The third measure of the government still remains to be noticed,—the regulation of the elective franchise in Ireland. The abuses of the 40s. freehold franchise had already been exposed; and were closely connected with Catholic emancipation.[3] The Protestant landlords had encouraged the multiplication of small freeholds,—being, in fact, leases held of middlemen,—in order to increase the number of dependent voters, and extend their own political influence. Such an abuse would, at any time, have demanded correction: but now these voters had transferred their allegiance from the landlord to the Catholic priest. 'That

Elective franchise in Ireland.

---

[1] Contents, 213; Non-contents, 109. Hans. Deb., 2nd Ser., xxi. 614–694.

[2] Twiss's Life of Eldon, iii. 84, *et seq.* Court and Cabinets of Geo. IV., ii. 395.

[3] *Supra*, p. 155; and Reports of Committees in Lords and Commons, 1825.

weapon,' said Mr. Peel, 'which the landlord has forged with so much care, and has heretofore wielded with such success, has broke short in his hand.' To leave such a franchise without regulation, was to place the county representation at the mercy of priests and agitators. It was therefore proposed to raise the qualification of a freeholder, from 40s. to 10l., to require due proof of such qualification, and to introduce a system of registration.

So large a measure of disfranchisement was, in itself, open to many objections. It swept away existing rights without proof of misconduct or corruption, on the part of the voters. So long as they had served the purposes of Protestant landlords, they were encouraged and protected: but when they asserted their independence, they were to be deprived of their franchise. Strong opinions were pronounced that the measure should not be retrospective; and that the *bonâ fide* 40s. freeholders, at least, should be protected:[1] but the connection between this and the greater measure, then in progress, saved it from any effective opposition; and it was passed rapidly through both Houses.[2] By one party, it was hailed as a necessary protection against the Catholic priests and leaders: and by the other, it was reluctantly accepted as the price of Catholic emancipation.

On the 28th April, the Duke of Norfolk, Lord

---

[1] See especially the speeches of Mr. Huskisson, Viscount Palmerston, and the Marquess of Lansdowne, Hans. Deb., 2nd Ser., xx. 1373, 1468; xxi. 407, 574.

[2] *Ibid.*, xx. 1329.

Clifford, and Lord Dormer came to the House of Lords, and claimed their hereditary seats among the peers, from which they had been so long excluded; and were followed, a few days afterwards, by Lord Stafford, Lord Petre, and Lord Stourton.[1] Respectable in the antiquity of their titles, and their own character, they were an honourable addition to the Upper House; and no one could affirm that their number was such as to impair the Protestant character of that assembly.

<small>Roman Catholic peers take the oaths, April 28th, May 1st, 1829.</small>

Mr. O'Connell, as already stated, had been returned in the previous year for the county of Clare: but the privilege of the new oath was restricted to members returned after the passing of the Act. That Mr. O'Connell would be excluded from its immediate benefit, had been noticed while the bill was in progress; and there can be little doubt that its language had been framed for that express purpose. So personal an exclusion was a petty accompaniment of this great remedial measure. By Mr. O'Connell it was termed 'an outlawry' against himself. He contended ably, at the bar, for his right of admission; but the Act was too distinct to allow of an interpretation in his favour. Not being permitted to take the new oath, and refusing, of course, to take the oath of supremacy,—a new writ was issued for the county of Clare.[2] Though returned again without opposition, Mr. O'Connell

<small>Mr. O'Connell and the Clare elections.</small>

<small>May 15th, 18th.</small>

<small>May 19th, 21st.</small>

---

[1] Lords' Journ., lxi. 402, 408.
[2] Hans. Deb., 2nd Ser., xxi. 1395, 1459, 1510.

made his exclusion the subject of unmeasured invective; and he entered the House of Commons, embittered against those by whom he had been enfranchised.

At length this great measure of toleration and justice was accomplished. But the concession came too late. Accompanied by one measure of repression, and another of disfranchisement, it was wrung by violence from reluctant and unfriendly rulers. Had the counsels of wiser statesmen prevailed, their political foresight would have averted the dangers before which the government, at length, had quailed. By rendering timely justice, in a spirit of conciliation and equity, they would have spared their country the bitterness, the evil passions, and turbulence of this protracted struggle. But thirty years of hope deferred, of rights withheld, of discontents and agitation, had exasperated the Catholic population of Ireland against the English government. They had overcome their rulers; and owing them no gratitude, were ripe for new disorders.[1]

Emancipation too long deferred.

Catholic emancipation, like other great measures, fell short of the anticipations, alike of supporters and opponents. The former were disappointed to observe the continued distractions of Ireland,—the fierce contentions between Catholics and Orangemen,—the coarse and truculent agitation by which the ill-will of the people was excited against their rulers—the perverse spirit in which every effort for the improvement of Ireland

Sequel of emancipation.

[1] See *supra*, Vol. II. 374.

was received,—and the unmanageable elements of Irish representation. But a just and wise policy had been initiated; and henceforth statesmen strove to correct those social ills which had arrested the prosperity of that hopeful country. With the Catholic Relief Act commenced the regeneration of Ireland.

On the other hand, the fears of the anti-Catholic party for the safety of the church and constitution were faintly realised. They dreaded the introduction of a dangerous proportion of Catholic members into the House of Commons. The result, however, fairly corresponded with the natural representation of the three countries. No more than six Catholics have sat, in any parliament, for English constituencies. Not one has ever been returned for Scotland. The largest number representing Catholic Ireland, in any parliament, amounted to fifty-one,—or less than one-half the representation of that country,—and the average, in the last seven parliaments, to no more than thirty-seven.[1] In these parliaments

<small>Number of Catholic members in the House of Commons.</small>

[1] *Number of Roman Catholic Members returned for England and Ireland since the year* 1835: *from the Test Rolls of the House of Commons; the earlier Test Rolls having been destroyed by fire, in* 1834.

		ENGLAND	IRELAND
New Parliament	1835	2	38
Do.	1837	2	27
Do.	1841	6	33
Do.	1847	5	44
Do.	1852	3	51
Do.	1857 to 1858	1 } Arundel	34
Do.	1859	1	34

These numbers, including members returned for vacancies, are sometimes slightly in excess of the Catholics sitting at the same time.

again, the total number of Roman Catholic members may be computed at about one-sixteenth of the House of Commons. The Protestant character of that assembly was unchanged.

To complete the civil enfranchisement of dissenters, a few supplementary measures were still required. They could only claim their rights on taking an oath; and some sects entertained conscientious objections to an oath, in any form. Numerous statutes had been passed to enable Quakers to make affirmations instead of oaths;[1] and in 1833, the House of Commons, giving a wide interpretation to these statutes, permitted Mr. Pease,—the first Quaker who had been elected for 140 years,—to take his seat on making an affirmation.[2] In the same year, Acts were passed to enable Quakers, Moravians, and Separatists, in all cases, to substitute an affirmation for an oath.[3] The same privilege was conceded, a few years later, to dissenters of more dubious denomination, who, having been Quakers or Moravians, had severed their connection with those sects, but retained their scruples concerning the taking of an oath.[4] Nor have these been barren concessions; for several members of these sects have since been admitted to Parliament; and one, at least, has taken a distinguished part in its debates.

Relief to dissenters and Roman Catholics had been

---

[1] 6 Anne, c. 23; 1 Geo. I. st. 2, c. 6 and 13; 8 Geo. I. c. 6; 22 Geo. II. c. 46.
[2] See Report of the Select Committee on his Case, Sess. 1833, No. 6.
[3] 3 & 4 Will. IV. c. 49, 82.   [4] 1 & 2 Vict. c. 77.

claimed on the broad ground that, as British subjects, they were entitled to their civil rights, without the condition of professing the religion of the state. And in 1830, Mr. Robert Grant endeavoured to extend this principle to the Jews. The cruel persecutions of that race form a popular episode in the early history of this country: but at this time they merely suffered, in an aggravated form, the disabilities from which Christians had recently been liberated. They were unable to take the oath of allegiance, as it was required to be sworn upon the Evangelists. Neither could they take the oath of abjuration, which contained the words, 'on the true faith of a Christian.' Before the repeal of the Corporation and Test Acts, they had been admitted to corporate offices, in common with dissenters, under cover of the annual indemnity Acts: but that measure, in setting dissenters free, had forged new bonds for the Jew. The new declaration was required to be made 'on the true faith of a Christian.' The oaths of allegiance and abjuration had not been designed, directly or indirectly, to affect the legal position of the Jews. The declaration had, indeed, been sanctioned with a forecast of its consequences: but was one of several amendments which the Commons were constrained to accept from the Lords, to secure the passing of an important measure.[1] The operation of the law was fatal to nearly all the rights of a citizen. A Jew could not hold any office, civil, military, or corporate. He could not follow

Jewish disabilities.

Mr. R. Grant's motion, April 5th, 1830.

[1] See *supra*, p. 161.

the profession of the law, as barrister or attorney, or attorney's clerk: he could not be a schoolmaster, or usher at a school. He could not sit as a member of either House of Parliament; nor even exercise the elective franchise, if called upon to take the electors' oath.

Mr. Grant advocated the removal of these oppressive disabilities in an admirable speech, embracing nearly every argument which was afterwards repeated, again and again, in support of the same cause. He was brilliantly supported, in a maiden speech, by Mr. Macaulay, who already gave promise of his future eminence. In the hands of his opponents, the question of religious liberty now assumed a new aspect. Those who had resisted, to the last, every concession to Catholics, had rarely ventured to justify their exclusion from civil rights, on the ground of their religious faith. They had professed themselves favourable to toleration; and defended a policy of exclusion, on political grounds alone. The Catholics were said to be dangerous to the state,—their numbers, their organisation, their allegiance to a foreign power, the ascendency of their priesthood, their peculiar political doctrines, their past history,—all testified to the political dangers of Catholic emancipation. But nothing of the kind could be alleged against the Jews. They were few in number, being computed at less than 30,000, in the United Kingdom. They were harmless and inactive in their relations to the state; and without any distinctive political character. It was, indeed, difficult to conceive any poli-

Arguments on either side.

tical objections to their enjoyment of civil privileges,—yet some were found. They were so rich, that, like the nabobs of the last century, they would buy seats in Parliament,—an argument, as it was well replied, in favour of a reform in Parliament, rather than against the admission of Jews. If of any value, it applied with equal force to all rich men, whether Jews or Christians. Again, they were of no country,—they were strangers in the land, and had no sympathies with its people. Relying upon the spiritual promises of restoration to their own Holy Land, they were not citizens, but sojourners, in any other. But if this were so, would they value the rights of citizenship, which they were denied? Would they desire to serve a country, in which they were aliens? And was it the fact that they were indifferent to any of those interests, by which other men were moved? Were they less earnest in business, less alive to the wars, policy, and finances of the state; less open to the refining influences of art, literature, and society? How did they differ from their Christian fellow-citizens, 'save these bonds'? Political objections to the Jews were, indeed, felt to be untenable; and their claims were therefore resisted on religious grounds. The exclusion of Christian subjects from their civil rights, had formerly been justified because they were not members of the established church. Now that the law had recognised a wider toleration, it was said that the state, its laws and institutions being Christian, the Jews, who denied Christ, could not be suffered to share, with Christians, the government of the state. Especially was it urged, that to admit them to Parliament would unchristianise the legislature.

The House of Commons, which twelve months before had passed the Catholic Relief Bill by vast majorities, permitted Mr. Grant to bring in his bill by a majority of eighteen only;[1] and afterwards refused it a second reading by a majority of sixty-three.[2] The arguments by which it was opposed were founded upon a denial of the broad principle of religious liberty; and mainly on that ground were the claims of the Jews for many years resisted. But the history of this long and tedious controversy must be briefly told. To pursue it through its weary annals were a profitless toil.

Jewish Relief Bill lost on second reading. May 17th, 1830.

In 1833, Mr. Grant renewed his measure; and succeeded in passing it through the Commons: but the Lords rejected it by a large majority.[3] In the next year, the measure met a similar fate.[4] The determination of the Lords was clearly not to be shaken; and, for some years, no further attempts were made to press upon them the re-consideration of similar measures. The Jews were, politically, powerless: their race was unpopular, and exposed to strongly-rooted prejudice; and

Jewish disabilities bills, 1833-4.

---

[1] Hans. Deb., 2nd Ser., xxiii. 1287.
[2] *Ibid.*, xxiv. 785. See also Macaulay's Essays, i. 308; Goldsmid's Civil Disabilities of British Jews, 1830; Blunt's Hist. of the Jews in England; First Report of Criminal Law Commission, 1845, p. 13.
[3] Contents, 54; Non-contents, 104. Hans. Deb., 3rd Ser., xvii. 205; xviii. 59; xx. 249.
[4] The second reading was lost in the Lords by a majority of 92. Hans. Deb., 3rd Ser., xxii. 1372; *Ibid.*, xxiii. 1158, 1349; *Ibid.*, xxiv. 382, 720.

their cause,—however firmly supported on the ground of religious liberty,—had not been generally espoused by the people, as a popular right.

But while vainly seeking admission to the legislature, the Jews were relieved from other disabilities. In 1839, by a clause in Lord Denman's Act for amending the laws of evidence all persons were entitled to be sworn in the form most binding on their conscience.[1] Henceforth the Jews could swear upon the Old Testament the oath of allegiance, and every other oath not containing the words 'on the true faith of a Christian.' These words, however, still excluded them from corporate offices, and from Parliament. In 1841, Mr. Divett succeeded in passing through the Commons a bill for the admission of Jews to corporations: but it was rejected by the Lords.[2] In 1845, however, the Lords, who had rejected this bill, accepted another, to the same effect, from the hands of Lord Lyndhurst.[3]

Jews admitted to corporations.

Parliament alone was now closed against the Jews. In 1848, efforts to obtain this privilege were renewed without effect. The Lords were still inexorable. Enfranchisement by legislative authority appeared as remote as ever; and attempts were therefore made to bring the claims of Jewish subjects to an issue, in another form.

In 1847, Baron Lionel Nathan de Rothschild was

---

[1] 1 & 2 Vict. c. 105.
[2] Hans. Deb., 3rd Ser., lvi. 504; lvii. 99; lviii. 1458.
[3] 8 & 9 Vict. c. 52; Hans. Deb., 3rd Ser., lxxviii. 407, 415; First Report of Criminal Law Commission, 1845 (Religious Opinions), 43.

returned as one of the members for the city of London. The choice of a Jew to represent such a constituency attested the state of public opinion, upon the question in dispute between the two Houses of Parliament. It may be compared to the election of Mr. O'Connell, twenty years before, by the county of Clare. It gave a more definite and practical character to the controversy. The grievance was no longer theoretical: there now sat below the bar a member legally returned by the wealthiest and most important constituency in the kingdom: yet he looked on as a stranger. None could question his return: no law affirmed his incapacity; then how was he excluded? By an oath designed for Roman Catholics, whose disabilities had been removed. He sat there, for four sessions, in expectation of relief from the legislature: but being again disappointed, he resolved to try his rights under the existing law. Accordingly, in 1850, he presented himself, at the table, for the purpose of taking the oaths. Having been allowed, after discussion, to be sworn upon the Old Testament,—the form most binding upon his conscience,—he proceeded to take the oaths. The oaths of allegiance and supremacy were taken in the accustomed form: but from the oath of abjuration he omitted the words 'on the true faith of a Christian,' as not binding on his conscience. He was immediately directed to withdraw; when, after many learned arguments, it was resolved that he was not entitled to sit or vote until he had taken

Baron Lionel de Rothschild returned for the city of London, 1847.

Claims to be sworn, July 26th, 29th, 30th, and Aug. 5th, 1850.

the oath of abjuration in the form appointed by law.[1]

In 1851, a more resolute effort was made to overcome the obstacle offered by the oath of abjuration. Mr. Alderman Salomons, a Jew, having been returned for the borough of Greenwich, omitted from the oath the words which were the Jews' stumbling block. Treating these words as immaterial, he took the entire substance of the oath, with the proper solemnities. He was directed to withdraw: but on a later day, while his case was under discussion, he came into the House, and took his seat within the bar, whence he declined to withdraw, until he was removed by the Sergeant at Arms. The House agreed to a resolution, in the same form as in the case of Baron de Rothschild. In the meantime, however, he had not only sat in the House, but had voted in three divisions;[2] and if the House had done him an injustice, there was now an opportunity for obtaining a judicial construction of the statutes, by the courts of law. By the judgment of the Court of Exchequer, affirmed by the Court of Exchequer Chamber, it was soon placed beyond further doubt, that no authority, short of a statute, was competent to dispense with those words which Mr. Salomons had omitted from the oath of abjuration.

Mr. Alderman Salomons, July 18th, 1851.

There was now no hope for the Jews, but in overcoming the steady repugnance of the Lords; and this was vainly attempted, year after

Further legislative efforts.

---

[1] Commons' Journ., cv. 584, 590, 612; Hans. Deb., 3rd Ser., cxiii. 297, 396, 486, 769.

[2] Commons' Journ., cvi. 372, 373, 381, 407; Hans. Deb., 3rd Ser., cxviii. 979, 1320.

year. Recent concessions, however, had greatly strengthened the position of the Jews. When the Christian character of our laws and constitution were again urged as conclusive against their full participation in the rights of British subjects,[1] Lord John Russell and other friends of religious liberty were able to reply:—Let us admit to the fullest extent that our country is Christian,—as it is: that our laws are Christian,—as they are; that our government, as representing a Christian country, is Christian,—as it is,—what then? Will the removal of civil disabilities from the Jews, unchristianise our country, our laws, and our government? They will all continue the same, unless you can argue that because there are Jews in England, therefore the English people are not Christian; and that because the laws permit Jews to hold land and houses, to vote at elections, and to enjoy municipal offices, therefore our laws are not Christian. We are dealing with civil rights; and if it be unchristian to allow a Jew to sit in Parliament,—not as a Jew, but as a citizen,—it is equally unchristian to allow a Jew to enjoy any of the rights of citizenship. Make him once more an alien, or cast him out from among you altogether.[2]

Baron de Rothschild continued to be returned again and again for the city of London,— a testimony to the settled purpose of his *Attempt to admit the Jews by a*

---

[1] See especially the speeches of Mr. Whiteside and Mr. Walpole, April 15th, 1853, on this view of the question.—Hans. Deb., 3rd Ser., cxxv. 1230, 1263.

[2] See especially Lord J. Russell's speech, April 15th, 1853.—*Ibid.*, 1283.

constituents: but there appeared no prospect of relief. In 1857, however, another loophole of the law was discovered, through which a Jew might possibly find his way into the House of Commons. The annual bill for the removal of Jewish disabilities had recently been lost, as usual, in the House of Lords, when Lord John Russell called attention to the provisions of a statute,[2] by which it was contended that the Commons were empowered to substitute a new form of declaration, for the abjuration oath. If this were so, the words 'on the true faith of a Christian,' might be omitted; and the Jew would take his seat, without waiting longer for the concurrence of the Lords.[3] But a committee, to whom the matter was referred, did not support this ingenious construction of the law;[4] and again the case of the Jews was remitted to legislation.

declaration, Aug. 3rd, 1857.

In the following year, however, this tedious controversy was nearly brought to a close. The Lords, yielding to the persuasion of the Conservative premier, Lord Derby, agreed to a concession. The bill, as passed by the Commons, at once removed the only legal obstacle to the admission of the Jews to Parliament. To this general enfranchisement the Lords declined to assent: but they allowed either House, by resolution, to omit the excluding words from the oath of abjuration. The Commons would thus be able to admit a Jewish

Jewish Relief Act, 1858.

---

[1] In 1849, and again in 1857, he placed his seat at the disposal of the electors, by accepting the Chiltern Hundreds, but was immediately re-elected. Commons' Journ., cxii. 343; Ann. Reg., Chron., 141.

[2] 5 & 6 Will. IV. c. 62.   [3] Hans. Deb., 3rd Ser., clvii. 933.

[4] Report of Committee, Sess. 2, 1857, No. 253.

member,—the Lords to exclude a Jewish peer. The immediate object of the law was secured: but what was the principle of this compromise? Other British subjects held their rights under the law: the Jews were to hold them at the pleasure of either House of Parliament. The Commons might admit them to-day, and capriciously exclude them to-morrow. If the crown should be advised to create a Jewish peer, assuredly the Lords would deny him a place amongst them. On these grounds, the Lords' amendments found little favour with the Commons: but they were accepted, under protest, and the bill was passed.[1] The evils of the compromise were soon apparent. The House of Commons was, indeed, open to the Jew: but he came as a suppliant. Whenever a resolution was proposed, under the recent Act,[2] invidious discussions were renewed,—the old sores were probed. In claiming his new franchise, the Jew might still be reviled and insulted. Two years later, this scandal was corrected; and the Jew, though still holding his title by a standing order of the Commons, and not under the law, acquired a permanent settlement.[3] Few of the ancient race have yet profited by their enfranchisement:[4] but their wealth, station, abilities, and character have amply attested their claims to a place in the legislature.

[1] 21 & 22 Vict. c. 48, 49; Comm. Journ., cxiii. 338; Hans. Deb., 3rd Ser., cli. 1905.
[2] A resolution was held not to be in force after a prorogation; Report of Committee, Sess. 1, 1859, No. 205.
[3] 23 & 24 Vict. c. 63. By the 29 & 30 Vict. c. 19, a new form of oath was established, from which the words 'on the true faith of a Christian' were omitted; and thus, at length, all distinctions between the Jews and other members were obliterated.

CHAPTER XIV.

FURTHER MEASURES OF RELIEF TO DISSENTERS:—CHURCH RATES:—LATER HISTORY OF THE CHURCH OF ENGLAND:—PROGRESS OF DISSENT:—THE PAPAL AGGRESSION, 1850:—THE CHURCH OF SCOTLAND:—THE PATRONAGE QUESTION:—CONFLICT OF CIVIL AND ECCLESIASTICAL JURISDICTIONS:—THE SECESSION, 1843:—THE FREE CHURCH OF SCOTLAND:—THE CHURCH OF IRELAND.

Other questions affecting the church and religion.

THE code of civil disabilities had been at length condemned: but during the protracted controversy which led to this result, many other questions affecting religious liberty demanded a solution. Further restraints upon religious worship were renounced; and the relations of the church to those beyond her communion reviewed in many forms. Meanwhile, the later history of the established churches, in each of the three kingdoms, was marked by memorable events, affecting their influence and stability.

Dissenters' births, marriages, and burials.

When Catholics and dissenters had shaken off their civil disabilities, they were still exposed to grievances affecting the exercise of their religion and their domestic relations, far more galling, and savouring more of intolerance. Their marriages were announced by the publication of bans in the parish church; and solemnised at its altar, according to a ritual which they repudiated. The births of their children were without legal evidence, unless they were baptised by a clergyman of the church, with a service obnoxious to their consciences; and even their dead could not obtain a Christian burial, except by the offices of the church. Even apart from religious scruples upon these matters, the enforced attendance of dissenters at the services of the church was a badge of inferiority and dependence, in the eye of the law. Nor was it without evils and embarrassments to the church herself. To perform her sacred offices for those who denied their sanctity, was no labour of love to the clergy. The marriage ceremony had sometimes provoked remonstrances; and the sacred character of all these services was impaired when addressed to unwilling ears, and used as a legal form, rather than a religious ceremony. It is strange that such grievances had not been redressed even before dissenters had been invested with civil privileges. The law had not originally designed to inflict them: but simply assuming all the subjects of the realm to be members of the Church of England, had made no provision for exceptional cases of conscience. Yet when the oppression of the marriage law had been formerly exposed,[1] intolerant Parliaments had obstinately refused relief. It was reserved for the reformed Parliament to extend to all religious sects entire freedom of conscience, coupled with great improvements in the general law of registration. As the church alone performed the religious services incident to all baptisms, marriages, and deaths; so was she entrusted with the sole management and custody of the registers. The relief of dissenters,

[1] *Supra*, p. 151.

therefore, involved a considerable interference with the privileges of the church, which demanded a judicious treatment.

The marriage law was first approached. In 1834, Lord John Russell,—to whom dissenters already owed so much,—introduced a bill to permit dissenting ministers to celebrate marriages in places of worship licensed for that purpose. It was proposed, however, to retain the accustomed publication of bans in church, or a licence. Such marriages were to be registered in the chapels where they were celebrated. There were two weak points in this measure,—of which Lord John himself was fully sensible,—the publication of bans, and the registry. These difficulties could only be completely overcome by regarding marriage, for all legal purposes, as a civil contract, accompanied by a civil registry: but he abstained from making such a proposal, in deference to the feelings of the church and other religious bodies.[1] The bill, in such a form as this, could not be expected to satisfy dissenters; and it was laid aside.[2] It was clear that a measure of more extensive scope would be required, to settle a question of so much delicacy.

Dissenters' Marriage Bill, Feb. 25th, 1834.

In the next session, Sir Robert Peel, having profited by this unsuccessful experiment, offered another measure, based on different principles. Reverting to the principle of the law, prior to Lord Hardwicke's Act of 1754, which viewed marriage, for certain purposes

Sir Robert Peel's Dissenters' Bill. March 17th, 1835.

---

[1] Hans. Deb., 3rd Ser., xxi. 776.   [2] Com. Journ., lxxxix. 226.

at least, as a civil contract, he proposed that dissenters objecting to the services of the church should enter into a civil contract of marriage, before a magistrate,—to be followed by such religious ceremonies elsewhere, as the parties might approve. For the publication of bans he proposed to substitute a notice to the magistrate, by whom also a certificate was to be transmitted to the clergyman of the parish for registration. The liberal spirit of this measure secured it a favourable reception: but its provisions were open to insuperable objections. To treat the marriage of members of the church as a religious ceremony, and the marriage of dissenters as a mere civil contract, apart from any religious sanction, raised an offensive distinction between the two classes of marriages. And again, the ecclesiastical registry of a civil contract, entered into by dissenters, was a very obvious anomaly. Lord John Russell expressed his own conviction that no measure would be satisfactory until a general system of civil registration could be established,—a subject to which he had already directed his attention.[1] The progress of this bill was interrupted by the resignation of Sir R. Peel. The new ministry, having May 22nd, 1835. consented to its second reading, allowed it to drop: but measures were promised in the next session for the civil registry of births, June 29th. marriages, and deaths, and for the marriage of dissenters.[2]

Early in the next session, Lord John Russell in-

---

[1] Hans. Deb., **3rd Ser.**, xxvi. 1073.   [2] *Ibid.*, 3rd Ser., xxix. 11.

troduced two bills to carry out these objects. The first was for the registration of births, marriages, and deaths. Its immediate purpose was to facilitate the granting of relief to dissenters: but it also contemplated other objects of state policy, of far wider operation. An accurate record of such events is important as evidence in all legal proceedings; and its statistical and scientific value cannot be too highly estimated. The existing registry being ecclesiastical took no note of births, but embraced the baptisms, marriages, and burials, which had engaged the services of the church. It was now proposed to establish a civil registration of births, marriages, and deaths, for which the officers connected with the new poor law administration afforded great facilities. The record of births and deaths was to be wholly civil; the record of marriages was to be made by the minister performing the ceremony, and transmitted to the registrar. The measure further provided for a general register office in London, and a division of the country into registration districts.[1]

Register of births, marriages, and deaths, Feb. 12th, 1836.

The Marriage Bill was no less comprehensive. The marriages of members of the Church of England were not affected, except by the necessary addition of a civil registry. The publication of bans, or licence, was continued, unless the parties themselves preferred giving notice to a registrar. The marriages of dissenters were allowed to be solemnised in their own chapels, registered for that purpose, after due notice to the registrar of the

Dissenters' Marriage Bill, Feb. 12th, 1836.

[1] Hans. Deb., 3rd Ser., xxxi. 367.

district; while those few dissenters who desired no religious ceremony, were enabled to enter into a civil contract before the superintendent registrar.[1] Measures so comprehensive and well considered could not fail to obtain the approval of Parliament. Every religious sect was satisfied: every object of state policy attained. The church, indeed, was called upon to make sacrifices: but she made them with noble liberality. Her clergy bore their pecuniary losses without a murmur, for the sake of peace and concord. Fees were cheerfully renounced with the services to which they were incident. The concessions, so gracefully made, were such as dissenters had a just right to claim, and the true interests of the church were concerned no longer in withholding.

In baptism and marriage, the offices of the church were now confined to her own members, or to such as sought them willingly. But in death, they were still needed by those beyond her communion. The church claimed no jurisdiction over the graves of her nonconformist brethren: but every parish burial-place was hers. The churchyard, in which many generations of churchmen slept, was no less sacred than the village church itself; yet here only could the dissenter find his last resting place. Having renounced the communion of the church while living, he was restored to it in death. The last offices of Christian burial were performed

Dissenters' burials.

---

[1] Hans. Deb., 3rd Ser., xxxi. 367; 6 & 7 Will. IV. c. 85, 86, amended by 1 Vict. c. 22. In 1852 the registration of chapels for all other purposes as well as marriages was transferred to the registrar-general.—15 & 16 Vict. c. 36.

over him, in consecrated ground, by the clergyman of the parish, and according to the ritual of the church. Nowhere was the painfulness of schism more deeply felt, on either side. The clergyman reluctantly performed the solemn service of his church, in presence of mourners who seemed to mock it, even in their sorrow. Nay, some of the clergy,—having scruples, not warranted by the laws of their church,—even refused Christian burial to those who had not received baptism at the hands of a priest, in holy orders.[1] On his side the dissenter recoiled from the consecrated ground, and the offices of the church. Bitterness and discord followed him to the grave, and frowned over his ashes.

In country parishes this painful contact of the church with nonconformity was unavoidable: but in populous towns, dissenters were earnest in providing themselves with separate burial grounds, and unconsecrated parts of cemeteries.[2] And latterly they have further sought, for their own ministers, the privilege of performing the burial service in the parish churchyard, with the permission of the incumbent.[3] In Ireland ministers of all denominations have long had access to the parish burial grounds.[4] Such a concession was necessary to meet

---

[1] Kemp *v.* Wickes, 1809, Phil., iii. 264; Escott *v.* Masten, 1842; Notes of Eccl. Cases, i. 552; Titchmarsh *v.* Chapman, 1844; *Ibid.,* iii. 370.

[2] Local Cemetery Acts, and 16 & 17 Vict. c. 134, s. 7. The Bishop of Carlisle having refused to consecrate a cemetery unless the unconsecrated part was separated by a wall, the legislature interfered to prevent so invidious a separation.—20 & 21 Vict. c. 81, s. 11.

[3] Feb. 19th and April 24th, 1861 (Sir Morton Peto); Hans. Deb., 3rd Ser., clxi. 650; clxii. 1051; May 2nd, 1862; *Ibid.,* clxvi. 1189.

[4] 5 Geo. IV. c. 25.

the peculiar relations of the population of that country to the church: but in England, it has not hitherto found favour with the legislature.

In 1834, another conflict arose between the church and dissenters, when the latter claimed to participate, with churchmen, in the benefits of those great schools of learning and orthodoxy,—the English universities. *Admission of dissenters to the Universities, 1834.* The position of dissenters was not the same in both universities. At Oxford, subscription to the thirty-nine articles had been required on matriculation, since 1581; and dissenting students had thus been wholly excluded from that university. It was a school set apart for members of the church. Cambridge had been less exclusive. It had admitted nonconformists to its studies, and originally even to its degrees. But since 1616, it had required subscription on proceeding to degrees. Dissenters, while participating in all its studies, were debarred from its honours and endowments,—its scholarships, degrees, and fellowships,—and from any share in the government of the university. From this exclusion resulted a *quasi* civil disability, for which the universities were not responsible. The inns of court admitted graduates to the bar in three years, instead of five; graduates articled to attorneys were admitted to practice after three years; the Colleges of Physicians and Surgeons admitted none but graduates as fellows. The exclusion of dissenters from universities was confined to England. Since 1793, the University of Dublin had been thrown open to Catholics and dissenters,[1] who

---
[1] 33 Geo. III. c. 21 (Irish).

were admitted to degrees in arts and medicine; and in the universities of Scotland there was no test to exclude dissenters.

Several petitions concerning these claims elicited full discussion in both Houses. Of these petitions, the most remarkable was signed by sixty-three members of the senate of the University of Cambridge, distinguished in science and literature, and of eminent position in the university. It prayed that dissenters should be admitted to take the degrees of bachelors, masters, or doctors in arts, law, and physic. Earl Grey, in presenting it to the House of Lords, opened the case of the dissenters in a wise and moderate speech, which was followed by a fair discussion of the conflicting rights of the church and dissenters.[1] In the Commons, Mr. Spring Rice ably represented the case of the dissenters, which was also supported by Mr. Secretary Stanley and Lord Palmerston, on behalf of the Government; and opposed by Mr. Goulburn, Sir R. Inglis, and Sir Robert Peel.[2] Petitions against the claims of dissenters were also discussed, particularly a counter-petition, signed by 259 resident members of the University of Cambridge.[3]

Petitions to both Houses.

March 21st, 1834.

March 24th.

Apart from the discussions to which these petitions gave rise, the case of the dissenters was presented in the more definite shape of a bill, introduced by Mr. George Wood.[4] Against

Universities Bill, April 17th, 1834.

---

[1] Hans. Deb., 3rd Ser., xxii. 497.   [2] Ibid., 570, 623, 674.
[3] Ibid., xxii. 1009.
[4] Ibid., xxii. 900. Ayes, 185; Noes, 44. Colonel Williams having

the admission of dissenters, it was argued that the religious education of the universities must either be interfered with or else imposed upon dissenters. It would introduce religious discord and controversies, violate the statutes of the universities, and clash with the internal discipline of the different colleges. The universities were instituted for the religious teaching of the Church of England; and were corporations enjoying charters and Acts of Parliament, under which they held their authority and privileges, for that purpose. If the dissenters desired a better education for themselves, they were rich and zealous, and could found colleges of their own, to vie with Oxford and Cambridge in learning, piety, and distinction.

On the other hand, it was contended that the administration of dissenters would introduce a better feeling between that body and the church. Their exclusion was irritating and invidious. The religious education of the universities was one of learning rather than orthodoxy; and it was more probable that dissenters would become attracted to the church, than that the influence of the church and its teaching would be impaired by their presence in the universities. The experience of Cambridge proved that discipline was not interfered with by their admission to its studies; and the denial of degrees to students who had distinguished themselves was a galling disqualification, upon which churchmen ought not to insist. The example of Dublin Univer-

moved for an address, the bill was ordered as an amendment to that question.

sity was also relied on, whose Protestant character had not been affected, nor its discipline interfered with, by the admission of Roman Catholics. This bill being warmly espoused by the entire Liberal party, was passed by the Commons, with large majorities.[1] In the Lords, however, it was received with marked disfavour. It was strenuously opposed by the Archbishop of Canterbury, the Duke of Gloucester, the Duke of Wellington, and the Bishop of Exeter; and even the new Premier, Lord Melbourne, who supported the second reading, avowed that he did not entirely approve of the measure. In his opinion its objects might be better effected by a good understanding and a compromise between both parties, than by the force of an Act of Parliament. The bill was refused a second reading by a majority of one hundred and two.[2]

June 20th.
July 28th.
Aug. 1st.

Not long afterwards, however, the just claims of dissenters to academical distinction were met, without trenching upon the church, or the ancient seats of learning,—by the foundation of the University of London,—open to students of every creed.[3] Some years later, the education, discipline, and endowments of the older universities called for the interposition of Parliament; and in considering their future regulation, the claims of dissenters were not overlooked. Provision was made for the opening

London University established, 1836.

Oxford and Cambridge Universities Act.

---

[1] On second reading—Ayes, 321; Noes, 147. On third reading—Ayes, 164; Noes, 75. Hans. Deb., 3rd Ser., xxiii. 632, 635.

[2] Contents, 85; Non-Contents, 187. Hans. Deb., 3rd Ser., xxv. 815.

[3] Debates, March 26th, 1835; Hans. Deb., 3rd Ser., xxvii. 279; London University Charters, Nov. 1836, and Dec. 1837.

of halls, for their collegiate residence and discipline; and the degrees of the universities were no longer withheld from their honourable ambition.[1]

The contentions hitherto related have been between the church and dissenters. But rival sects have had their contests: and in 1844 the legislature interposed to protect the endowments of dissenting communions from being despoiled by one another. Decisions of the Court of Chancery and the House of Lords, in the case of Lady Hewley's charity, had disturbed the security of all property held in trust by nonconformists, for religious purposes. The faith of the founder,—not expressly defined by any will or deed, but otherwise collected from evidence,—was held to be binding upon succeeding generations of dissenters. A change or development of creed forfeited the endowment; and what one sect forfeited, another might claim. A wide field was here opened for litigation. Lady Hewley's trustees had been dispossessed of their property, after a ruinous contest of fourteen years. In the obscure annals of dissent, it was difficult to trace out the doctrinal variations of a religious foundation; and few trustees felt themselves secure against the claims of rivals, encouraged at once by the love of gain and by religious hostility. An unfriendly legislature might have looked with complacency upon endowments wasted, and rivalries embittered. Dissent might have been put into

[1] Oxford University Act, 17 & 18 Vict. c. 81, s. 43, 44, &c.; Cambridge University Act, 19 & 20 Vict. c. 88, s. 45, &c. These degrees, however, did not entitle them to offices hitherto held by churchmen.

chancery, without a helping hand. But Sir Robert Peel's enlightened chancellor, Lord Lyndhurst, came forward to stay further strife. His measure provided that where the founder had not expressly defined the doctrines or form of worship to be observed, the usage of twenty-five years should give trustees a title to their endowment;[1] and this solution of a painful difficulty was accepted by Parliament. It was not passed without strong opposition on religious grounds, and fierce jealousy of Unitarians, whose endowments had been most endangered: but it was, in truth, a judicious legal reform rather than a measure affecting religious liberty.[2]

In the same spirit, Parliament has empowered the trustees of endowed schools to admit children of different religious denominations, unless the deed of foundation expressly limited the benefits of the endowment to the church, or some other religious communion.[3]

Endowed Schools Act, 1860.

Long after Parliament had frankly recognised complete freedom of religious worship, many intolerant enactments still bore witness to the rigour of our laws. Liberty had been conceded so grudgingly,—and clogged with so many conditions,—that the penal code had not yet disappeared from the statute-book. In 1845, the Criminal Law Commission enumerated the restraints and penalties which had hitherto escaped the vigilance of the legislature.[4] And Parliament

Repeal of penalties on religious worship.

---

[1] Hans. Deb., 3rd Ser., lxxiv. 579, 821.
[2] *Ibid.*, lxxv. 321, 383; lxxvi. 116; 7 & 8 Vict. c. 45.
[3] 23 Vict. c. 11.
[4] First Report of Crim. Law Commission (Religious Opinions), 1845.

has since blotted out many repulsive laws affecting the religious worship and education of Roman Catholics, and others not in communion with the church.[1]

The church honourably acquiesced in those just and necessary measures which secured to dissenters liberty in their religious worship and ministrations, and exemption from civil disabilities. But a more serious contention had arisen affecting her own legal rights,—her position as the national establishment,—and her ancient endowments. Dissenters refused payment of church rates. Many suffered imprisonment, or distraint of their goods, rather than satisfy the lawful demands of the church.[2] Others, more practical and sagacious, attended vestries, and resisted the imposition of the annual rate upon the parishioners. And during the progress of these local contentions, Parliament was appealed to by dissenters for legislative relief. *Church rates.*

The principles involved in the question of church rate, while differing in several material points from those concerned in other controversies between the church and dissenters, may yet be referred to one common origin,—the legal recognition of a national church, with all the rights *Principles involved.*

---

[1] See 2 & 3 Will. 4, s. 115 (Catholic Chapels and Schools); 7 & 8 Vict. c. 102; Hans. Deb., 3rd Ser., lxxiv. 691; lxxvi. 1165; 9 & 10 Vict. c. 59; *Ibid.*, lxxxiii. 495. Among the laws repealed by this Act was the celebrated statute or ordinance of Henry III., 'pro expulsione Judæorum.' 18 & 19 Vict. c. 86 (Registration of Chapels).

[2] See debates, July 30th, 1839; July 24th, 1840 (Thorogood's case); Hans. Deb., 3rd Ser., xlix. 998; lv. 939. Appendix to Report of Committee on Church Rates, 1851, p. 606–645.

incident to such an establishment, in presence of a powerful body of nonconformists. By the common law, the parishioners were bound to maintain the fabric of the parish church, and provide for the decent celebration of its services. The edifice consecrated to public worship was sustained by an annual rate, voted by the parishioners themselves assembled in vestry, and levied upon all occupiers of land and houses within the parish, according to their ability.[1] For centuries, the parishioners who paid this rate were members of the church. They gazed with reverence on the antique tower; hastened to prayers at the summons of the sabbath bells; sat beneath the roof which their contributions had repaired; and partook of the sacramental bread and wine which their liberality had provided. The rate was administered by lay churchwardens of their own choice; and all cheerfully paid what was dispensed for the common use and benefit of all. But times had changed. Dissent had grown, and spread and ramified throughout the land. In some parishes, dissenters even outnumbered the members of the church. Supporting their own ministers, building and repairing their own chapels, and shunning the services and clergy of the parish church, they resented the payment of church rate as at once an onerous and unjust tax, and an offence to their consciences. They insisted that the burden should be borne exclusively by members of the church. Such,

[1] Lyndwood, 53; Wilkins' Concil., i. 253; Coke's 2nd Inst., 489, 653; 13 Edw. I. (statute, *Circumspecte agatis*); Sir J. Campbell's letter to Lord Stanley, 1837; Report of Commission on Eccl. Courts, 1832.

they contended, had been the original design of church rate; and this principle should again be recognised, under altered conditions, by the state. The church stood firmly upon her legal rights. The law had never acknowledged such a distinction of persons as that contended for by dissenters; nay, the tax was chargeable, not so much upon persons, as upon property; and having existed for centuries, its amount was, in truth, a deduction from rent. If dissenting tenants were relieved from its payment, their landlords would immediately claim its equivalent in rental. But, above all, it was maintained that the fabric of the church was national property, —an edifice set apart by law for public worship, according to the religion of the state,—open to all, —inviting all to its services—and as much the common property of all, as a public museum or picture-gallery, which many might not care to enter, or were unable to appreciate.

Such being the irreconcilable principles upon which each party took its stand, contentions of increasing bitterness became rife in many parishes,—painful to churchmen, irritating to dissenters, and a reproach to religion. *Lord Althorp's scheme of commutation, April 21st, 1834.* In 1834, Earl Grey's ministry, among its endeavours to reconcile, as far as possible, all differences between the church and dissenters, attempted a solution of this perplexing question. Their scheme, as explained by Lord Althorp, was to substitute for the existing church rate an annual grant of 250,000*l.* from the consolidated fund, for the repair of churches. This sum, equal to about half the estimated rate, was to be distributed rateably to the several parishes. Church rate, in short, was to become national instead of parochial. This expedient found no favour with dissenters, who would still be liable to pay for the support of the church, in another form. Nor was it acceptable to churchmen, who deemed a fixed parliamentary subsidy, of reduced amount, a poor equivalent for their existing rights. The bill was, therefore, abandoned, having merely served to exemplify the intractable difficulties of any legislative remedy.[1]

In 1837, Lord Melbourne's government approached this embarrassing question with no better success. Their scheme provided a fund for the repair of churches out of surplus revenues, to arise from an improved administration of church lands.[2] This measure might well satisfy dissenters: but was wholly repudiated by the church.[3] It abandoned church rates, to which she was entitled; and appropriated her own revenues to purposes otherwise provided for, by law. She enjoyed both sources of income, and it was simply proposed to deprive her of one. If her revenues could be improved, she was herself entitled to the benefit of that improvement, for other spiritual objects. If church rates were to be surrendered, she claimed from the state another fund, as a reasonable equivalent.

Mr. Spring Rice's scheme for settling church rates, March 3rd, 1837.

But the legal rights of the church, and the means

---

[1] Hans. Deb., 3rd Ser., xx. 1012; Comm. Journ., lxxxix. 203, 207.
[2] Hans. Deb., 3rd Ser., xxxvi. 1207; xxxviii. 1073.
[3] Ann. Reg., 1837, p. 85.

of enforcing them, were about to be severely contested by a long course of litigation. In 1837, a majority of the vestry of Braintree having postponed a church rate for twelve months, the churchwardens took upon themselves, of their own authority, and in defiance of the vestry, to levy a rate. In this strange proceeding they were supported, for a time, by the Consistory Court,[1] on the authority of an obscure precedent.[2] But the Court of Queen's Bench restrained them, by prohibition, from collecting a rate, which Lord Denman emphatically declared to be 'altogether invalid, and a church rate in nothing but the name.'[3] In this opinion the Court of Exchequer Chamber concurred.[4] Chief Justice Tindal, however, in giving the judgment of this court, suggested a doubt whether the churchwardens, and a minority of the vestry together, might not concur in granting a rate, at the meeting of the parishioners assembled for that purpose. This suggestion was founded on the principle that the votes of the majority, who refused to perform their duty, were lost or thrown away; while the minority, in the performance of the prescribed duty of the meeting, represented the whole number.

The first Braintree case.

This subtle and technical device was promptly tried at Braintree. A rate being again refused by the majority, a monition was obtained from the Consistory Court, com-

The second Braintree case, 1841–1853.

---

[1] Veley v. Burder, Nov. 15th, 1837; App. to Report of Church Rates Co., 1851, p. 601.
[2] Gaudern v. Selby in the Court of Arches, 1799.
[3] Lord Denman's Judgment, May 1st, 1840; Burder v. Veley; Adolph. and Ellis, xii. 244.
[4] Feb. 8th, 1841; *Ibid.*, 300.

manding the churchwardens and parishioners to make a rate according to law.[1] In obedience to this monition, another meeting was assembled; and a rate being again refused by the majority, it was immediately voted in their presence, by the churchwardens and the minority.[2] A rate so imposed was of course resisted. The Consistory Court pronounced it illegal: the Court of Arches adjudged it valid. The Court of Queen's Bench, which had scouted the authority of the churchwardens, respected the right of the minority,—scarcely less equivocal,—to bind the whole parish; and refused to stay the collection of the rate by prohibition. The Court of Exchequer Chamber affirmed this decision. But the House of Lords,—superior to the subtilties by which the broad principles of the law had been set aside,—asserted the unquestionable rights of a majority. The Braintree rate which the vestry had refused, and a small minority had assumed to levy, was pronounced invalid.[3]

This construction of the law gravely affected the relations of the church to dissenters. From this time, church rates could not practically be raised in any parish, in which a majority of the vestry refused to impose them. The church, having an abstract legal title to receive them, was powerless to enforce it. The legal obligation to repair the parish church continued: but church rates assumed the form of a voluntary contribution, rather than a compulsory tax. It was

Its effect upon the rights of the church.

---

[1] June 22nd, 1841. [2] July 15th, 1841.
[3] Jurist, xvii. 939. Clark's House of Lords' Cases, iv. 679-814.

vain to threaten parishioners with the censures of ecclesiastical courts, and a whole parish with excommunication.[1] Such processes were out of date. Even if vestries had lost their rights, by any forced construction of the law, no rate could have been collected against the general sense of the parishioners. The example of Braintree was quickly followed. Wherever the dissenting body was powerful, canvassing and agitation were actively conducted, until, in 1859, church rates had been refused in no less than 1,525 parishes or districts.[2] This was a serious inroad upon the rights of the church.

While dissenters were thus active and successful in their local resistance to church rates, they were no less strenuous in their appeals to Parliament for legislative relief. Government having vainly sought the means of adjusting the question, in any form consistent with the interests of the church, the dissenters organised an extensive agitation for the total repeal of church rates. Proposals for exempting dissenters from payment were repudiated by both parties.[3] Such a compromise was regarded by churchmen as an encouragement to dissent, and by nonconformists as derogatory to their rights and pretensions, as independent religious

Bills for the abolition of church rates.

[1] Church Rates Committee, 1851: Dr. Lushington's Ev., Q. 2358-2365; Courtald's Ev., 489-491; Pritchard's Ev., Q. 660, 661; Terrell's Ev., Q. 1975-1982; Dr. Lushington's Ev. before Lords' Committee, 1859.
[2] Parl. Return, Sess. 2, 1359, No. 7.
[3] On Feb. 11th, 1840, a motion by Mr. T. Duncombe to this effect was negatived by a large majority. Ayes, 62; Noes, 117.—*Comm. Journ.*, xcv. 74. Again, on March 13th, 1849, an amendment to the same purpose found only twenty supporters. In 1852 a bill to relieve dissenters from the rate, brought in by Mr. Packe, was withdrawn.

bodies. The first bill for the abolition of church rates was introduced in 1841 by Sir John Easthope, but was disposed of without a division.[1] For several years similar proposals were submitted to the Commons without success.[2] In 1855, and again in 1856, bills for this purpose were read a second time by the Commons,[3] but proceeded no farther. In the latter year Sir George Grey, on behalf of ministers, suggested as a compromise between the contending parties, that where church rates had been discontinued in any parish for a certain period,—sufficient to indicate the settled purpose of the inhabitants,—the parish should be exempted from further liability.[4] This suggestion, however, founded upon the anomalies of the existing law, was not submitted to the decision of Parliament. The controversy continued; and at length, in 1858, a measure, brought in by Sir John Trelawny, for the total abolition of church rates, was passed by the Commons; and rejected by the Lords.[5] In 1859, another compromise was suggested, when Mr. Secretary Walpole brought in a bill to facilitate a voluntary provision for church rates; but it was refused a second reading by a large majority.[6] In 1860, another abolition bill was passed by one House, and rejected by the other.[7]

[1] May 26th, 1841; Comm. Journ., xcvi. 345, 414.
[2] June 16th, 1842; Comm. Journ., xcvii. 385; March 13th, 1849; Ibid., civ. 134; May 26th, 1853; Ibid., cviii. 516.
[3] May 16th, 1855: Ayes, 217; Noes, 189. Feb. 8th, 1856; Ayes, 221; Noes, 178.
[4] March 5th, 1856; Hans. Deb., 3rd Ser., cxl. 1900.
[5] The third reading of this bill was passed on June 8th by a majority of 63: Ayes, 266; Noes, 203.—Comm. Journ., cxiii. 216.
[6] March 9th, 1859. Ayes, 171; Noes, 254.—Comm. Journ., cxiv. 66.
[7] The third reading of this bill was passed by a majority of nine only. Ayes, 235; Noes, 226.—Comm. Journ., cv. 208.

Other compromises were suggested by friends of the church:[1] but none found favour, and total abolition was still insisted upon, by a majority of the Commons. With ministers it was an open question; and between members and their constituents, a source of constant embarrassment. Meanwhile, an active counter-agitation, on behalf of the church, began to exercise an influence over the divisions; and from 1858 the ascendency of the anti-church-rate party sensibly declined.[2] Such a reaction was obviously favourable to the final adjustment of the claims of dissenters, on terms more equitable to the church: but as yet the conditions of such an adjustment baffled the sagacity of statesmen. *Reaction in favour of the church.*

While these various contentions were raging between the church and other religious bodies, important changes were in progress in the church, and in the religious condition of the people. The church was growing in spiritual influence and temporal resources. Dissent was making advances still more remarkable. *State of the church to the end of last century.*

For many years after the accession of George III. the church continued her even course, with little change of condition or circumstances.[3] She was enjoying a tranquil, and apparently prosperous, existence. Favoured by the state and society: threatened by no visible dangers: dominant over

---

[1] Viz. the Archbishop of Canterbury, Mr. Alcock, Mr. Cross, Mr. Newdegate, and Mr. Hubbard.

[2] In 1861 (beyond the limits of this history) the annual bill was lost on the third reading by the casting vote of the Speaker; in 1862, by a majority of 17; and in 1863, by a majority of 10. See also Supplementary Chapter.

[3] *Supra*, p. 85.

Catholics and dissenters; and fearing no assaults upon her power or privileges, she was contented with the dignified security of a national establishment. The more learned churchmen devoted themselves to classical erudition and scholastic theology: the parochial clergy to an easy, but generally decorous, performance of their accustomed duties. The discipline of the church was facile and indulgent. Pluralities and non-residence were freely permitted, the ease of the clergy being more regarded than the spiritual welfare of the people. The parson farmed, hunted, shot the squire's partridges, drank his port wine, joined in the friendly rubber, and frankly entered into all the enjoyments of a country life. He was a kind and hearty man; and if he had the means, his charity was open-handed. Ready at the call of those who sought religious consolation, he was not earnest in searching out the spiritual needs of his flock. Zeal was not expected of him: society was not yet prepared to exact it.

While ease and inaction characterised the church, a great change was coming over the religious and social condition of the people. The religious movement, commenced by Wesley and Whitefield,[1] was spreading widely among the middle and humbler classes. An age of spiritual lethargy was passing away; and a period of religious emotion, zeal, and activity commencing. At the same time, the population of the country was attaining an extraordinary and unprecedented development. The church was ill prepared to meet these new conditions of society. Her clergy were slow to

Changes in the condition of the people.

[1] *Supra*, p. 85.

perceive them; and when pressed by the exigencies of the time, they could not suddenly assume the character of missionaries. It was a new calling, for which their training and habits unfitted them; and they had to cope with unexampled difficulties. A new society was growing up around them, with startling suddenness. A country village often rose, as if by magic, into a populous town: a town was swollen into a huge city. Artisans from the loom, the forge, and the mine were peopling the lone valley and the moor. How was the church at once to embrace a populous and strange community in her ministrations? The parish church would not hold them if they were willing to come: the parochial clergy were unequal, in number and in means, to visit them in their own homes. Spoliation and neglect had doomed a large proportion of the clergy to poverty; and neither the state nor society had yet come to their aid. If there were shortcomings on their part, they were shared by the state, and the laity. There was no organisation to meet the pressure of local wants, while population was outgrowing the ordinary agencies of the church. The field which was becoming too wide for her, was entered upon by dissent; and hitherto it has proved too wide for both.[1]

Sudden growth of population.

[1] It is computed that on the census Sunday, 1851, 5,288,294 persons able to attend religious worship once at least, were wholly absent. And it has been reckoned that in Southwark 68 per cent. of the population attend no place of worship whatever; in Sheffield, 62; in Oldham, 61½. In thirty-four great towns, embracing a population of 3,993,467, no less than 2,197,388, or 52½ per cent., are said to attend no places of worship.—*Dr. Hume's Ev. before Lords' Com. on Church Rates*, 1859, Q. 1290–1300.

Causes adverse to the clergy in presence of dissent.

In dealing with rude and industrial populations, the clergy laboured under many disadvantages compared with other sects,—particularly the Methodists,—by whom they were environed. However earnest in their calling, they were too much above working men in rank and education, to gain their easy confidence. They were gentlemen, generally allied to county families, trained at the universities, and mingling in refined society. They read the services of the church with grave propriety, and preached scholarlike discourses without emphasis or passion. Their well-bred calmness and good taste ministered little to religious excitement. But hard by the village church, a Methodist carpenter or blacksmith would address his humble flock with passionate devotion. He was one of themselves, spoke their rough dialect, used their wonted phrases; and having been himself converted to Methodism, described his own experience and consolations. Who can wonder that numbers forsook the decorous monotony of the church service for the fervid prayers and moving exhortations of the Methodist? Among the more enlightened population of towns, the clergy had formidable rivals in a higher class of nonconformist ministers, who attracted congregations, not only by doctrines congenial to their faith and sentiments, but by a more impassioned eloquence, greater warmth and earnestness, a plainer language, and closer relations with their flocks. Again, in the visitation of the sick, dissent had greater resources than the church. Its ministers were more familiar with their habits and religious feelings; were admitted with greater freedom to their homes; and were assisted by an active lay agency, which the church was slow to imitate.

Social causes further contributed to the progress of dissent. Many were not unwilling to escape from the presence of their superiors in station. Farmers and shopkeepers were greater men in the meeting-house, than under the shadow of the pulpit and the squire's pew. Working men were glad to be free, for one day in the week, from the eye of the master. It was a comfort to be conscious of independence, and to enjoy their devotions,—like their sports,—among themselves, without restraint or embarrassment. Even their homely dress tempted them from the church; as rags shut out a lower grade from public worship altogether. *Social causes of dissent.*

In Wales, there was yet another inducement to dissent. Like the Irish at the Reformation, the people were ignorant of the language in which the services of the church were too often performed. In many parishes, the English liturgy was read, and English sermons preached to Welshmen. Even religious consolations were ministered with difficulty, in the only language familiar to the people. Addressed by nonconformist teachers in their own tongue, numbers were soon won over. Doctrines and ceremonies were as nothing compared with an intelligible devotion. They followed Welshmen, rather than dissenters: but found themselves out of communion with the church.[1] *Dissent in Wales.*

[1] For an account of the condition of the church and dissent in Wales, see Wales, by Sir T. Phillips, ch. v. vi.

From these combined causes,—religious and social,—dissent marched onwards. The church lost numbers from her fold; and failed to embrace multitudes among the growing population, beyond her ministrations. But she was never forsaken by the rank, wealth, intellect, and influence of the country; and the poor remained her uncontested heritage. Nobles, and proprietors of the soil, were her zealous disciples and champions: the professions,—the first merchants and employers of labour, continued faithful. English society held fast to her. Aspirants to respectability frequented her services. The less opulent of the middle classes, and the industrial population, thronged the meeting-house: men who grew rich and prosperous forsook it for the church.

The church retained English society.

It was not until early in the present century, that the rulers and clergy of the church were awakened to a sense of their responsibilities, under these new conditions of society and religious feeling. Startled by the outburst of infidelity in France, and disquieted by the encroachments of dissent,—they at length discovered that the church had a new mission before her. More zeal was needed by her ministers; better discipline and organisation in her government; new resources in her establishment. The means she had must be developed; and the cooperation of the state and laity must be invoked, to combat the difficulties by which she was surrounded. The church of the sixteenth century must be adapted to the population and needs of the nineteenth.

Regeneration of the church.

The first efforts made for the regeneration of the church were not very vigorous, but they were in the right direction. In 1803, measures were passed to restrain clerical farming, to enforce the residence of incumbents, and to encourage the building of churches.[1]

Fifteen years later, a comprehensive scheme was devised for the building and endowment of churches in populous places. The disproportion between the means of the church and the growing population was becoming more and more evident;[2] and in 1818 provision was made by Parliament for a systematic extension of church accommodation. Relying mainly upon local liberality, Parliament added contributions from the public revenue, in aid of the building and endowment of additional churches.[3] Further encouragement was also given by the remission of duties upon building materials.[4] *Church Building Act, 1818.*

The work of church extension was undertaken with exemplary zeal. The piety of our ancestors, who had raised churches in every village throughout the land, was emulated by the laity, in the present century, who provided for the spiritual needs of their own time. New churches *Church extension, England.*

---

[1] 43 Geo. III. c. 84, 108; and see Stephen's Ecclesiastical Statutes, 892, 985.

[2] Lord Sidmouth's Life, iii. 138; Returns laid before the House of Lords, 1811.

[3] 58 Geo. III. c. 45; 3 Geo. IV. c. 72, &c. One million was voted in 1813, and 500,000l. in 1824. Exchequer bill loans to about the same amount were also made.—*Porter's Progress*, 619.

[4] In 1837 these remissions had amounted to 170,561l.; and from 1837 to 1845, to 165,778l.—Parl. Papers, 1838, No. 325; 1845, No. 322.

arose everywhere among a growing and prosperous population; parishes were divided; and endowments found for thousands of additional clergy.[1]

The poorer clergy have also received much welcome assistance from augmentations of the fund known as Queen Anne's Bounty.[2] Nor is it unworthy of remark, that the general opulence of the country has contributed, in another form, to the poorer benefices. Large numbers of clergy have added their private resources to the scant endowments of their cures; and with a noble spirit of devotion and self-sacrifice, have dedicated their lives and fortunes to the service of the church.

Other endowments of the church.

While the exertions of the church were thus encouraged by public and private liberality, the legislature was devising means for developing the existing resources of the establishment. Its revenues were large, but ill administered, and unequally distributed. Notwithstanding the spoliations of the sixteenth century, the net revenues

Ecclesiastical revenues.

---

[1] Between 1801 and 1831 about 500 churches were built at an expense of 3,000,000*l*. In twenty years, from 1831 to 1851, more than two thousand new churches were erected at an expense exceeding 6,000,000*l*. In this whole period of fifty years 2,529 churches were built at an expense of 9,087,000*l*., of which 1,663,429*l*. were contributed from public funds, and 7,423,571*l*. from private benefactions.—Census, 1851, Religious Worship, p. xxxix.; see also Lords' Debate, May 11th, 1854.—Hans. Deb., 3rd Ser., cxxxiii. 153. Between 1801 and 1858, it appears that 3,150 churches had been built at an expense of 11,000,000*l*.—Lords' Report on Spiritual Destitution, 1858; Cotton's Ev., Q. 141.

[2] 2 & 3 Anne c. 11; 1 Geo. I. st. 2, c. 10; 45 Geo. III. c. 84; 1 & 2 Will. IV. c. 45, &c. From 1809 to 1820, the governors of Queen Anne's bounty distributed no less than 1,000,000*l*. to the poorer clergy. From April 5th, 1831, to Dec. 31st, 1835, they disbursed 637,342*l*. From 1850 to 1860 inclusive, they distributed 2,502,747*l*.

amounted to 3,490,497*l.*; of which 435,046*l.* was appropriated by the bishops and other dignitaries; while many incumbents derived a scanty pittance from the ample patrimony of the church.[1] Sound policy, and the interests of the church herself, demanded an improved management and distribution of this great income; and in 1835 a commission was constituted, which, in five successive reports, recommended numerous ecclesiastical reforms. In 1836, the ecclesiastical commissioners were incorporated,[2] with power to prepare schemes for carrying these recommendations into effect. Many reforms in the church establishment were afterwards sanctioned by Parliament. The boundaries of the several dioceses were revised: the sees of Gloucester and Bristol were consolidated, and the new sees of Manchester and Ripon created: the episcopal revenues and patronage were re-adjusted.[3] The establishments of cathedral and collegiate churches were reduced, and their revenues appropriated to the relief of spiritual destitution. And the surplus revenues of the church, accruing from all these reforms, have since been applied, under the authority of the commissioners, to the augmentation of small livings, and other purposes designed to increase the efficiency of the church.[4] At the same

Ecclesiastical commission, 1836.

[1] Report of Ecclesiastical Duties and Revenues Comm., 1831.
[2] 6 & 7 Will. IV. c. 77. The constitution of the commissioners was altered in 1840 by 3 & 4 Vict. c. 113; 14 & 15 Vict. c. 104; 23 & 24 Vict. c. 124.
[3] See 6 & 7 Will. IV. c. 77; 3 & 4 Vict. c. 113. Originally the sees of St. Asaph and Bangor were also united; but the 10 and 11 Vict. c. 108, which constituted the bishopric of Manchester, repealed the provisions concerning the union of these sees.
[4] In 1860, no less than 1,388 benefices and districts had been aug-

time pluralities were more effectually restrained, and residence enforced, among the clergy.[1]

In extending her ministrations to a growing community, the church has further been assisted from other sources. Several charitable societies have largely contributed to this good work,[2] and private munificence,—in an age not less remarkable for its pious charity than for its opulence,—has nobly supported the zeal and devotion of the clergy.

Private munificence.

The principal revenues of the church, however, were derived from tithes; and these continued to be collected by the clergy, according to ancient usage, 'in kind.' The parson was entitled to the farmer's tenth wheat-sheaf, his tenth pig, and his tenth sack of potatoes! This primitive custom of the Jews was wholly unsuited to a civilised age. It was vexatious to the farmer, discouraging to agriculture, and invidious to the clergy. A large proportion of the land was tithe-free; and tithes were often the property of lay impropriators: yet the

Tithes commutation, England.

---

mented and endowed, out of the common fund of the commissioners, to the extent of 98,900*l.* a year; to which had been added land and tithe rent-charge amounting to 9,600*l.* a year.—14th Report of Commissioners, p. 5.

[1] 1 & 2 Vict. c. 106.

[2] In twenty-five years the Church Pastoral Aid Society raised and expended 715,624*l.*, by which 1015 parishes were aided. In twenty-four years the Additional Curates Society raised and expended 531,110*l.* In thirty-three years the Church Building Society expended 680,233*l.*, which was met by a further expenditure, on the part of the public, of 4,451,405*l.*—*Reports of these Societies for* 1861.

Independently of diocesan and other local societies, the aggregate funds of religious societies connected with the church amounted, in 1851, to upwards of 400,000*l.* a year, of which 250,000*l.* was applied to foreign missions.—Census of 1851, Religious Worship, p. xli.

church sustained all the odium of an antiquated and anomalous law. The evil had long been acknowledged. Prior to the Acts of Elizabeth restraining alienations of church property,[1] landowners had purchased exemption from tithes by the transfer of lands to the church; and in many parishes a particular custom prevailed, known as a *modus*, by which payment of tithes in kind had been commuted. The Long Parliament had designed a more general commutation.[2] Adam Smith and Paley had pointed out the injurious operation of tithes; and the latter had recommended their conversion into corn-rents.[3] This suggestion having been carried out in some local inclosure bills, Mr. Pitt submitted to the Archbishop of Canterbury, in 1791, the propriety of its general adoption: but unfortunately for the interests of the church, his wise counsels were not accepted.[4] It was not for more than forty years afterwards, that Parliament perceived the necessity of a general measure of commutation. In 1833 and 1834, Lord Althorp submitted imperfect schemes for consideration;[5] and in 1835, Sir Robert Peel proposed a measure to facilitate voluntary commutation, which was obviously inadequate.[6] But in 1836, a measure, more comprehensive, was framed by Lord Melbourne's government, and accepted by Parliament. It provided for the general commuta-

[1] 1 Eliz. c. 19; 13 Eliz. c. 10.
[2] Collier's Eccl. Hist., ii. 861.
[3] Moral and Political Philosophy, ch. xii.
[4] Lord Stanhope's Life of Pitt, ii. 131.
[5] April 18th, 1833; April 15th, 1834; Hans. Deb., 3rd Ser., xvii. 281; xxii. 834.
[6] March 24th, 1835; *Ibid.* xxvii. 183.

tion of tithes into a rent-charge upon the land, payable in money, but varying according to the average price of corn, for seven preceding years. Voluntary agreements upon this principle were first encouraged; and where none were made, a compulsory commutation was effected by commissioners appointed for that purpose.[1] The success of this statesmanlike measure was complete. In fifteen years, the entire commutation of tithes was accomplished in nearly every parish in England and Wales.[2] To no measure, since the Reformation, has the church owed so much peace and security. All disputes between the clergy and their parishioners, in relation to tithes, were averted; while their rights, identified with those of the lay-impropriators, were secured immutably upon the land itself.

Throughout the progress of these various measures the church was gaining strength and influence, by her own spiritual renovation. While the judicious policy of the legislature had relieved her from many causes of jealousy and ill-will, and added to her temporal resources, she displayed a zeal and activity worthy of her high calling and destinies. Her clergy,—earnest, intellectual, and accomplished,—have kept pace with the advancing enlightenment of their age. They have laboured,

Continued zeal of the church.

---

[1] Feb. 9th, 1836. Hans. Deb., 3rd Ser., xxxi. 185; 6 & 7 Will. IV. c. 71; 7 Will. IV. and 1 Vict. c. 69; 1 & 2 Vict. c. 64; 2 & 3 Vict. c. 32; 5 & 6 Vict. c. 54; 9 & 10 Vict. c. 73; 10 & 11 Vict. c. 104; 14 & 15 Vict. c. 53.

[2] In Feb. 1851, the commissioners reported that 'the great work of commutation is substantially achieved.'—1851, No. [1325]. In 1852, they speak of formal difficulties in about one hundred cases. 1852, No. [1447].

with all their means and influence, in the education of the people; and have joined heartily with laymen in promoting, by secular agencies, the cultivation and moral welfare of society. At one time there seemed danger of further schisms, springing from controversies which had been fruitful of evil at the Reformation. The high church party leaning, as of old, to the imposing ceremonial of Catholic worship, aroused the apprehensions of those who perceived in every symbol of the Romish church, a revival of her errors and superstitions. But the extravagance of some of the clergy was happily tempered by the moderation of others, and by the general good sense and judgment of the laity; and schism was averted. Another schism, arising out of the Gorham controversy, was threatened by members of the evangelical, or low church party: but was no less happily averted. The fold of the church has been found wide enough to embrace many diversities of doctrine and ceremony. The convictions, doubts, and predilections of the sixteenth century still prevail, with many of later growth: but enlightened churchmen, without absolute identity of opinion, have been proud to acknowledge the same religious communion,—just as citizens, divided into political parties, are yet loyal and patriotic members of one state. And if the founders of the reformed church erred in prescribing too strait a uniformity, the wisest of her rulers, in an age of active thought and free discussion, have generally shown a tolerant and cautious spirit in dealing with theological controversies. The ecclesiastical courts have also striven to give breadth to her articles and liturgy. Never was comprehension more politic. The time has come, when any serious schism might bring ruin on the church.

Such having been the progress of the church, what have been the advances of dissent? We have seen how wide a field lay open to the labours of pious men. A struggle had to be maintained between religion and heathenism in a Christian land; and in this struggle dissenters long bore the foremost part. They were at once preachers and missionaries. Their work prospered, and in combating ignorance and sin, they grew into formidable rivals of the church. The old schisms of the Reformation had never lost their vitality. There had been persecution enough to alienate and provoke nonconformists: but not enough to repress them. And when they started on a new career, in the last century, they enjoyed toleration. The doctrines for which many had formerly suffered, were now freely preached, and found crowds of new disciples. At the same time, freedom of worship and discussion favoured the growth of other diversities of faith, ceremonial, and discipline.

Progress of dissent.

The later history of dissent,—of its rapid growth and development,—its marvellous activity and resources,—is to be read in its statistics The church in extending her ministrations had been aided by the state; and by the liberality of her wealthy flocks. Dissent received no succour or encouragement from the state; and its disciples were generally drawn from the less opulent classes of

Statistics of dissent.

society. Yet what has it done for the religious instruction of the people? In 1801, the Wesleyans had 825 chapels or places of worship: in 1851, they had the extraordinary number of 11,007, with sittings for 2,194,298 persons! The original connection alone numbered 1,034 ministers, and upwards of 13,000 lay or local preachers. In 1801, the Independents had 914 chapels: in 1851, they had 3,244, with sittings for 1,067,760 members. In 1801, the Baptists had 652 places of worship: in 1851, they had 2,789, with sittings for 752,346. And numerous other religious denominations swelled the ranks of Protestant dissent.

The Roman Catholics,—forming a comparatively small body,—have yet increased of late years in numbers and activity. Their chapels grew from 346 in 1824, to 574 in 1851, with accommodation for 186,111 persons. Between 1841 and 1853 their religious houses were multiplied from 17 to 88; and their priests from 557 to 875. Their flocks have naturally been enlarged by considerable numbers of Irish and foreigners who have settled, with their increasing families, in the metropolis and other large towns.

For the population of England and Wales, amounting in 1851 to 17,927,609, there were 34,467 places of worship, of which 14,077 belonged to the church of England. Accommodation was provided for 9,467,738 persons, of whom 4,922,412 were in the establishment. On the 30th of March, 4,428,338 attended morning service, of whom 2,371,732 were members of the

Statistics of places of worship.

church.[1] Hence it has been computed that there were 7,546,948 members of the establishment habitually attending religious worship; and 4,466,266 nominal members rarely, if ever, attending the services of their church. These two classes united, formed about 67 per cent. of the population. The same computation reckoned 2,264,324 Wesleyans, and 610,786 Roman Catholics.[2] The clergy of the established church numbered 17,320: ministers of other communions, 6,405.[3]

So vast an increase of dissent has seriously compromised the position of the church, as a national establishment. Nearly one-third of the present generation have grown up out of her communion. But her power is yet dominant. She holds her proud position in the state and society: she commands the parochial organisation of the country: she has the largest share in the education of the people;[4] and she has long been straining every nerve to extend her influence. The traditions and sentiment of the nation are on her side. And while she comprises a united body of faithful members, dissenters are divided into up-

Relations of the church to dissent.

---

[1] Census of Great Britain, 1851, Religious Worship. The progressive increase of dissent is curiously illustrated by a return of temporary and permanent places of worship registered in decennial periods.—Parl. Paper, 1853, No. 156.

[2] Dr. Hume's Ev. before Lords' Com. on Church Rates, 1859, Q. 1291, and map. Independents and Baptists together are set down as $9\frac{3}{4}$ per cent., and other sects $6\frac{3}{4}$ on the population.

[3] Census, 1851: occupations, table 27.

[4] In 1860 she received about 77 per cent. of the education grant from the Privy Council; and of 1,549,312 pupils in day-schools, she had no less than 1,187,086; while of Sunday-school pupils dissenters had a majority of 200,000.—Rep. of Education Com., 1861, p. 593, 594; Bishop of London's Charge, 1862, p. 35.

wards of one hundred different sects, or congregations, without sympathy or cohesion, and differing in doctrines, polity, and forms of worship. Sects, not bound by subscription to any articles of faith, have been rent asunder by schisms. The Wesleyans have been broken up into nine divisions:[1] the Baptists into five.[2] These discordant elements of dissent have often been united in opposition to the church, for the redress of grievances common to them all. But every act of toleration and justice, on the part of the state, has tended to dissolve the combination. The odium of bad laws weighed heavily upon the church; and her position has been strengthened by the reversal of a mistaken policy. Nor has the church just cause of apprehension from any general sentiment of hostility on the part of Protestant nonconformists. Numbers frequent her services, and are still married at her altars.[3] The Wesleyans, dwelling just outside her gates, are friends and neighbours, rather than adversaries. The most formidable and aggressive of her opponents are the Independents. With them the 'voluntary principle' in religion is a primary article of faith. They condemn all church establishments; and the Church of England is the foremost example to be denounced and assailed.

---

[1] The Original Connexion, New Connexion, Primitive Methodists, Bible Christians, Wesleyan Methodist Association, Independent Methodists, Wesleyan Reformers, Welsh Calvinistic Methodists, and Countess of Huntingdon's Connexion.

[2] General, Particular, Seventh-day, Scotch, New Connexion General.

[3] Eighty per cent. of all marriages are celebrated by the church.—Rep. of Registrar-Gen., 1862, p. viii.

Whatever the future destinies of the church, the gravest reflections arise out of the later development of the Reformation. The church was then united to the state. Her convocation, originally dependent, has since lost all but a nominal place in the ecclesiastical polity of the realm. And what have become the component parts of the legislature which directs the government, discipline, revenues,— nay even the doctrines, of the church? The Commons, who have attained a dominant authority, are representatives of England,—one-third nonconformists,—of Presbyterian Scotland,—and of Catholic Ireland. In the union of church and state no such anomaly had been foreseen; yet has it been the natural consequence of the Reformation,—followed by the consolidation of these realms, and the inevitable recognition of religious liberty in a free state.

Relations of the church to Parliament.

However painful the history of religious schisms and conflicts, they have not been without countervailing uses. They have extended religious instruction; and favoured political liberty. If the church and dissenters, united, have been unequal to meet the spiritual needs of this populous land,—what could the church, alone and unaided, have accomplished? Even if the resources of dissent had been placed in her hands, rivalry would have been wanting, which has stimulated the zeal of both. Liberty owes much to schism. It brought down the high prerogatives of the Tudors and Stuarts; and in later times, has been a powerful auxiliary in many popular movements.

Influence of dissent upon political liberty.

The undivided power of the church, united to that of the crown and aristocracy, might have proved too strong for the people. But while she was weakened by dissent, a popular party was growing up, opposed to the close political organisation with which she was associated. This party was naturally joined by dissenters; and they fought side by side in the long struggle for civil and religious liberty.

The church and dissenters, generally opposed on political questions affecting religion, have been prompt to make common cause against the church of Rome. *The Papal aggression, 1850.* The same strong spirit of Protestantism which united them in resistance to James II. and his House, has since brought them together on other occasions. Dissenters, while seeking justice for themselves, had been no friends to Catholic emancipation; and were far more hostile than churchmen to the endowment of Maynooth.[1] And in 1851, they joined the church in resenting an aggressive movement of the Pope, which was felt to be an insult to the Protestant people of England.

For some time irritation had been growing, in the popular mind, against the church of Rome. The activity of the priesthood was everywhere apparent. Chapels were built, and religious houses founded.[2] A Catholic cathedral was erected in London. Sisters of mercy, in monastic robes, offended the eyes of Protestants. Tales of secret proselytism abounded. No family was believed to be safe from the designs of priests and Jesuits. Protestant heiresses had

---

[1] See *infra*, p. 270.   [2] See *supra*, p. 223.

taken the veil, and endowed convents: wives of Protestant nobles and gentlemen had secretly renounced the faith in which their marriage vows were given: fathers, at the point of death, had disinherited their own flesh and blood, to satisfy the extortion of confessors. Young men at Oxford, in training for the church, had been perverted to Romanism. At the same time, in the church herself, the tractarian, or high church clergy, were reverting to ceremonies associated with that faith; and several had been gained over to the church of Rome. While Protestants, alarmed by these symptoms, were disposed to overestimate their significance, the ultramontane party among the Catholics, encouraged by a trifling and illusory success, conceived the extravagant design of reclaiming Protestant England to the fold of the Catholic church.

In September 1850, Pope Pius IX., persuaded that the time had come for asserting his ancient pretensions within this realm, published a brief, providing for the ecclesiastical government of England. Hitherto the church of Rome in England had been superintended by eight vicars apostolic: but now the Pope, considering the 'already large number of Catholics,' and 'how the hindrances which stood in the way of the spreading of the Catholic faith are daily being removed,' saw fit to establish 'the ordinary form of episcopal rule in that kingdom;' and accordingly divided the country into one metropolitan, and twelve episcopal sees. And to his archbishop and bishops he gave 'all the rights and privileges which the Catholic

The Pope's brief, 1850.

archbishops and bishops, in other states, have and use, according to the common ordinances of the sacred canons and apostolic constitutions.' Nor did the brief omit to state that the object of this change was 'the well-being and advancement of Catholicity throughout England.'[1]

This was followed by a pastoral of Cardinal Wiseman, on his appointment as Archbishop of Westminster, exulting in the supposed triumph of his church. 'Your beloved country,' said he, 'has received a place among the fair churches which, normally constituted, form the splendid aggregate of Catholic communion: Catholic England has been restored to its orbit in the ecclesiastical firmament, from which its light had long vanished, and begins now anew its course of regularly adjusted action round the centre of unity, the source of jurisdiction, of light, and of vigour.'[2]

Cardinal Wiseman's pastoral.

The enthronisation of the new bishops was celebrated with great pomp; and exultant sermons were preached on the revival of the Catholic church. In one of these, Dr. Newman,—himself a recent convert,—declared that 'the people of England, who for so many years had been separated from the see of Rome, are about, of their own will, to be added to the holy church.'

Catholic bishops enthroned.

No acts or language could have wounded more deeply the traditional susceptibilities of the English people. For three hundred years the papal supremacy had been renounced, and the

Popular indignation.

---

[1] Papal Brief, Sept. 30th, 1850; Ann. Reg., 1850, App. 405.
[2] Pastoral, Oct. 7th, 1850; Ann. Reg., 1850, App. 411.

Romish faith held in abhorrence. Even diplomatic relations with the sovereign of the Roman States,—as a temporal prince,—had until lately been forbidden.[1] And now the Pope had assumed to parcel out the realm into Romish bishoprics; and to embrace the whole community in his jurisdiction. Never, since the Popish plot, had the nation been so stirred with wrath and indignation. Early in November, Lord John Russell, the Premier, increased the public excitement by a letter to the Bishop of Durham, denouncing the 'aggression of the Pope as insolent and insidious,' and associating it with the practices of the tractarian clergy of the Church of England.[2] Clergy and laity, churchmen and dissenters, vied with one another in resentful demonstrations; and in the bonfires of the 5th of November,—hitherto the sport of children,—the obnoxious effigies of the Pope and Cardinal Wiseman were immolated, amidst the execrations of the multitude. No one could doubt the Protestantism of England. Calm observers saw in these demonstrations ample proof that the papal pretensions, however insolent, were wholly innocuous; and Cardinal Wiseman, perceiving that in his over-confidence he had mistaken the temper of the people, sought to moderate their anger by a conciliatory address. The ambitious episcopate now assumed the modest proportions of an arrangement for the spiritual care of a small body of Roman Catholics.

---

[1] In 1848 an Act was passed, with some difficulty, to allow diplomatic relations with the sovereign of the Roman States.—11 & 12 Vict. c. 108; Hans. Deb., 3rd Ser., xcvi. 169; ci. 227, 234.

[2] Nov. 4th, 1850; Ann. Reg., 1850, p. 198.

Meanwhile, the government and a vast majority of the people were determined that the papal aggression should be repelled; but how? If general scorn and indignation could repel an insult, it had already been amply repelled: but action was expected on the part of the state; and how was it to be taken? Had the laws of England been violated? The Catholic Relief Act of 1829 forbade the assumption of any titles belonging to the bishops of the Church of England and Ireland:[1] but the titles of these new bishops being taken from places not appropriated by existing sees, their assumption was not illegal. Statutes, indeed, were still in force prohibiting the introduction of papal bulls or letters into this country.[2] But they had long since fallen into disuse; and such communications had been suffered to circulate, without molestation, as natural incidents to the internal discipline of the church of Rome. To prosecute Cardinal Wiseman for such an offence would have been an act of impotent vengeance. Safe from punishment, he would have courted martyrdom. The Queen's supremacy in all matters, ecclesiastical and temporal, was undoubted: but had it been invaded? When England professed the Catholic faith, the jurisdiction of the Pope had often conflicted with that of the crown. Both were concerned in the government of the same church: but now the spiritual supremacy of the crown was exercised over the church of England

Difficulties of the case.

[1] 10 Geo. IV. c. 7, s. 24.
[2] In 1846, that part of the 13th Eliz. which attached the penalties of treason to this offence had been repealed, but the law continued in force.

only. Roman Catholics,—in common with all other subjects not in communion with the church,—enjoyed full toleration in their religious worship; and it was an essential part of their faith and polity to acknowledge the spiritual authority of the Pope. Could legal restraints, then, be imposed upon the internal government of the church of Rome, without an infraction of religious toleration? True, the papal brief, in form and language, assumed a jurisdiction over the whole realm; and Cardinal Wiseman had said of himself, 'We govern, and shall continue to govern, the counties of Middlesex, Hertford, and Essex.' But was this more than an application of the immutable forms of the church of Rome to altered circumstances? In governing Roman Catholics, did the Pope wrest from the Queen any part of her ecclesiastical supremacy?

Such were the difficulties of the case; and ministers endeavoured to solve them by legislation. Drawing a broad distinction between the spiritual jurisdiction of the Pope over the members of his church, and an assumption of sovereignty over the realm, they proposed to interdict all ecclesiastical titles derived from places in the United Kingdom. Let the Catholics, they argued, be governed by their own bishops: let the Pope freely appoint them: leave entire liberty to Catholic worship and polity: but reserve to the civil government of this country alone, the right to create territorial titles. Upon this principle a bill was introduced into the House of Commons by Lord John Russell. The titles assumed by

Ecclesiastical Titles Bill, Feb. 7th, 1851.

the Catholic bishops were prohibited: the brief or rescript creating them was declared unlawful: the acts of persons bearing them were void; and gifts or religious endowments acquired by them, forfeited to the crown.[1] These latter provisions were subsequently omitted by ministers;[2] and the measure was confined to the prohibition of territorial titles. It was shown that in no country in Europe,— whether Catholic or Protestant,—would the Pope be suffered to exercise such an authority, without the consent of the state; and it was not fit that England alone should submit to his encroachments upon the civil power. But as the bill proceeded, the difficulties of legislation accumulated. The bill embraced Ireland, where such titles had been permitted, without objection, since the Relief Act of 1829. It would, therefore, withdraw a privilege already conceded to Roman Catholics, and disturb that great settlement. Yet, as the measure was founded upon the necessity of protecting the sovereignty of the crown, no part of the realm could be excepted from its operation. And thus, for the sake of repelling an aggression upon Protestant England, Catholic Ireland was visited with this new prohibition.

The bill encountered objections, the most opposite and contradictory. On one side, it was condemned as a violation of religious liberty. *Objections to the bill.* The Catholics, it was said, were everywhere governed by bishops, to whom districts were assigned, universally known as dioceses, and distinguished by some

---

[1] Feb. 7th, 1851. Hans. Deb., 3rd Ser., cxiv. 187.
[2] March 7th; *Ibid.*, 1123.

local designation. To interfere with the internal polity of the church of Rome was to reverse the policy of toleration, and might eventually lead to the revival of penal laws. If there was insolence in the traditional language of the Court of Rome, let it be repelled by a royal proclamation, or by addresses from both Houses, maintaining Her Majesty's undoubted prerogatives: but let not Parliament renew its warfare with religious liberty. On the other hand, it was urged that the encroachments of the church of Rome upon the temporal power demanded a more stringent measure than that proposed,—severer penalties, and securities more effectual.

These opposite views increased the embarrassments of the government, and imperilled the success of the measure. For a time ministers received the support of large majorities who,—differing upon some points,—were yet agreed upon the necessity of a legislative condemnation of the recent measures of the church of Rome. But on the report of the bill, amendments were proposed, by Sir F. Thesiger, to increase the stringency of its provisions. They declared illegal, not only the particular brief, but all similar briefs; extended to every person the power of prosecuting for offences, with the consent of the attorney-general; and made the introduction of bulls or rescripts a penal offence.

Such stringency went far beyond the purpose of ministers, and they resisted the amendments: but a considerable number of members,—chiefly Roman Catholics,—hoping that ministers, if overborne by the opposition, would abandon the bill, retired from the House and left ministers in a minority. The amendments, however, were accepted, and the bill was ultimately passed.[1]

It was a protest against an act of the Pope which had outraged the feelings of the people of England: but as a legislative measure, it was a dead letter. The church of Rome receded not a step from her position; and Cardinal Wiseman and the Catholic bishops,—as well in England as in Ireland,—continued to bear, without molestation, the titles conferred upon them by the Pope. The excitement of the people, and acrimonious discussions in Parliament, revived animosities which recent legislation had tended to moderate: yet these events were not unfruitful of good. They dispelled the wild visions of the ultramontane party: checked the tractarian movement in the Church of England; and demonstrated the sound and faithful Protestantism of the people. Nor had the ultramontane party any cause of gratulation, in their apparent triumph over the state. They had given grave offence to the foremost champions of the Catholic cause: their conduct was deplored by the laity of their own church; and they had increased the repugnance of the people to a faith which they had scarcely yet learned to tolerate.

Results of the bill.

The church of Scotland, like her sister church of England, has also been rent by schisms. The protracted efforts of the English government to sustain episcopacy in the

Church of Scotland: schisms and dissent.

[1] 14 & 15 Vict. c. 60; Hans. Deb., 3rd Ser., cxiv. cxv. cxvi. *passim*; Ann. Reg., 1851. ch. ii. iii.

establishment,[1] resulted in the foundation of a distinct episcopalian church. Comparatively small in numbers, this communion embraced a large proportion of the nobility and gentry who affected the English connexion, and disliked the democratic spirit and constitution of the Presbyterian church. In 1732, the establishment was further weakened by the retirement of Ebenezer Erskine, and an ultra-puritanical sect, who founded the Secession Church of Scotland.[2] This was followed by the foundation of another seceding church, called the Presbytery of Relief, under Gillespie, Boston, and Colier;[3] and by the growth of independents, voluntaries, and other sects. But the widest schism is of recent date; and its causes illustrate the settled principles of Presbyterian polity; and the relations of the church of Scotland to the state.

Lay patronage had been recognised by the Catholic church in Scotland, as elsewhere; but the Presbyterian church soon evinced her repugnance to its continuance. Wherever lay patronage has been allowed, it has been the proper office of the church to judge of the qualifications of the clergy, presented by patrons. The patron nominates to a benefice; the church approves and inducts the nominee. But this limited function, which has ever been exercised in the church of England, did not

History patronage.

---

[1] *Supra*, p. 71.
[2] Cunningham's Church Hist. of Scotland, ii. 427–440, 450–455; Moncrieff's Life of Erskine; Fraser's Life of Erskine; Thomson's Hist. of the Secession Church.
[3] Cunningham's Ch. Hist., ii. 501, 513. In 1847 the Secession Church and the Relief Synod were amalgamated under the title of the 'United Presbyterian Church.'

satisfy the Scottish reformers, who, in the spirit of other Calvinistic churches, claimed for the people a voice in the nomination of their own ministers. Knox went so far as to declare, in his First Book of Discipline,—which, however, was not adopted by the church,—' that it appertaineth unto the people, and to every several congregation, to elect their minister.'[1] The Second Book of Discipline, adopted as a standard of the church in 1578, qualified this doctrine: but declared 'that no person should be intruded in any offices of the kirk contrary to the will of the congregation, or without the voice of the eldership.'[2] But patronage being a civil right, the state undertook to define it, and to prescribe the functions of the church. In 1567, the Parliament declared that the presentation to benefices 'was reserved to the just and ancient patrons,' while the examination and admission of ministers belonged to the church. Should the induction of a minister be refused, the patron might appeal to the General Assembly.[3] And again, by an Act of 1592, presbyteries were required to receive and admit whatever qualified minister was presented by the crown or lay patrons.[4] In the troublous times of 1649, the church being paramount, Parliament swept away all lay patronage as a 'popish custom.'[5] On the Restoration it was revived, and rendered doubly odious by

---

[1] A.D. 1560, ch. iv. s. ii. Robertson's Auchterarder Case, i. 22 (Mr. Whigham's argument), &c. Buchanan's Ten Years' Conflict, i. 47.
[2] Ch. iii. s. 4 & 5; and again, in other words, ch. xii. s. 9 & 10.
[3] Scots Acts, 1567, c. 7.
[4] James VI., Parl., xii. c. 116.
[5] Scots Acts, 1649, c. 171; Buchanan, i. 98–105.

the persecutions of that period. The Revolution restored the ascendency of the Presbyterian Church and party; and again patronage was overthrown. By an Act of 1690, the elders and heritors were to choose a minister for the approval of the congregation; and if the latter disapproved the choice, they were to state their reasons to the presbytery, by whom the matter was to be determined.[1] Unhappily this settlement, so congenial to Presbyterian traditions and sentiment, was not suffered to be permanent. At the Union, the constitution and existing rights of the church of Scotland were guaranteed: yet within five years, the heritors determined to reclaim their patronage. The time was favourable: Jacobites and high church Tories were in the ascendant, who hated Scotch Presbyterians no less than English dissenters; and an Episcopalian Parliament naturally favoured the claims of patrons. An Act was therefore obtained in 1712, repealing the Scotch Act of 1690, and restoring the ancient rights of patronage.[2] It was an untoward act, conceived in the spirit of times before the Revolution. The General Assembly then protested against it as a violation of the treaty of union; and long continued to record their protest.[3] The people of Scotland were outraged. Their old strife with Episcopalians was still raging; and to that communion most of the patrons belonged. For some time patrons did

---

[1] Scots Acts, 1690, c. 23.   [2] 10 Anne, c. 12.
[3] Carstares State Papers, App. 796-800; Cunningham's Church Hist. of Scotland, ii. 362. Claim of Rights of the Church of Scotland, May, 1842, p. 9; D'Aubigné's Germany, England, and Scotland, 377-385; Buchanan's Ten Years' Conflict, i. 124-133.

not venture to exercise their rights: ministers continued to be called by congregations; and some who accepted presentations from lay patrons were degraded by the church.[1] Patronage, at first a cause of contention with the state and laity, afterwards brought strifes into the church herself. The Assembly was frequently at issue with presbyteries concerning the induction of ministers. The church was also divided on the question of presentations; the moderate party, as it was called, favouring the rights of patrons, and the popular party the calls of the people. To this cause was mainly due the secession of Ebenezer Erskine[2] and Gillespie,[3] and the foundation of their rival churches. But from about the middle of the last century the moderate party, having obtained a majority in the Assembly, maintained the rights of patrons; and thus, without any change in the law, the Act of 1712 was, at length, consistently enforced.[4] A call by the people had always formed part of the ceremony of induction; and during the periods in which lay patronage had been superseded, it had unquestionably been a substantial election of a minister by his congregation.[5] A formal call continued to be recognised: but presbyteries did not venture to reject

---

[1] Cunningham's Church Hist., ii. 420.
[2] Cunningham's Church Hist. of Scotland, ii. 419-446, 450-455; Thomson's Hist. of the Secession Church; Moncrieff's Life of Erskine; Fraser's Life of Erskine.
[3] Cunningham's Church Hist., ii. 501, 513.
[4] Cunningham's Church Hist. of Scotland, ii. 491-500, 511, 537, 558; D'Aubigné's Germany, England, and Scotland, 388-394; Judgments in first Auchterarder case; Buchanan's Ten Years' Conflict, i. 145-165.
[5] Judgments of Lord Brougham and the Lord Chancellor in the first Auchterarder case, p. 239, 334, 335.

any qualified person duly presented by a patron. At the end of the century, the patronage question appeared to have been set at rest.[1]

Lay patronage a cause of dissent. But the enforcement of this law continued to be a fertile cause of dissent from the establishment. When a minister was forced upon a congregation by the authority of the Presbytery or General Assembly, the people, instead of submitting to the decision of the church, joined the Secession Church, the Presbytery of Relief, or the Voluntaries.[2] No people in Christendom are so devoted to the pulpit as the Scotch. There all the services of their church are centred. No liturgy directs their devotion: the minister is all in all to them,—in prayer, in exposition, and in sermon. If acceptable to his flock, they join devoutly in his prayers, and are never weary of his discourses: if he finds no favour, the services are without interest or edification. Hence a considerable party in the church were persuaded that a revival of the ancient principles of their faith, which recognised the potential voice of the people in the appointment of ministers, was essential to the security of the establishment.

The Veto Act, 1834. Hostility to lay patronage was continually increasing, and found expression in petitions and parliamentary discussion.[3] Meanwhile the 'non-intrusion party,' led by Dr. Chalmers, were gaining ground in the General Assembly: in 1834,

---

[1] Cunningham's Church Hist. of Scotland, ii. 581.
[2] *Ibid.*; Report on Church Patronage (Scotland), 1834, Evidence.
[3] July 16th, 1833, on Mr. Sinclair's motion.—Hans. Deb., 3rd Ser., xix. 704.

they had secured a majority; and, without awaiting remedial measures from Parliament, they succeeded in passing the celebrated 'Veto Act.'[1] This Act declared it to 'be a fundamental law of the church that no pastor shall be intruded on a congregation, contrary to the will of the people;' and provided that if, without any special objections to the moral character, doctrine, or fitness of a presentee, the majority of the male heads of families signified their dissent, the presbytery should, on that ground alone, reject him. Designed, in good faith, as an amendment of the law and custom of the church, which the Assembly was competent to make, it yet dealt with the rights already defined by Parliament. Patronage was border land, which the church had already contested with the state; and it is to be lamented that the Assembly,—however well advised as to its own constitutional powers,[2]—should thus have entered upon it, without the concurrence of Parliament. Never was time so propitious for the candid consideration of religious questions. Reforms were being introduced into the church; the grievances of dissenters were being redressed; a popular party were in the ascendant; and agitation had lately shown its power over the deliberations of the legislature. A Veto Act, or other compromise sanctioned by Parliament, would have brought peace to the church. But now the state had made one law: the

---

[1] For a full narrative of all the circumstances connected with the state of parties in the Church, and the passing of this Act, see Buchanan's Ten Years' Conflict, i. 174-296.

[2] The jurisdiction of the Assembly had been supported by the opinion of the law officers of the crown in Scotland.—*Buchanan*, i. 442.

church another; and how far they were compatible was soon brought to a painful issue.

In the same year, Lord Kinnoull presented Mr. Young to the vacant parish of Auchterarder: but a majority of the male heads of families having objected to his presentation, without stating any special grounds of objection, the presbytery refused to proceed with his trials, in the accustomed form, and judge of his qualifications. Mr. Young appealed to the synod of Perth and Stirling, and thence to the General Assembly; and the presbytery being upheld by both these courts, rejected Mr. Young.

Auchterarder case, 1834–1839.

Having vainly appealed to the superior church courts, Lord Kinnoull and Mr. Young claimed from the Court of Session an enforcement of their civil rights. They maintained that the presbytery, as a church court, were bound to adjudge the fitness of the presentee, and not to delegate that duty to the people, whose right was not recognised by law; and that his rejection, on account of the veto, was illegal. The presbytery contended that admission to the pastoral office being the function of the church, she had a right to consider the veto of the congregation as a test of fitness, and to prescribe rules for the guidance of presbyteries. In the exercise of such functions the jurisdiction of the church was supreme, and beyond the control of the civil tribunals. The court, however, held that neither the law of the church, prior to the Veto Act, nor the law of the land, recognised the right of a congregation to

Adverse judgments of the civil courts.

reject a qualified minister. It was the duty of the presbytery to judge of his fitness, on grounds stated and examined; and the Veto Act, in conferring such a power upon congregations, violated the civil and patrimonial rights of patrons, secured to them by statute, and hitherto protected by the church herself. Upon the question of jurisdiction, the court maintained its unquestionable authority to give redress to suitors who complained of a violation of their civil rights; and while admitting the competency of the church to deal with matters of doctrine and discipline, declared that in trenching upon civil rights she had transgressed the limits of her jurisdiction. To deny the right of the Court of Session to give effect to the provisions of the statute law, when contravened by church courts, was to establish the supremacy of the church over the state.[1] From this decision the presbytery appealed to the House of Lords, by whom, after able arguments at the bar, and masterly judgments from Lord Chancellor Cottenham and Lord Brougham, it was, on every point affirmed.[2]

Submission to the law, even under protest, and an appeal to the remedial equity of Parliament, might now have averted an irreconcilable conflict between the civil and ecclesiastical powers, without an absolute surrender of principles for which the church was contending. But this occasion was lost. The Assembly, indeed,

Resistance of the General Assembly.

[1] Robertson's Report of the Auchterarder Case, 2 vols. 8vo. 1838; Buchanan, i. 340–487.
[2] Maclean and Robinson's cases decided in the House of Lords, 1839, i. 220.

suspended the operation of the Veto Act for a year; and agreed that, so far as the temporalities of Auchterarder were concerned, the case was concluded against the church. The manse, the glebe, and the stipend should be given up : but whatever concerned the duties of a presbytery, in regard to the cure of souls, and the ministry of the gospel, was purely ecclesiastical and beyond the jurisdiction of any civil court. A presbytery being a church court, exercising spiritual powers, was amenable to the Assembly only, and was not to be coerced by the civil power. On these grounds it was determined to refuse obedience to the courts ; and the hopeless strife continued between the two jurisdictions, embittered by strong party differences in the Assembly, and among the laity of Scotland. Parliament alone could have stayed it : but the resistance of the church forbade its interposition ; and a compromise, proposed by Lord Aberdeen, was rejected by the Assembly.

The judgment of the Court of Session having been affirmed, the presbytery were directed to make trial of the qualifications of Mr. Young: but they again refused. For this refusal Lord Kinnoull and Mr. Young brought an action for damages, in the Court of Session, against the majority of the presbytery; and obtained a unanimous decision that they were entitled to pecuniary redress for the civil wrongs they had sustained. On appeal to the House of Lords, this judgment also was unanimously affirmed.[1] In other cases, the Court of Ses-

Second Auchterarder case.

---

[1] July 11th, 1842. Bell's Cases decided in the House of Lords, i. 662.

sion interfered in a more peremptory form. The presbytery of Dunkeld, having inducted a minister to the parish of Lethendy, in defiance of an interdict from the Court of Session, were brought up before that court, and narrowly escaped imprisonment.[1] The crown presented Mr. Mackintosh to the living of Daviot and Dunlichity: when several parishioners, who had been canvassing for another candidate, whose claims they had vainly pressed upon the secretary of state, prepared to exercise a veto. But as such a proceeding had been pronounced illegal by the House of Lords, Mr. Mackintosh obtained from the Court of Session a decree interdicting the heads of families from appearing before the presbytery, and declaring their dissent without assigning special objections.[2]

Lethendy case.

Daviot case, Dec. 17th, 1839.

While this litigation was proceeding, the civil and ecclesiastical authorities were brought into more direct and violent collision. Mr. Edwards was presented, by the trustees of Lord Fife, to the living of Marnoch, in the presbytery of Strathbogie: but a majority of the male heads of families having signified their veto, the seven ministers constituting the presbytery, in obedience to the law of the church and an order of the General Assembly, refused to admit him to his trials. Mr. Edwards appealed to the Court of Session, and obtained a decree directing the presbytery to admit him to the living, if found qualified. The ministers

The Strathbogie cases.

---

[1] Buchanan, ii. 1–17.
[2] Dunlop, Bell, and Murray's Reports, ii. 253.

of the presbytery were now placed in the painful dilemma of being obliged to disobey either the decree of the civil court, or the order of the supreme court of the church. In one case they would be punished for contempt; in the other for contumacy. Prohibited by a commission of Assembly from proceeding further, before the next General Assembly, they nevertheless resolved, as ministers of the established church, sworn to pay allegiance to the crown, to render obedience to the law, constitutionally interpreted and declared. For this offence against the church they were suspended by the commission of Assembly; and their proceedings as a presbytery were annulled.[1]

The Court of Session, thus defied by the church, suspended the execution of the sentence of the commission of Assembly against the suspended ministers, prohibited the service of the sentence of suspension, and forbade other ministers from preaching or intruding into their churches or schools.[2] These proceedings being reported to the General Assembly, that body approved of the acts of the commission,—further suspended the ministers, and again provided for the performance of their parochial duties. Again the Court of Session interfered, and prohibited the execution of these acts of the Assembly, which were in open

The Strathbogie ministers, Feb. 14th, 1840.

---

[1] Dec. 11th, 1839.

[2] Dunlop, Bell, and Murray's Reports, ii. 258, 585. Lord Gillies on the question of jurisdiction, said: 'The pretensions of the church of Scotland, at present, are exactly those of the Papal See a few centuries ago. They not only decline the jurisdiction of the civil courts, but they deny that Parliament can bind them by a law which they choose to say is inconsistent with the law of Christ.'

defiance of its previous interdicts.[1] The church was in no mood to abate her pretensions. Hitherto the members of the Strathbogie presbytery had been under sentence of suspension only. They had vainly sought protection from Parliament; and on the 27th of May 1841, the General Assembly deposed them from the ministry. Dr. Chalmers, in moving their deposition, betrayed the spirit which animated that Assembly, and the dangers which were now threatening the establishment. 'The church of Scotland,' he said, 'can never give way, and will sooner give up her existence as a national establishment, than give up her powers as a self-acting and self-regulating body, to do what in her judgment is best for the honour of the Redeemer, and the interest of his kingdom upon earth.'[2] It was evident that the ruling party in the Assembly were prepared to resist the civil authority at all hazards.

The contest between the civil and ecclesiastical jurisdictions was now pushed still further. *The Strathbogie commissioners.* The majority of the presbytery of Strathbogie, who had been deposed by the General Assembly, but reinstated by the Court of Session, elected commissioners to the General Assembly: the minority elected others. The Court of Session interdicted the commissioners elected by the minority, from taking their seats in the Assembly.[3] And in

[1] June 11th, 1840. Dunlop, Bell, and Murray's Reports, ii. 1047, 1380.
[2] Ann. Reg., 1841, p. 71–73; Hans. Deb., 3rd Ser., lvii. 1377; lviii. 1503; Buchanan, ii. 17–285.
[3] May 27th, 1842. Dunlop, Bell, and Murray's Report, iv. 1298. Lord Fullerton, who differed from the majority of the court, said: 'According to my present impression, this court has no more right

restraining the contumacy of these refractory commissioners, the civil court was forced to adjudge the constitution and rights of the Ecclesiastical Assembly. All these decisions were founded on the principle that ministers and members of the Church of Scotland were not to be permitted to refuse obedience to the decrees of the civil courts of the realm, or to claim the exercise of rights which those courts had pronounced illegal. The church regarded them as encroachments upon her spiritual functions.

It was plain that such a conflict of jurisdictions could not endure much longer. One or the other must yield: or the legislature must interfere to prevent confusion and anarchy. In May 1842, the General Assembly presented to Her Majesty a claim, declaration, and protest, complaining of encroachments by the Court of Session; and also an address, praying for the abolition of patronage. These communications were followed by a memorial to Sir Robert Peel and the other members of his government, praying for an answer to the complaints of the church, which, if not redressed, would inevitably result in the disruption of the establishment. On behalf of the government, Sir James Graham, Secretary of State for the Home Department, returned a reply, stern and unbending in tone, and with more of rebuke than conciliation. The aggression, he said, had originated with the Assembly, who had passed

Claim and declaration of General Assembly, May 1842.

Answer of Sir James Graham, Jan. 4th, 1843.

to grant such an interdict, than to interdict any persons from taking their seats and acting and voting as members of the House of Commons.'—*Ibid.*

the illegal Veto Act, which was incompatible with the rights of patrons as secured by statute. By the standards of the church, the Assembly were restrained from meddling with civil jurisdiction: yet they had assumed to contravene an Act of Parliament, and to resist the decrees of the Court of Session,—the legal expositor of the intentions of the legislature. The existing law respected the rights of patrons to present, of the congregation to object, and of the church courts to hear and judge,—to admit or reject the candidate. But the Veto Act deprived the patrons of their rights, and transferred them to the congregations. The government were determined to uphold established rights, and the jurisdiction of the civil courts: and would certainly not consent to the abolition of patronage. To this letter the General Assembly returned an answer of extraordinary logical force: but the controversy had reached a point beyond the domain of argument.[1]

The church was hopelessly at issue with the civil power. Nor was patronage the only ground of conflict. The General Assembly had admitted the ministers of *quoad sacra* parishes and chapels of ease, to the privileges of the parochial clergy, including the right of sitting in the Assembly, and other church courts.[2] The legality of the acts of the Assembly was called in question; and in January 1843, the Court of Session adjudged them to be illegal.[3] On the meeting of

Quoad sacra ministers, Jan. 20th, 1843.

---

[1] Papers presented in answer to addresses of the House of Commons, Feb. 9th and 10th, 1843; Buchanan, ii. 357.
[2] Acts of Assembly, 1833, 1834, 1837, and 1839.
[3] Stewarton Case, Bell, Murray, &c., Reports, iv. 427.

the Assembly on the 31st of January, a motion was made, by Dr. Cook, to exclude the *quoad sacra* ministers from that body, as disqualified by law: but it was lost by a majority of ninety-two. Dr. Cook, and the minority, protesting against the illegal constitution of the Assembly, withdrew; and the *quoad sacra* ministers retained their seats, in defiance of the Court of Session. The conflict was approaching its crisis; and, in the last resort, the Assembly agreed upon a petition to Parliament, complaining of the encroachments of the civil courts upon the spiritual jurisdiction of the church, and of the grievance of patronage.

This petition was brought under the consideration of the Commons, by Mr. Fox Maule. He ably presented the entire case for the church; and the debate elicited the opinions of ministers, and the most eminent members of all parties. Amid expressions of respect for the church, and appreciation of the learning, piety, and earnestness of her rulers, a sentiment prevailed that until the General Assembly had rescinded the Veto Act, in deference to the decision of the House of Lords, the interposition of Parliament could scarcely be claimed, on her behalf. She had taken up her position, in open defiance of the civil authority; and nothing would satisfy her claims but submission to her spiritual jurisdiction. Some legislation might yet be possible: but this petition assumed a recognition of the claims of the church, to which the majority of the House were not prepared to assent. Sir Robert Peel regarded these claims as involving

[marginal note: Petition of General Assembly, March 7th, 1843.]

'the establishment of an ecclesiastical domination, in defiance of law,' which 'could not be acceded to without the utmost ultimate danger, both to the religious liberties and civil rights of the people.' The House concurred in this opinion, and declined to entertain the claims of the church by a majority of one hundred and thirty-five.[1]

This decision was accepted by the non-intrusion party as conclusive; and preparations were immediately made for their secession from the church.[2] The General Assembly met on the 18th May, when a protest was read by the moderator, signed by 169 commissioners of the Assembly, including *quoad sacra* ministers and lay elders. This protest declared the jurisdiction assumed by the civil courts to be 'inconsistent with Christian liberty, and with the authority which the Head of the church hath conferred on the church alone.' It stated that the word and will of the state having recently been declared that submission to the civil courts formed a condition of the establishment, they could not, without sin, continue to retain the benefits of the establishment to which such condition was attached, and would therefore withdraw from it,—retaining, however, the confession of faith and standards of the church. After the reading of this protest, the remonstrants with-

The secession, May 18th, 1843.

---

[1] Ayes, 76; Noes, 211. Hans. Deb., 3rd Ser., lxvii. 354, 441. See also debate in the Lords on Lord Campbell's resolutions, March 31; *Ibid.*, lxviii. 218; Debate on *Quoad Sacra* Ministers, May 9th; *Ibid.*, lxix. 12.

[2] Minute of Special Commission of the General Assembly, March 20th; Ann. Reg., 1843, p. 245; Buchanan, ii. 427.

drew from the Assembly; and joined by many other ministers, constituted the 'Free Church of Scotland.' Their schism was founded on the first principles of the Presbyterian polity,—repugnance to lay patronage, and repudiation of the civil jurisdiction, in ecclesiastical affairs. These principles,—at issue from the very foundation of the church,—had now torn her asunder.[1]

Veto Act rescinded. A few days afterwards, the General Assembly rescinded the Veto Act, and the act admitting *quoad sacra* ministers to that court; and annulled the sentences upon the Strathbogie ministers. The seceders were further declared to have ceased to be members of the church, and their endowments were pronounced vacant.[2] The church thus submitted herself, once more, to the authority of the law; and renewed her loyal alliance with the state.

The Free Church of Scotland. The secession embraced more than a third of the clergy of the church of Scotland, and afterwards received considerable accessions of strength.[3] Some of the most eminent of the clergy,—including Dr. Chalmers and Dr. Candlish,—were its leaders. Their eloquence and character insured the popularity of the movement; and those who denied the justice of their cause, and blamed them

---

[1] Sydow's Scottish Church Question, 1845; D'Aubigné's Germany, England, and Scotland, 377–459; Buchanan's Ten Years' Conflict, 433–449.

[2] Ann. Reg., 1843, p. 250; D'Aubigné's Germany, England, and Scotland, 443–459.

[3] Of 947 parish ministers, 214 seceded; and of 246 *quoad sacra* ministers, 144 seceded.—Ann. Reg., 1843, p. 255; Speech of Lord Aberdeen, June 13th, 1843; Hans. Deb., 3rd Ser., lxix. 1414; Buchanan, ii. 464, 468; Hannay's Life of Dr. Chalmers.

as the authors of a grievous schism, could not but admire their earnestness and noble self-denial. Men highly honoured in the church, had sacrificed all they most valued, to a principle which they conscientiously believed to demand that sacrifice. Their once crowded churches were surrendered to others, while they went forth to preach on the hill-side, in tents, in barns, and stables. But they relied, with just confidence, upon the sympathies and liberality of their flocks;[1] and in a few years the spires of their free kirks were to be seen in most of the parishes of Scotland.

When this lamentable secession had been accomplished, the government at length undertook to legislate upon the vexed question of patronage. In 1840, Lord Aberdeen had proposed a bill, in the vain hope of reconciling the conflicting views of the two parties in the church; and this bill he now offered, with amendments, as a settlement of the claims of patrons, the church, and the people. The Veto Act had been pronounced illegal, as it delegated to the people the functions of the church courts; and in giving the judgment of the House of Lords, it had been laid down that a presbytery in judging of the qualifications of a minister were restricted to an inquiry into his 'life, literature, and doctrine.' The bill, while denying a capricious veto to the people, recognised their right of objecting

Patronage Act, 1843.

---

[1] In eighteen years they contributed 1,251,458*l*. for the building of churches, manses, and schools; and for all the purposes of their new establishment no less a sum than 5,229,631*l*.—Tabular abstracts of sums contributed to Free Church of Scotland to 1858–1859, with MS. additions for the two following years, obtained through the kindness of Mr. Dunlop, M.P.

to a presentation, in respect of 'ministerial gifts and qualities, either in general, or with reference to that particular parish;' of which objections the presbytery were to judge. In other words, they might show that a minister, whatever his general qualifications, was unfitted for a particular parish. He might be ignorant of Gaelic, among a Gaelic population: or too weak in voice to preach in a large church: or too infirm of limb to visit the sick in rough Highland glens. It was argued, that with so wide a field of objection, the veto was practically transferred from the people to the presbytery; and that the bill being partly declaratory, amounted to a partial reversal of the judgment of the Lords in the Auchterarder case. But after learned discussions in both Houses, it was passed by Parliament, in the hope of satisfying the reasonable wishes of the moderate party in the church, who respected the rights of patrons, yet clung to the Calvinistic principle which recognised the concurrence of the people.[1] To the people was now given the full privilege of objection; and to the church judicatories the exclusive right of judgment.

The secession of 1843, following prior schisms, augmented the religious disunion of Scotland; and placed a large majority of the people out of communion with the state church,—which the nation itself had founded at the Reformation.[2]

Religious disunion in Scotland.

---

[1] Lords' Deb., June 13th, July 3rd, 17th, 1843; Hans. Deb., 3rd Ser., lxix. 1400; lxx. 534, 1202; Commons Deb., July 31st, Aug. 10th, 1843; Hans. Deb., lxxi. 10, 517; 6 & 7 Vict. c. 61; Buchanan, ii. 458.

[2] In 1851, of 3,395 places of worship, 1,183 belonged to the Estab-

Let us now turn, once more, to the history of the church in Ireland. Originally the church of a minority, she had never extended her fold. On the contrary, the rapid multiplication of the Catholic peasantry had increased the disproportion between the members of her communion, and a populous nation. At the Union, indeed, she had been united to her powerful sister church in England;[1] and the weakness of one gained support from the strength of the other. The law had joined them together; and constitutionally they became one church. But no law could change the essential character of the Irish Establishment, or its relations to the people of that country. In vain were English Protestants reckoned among its members. No theory could disturb the proportion of Protestants and Catholics in Ireland. While the great body of the people were denied the rights of British subjects, on account of their religion, that grievance had caused the loudest complaints. But in the midst of the sufferings and discontents of that unhappy land, jealousy of the Protestant church, aversion to her endowed clergy, and repugnance to contribute to the maintenance of the established religion, were ever proclaimed as prominent causes of disaffection and outrage.

Church in Ireland.

---

lished Church; 889 to the Free Church; 465 to the United Presbyterian Church; 112 to the Episcopal Church; 104 to Roman Catholics; and 642 to other religious denominations, embracing most of the sects of English dissenters. On the census Sunday 228,757 attended the morning service of the Established Church; and no less than 255,482 that of the Free Church (Census Returns, 1851). In 1860, the latter had 234,953 communicants.

[1] Act of Union, Art. 5.

Foremost among the evils by which the church and the people were afflicted, was the law of tithes. However impolitic in England,[1] its policy was aggravated by the peculiar condition of Ireland. In the one country, tithes were collected from a few thriving farmers,—generally members of the church: in the other, they were levied upon vast numbers of cottier tenants,—miserably poor, and generally Catholics.[2] Hence, the levy of tithes, in kind, provoked painful conflicts between the clergy and the peasantry. Statesmen had long viewed the law of tithes with anxiety. So far back as 1786, Mr. Pitt had suggested the propriety of a general commutation, as a measure calculated to remove grievances and strengthen the interests of the church.[3] In 1807, the Duke of Bedford, attributing most of the disorders of the country to the rigid exaction of tithes, had recommended their conversion into a land tax, and ultimately into land.[4] Repeated discussions in Parliament had revealed the magnitude of the evils incident to the law. Sir John Newport, in 1822,[5] and Sir Henry Parnell, in 1823,[6] had exposed them. In 1824, Lord Althorp

Resistance to tithes.

---

[1] *Supra*, p. 218.

[2] In one parish 200*l.* were contributed by 1,600 persons; in another 700*l.*, by no less than 2,000.—Second Report of Commons Committee, 1832. In a parish in the county of Carlow, out of 446 tithe-payers 221 paid sums under 9*d.*; and out of a body of 7,005, in several parishes, one-third paid less than 9*d.* each.—*Mr. Littleton's Speech*, Feb. 20th, 1834.

[3] Letter to the Duke of Rutland; Lord Stanhope's Life, i. 319. See also Lord Castlereagh's Corr., iv. 193 (1801).

[4] Speech of Lord J. Russell, June 23rd, 1834; Hans. Deb., 3rd Ser., xxiv. 798.

[5] Hans. Deb., 2nd Ser., vi. 1475; Mr. Hume also, March 4th, 1823; *Ibid.*, viii. 367.

[6] *Ibid.*, ix. 1175.

and Mr. Hume had given them a prominent place among the grievances of Ireland.[1] The evils were notorious, and remaining without correction, grew chronic and incurable. The peasants were taught by their own priesthood, and by a long course of political agitation, to resent the demands of the clergy as unjust: their poverty aggravated the burden; and their numbers rendered the collection of tithes not only difficult, but dangerous. It could only be attempted by tithe-proctors,—men of desperate character and fortunes, whose hazardous services hardened their hearts against the people,—and whose rigorous execution of the law increased its unpopularity. To mitigate these disorders, an Act was passed, in 1824, for the voluntary composition of tithes: but the remedy was partial; and resistance and conflicts continued to increase with the bitterness of the strife, that raged between Protestants and Catholics. At length, in 1831, the collection of tithes in many parishes became impracticable. The clergy received the aid of the police, and even of the military: but in vain. Tithe-proctors were murdered; and many lives were lost, in collisions between the police and the peasantry. Men, not unwilling to pay what they knew to be lawful, were intimidated and coerced by the more violent enemies of the church. Tithes could only be collected at the point of the bayonet; and a civil war seemed impending over a country, which for centuries had been wasted by conquests, rebellions, and internecine strife. The clergy shrank from the

---

[1] Hans. Deb., 2nd Ser., xi. 547, 660.

shedding of blood in their service; and abandoned their claims upon a refractory and desperate people.

The law was at fault; and the clergy, deprived of their legal maintenance, were starving, or dependent upon private charity.[1] That the law must be reviewed, was manifest: but in the meantime, immediate provision was needed for the clergy. The state, unable to protect them in the enforcement of their rights, deemed itself responsible for their sufferings, and extended its helping hand. In 1832, the Lord-lieutenant was empowered to advance 60,000*l.* to the clergy who had been unable to collect the tithes of the previous year;[2] and the government rashly undertook to levy the arrears of that year, in repayment of the advance. Their attempt was vain and hopeless. They went forth, with an array of tithe-proctors, police, and military: but the people resisted. Desperate conflicts ensued: many lives were lost: the executive became as hateful as the clergy: but the arrears were not collected. Of 100,000*l.*, no more than 12,000*l.* were recovered, at the cost of tumults and bloodshed.[3] The people were in revolt against the law, and triumphed. The government, confessing their failure, abandoned their fruitless efforts; and in 1833, obtained from Parliament the advance of a million, to maintain the destitute clergy, and cover the arrears of tithes, for that and the two previous years. Indemnity

Provision for the clergy, 1832–1833.

---

[1] Reports of Committees in Lords and Commons, 1832. Ann. Reg., 1831, p. 324; 1832, p. 281.
[2] Act, 2 & 3 Will. IV. c. 41.
[3] Speech of Mr. Littleton; Hans. Deb., 3rd Ser., xx. 342.

for this advance, however, was sought in the form of a land tax, which, it needed little foresight to conjecture, would meet with the same resistance as tithes.[1] These were temporary expedients, to meet the immediate exigencies of the Irish clergy; and hitherto the only general measure which the legislature had sanctioned, was one for making the voluntary tithe compositions compulsory and permanent.[2]

Meanwhile, the difficulties of the tithe question were bringing into bold relief the anomalous condition of the Irish Church. Resistance to the payment of tithes was accompanied by fierce vituperation of the clergy, and denunciations of a large Protestant establishment, in the midst of a Catholic people. The Catholic priests and agitators would have trampled upon the church as an usurper: the Protestants and Orangemen were prepared to defend her rights with the sword. Earl Grey's government, leaning to neither extreme, recognised the necessity of extensive reforms and reductions in the establishment. Notwithstanding the spoliations of Henry VIII. and Elizabeth, its endowments were on the ambitious scale of a national church. With fewer members than a moderate diocese in England, it was governed by no less than four archbishops and eighteen bishops. Other dignitaries enjoyed its temporalities in the same proportion; and many sinecure benefices were even without Protestant flocks.

Irish church reform.

[1] 3 & 4 Will. IV. c. 100; Hans. Deb., 3rd Ser., xx. 350.
[2] 2 & 3 Will. IV. c. 119.

Such an establishment could not be defended;
and in 1833, ministers introduced an extensive measure of reform. It suppressed, after the interests of existing incumbents, two archbishoprics, and eight separate sees; and reduced the incomes of some of the remaining bishops. All sinecure stalls in cathedrals were abolished, or associated with effective duties. Livings, in which no duties had been performed for three years, were not to be filled up. First fruits were abolished. Church cess,—an unpopular impost, similar to church rates in England,—levied upon Catholics, but managed by Protestant vestries,—was discontinued; and the repair of churches provided for out of a graduated tax upon the clergy. Provision was made for the improvement of church lands; for the augmentation of small livings, and for the building of churches and glebe houses, under the superintendence of a commission, by whom the surplus revenues of the church were to be administered.[1]

Church Temporalities (Ireland) Bill, 1833.

So bold were these reforms, that even Mr. O'Connell at first expressed his satisfaction: yet while they discontinued the most prominent abuses of the establishment, they increased its general efficiency. In the opinion of some extreme Tories, indeed, the measure was a violation of the coronation oath, and the stipulations of the Union with Ireland: it was an act of spoliation: its principles were revolutionary. But by men of more moderate views,

---

[1] Lord Althorp's Speech, Feb. 12th, 1833; Hans. Deb., 3rd Ser., xv. 561.

its justice and necessity were generally recognised.[1]

One principle, however, involved in the scheme became the ground of painful controversy; and long interfered with the progress of other measures conceived in the interests of the church. *Principle of appropriation.* A considerable sum was expected to be derived from the grant of perpetual leases of church lands; and the question was naturally raised, how was it to be disposed of? Admitting the first claims of the church,—what was to become of any surplus, after satisfying the needs of the establishment? On one side, it was maintained that the property of the church was inalienable; and that nothing but its redistribution, for ecclesiastical purposes, could be suffered. On the other, it was contended that the church had no claim to the increased value given to her lands by an Act of Parliament; and that, in any case, the legislature was free to dispose of church revenues, for the public benefit. The bill provided that the monies accruing from the grant of these perpetuities should be applied, in the first instance, in redemption of charges upon parishes, for building churches; and any surplus, to such purposes as Parliament might hereafter direct.[2] Ministers, fearing that the recognition of this principle of appropriation, even in so vague a form, would endanger their measure in the House of Lords, abandoned it in committee,—to the *June 21st, 1833.* disgust of Mr. O'Connell and his followers, and of

---

[1] Debate on second reading, May 6th; Hans. Deb., 3rd Ser., xvii. 966. [2] Clause 147.

many members of the liberal party. Mr. O'Connell asked what benefit the Irish people could now hope to derive from the measure, beyond the remission of the church cess? The church establishment would indeed be reduced; but the people would not save a single shilling by the reduction.[1] In truth, however, the clause had not expressly declared that the revenues of the church were applicable to state purposes. Its retention would not have affirmed the principle: its omission did not surrender any rights which the legislature might, hereafter, think fit to exercise. Whenever the surplus should actually arise, Parliament might determine its appropriation. Yet both parties otherwise interpreted its significance; and it became the main question at issue between the friends and opponents of the church, who each foresaw, in the recognition of an abstract principle, the ultimate alienation of the revenues of the Irish establishment. For the present, a concession being made to the fears of the church party, the bill was agreed to by both Houses.[2] But the conflict of parties, upon the controverted principle, was by no means averted.

In the next session, Mr. Ward, in a speech of singular ability, called upon the House of Commons to affirm a resolution that the church establishment in Ireland exceeded the spiritual wants of the Protestant population; and that it being the right of the state to

Church in Ireland: Mr. Ward's motion, May 27th, 1834.

---

[1] Hans. Deb., 3rd Ser., xviii. 1073; Ann. Reg., 1833, p. 104.
[2] Church Temporalities (Ireland) Act, 3 & 4 Will. IV. c. 37.

regulate the distribution of church property, the temporal possessions of the church in Ireland ought to be reduced.[1] This resolution not only asserted the principle of appropriation: but disturbed the recent settlement of the ecclesiastical establishment in Ireland. It was fraught with political difficulties. The cabinet had already been divided upon the principles involved in this motion; and the discussion was interrupted for some days by the resignation of Mr. Stanley, Sir James Graham, the Duke of Richmond, and the Earl of Ripon. The embarrassment of ministers was increased by a personal declaration of the King against innovations in the church, in reply to an address of the Irish bishops and clergy.[2] The motion, however, was successfully met by the appointment of a commission to inquire into the revenues and duties of the church, and the general state of religious instruction in Ireland. *Superseded by appointment of a commission, June 2nd, 1834.* Hitherto there had been no certain information either as to the revenues of the church, or the numbers of different religious communions in the country; and ministers argued that, until these facts had been ascertained, it could not with propriety be affirmed that the establishment was excessive. At the same time, the appointment of the commission implied that Parliament would be prepared to deal with any surplus which might be proved to exist, after providing for the wants of the Protestant population.

[1] Hans. Deb., 3rd Ser., xxiii. 1368.
[2] May 28th, 1834; Ann. Reg., 1834, 43.

On these grounds the previous question was moved, and carried by a large majority.[1]

A few days afterwards, the propriety of issuing this commission, and the rights of the state over the distribution of church property, were warmly debated in the House of Lords.

<small>Lords' debate on appropriation. June 6th, 1834.</small>

While one party foresaw spoliation as the necessary result of the proposed inquiry, and the other disclaimed any intentions hostile to the church, it was agreed on all sides that such an inquiry assumed a discretionary power in the state, over the appropriation of church property.[2] Earl Grey boldly avowed, that if it should appear that there was a considerable excess of revenue, beyond what was required for the efficiency of the church and the propagation of divine truth, 'the state would have a right to deal with it with a view to the exigencies of the state and the general interests of the country.'[3]

Meanwhile, the difficulties of the question of Irish tithes were pressing. Ministers had introduced a bill, early in the session, for converting tithes into a land tax, payable to the government by the landlords, and subject to redemption. When redeemed, the proceeds were to be invested in land for the benefit of the church.[4] The merits of this measure were repeatedly discussed, and the scheme itself materially modified in its pro-

<small>Irish tithes associated with appropriation.</small>

---

[1] For the motion, 120; for the previous question, 396.—Hans. Deb., 3rd Ser., xxiv. 10.

[2] Hans. Deb., 3rd Ser., xxiv. 243.

[3] Hans. Deb., 3rd Ser., xxiv. 254.

[4] Mr. Littleton's Explanation, Feb. 20th, 1834.—Hans. Deb., 3rd Ser., xxi. 572.

gress: but the question of appropriation bore a foremost place in the discussions. Mr. O'Connell viewed with alarm a plan securing to the church a perpetual vested interest in tithes, which could no longer be collected; and threatened the landlords with a resistance to rent, when it embraced a covert charge for the maintenance of the Protestant church. Having opposed the measure itself, on its own merits, he endeavoured to pledge the House to a resolution, that any surplus of the funds to be raised in lieu of tithes, after providing for vested interests and the spiritual wants of the church, should be appropriated to objects of public utility.[1] Disclaiming any desire to appropriate these funds for Catholic or other religious uses, he proposed that they should be applied to purposes of charity and education. On the part of ministers, Lord Althorp and Lord John Russell again upheld the right of the state to review the distribution of church property, and apply any surplus according to its discretion. Nor did they withhold their opinion, that the proper appropriation would be to kindred purposes, connected with the moral and religious instruction of the people. But they successfully resisted the motion as an abstract proposition, prematurely offered.[2] Soon afterwards, Lord Grey's administration was suddenly dissolved: but the Tithe Bill was continued by Lord Melbourne. Many amendments, however, were made,—including one

June 23rd, 1834.

---

[1] Amendment on going into committee.—Hans. Deb., 3rd Ser., xxiv. 734.

[2] It was negatived by a majority of 261. Ayes, 99; Noes, 360.—Hans. Deb., 3rd Ser., xxiv. 805.

forced upon ministers by Mr. O'Connell, by which the tithe-payer was immediately relieved to the extent of forty per cent. After all these changes, the bill was rejected, on the second reading, by the House of Lords.[1] Again the clergy were left to collect their tithes, under increased difficulties and discouragement.

In the next session, Sir Robert Peel had succeeded to the embarrassments of Irish tithes and the appropriation question. As to the first, he offered a practical measure for the commutation of tithes into a rent-charge upon the land, with a deduction of twenty-five per cent. Provision was also made for its redemption, and the investment of the value in land, for the benefit of the church. He further proposed to make up the arrears of tithes in 1834, out of the million already advanced to the clergy.[2] But the commutation of tithes was not yet destined to be treated as a practical measure. It had been associated, in the late session, with the controverted principle of appropriation,— which now became the rallying point of parties. It had severed from Lord Grey some of his ablest colleagues, and allied them with the opposite party.

Sir Robert Peel's measure for commuting Irish tithes, 1835.

Sir Robert Peel, on accepting office, took an early opportunity of stating that he would not give his 'consent to the alienation of church property, in any part of the United Kingdom, from strictly ecclesiastical purposes.' On the other hand, in the first discussion upon

Appropriation question adopted by the Whigs in opposition, 1835.

---

[1] Aug. 11th, 1834. Hans. Deb., 3rd Ser., xxv. 1143.
[2] Hans. Deb., *Ibid.*, xxvii. 13.

Irish tithes, Lord John Russell expressed his doubts whether any advantage would result from the abolition of tithes, without a prior decision of the appropriation question: and Mr. O'Connell proclaimed that the word 'appropriation would exert a magical influence in Ireland.' The Whigs, exasperated by their sudden dismissal,[1] were burning to recover their ground: but the liberal measures of the new ministry afforded few assailable points. Sir Robert Peel, however, had taken his stand upon the inviolability of church property; and the assertion of the contrary doctrine served to unite the various sections of the opposition. The Whigs, indeed, were embarrassed by the fact that they had themselves deprecated the adoption of any resolution, until the commission had made its report; and this report was not yet forthcoming. But the exigencies of party demanded a prompt and decisive trial of strength. Lord John Russell, therefore, pressed forward with resolutions affirming that any surplus revenues of the church of Ireland, not required for the spiritual care of its members, should be applied to the moral and religious education of all classes of the people; and that no measure on the subject of tithes would be satisfactory which did not embody that principle. These resolutions were affirmed by small majorities;[2] and Sir Robert Peel was driven from power.

[1] *Supra*, Vol. I. p. 145.
[2] On April 2nd a committee of the whole House was obtained by a majority of 33.—Hans. Deb., 3rd Ser., xxvii. 362, 770, &c. On April 6th, the first resolution was agreed to in committee by a majority of 25; and on the 7th, the second resolution was affirmed by

It was an untoward victory. The Whigs had pledged themselves to connect the settlement of tithes with the appropriation of the surplus revenues of the church of Ireland. The Conservatives were determined to resist that principle; and having a large majority in the House of Lords, their resistance was not to be overcome.

Appropriation under Lord Melbourne.

Meanwhile, the position of ministers was strengthened by the disclosure of the true state of the church. Out of a population of 7,943,940 persons, there were 852,064 members of the establishment; 6,427,712 Roman Catholics, 642,356 Presbyterians; and 21,808 Protestant dissenters of other denominations. The state church embraced little more than a tenth of the people.[1] Her revenues amounted to 865,525*l.* In 151 parishes there was not a single Protestant: in 194 there were less than ten: in 198 less than twenty: and in 860 parishes there were less than fifty.[2]

Revenues of the church of Ireland.

These facts were dwelt upon in support of appropriation, which formed part of every bill for the commutation of tithes. But the Lords had taken their stand upon a principle; and were not to be shaken. Tithes were still withheld from the clergy; and the feelings of the people

Appropriation abandoned, 1838.

---

the House on the report by a majority of 27.—Comm. Journ., xc. 202, 208; Hans. Deb., 3rd Ser., xxvii. 790, 837, 878.

[1] 1st Report of Commissioners on Public Instruction, Ireland (1835), p. 7.

[2] Lord Morpeth's Speech, 1835; Hans. Deb., 3rd Ser., xxviii. 1339. The latter number comprises the parishes previously enumerated.

were embittered by continual discussions relating to the church; while bill after bill was sacrificed to clauses of appropriation. This mischievous contest between the two Houses was brought to a close in 1838, by the abandonment of the appropriation clause by ministers themselves. It was, indeed, bitter and humiliating: but it was unavoidable. The settlement of tithes could no longer be deferred; and any concession from the Lords was hopeless. But the retirement of the Whigs from a position, which they had chosen as their own battlefield, was a grievous shock to their influence and reputation. They lost the confidence of many of their own party, —forfeited public esteem,—and yielded to the opposition an exultant triumph which went far to restore them to popular favour, and ultimately to power.[1]

But if ruin awaited the Whigs, salvation was at hand for the church of Ireland. Tithes were at length commuted into a permanent rent-charge upon the land; and the clergy amply indemnified for a sacrifice of one-fourth the amount, by unaccustomed security and the peaceable enjoyment of their rights. They were further compensated for the loss of arrears, out of the balance of the million, advanced by Parliament as a loan in 1833, and eventually surrendered as a free gift.[2] The church had passed through a period of trials and danger; and was again at peace. The grosser abuses of her establishment were gradually corrected,

Commutation of Irish tithes, 1838.

[1] See especially Debates, May 14th and July 2nd, 1838. Hans. Deb., 3rd Ser., xlii. 1203; xliii. 1177.
[2] 1 & 2 Vict. c. 109.

under the supervision of the ecclesiastical commissioners: but its diminished revenues were devoted exclusively to the promotion of its spiritual efficiency.

While the state protected the Protestant church, it had not been unmindful of the interests of the great body of the people, who derived no benefit from her ministrations. In 1831 a national system of education was established, embracing the children of persons of all religious denominations.[1] It spread and flourished, until, in 1860, 803,364 pupils received instruction,—of whom 663,145 were Catholics,[2]—at an annual cost to the state of 270,000*l*.[3]

National education in Ireland.

In 1845, Sir Robert Peel adventured on a bold measure for promoting the education of Catholic priests in Ireland.[4] Prior to 1795, the laws forbade the endowment of any college or seminary for the education of Roman Catholics in Ireland; and young men in training for the priesthood were obliged to resort to colleges on the continent, and chiefly to France, to prepare themselves for holy orders. But the French revolutionary war having nearly closed Europe against them, the government were induced to found the Roman Catholic College of Maynooth.[5] It was a friendly

Maynooth College, 1845.

---

[1] On Sept. 9th, 1831, 30,000*l*. were first voted for this purpose.—Hans. Deb., 3rd Ser., vi. 1249. Commissioners were appointed by the Lord-lieutenant to administer the system in 1832, and incorporated by letters patent in 1845.

[2] 28th Report of Commissioners, 1861, No. [3026], pp. 10, 11, &c.

[3] The sum voted in 1860 was 270,722*l*.

[4] April 3rd, 1845. Hans. Deb., lxxix. 18.

[5] Irish Act, 35 Geo. III. c. 21; Cornwallis Corr., iii. 365-375; Lord Stanhope's Life of Pitt, ii. 311.

concession to the Catholics; and promised well for the future loyalty of the priesthood. The college was supported by annual grants of the Parliament of Ireland, which were continued by the United Parliament, after the Union. The connection of the state with this college had been sanctioned in the days of Protestant ascendency in Ireland; and was continued without objection by George III.,—the most Protestant of kings,—and by the most Protestant of his ministers, at a time when prejudices against the Catholics had been fomented to the utmost. But when more liberal sentiments prevailed concerning the civil rights of the Catholics, a considerable number of earnest men, both in the church and in other religious bodies, took exceptions to the endowment of an institution, by the state, for teaching the doctrines of the church of Rome. 'Let us extend to Catholics,' they said, 'the amplest toleration: let us give them every encouragement to found colleges for themselves: but let not a Protestant state promote errors and superstitions: ask not a Protestant people to contribute to an object abhorrent to their feelings and consciences.' On these grounds the annual grant had been for some time opposed, while the college,—the unfortunate object of discussion,—was neglected and falling into decay. In these circumstances, Sir Robert Peel proposed to grant 30,000*l.* for buildings and improvements,—to allow the trustees of the college to hold lands to the value of 3,000*l.* a year,—and to augment the endowment from less than 9,000*l.* a year to 26,360*l.* To give permanence to this endowment, and to avoid irritating discussions, year after year, it was charged upon the Consolidated Fund.[1]

Having successfully defended the revenues of the Protestant church, he now met the claims of the Catholic clergy in a liberal and friendly spirit. The concession infringed no principle which the more niggardly votes of former years had not equally infringed: but it was designed at once to render the college worthy of the patronage of the state, and to conciliate the Catholic body. He was supported by the first statesmen of all parties, and by large majorities in both Houses: but the virulence with which his conciliatory policy was assailed, and the doctrines of the church of Rome denounced, deprived a beneficent act of its grace and courtesy.

If the consciences of Protestants were outraged by contributing, however little, to the support of the Catholic faith, what must have been the feelings of Catholic Ireland towards a Protestant church, maintained for the use of a tenth of the people! It would have been well to avoid so painful a controversy: but it was raised; and the Act of 1845, so far from being accepted as the settlement of a vexed question, appeared for several years to aggravate the bitterness of the strife. But the state, superior to sectarian animosities, calmly acknowledged the claims of Catholic subjects upon its justice and liberality. Governing a vast empire, and ruling over men of different races and religions, it had already aided the propa-

State aid given to other religions.

---

[1] April 3rd, 1845. Hans. Deb., 3rd Ser., lxxix. 18. See also Supplementary Chapter.

gation of doctrines which it disowned. In Ireland itself, the state has provided for the maintenance of Roman Catholic chaplains in prisons and workhouses. A different policy would have deprived the inmates of those establishments, of all the offices and consolations of religion. It has provided for the religious instruction of Catholic soldiers; and since the reign of William III. the Presbyterians of Ireland received aid from the state, known as the Regium Donum. In Canada, Malta, Gibraltar, the Mauritius and other possessions of the crown, the state has assisted Catholic worship. Its policy has been imperial and secular,—not religious.

In the same enlarged spirit of equity, Sir Robert Peel secured, in 1845, the foundation of three new colleges in Ireland, for the improvement of academical education, without religious distinctions. *Queen's colleges, Ireland, 1845.* These liberal endowments were mainly designed for Catholics, as composing the great body of the people: but they who had readily availed themselves of the benefits of national education,—founded on the principle of a combined literary and separate religious instruction,—repudiated these new institutions. Being for the use of all religious denominations, the peculiar tenets of no particular sect could be allowed to form part of the ordinary course of instruction: but lecture-rooms were assigned for the purpose of religious teaching, according to the creed of every student.[1] The Catholics, however, withheld their confidence from a system in which their own faith was not recognised

---

[1] Hans. Deb., 3rd Ser., lxxx. 345; 8 & 9 Vict. c. 66.

as predominant; and denounced the new colleges as 'godless.' The Roman Catholic Synod of Thurles prohibited the clergy of their communion from being concerned in the administration of these establishments;[1] and their decrees were sanctioned by a rescript of the Pope.[2] The colleges were everywhere discountenanced as seminaries for the sons of Catholic parents. The liberal designs of Parliament were so far thwarted; yet, even under these discouragements, the colleges enjoyed a fair measure of success. A steady increase of pupils of all denominations has been maintained;[3] the education is excellent; and the best friends of Ireland are still hopeful that a people of rare aptitude for learning will not be induced, by religious jealousies, to repudiate the means of intellectual cultivation, which the state has invited them to accept.[4]

[1] August, 1850.   [2] May 23rd, 1851.
[3] In 1858 the commissioners of inquiry reported:—'The colleges cannot be regarded otherwise than as successful.'—*Report of Commissioners*, 1858, No. [2413.] In 1860, the entrances had increased from 168 to 309; and the numbers attending lectures, from 454 to 752. Of the latter number, 207 were members of the Established Church; 204, Roman Catholics; 247, Presbyterians; and 94 of other persuasions.—*Report of President* for 1860–61, 1862, No. [2999].
[4] As to recent legislation concerning religious establishments in Ireland, see Supplementary Chapter.

CHAPTER XV.

LOCAL GOVERNMENT THE BASIS OF CONSTITUTIONAL FREEDOM:—VESTRIES:—MUNICIPAL CORPORATIONS IN ENGLAND, SCOTLAND, AND IRELAND:—LOCAL IMPROVEMENT AND POLICE ACTS:—LOCAL BOARDS CONSTITUTED UNDER GENERAL ACTS:—COURTS OF QUARTER SESSIONS.

THAT Englishmen have been qualified for the enjoyment of political freedom, is mainly due to those ancient local institutions by which they have been trained to self-government. The affairs of the people have been administered, not in Parliament only, but in the vestry, the town-council, the board-meeting, and the Court of Quarter Sessions. England alone among the nations of the earth has maintained for centuries a constitutional polity; and her liberties may be ascribed, above all things, to her free local institutions. Since the days of their Saxon ancestors,[1] her sons have learned, at their own gates, the duties and responsibilities of citizens. Associating, for the common good, they have become exercised in public affairs. Thousands of small communities have enjoyed the privileges of self-government: taxing themselves, through their representatives, for local objects: meeting for discussion and business; and animated by local rivalries and ambitions. The

Local government the basis of constitutional freedom.

[1] Palgrave's English Commonwealth, i. 628; Allen's Prerog., 128.

history of local government affords a striking parallel to the general political history of the country. While the aristocracy was encroaching upon popular power in the government of the state, it was making advances, no less sure, in local institutions. The few were gradually appropriating the franchises which were the birthright of the many; and again, as political liberties were enlarged, the rights of self-government were recovered.

Every parish is the image and reflection of the state. The land, the church, and the commonalty share in its government: the aristocratic and democratic elements are combined in its society. The common law,—in its grand simplicity,—recognised the right of all the rated parishioners to assemble in vestry, and administer parochial affairs.[1] But in many parishes this popular principle gradually fell into disuse; and a few inhabitants, — self-elected and irresponsible,— claimed the right of imposing taxes, administering the parochial funds, and exercising all local authority. This usurpation, long acquiesced in, grew into a custom, which the courts recognised as a legal exception from the common law. The people had forfeited their rights; and select vestries ruled in their behalf. So absolute was their power, that they could assemble without notice, and bind all the inhabitants of the parish by their vote.[2]

The parish.

The vestry.

The select vestry.

This single abuse was corrected by Mr. Sturges

---

[1] Shaw's Par. Law, c. 17; Steer's Par. Law, 253; Toulmin Smith's Parish, 2nd edn., 15–23, 46–52, 288–330.

[2] Gibson's Codex, 219; Burn's Eccl. Law, iv. 10, &c.; Steer, 251.

Bourne's Act in 1818:[1] but this same act, while it left select vestries otherwise un-reformed, made a further inroad upon the popular constitution of open vestries. Hitherto every person entitled to attend, had enjoyed an equal right of voting; but this act multiplied the votes of vestrymen according to the value of their rated property: one man could give six votes: others no more than one. *Mr. Sturges Bourne's Act, 1818.*

An important breach, however, was made in the exclusive system of local government, by Sir John Hobhouse's Vestry Act, passed during the agitation for parliamentary reform.[2] The majority of ratepayers, in any parish, within a city or town, or any other parish comprising 800 householders rated to the poor, were empowered to adopt this act. Under its provisions, vestries were elected by every rated parishioner: the votes of the electors were taken by ballot: every ten-pound householder, except in certain cases,[3] was eligible as a vestryman: and no member of the vestry was entitled to more than a single vote. This measure, however democratic in principle, did little more than revert to the policy of the common law. It was adopted in some populous parishes in *Sir John Hobhouse's Act, 1831.*

---

[1] 58 Geo. III. c. 69, amended by 59 Geo. III. c. 85, 7 Will. IV. and 1 Vict. c. 35; Report on Poor Laws, 1818.—Hans. Deb., 1st Ser., xxxviii. 573.

[2] 1 & 2 Will. IV. c. 60; Oct. 20th, 1831; Toulmin Smith's Parish, 240.

[3] In the metropolis, or in any parish having more than 3,000 inhabitants, a 40*l.* qualification was required. In the metropolis, however, the act was superseded by the Metropolis Local Management Act, 1855.—*Infra,* 297.

the metropolis and elsewhere: but otherwise has had a limited operation.[1]

Municipal corporations, England. The history of municipal corporations affords another example of encroachments upon popular rights. The government of towns, under the Saxons, was no less popular than the other local institutions of that race;[2] and the constitution of corporations, at a later period, was founded upon the same principles. All the settled inhabitants and traders of corporate towns, who contributed to the local taxes, had a voice in the management of their own municipal affairs.[3] The community, enjoying corporate rights and privileges, was continually enlarged by the admission of men connected with the town by birth, marriage, apprenticeship or servitude, and of others, not so connected, by gift or purchase. For some centuries after the conquest, the burgesses assembled in person, for the transaction of business. They elected a mayor, or other chief magistrate: but no governing body, or town-council, to whom their authority was delegated. The burgesses only were known to the law. But as towns and trade increased, the more convenient practice of representation was introduced for municipal as well as for parliamentary government. The most wealthy and influential inhabitants being

[1] In 1842, nine parishes only had adopted it.—Parl. Paper, 1842, No. 564.
[2] Palgrave's English Commonwealth, i. 629; Merewether and Stephens' Hist. of Boroughs, Introd. viii.; Kemble's Hist., ii. 262; Lappenberg's England, App.; Hallam's Middle Ages, ii. 153.
[3] Report of Commissioners on Municipal Corporations, 1835, p. 16; Merewether and Stephens' Hist., Introd. v. 1, 10, &c.; Hallam's Middle Ages, ii. 155.

chosen, gradually encroached upon the privileges of the inferior townsmen, assumed all municipal authority, and substituted self-election for the suffrages of burgesses and freemen. This encroachment upon popular rights was not submitted to without many struggles: but at the close of the fifteenth century, it had been successfully accomplished in a large proportion of the corporations of England.

Until the reign of Henry VII., these encroachments had been local and spontaneous. The people had submitted to them: but the law had not enforced them. From this time, however, popular rights were set aside in a new form. The crown began to grant charters to boroughs,—generally conferring or reviving the privilege of returning members to Parliament; and most of these charters vested all the powers of municipal government in the mayor and town council,—nominated in the first instance by the crown itself, and afterwards self-elected. Nor did the contempt of the Tudors for popular rights stop here. By many of their charters, the same governing body was intrusted with the exclusive right of returning members to Parliament. For national as well as local government, the burgesses were put beyond the pale of the constitution. And in order to bring municipalities under the direct influence of the crown and the nobility, the office of high steward was often created: when the nobleman holding that office became the patron of the borough, and returned its members to Parliament. The power of the crown and aristocracy was increased, at the ex-

Charters from Henry VII. to the Revolution.

pense of the liberties of the people. The same policy was pursued by the Stuarts; and the two last of that race violated the liberties of the few corporations which still retained a popular constitution, after the encroachments of centuries.[1]

After the Revolution, corporations were free from the intrusion of prerogative: but the policy of municipal freedom was as little respected as in former times. A corporation had come to be regarded as a close governing body, with peculiar privileges. The old model was followed; and the charters of George III. favoured the municipal rights of burgesses no more than the charters of Elizabeth or James I.[2] Even where they did not expressly limit the local authority to a small body of persons,—custom and usurpation restricted it either to the town council, or to that body and its own nominees, the freemen. And while this close form of municipal government was maintained, towns were growing in wealth and population, whose inhabitants had no voice in the management of their own affairs Two millions of people were denied the constitutional privilege of self-government.

Corporations from the Revolution to George III.

Self-elected and irresponsible corporations were suffered to enjoy a long dominion. Composed of local, and often hereditary cliques and family connexions, they were absolute masters over their own townsmen. Generally of one political party, they excluded men of different opinions,

Abuses of close corporations.

---

[1] Case of Quo Warranto, 1683; St. Tr., viii. 1039; Hume's Hist., vi. 201; remodelling the corporations, 1687; Hallam's Const. Hist., ii. 238.
[2] Report of Commissioners, p. 17.

—whether in politics or religion,—and used all the influence of their office for maintaining the ascendency of their own party. Elected for life, it was not difficult to consolidate their interest; and they acted without any sense of responsibility.[1] Their proceedings were generally secret: nay, secrecy was sometimes enjoined by an oath.[2]

Despite their narrow constitution, there were some corporations which performed their functions worthily. Maintaining a mediæval dignity and splendour, their rule was graced by public virtue, courtesy and refinement. Nobles shared their councils and festivities: the first men of the county were associated with townsmen: and while ruling without responsibility, they retained the willing allegiance of the people, by traditions of public service, by acts of munificence and charity, and by the respect due to their eminent station. But the greater number of corporations were of a lower type. Neglecting their proper functions,—the superintendence of the police, the management of the gaols, the paving and lighting of the streets, and the supply of water,—they thought only of the personal interests attached to office. They grasped all patronage, lay and ecclesiastical, for their relatives, friends, and political partisans; and wasted the corporate funds in greasy feasts and vulgar revelry.[3] Many were absolutely insolvent. Charities were despoiled, and public trusts neglected and misapplied: jobbery and corruption in every form were

[1] Report of Commissioners, p. 36.   [2] Ibid., 36.
[3] Ibid., p. 46.

fostered.[1] Townsmen viewed with distrust the proceedings of councils, over whom they had no control,—whose constitution was oligarchical,—and whose political sentiments were often obnoxious to the majority. In some towns the middle classes found themselves ruled by a close council alone: in others by the council and a rabble of freemen,—its creatures,—drawn mainly from the lower classes, and having no title to represent the general interests of the community. Hence important municipal powers were often intrusted, under Local Acts, to independent commissioners, in whom the inhabitants had confidence.[2] Even the administration of justice was tainted by suspicions of political partiality.[3] Borough magistrates were at once incompetent, and exclusively of one party; and juries were composed of freemen, of the same close connexion. This favoured class also enjoyed trading privileges, which provoked jealousy and fettered commerce.[4]

But the worst abuse of these corrupt bodies, was *Monopoly of electoral rights.* that which too long secured their impunity. They were the strongholds of Parliamentary interest and corruption. The electoral privileges which they had usurped, or had acquired by charter, were convenient instruments in the hands of both the political parties, who were contending for power. In many of the corporate towns the representation was as much at the disposal of particular families, as that of nomination boroughs: in

---

[1] Rep. of Commissioners, 31, 46, 47, 48.
[2] Ibid., 43.
[3] Ibid., 26-29, 39.
[4] Ibid., 40.

others it was purchased by opulent partisans, whom both parties welcomed to their ranks. In others, again, where freemen enjoyed the franchise, it was secured by bribery, in which the corporations too often became the most active agents,—not scrupling even to apply their trust funds to the corruption of electors.[1] The freemen were generally needy and corrupt, and inferior, as well in numbers as in respectability, to the other inhabitants:[2] but they often had an exclusive right to the franchise; and whenever a general election was anticipated, large additions were made to their numbers.[3] The freedom of a city was valued according to the length of the candidate's purse. Corporations were safe so long as society was content to tolerate the notorious abuses of Parliamentary representation. The municipal and Parliamentary organisations were inseparable: both were the instruments by which the crown, the aristocracy, and political parties had dispossessed the people of their constitutional rights; and they stood and fell together.

The Reform Act wrested from the corporations their exclusive electoral privileges, and restored them to the people. This tardy act of retribution was followed by the appointment of a commission of inquiry, which roughly exposed the manifold abuses of irresponsible power, wherever it had been suffered to prevail. And in 1835, Parliament was called upon to overthrow these municipal oligarchies. The measure was fitly intro-

The Municipal Corporations Bill, 1835.

---

[1] Rep. of Comm., 45.   [2] Ibid., 33.
[3] Ibid., 34, 35. (See table of freemen created.)

duced by Lord John Russell, who had been foremost in the cause of Parliamentary reform.[1] It proposed to vest the municipal franchise in rated inhabitants who had paid poor-rates within the borough for three years. By them the governing body, consisting of a mayor and common council, were to be elected. The ancient order of aldermen was to be no longer maintained. The pecuniary rights of existing freemen were preserved during their lives: but their municipal franchise was superseded; and as no new freemen were to be created, the class would be eventually extinguished. Exclusive rights of trading were to be discontinued. To the councils, constituted so as to secure public confidence, more extended powers were intrusted, for the police and local government of the town, and the administration of justice; while provision was made for the publicity of their proceedings, the proper administration of their funds, and the publication and audit of their accounts.

No effective opposition could be offered to the general principles of this measure. The propriety of restoring the rights of self-government to the people, and sweeping away the corruptions of ages, was generally admitted: but strenuous efforts were made to give further protection to existing rights, and to modify the popular character of the measure. These efforts, ineffectual in the Commons, were successful in the Lords Counsel was heard, and witnesses examined, on behalf of several of the corporations: but the main principles of the bill were not contested. Important

Amended by the Lords.

---

[1] June 5th, 1835.—Hans. Deb., 3rd Ser., xxviii. 541.

amendments, however, were inserted. The pecuniary rights and parliamentary franchise of freemen received more ample protection. With a view to modify the democratic constitution of the councils, a property qualification was required for town councillors; and aldermen were introduced into the council, to be elected for life; the first aldermen being chosen from the existing body of aldermen.[1] Those amendments were considered by ministers and the Commons, in a spirit of concession and compromise. The more zealous advocates of popular rights urged their unconditional rejection, even at the sacrifice of the bill: but more temperate councils prevailed, and the amendments were accepted with modifications. A qualification for councillors was agreed to, but in a less invidious form: aldermen were to be elected for six years, instead of for life; and the exclusive eligibility of existing aldermen was not insisted on.[2] And thus was passed a popular measure, second in importance to the Reform Act alone.[3] The municipal bodies which it created, if less popular than under the original scheme, were yet founded upon a wide basis of representation, which has since been further extended.[4] Local self-government was effectually restored. Elected rulers have since generally secured the confidence of their constituents: municipal office has become an object of honourable ambition to public-spirited townsmen; and local administration,—if not free from

[1] Hans. Deb., 3rd Ser., xxx. 426, 480, 579, &c.
[2] *Ibid.*, xxx. 1132, 1194, 1335.
[3] 5 & 6 Will. IV. c. 76.
[4] Municipal Corporations Act, 1859, 22 Vict. c. 35.

abuses,[1] has been exercised under responsibility and popular control. And further, the enjoyment of municipal franchises has encouraged and kept alive a spirit of political freedom, in the inhabitants of towns.

Corporation of London. One ancient institution alone was omitted from this general measure of reform,—the corporation of the City of London. It was a municipal principality,—of great antiquity, of wide jurisdiction, of ample property and revenues,—and of composite organisation. Distinguished for its public spirit, its independent influence had often been the bulwark of popular rights. Its magistrates had braved the resentment of kings and Parliaments: its citizens had been foremost in the cause of civil and religious liberty. Its traditions were associated with the history and glories of England. Its civic potentates had entertained, with princely splendour, kings, conquerors, ambassadors and statesmen. Its wealth and stateliness, its noble old Guildhall and antique pageantry, were famous throughout Europe. It united, like an ancient monarchy, the memories of a past age, with the pride and powers of a living institution.

Efforts to reform it. Such a corporation as this could not be lightly touched. The constitution of its governing body: its powerful companies or guilds: its courts of civil and criminal jurisdiction: its varied municipal functions: its peculiar customs: its extended powers of local taxation,—all these

---

[1] See Reports of Lords' Committees on Rates and Municipal Franchise, 1859, and Elective Franchise, 1860.

demanded careful inquiry and consideration. It was not until 1837 that the commissioners were able to prepare their report; and it was long before any scheme for the reconstitution of the municipality was proposed. However superior to the close corporations which Parliament had recently condemned, many defects and abuses needed correction. Some of these the corporation itself proceeded to correct; and others it sought to remedy, in 1852, by means of a private bill. In 1853, another commission of eminent men was appointed, whose able report formed the basis of a government measure in 1856.[1] This bill, however, was not proceeded with; nor have later measures, for the same purpose hitherto been accepted by Parliament.[2] Yet it cannot be doubted that this great institution will be eventually brought into harmony with the recognised principles of free municipal government.

The history of municipal corporations in Scotland resembles that of England, in its leading characteristics. The royal burghs, being the property of the crown, were the first to receive corporate privileges. The earlier burgesses were tenants of the crown, with whom were afterwards associated the trades or crafts of the place, which comprised the main body of inhabitants. In the fourteenth century, the constitution of these municipalities appears to have become popular; and the growing influence and

Corporations in Scotland.
Royal burghs.

[1] Sir George Grey, April 1st, 1856.—Hans. Deb., 3rd Ser., cxli. 314.
[2] Sir George Grey, 1858.—Hans. Deb., 3rd Ser., cxlviii. 738; Sir George Lewis, 1859 and 1860. *Ibid.*, cliv. 946; clvi. 282.

activity of the commonalty excited the jealousy of more powerful interests.[1] The latter, without waiting for the tedious expedient of usurpation, obtained an Act of the Scottish Parliament in 1469, which deprived the burgesses of their electoral rights, and established a close principle of self-election. The old council of every burgh was to choose the new council for the year, and the two councils together, with one person representing each craft, were to elect the burgh officers.[2]

Other burghs. Municipal privileges were also granted to other burghs, under the patronage of territorial nobles, or the church. The rights of burgesses varied in different places: but they were generally dependent upon their patrons.

Close character of these municipalities. Neither of these two classes of municipalities had enjoyed for centuries the least pretence of a popular constitution. Their property and revenues, their rights of local taxation, their patronage, their judicature, and the election of representatives in Parliament, were all vested in small self-elected bodies. The administration of these important trusts was characterised by the same abuses as those of English corporations. The property was corruptly alienated and despoiled: sold to nobles and other favoured persons,—sometimes even to the provost himself,—at inadequate prices: leased at nominal rents to members of the council; and improvidently charged with debts.[1] The revenues were wasted by extravagant salaries,—jobbing con-

---

[1] Rep. of Commrs, 1835, p. 18. [2] Scots Acts, 1469, c. 5.
[3] Rep., 1835, p. 30.

tracts, — public works executed at an exorbitant cost,—and civic entertainments.[1] By such maladministration several burghs were reduced to insolvency.[2] Charitable funds were wasted and misapplied:[3] the patronage, distributed among the ruling families, was grossly abused. Incompetent persons, and even boys, were appointed to offices of trust. At Forfar, an idiot performed for twenty years the responsible duties of town clerk. Lucrative offices were sold by the councils.[4] Judicature was exercised without fitness or responsibility. The representation formed part of the narrow parliamentary organisation by which Scotland, like her sister kingdoms, was then governed.

Many of these abuses were notorious at an early period; and the Scottish Parliament frequently interposed to restrain them.[5] They continued, however, to flourish; and were exposed by parliamentary inquiries in 1793, and again in 1819, and the two following years.[6] The latter were followed by an Act in 1822, regulating the accounts and administration of the royal burghs, checking the expenditure, and restraining abuses in the sale and leasing of property, and the contracting of debts.[7] But it was reserved for the first reformed Parliament to deal with the greatest evil,

Municipal reforms, Scotland. 1833.

---

[1] Rep., 1821, p. 14; Rep., 1835, p. 34.
[2] Rep., 1819, p. 15, 23; *Ibid.*, 1835, p. 36.
[3] Rep., 1819, p. 23; *Ibid.*, 1835, p. 38.
[4] Rep., 1820, p. 4; *Ibid.*, 1835, p. 67.
[5] Scots Acts, 1491, c. 19; 1503, c. 36, 37; 1535, c. 35; 1593, c. 39; 1693, c. 45; Rep. of 1835, p. 22–28.
[6] Rep. of Comm. Committees, 1819, 1820, and 1821.
[7] 3 Geo. IV. c. 91.

and the first cause of all other abuses—the close constitution of these burghs. The Scotch Reform Act had already swept away the electoral monopoly which had placed the entire representation of the country in the hands of the government and a few individuals; and in the following year, the ten pound franchise was introduced as the basis of new municipal constitutions. The system of self-election was overthrown, and popular government restored. The people of Scotland were impatient for this remedial measure; and, the abuses of the old corporate bodies being notorious, Parliament did not even wait for the reports of commissioners appointed to inquire into them: but proceeded at once to provide a remedy. The old fabric of municipal administration fell without resistance, and almost in silence: its only defence being found in the protest of a solitary peer.[1]

In the corporations of Ireland, popular rights had been recognised, at least in form,—though the peculiar condition of that country had never been favourable to their exercise. Even the charters of James I., designed to narrow the foundations of corporate authority, usually incorporated the inhabitants, or commonalty of boroughs.[2] The ruling bodies, however, having the power of admitting freemen, whether resident or not, readily appropriated all the power and patronage of local administration. In the greater number of boroughs, the council, or other ruling body, was practically self-

Corporations, Ireland.

---

[1] Hans. Deb., 3rd Ser., xx. 563-576; 3 & 4 Will. IV. c. 76, 77.
[2] Rep. of Commrs. 1835, p. 7.

elected. The freemen either had no rights, or were debarred, by usurpation, from asserting them. In other boroughs, where the rights of freemen were acknowledged, the council were able to overrule the inhabitants by the voices of non-resident freemen, —their own nominees and creatures. Close self-election, and irresponsible power, were the basis of nearly all the corporations of Ireland.[1] In many boroughs, patrons filled the council with their own dependents, and exercised uncontrolled authority over the property, revenues, and government of the municipality.

It were tedious to recount the more vulgar abuses of this system. Corporate estates appropriated, or irregularly acquired by patrons, and others in authority: leases corruptly granted: debts recklessly contracted: excessive tolls levied, to the injury of trade and the oppression of the poor: exclusive trading privileges enjoyed by freemen, to the detriment of other inhabitants: the monopoly of patronage by a few families: the sacrifice of the general welfare of the community to the particular interests of individuals: such were the natural results of close government in Ireland, as elsewhere.[2] The proper duties of local government were neglected or abused; and the inhabitants of the principal towns were obliged to seek more efficient powers for paving, lighting, and police, under separate boards constituted by local Acts, or by a general measure of 1828, enacted for that pur-

Their abuses.

[1] Rep. of Commrs., p. 13-18.
[2] *Ibid.*, 17-38.

pose.[1] But there were constitutional evils greater than these. Corporate towns returned members to Parliament; and the patrons, usurping the franchises of the people, reduced them to nomination boroughs.

Exclusion of Catholics. But, above all, Catholics were everywhere excluded from the privileges of municipal government. The remedial law of 1793, which restored their rights,[2] was illusory. Not only were they still denied a voice in the council: but even admission to the freedom of their own birthplaces. A narrow and exclusive interest prevailed,—in politics, in local administration, and in trade,—over Catholic communities, however numerous and important.[3] Catholics could have no confidence either in the management of municipal trusts, or in the administration of justice. Among their own townsmen, their faith had made them outlaws.

The Reform Act established a new elective franchise on a wider basis; and the legislature soon afterwards addressed itself to the consideration of the evils of municipal misgovernment. But the Irish corporations were not destined to fall, like the Scotch burghs, without a struggle.

Irish Corporations Bills.

In 1835, Lord Melbourne's government introduced a bill for the reconstitution of the Irish corporations, upon the same principles as those already applied to other parts of the United Kingdom. It was passed by the Commons without much discussion: but was not proceeded

Corporations (Ireland) Bill. 1835.

---

[1] 9 Geo. IV. c. 82; Rep. of Commrs., p. 21.
[2] 33 Geo. III. c. 21 (Irish). *Supra*, p. 111.
[3] Rep. of Commrs., p. 16.

with in the Lords, on account of the late period of the session.[1] In the following year it was renewed, with some modifications:[2] when it encountered new obstacles. The Protestant party in Ireland were suffering under grave discouragements. Catholic emancipation and Parliamentary. reform had overthrown their dominion : their church was impoverished by the refusal of tithes, and threatened with an appropriation of her revenues ; and now their ancient citadels, the corporations, were invested. Here they determined to take their stand. Their leaders, however, unable openly to raise this issue, combated the measure on other grounds. Adverting to the peculiar condition of Ireland, they claimed an exceptional form of local government. Hitherto, it was said, all local jurisdiction had been exercised by one exclusive party. Popular election would place it in the hands of another party, no less dominant. If the former system had caused distrust in local government and in the administration of justice, the proposed system would cause equal jealousy on the other side. Catholic ascendency would now be the rule of municipal government. Nor was there a middle class in Ireland equal to the functions proposed to be intrusted to them. The wealth and intelligence of Protestants would be overborne and outnumbered by an inferior class of Catholic townsmen. It was denied that boroughs had ever enjoyed a popular franchise. The corporations prior to James I. had

Renewed in 1836.

[1] Hans. Deb., 3rd Ser., xxx. 230, 614, &c.
[2] *Ibid.*, xxxi. 496, 1019.

been founded as outworks of English authority, among a hostile people; and after that period, as citadels of Protestant ascendency. It was further urged that few of the Irish boroughs required a municipal organisation. On these grounds Sir Robert Peel and the opposition proposed a fundamental change in the ministerial scheme. They consented to the abolition of the old corporations: but declined to establish new municipal bodies in their place. They proposed to provide for the local administration of justice by sheriffs and magistrates appointed by the crown: to vest all corporate property in royal commissioners, for distribution for municipal purposes; and to intrust the police and local government of towns to boards elected under the General Lighting and Watching Act of 1828.[1]

The Commons would not listen to proposals for denying municipal government to Ireland, and vesting local authority in officers appointed by the crown: but the Lords eagerly accepted them; and the bill was lost.[2]

In the following year, a similar measure was again passed by the Commons, but miscarried in the other House by reason of delays, and the king's death. In 1838, the situation of parties and the determined resistance of the Lords to the Irish policy of the government, brought about concessions and compromise. Ministers, by abandoning the principle of appropriation,

Bill of 1837.

Bill of 1838-9.

---

[1] Debates on second reading, Feb. 29th, and on Lord F. Egerton's instruction, March 7th.—Hans. Deb., 3rd Ser., xxxi. 1050, 1308.
[2] Hans. Deb., 3rd Ser., xxxiv. 963, &c.

in regard to the Irish Church revenues, at length attained a settlement of the tithe question; and it was understood that the Lords would accept a corporation bill. Yet in this and the following years the two Houses disagreed upon the municipal franchise and other provisions; and again the ministerial measures were abandoned. In 1840, a sixth bill was introduced, in which large concessions were made to the Lords.[1] Further amendments, however, were introduced by their lordships, which ministers and the Commons were constrained to accept. The tedious controversy of six years was at length closed: but the measure virtually amounted to a scheme of municipal disfranchisement.

Bill of 1840.

Ten corporations only were reconstituted by the bill, with a ten pound franchise. Fifty-eight were abolished:[2] but any borough with a population exceeding 3,000 might obtain a charter of incorporation. The local affairs and property of boroughs, deprived of corporations, were to be under the management of commissioners elected according to the provisions of the General Lighting and Watching Act, or of the poor-law guardians.[3] The measure was a compromise; and, however imperfect as a general scheme of local government, it at least corrected the evils of the old system, and closed an irritating contest between two powerful parties.

The Irish Corporations Act, 1840.

The reconstitution of municipal corporations,

---

[1] Hans. Deb., 3rd Ser., li. 641; liii. 1160; lv. 183, 1216.
[2] Schedules B and C of Act.   [3] 3 & 4 Vict. c. 108.

upon a popular basis, has widely extended the principle of local self-government. The same principle has been applied, without reserve, to the management of other local affairs. Most of the principal towns of the United Kingdom have obtained Local Acts, at different times, for improvements,—for lighting, paving, and police,—for waterworks,—for docks and harbours; and in these measures, the principle of elected and responsible boards has been accepted as the rule of local administration. The functions exercised under these Acts are of vast importance, not only to the localities immediately concerned, but to the general welfare of the community. The local administration of Liverpool resembles that of a maritime state. In the order and wise government of large populations, by local authority, rests the general security of the realm. And this authority is everywhere based upon representation and responsibility. In other words, the people who dwell in towns have been permitted to govern themselves.

Local Improvement and Police Acts.

Extensive powers of administration have also been intrusted to local boards constituted under general statutes for the sanitary regulation, improvement, and police of towns and populous districts.[1] Again, the same principle was adopted in the election of boards of guardians for the administration of the new poor

Local boards constituted under General Acts.

---

[1] Public Health Act, 1848; Local Government Act, 1858; Toulmin Smith's Local Government Act, 1858; Glen's Law of Public Health and Local Government; Police (Scotland) Acts, 1850; Towns' Improvement (Scotland) Act, 1860; Police and Improvement (Scotland) Act, 1862, consolidating previous Acts.

laws, throughout the United Kingdom. And lastly, in 1855, the local affairs of the metropolis were intrusted to the Metropolitan Board of Works,—a free municipal assembly,—elected by a popular constituency, and exercising extended powers of taxation and local management.[1]

The sole local administration, indeed, which has still been left without representation, is that of counties; where rates are levied and expenditure sanctioned by magistrates appointed by the crown. Selected from the nobles and gentry of the county for their position, influence, and character, the magistracy undoubtedly afford a virtual representation of its interests. The foremost men assemble and discuss the affairs in which they have themselves the greatest concern: but the principles of election and responsibility are wanting. This peculiarity was noticed in 1836 by the commission on county rates;[2] and efforts have since been made, first by Mr. Hume,[3] and afterwards by Mr. Milner Gibson,[4] to introduce responsibility into county administration. It was proposed to establish financial boards, constituted of members elected by boards of guardians, and of magistrates chosen by themselves. To the representative principle itself few objections were offered; but no scheme for

Courts of Quarter Sessions.

---
[1] Metropolis Local Management Acts, 1855, 1862. Toulmin Smith's Metropolis Local Management Act.
[2] The Commissioners said: 'No other tax of such magnitude is laid upon the subject, except by his representatives.' . . . 'The administration of this fund is the exercise of an irresponsible power intrusted to a fluctuating body.'
[3] In 1837 and 1839.—Hans. Deb., 3rd Ser., cvi. 125.
[4] In 1840, and subsequently.—*Ibid.*, cviii. 738.

carrying it into effect has yet found favour with the legislature.

Counties represent the aristocratic, towns the democratic, principles of our constitution. In counties, territorial power, ancestral honours, family connexions, and local traditions have dominion. The lords of the soil still enjoy influence and respect, little less than feudal. Whatever forms of administration may be established, their ascendency is secure. Their power is founded upon the broad basis of English society: not upon laws or local institutions. In towns, power is founded upon numbers and association. The middle classes,—descendants and representatives of the stout burghers of olden times,—have sway. The wealth, abilities, and public virtues of eminent citizens may clothe them with influence: but they derive authority from the free suffrages of their fellow-citizens, among whom they dwell. The social differences of counties and towns have naturally affected the conditions of their local administration and political tendencies: but both have contributed, in different ways, to the good government of the state.

Distinctive character of counties and towns.

CHAPTER XVI.

GOVERNMENT OF IRELAND BEFORE THE UNION : — THE LEGISLATURE AND THE EXECUTIVE : — PROTESTANT ASCENDENCY : — IRELAND A DEPENDENCY :—COMMERCIAL RESTRICTIONS :—THE VOLUNTEERS :— LEGISLATIVE AND JUDICIAL INDEPENDENCE GRANTED 1782 :—THE UNITED IRISHMEN AND OTHER ASSOCIATIONS :—THE REBELLION OF 1798 :—THE UNION :—ITS BENEFITS DEFERRED :—FREEDOM AND EQUALITY FINALLY ASSURED.

WE have seen liberty steadily advancing, in every form, and under every aspect, throughout our political and religious institutions. And nowhere has its advance been more conspicuous than in Ireland. In that country, the English laws and constitution had been established as if in mockery.[1] For ages its people were ruled, by a conquering and privileged race, as aliens and outlaws.[2] Their lands were wrested from them: their rights trampled under foot: their blood and their religion proscribed.[3]

Progress of liberty in Ireland.

Before George III, commenced his reign, the dawn of better days was brightening the horizon; yet, what was then the political condition of his Irish subjects? They were governed by a Parliament, whence every

Government of Ireland before the Union.

---

[1] Leland, Hist., i. 80, &c.; Plowden's Hist., i. 33.
[2] Davis, 100, 109.
[3] For the earlier history of Ireland, see Plowden, i. 1-332; Leland, Prelim. Discourse; O'Halloran; Moore ; and a succinct but comprehensive outline by Hallam, Const. Hist., chap. xviii.

Catholic was excluded. The House of Lords was composed of prelates of the Protestant church, and of nobles of the same faith,—owners of boroughs, patrons of corporations, masters of the representation, and in close alliance with the Castle.[1]

The Lords.

The House of Commons assumed to represent the country: but the elective franchise,—narrow and illusory in other respects,—was wholly denied to five-sixths of the people,[2]—on account of their religion.[3] Every vice of the English representative system was exaggerated in Ireland. Nomination boroughs had been more freely created by the crown:[4] in towns, the members were returned by patrons or close corporations: in counties, by great proprietors. In an assembly of 300, twenty-five lords of the soil alone returned no less than 116 members.[5] A comparatively small number of patrons returned a majority; and, acting in concert, were able to dictate their own terms to the government. So well were their influence and tactics recognised, that they were known as the 'Parliamentary undertakers.'[6] Theirs was not an ambition to be satisfied with political power and ascen-

The Commons.

---

[1] Hardy's Life of Lord Charlemont, i. 102.

[2] Primate Boulter admitted that there were five Catholics to one Protestant in the reign of George II.—Plowden's Hist., i. 269, 271; Grattan's Life, i. 64.

[3] 2 Geo. I. c. 19; 1 Geo. II. c. 9, s. 7.

[4] Leland, ii. 437; Plowden's Hist., i. 109; App. xv. xvi.; Carte's Ormond, i. 18; Lord Mountmorres' Hist. of the Irish Parliament, i. 166, &c.; Desiderata Curiosa Hibernica, 308; Moore's Hist., iv. 164.

[5] Massey (on the authority of the Bolton MSS.) Hist., iii. 264. See also Wakefield's Statistical and Political Account of Ireland, ii. 301.

[6] Wilkinson's Survey of South of Ireland, 57; Adolphus' Hist., i. 161.

dency: they claimed more tangible rewards,—titles, offices, pensions,—for themselves, their relatives and dependents. Self-interest and corruption were all but universal, in the entire scheme of parliamentary government. Two-thirds of the House of Commons, on whom the government generally relied, were attached to its interest by offices, pensions, or promises of preferment.[1] Patrons and nominees alike exacted favours; and in five-and-twenty years, the Irish pension list was trebled.[2] Places and pensions, the price of parliamentary services, were publicly bought and sold in the market.[3] But these rewards, however lavishly bestowed, failed to satisfy the more needy and prodigal, whose fidelity was purchased from time to time with hard cash.[4] Parliamentary corruption was a recognised instrument of government: no one was ashamed of it. Even the Speaker, whose office should have raised him above the low intrigues and sordid interests of faction, was mainly relied upon for the management of the House of Commons.[5] And this corrupt and servile assembly, once intrusted with power, might continue to abuse it for an indefinite period. If not subservient to the crown, it was dissolved: but, however neglectful of the rights and interests of the people, it was firmly installed as

Parliament expired only on demise of crown.

---

[1] Plowden's Hist., i. 360, 375. See also analysis of the ministerial majority in 1784, in the Bolton MSS., Massey's Hist., iii. 265.
[2] Plowden's Hist., i. 451; *supra*, Vol. I. p. 256.
[3] Plowden's Hist., i. 364, 378.
[4] Plowden's Hist., i. 374; Irish Debates, i. 139; Grattan's Life, i. 97; Walpole's Journ., i. 399.
[5] Hardy's Life of Lord Charlemont, i. 88.

their master. The law made no provision for its expiration, save on the demise of the crown itself.

Such being the legislature, to whom the rights of the people were intrusted,—the executive power was necessarily in the hands of those who corruptly wielded its authority. The lord-lieutenant, selected from English nobles of the highest rank, was generally superior to the petty objects of local politicians: but he was in the hands of a cabinet consisting of men of the dominant faction,—intent upon continuing their own power,—and ministering to the ambition and insatiable greed of their own families and adherents. Surrounded by intrigues and troubles, he escaped as much as possible from the intolerable thraldom of a residence in Ireland; and, in his absence, three men governed the country absolutely, as lords justices. Contending among themselves for influence and patronage, they agreed in maintaining the domination of a narrow oligarchy, and the settled policy of Protestant ascendency.[1] As if to mark the principles of such a rule, the primate bore the foremost place in the administration of affairs.[2]

The executive.

The proscription of Catholics at once insured the power, and ministered to the cupidity of the ruling party. Every judge, every magistrate, every officer,—civil, military and corporate,—was a

Monopoly of power and office.

---

[1] Plowden's Hist., i. 370; Adolphus' Hist., 159-161; Grattan's Life, i. 97.
[2] On the accession of George III., the lords justices were the primate, Dr. Stone, Lord Shannon, a former speaker, and Mr. Ponsonby, then holding the office of Speaker.

churchman. No Catholic could practise the law,[1] or serve upon a jury. The administration of justice, as well as political power, was monopolised by Protestants. A small junto distributed among their select band of followers all the honours and patronage of the state. Every road to ambition was closed against Catholics,—the bar, the bench, the army, the senate, and the magistracy. And Protestant nonconformists, scarcely inferior in numbers to churchmen, fared little better than Catholics. They were, indeed, admitted to a place in the legislature, but they were excluded, by a Test Act, from every civil office, from the army, and from corporations, and, even where the law failed to disqualify them, they might look in vain for promotion to a clique who discerned merit in none but churchmen. Such were the rights and liberties of the Irish people; and such the character and policy of their rulers.

And while the internal polity of Ireland was exclusive, illiberal, and corrupt, the country, in its relations to England, still bore the marks of a conquered province. The Parliament was not a free legislature, with ample jurisdiction in making laws and voting taxes. By one of 'Poynings' Acts,'[2] in the reign of Henry VII., the Irish Parliament was not summoned until the Acts it was called upon to pass had already been approved and certified, under the great seal, in England. Such Acts it might discuss and reject, but could not amend. This restriction, however, was afterwards relaxed; and laws were certified in the

Subordination of Ireland to the English government.

---

[1] Plowden's Hist., i. 271.   [2] 10 Henry VII. c. 4 (Irish).

same manner, after the opening of Parliament.'[1] Parliament could say 'aye' or 'no' to the edicts of the crown: but could originate nothing itself. Even money bills were transmitted to the Commons in the same imperial form. Soon after the revolution, the Commons had vainly contended for the privilege of originating grants to the crown, like their English prototypes: but their presumption was rebuked by the chief governor, and the claim pronounced unfounded by the judges of both countries.[2] The rejection of a money bill was also visited with rebuke and protest.[3]

The Irish Parliament, however, released itself from this close thraldom by a procedure more consonant with English usage, and less openly obnoxious to their independence. Heads of bills were prepared by either House, and submitted to the Privy Council in Ireland, by whom they were transmitted to the king, or withheld at their pleasure. If approved by His Majesty, with or without amendments, they were returned to the House in which they had been proposed, where they were read three times, but could not be amended.[4] The crown, however, relinquished no part of its prerogative; and money bills continued to be transmitted from the Privy Council, and were accepted by the Commons.[5]

[1] 3 & 4 Philip and Mary, c. 4 (Irish); Lord Mountmorres' Hist. of Irish Parl., i. 48–50; Blackstone's Comm. (Kerr), 1, 84.
[2] Lord Mountmorres' Hist., i. 47; ii. 142, 184.
[3] In 1692.—Com. Journ. (Ireland), ii. 35; Lord Mountmorres' Hist., i. 54; Hardy's Life of Lord Charlemont, i. 246.
[4] Lord Mountmorres' Hist., i. 58, 63; Plowden's Hist., i. 395, n.
[5] In 1760 a Bill was so transmitted and passed.—Grattan's Life, i. 57.

These restrictions were marks of the dependence of the legislature upon the crown: other laws and customs proclaimed its subordination to the Parliament of England. That imperial senate asserted and exercised the right of passing laws 'to bind the people and kingdom of Ireland;' and in the sixth of George I. passed an Act explicitly affirming this right, in derogation of the legislative authority of the national council sitting in Dublin.[1] Its judicature was equally overborne. The appellate jurisdiction of the Irish House of Lords was first adjudged to be subordinate to that of the highest court of appeal in England, and then expressly superseded and annulled by a statute of the English Parliament.[2] The legislature of Ireland was that of a British dependency. Whether such a Parliament were free or not, may have little concerned the true interests of the people of Ireland, who owed it nothing but bondage: but the national pride was stung by a sense of inferiority and dependence.

Supremacy of the Parliament of England.

The subordination of Ireland was further testified in another form, at once galling to her pride, and injurious to her prosperity. To satisfy the jealous instincts of English traders, her commerce had been crippled with intolerable prohibitions and restraints. The export of her produce

Commercial restrictions.

---

[1] 10 Henry VII. c. 22 (Irish); Carte's Life of Ormond, iii. 55; Lord Mountmorres' Hist., i. 360; Comm. Journ. (England), June 27th and 30th, 1698; Parl. Hist., v. 1181; Plowden's Hist., i. 244; Statute 6 Geo. I. c. 5.

[2] 6 Geo. I. c. 5.—Parl. Hist., vii. 642; Lord Mountmorres' Hist., i. 339.

and manufactures to England was nearly interdicted: all direct trade with foreign countries and British possessions prohibited. Every device of protective and prohibitory duties had been resorted to, for insuring a monopoly to English commerce and manufactures. Ireland was impoverished, that English traders should be enriched.[1]

Such were the laws and government of Ireland when George III. succeeded to its crown; and for many years afterwards. Already a 'patriot' party had arisen to expose the wrongs of their country, and advocate her claims to equality: but hitherto their efforts had been vain. A new era, however, was now about to open; and a century of remedial legislation to be commenced, for repairing the evils of past misgovernment.

New era opened under George III.

One of the first improvements in the administration of Ireland was a more constant residence of the lord-lieutenant. The mischievous rule of the lords justices was thus abated, and even the influence of the Parliamentary undertakers impaired: but the viceroy was still fettered by his exclusive cabinet.[2]

Residence of lord-lieutenant.

Attempts were made so early as 1761 to obtain a septennial Act for Ireland, which resulted in the passing of an octennial bill, in 1768.[3]

Octennial Act, 1768.

---

[1] 32 Charles II. c. 2, prohibited the export of cattle, sheep, and live stock; 10 & 11 Will. III. c. 10, interdicted the export of wool; and other statutes imposed similar restraints. See Parl. Hist., xix. 1100, *et seq.*; Swift's Tract on Irish Manufactures, 1720; Works, vii. 15; Short View of the State of Ireland, 1727.—*Ibid.*, 324.

[2] Adolphus' Hist., i. 331.

[3] This difference between the law of the two countries was introduced to prevent the confusion of a general election, on both sides of the Channel, at the same time.—Walpole's Mem., iii. 155; Lord

Without popular rights of election, this new law was no great security for freedom, but it disturbed, early in the reign of a young king, the indefinite lease of power, hitherto enjoyed by a corrupt confederacy; while discussion and popular sentiments were beginning to exercise greater influence over the legislature.

A new Parliament was called, after the passing of the Act, in which the country party gained ground. The government vainly attempted to supplant the undertakers in the management of the Commons, and were soon brought into conflict with that assembly. The Commons rejected a money bill, 'because it did not take its rise in that House;' and in order to prove that they had no desire to withhold supplies from the crown, they made a more liberal provision than had been demanded. The lord-lieutenant, however, Lord Townshend, marked his displeasure at this proceeding, by proroguing Parliament as soon as the supplies were voted; and protesting against the vote and resolution of the Commons, as a violation of the law, and an invasion of the just rights of the crown.[1] So grave was this difference, that the lord-lieutenant suspended the further sitting of Parlia- *Conflict between the Executive and the Commons, 1769.* *Claim to originate money bills, 1769.* *Repeated prorogations.*

Chesterfield's Letters, iv. 468; Plowden's Hist., i. 352, 387; Hardy's Life of Lord Charlemont, i. 248-261.

[1] Lords' Journ. (Ireland), iv. 538. The lord-lieutenant, not contented with this speech on the prorogation, further entered a separate protest in the Lords' Journal.—Commons' Journal (Ireland), viii. 323; Debates of Parliament of Ireland, ix. 181; Plowden's Hist. of Ireland, i. 396; ii. 251; Grattan's Mem., i. 98-101; Lord Mountmorres' Hist., i. 54; Hardy's Life of Lord Charlemont, i. 290.

ment, by repeated prorogations, for fourteen months,[1] —a proceeding which did not escape severe animadversion in the English Parliament.[2] Parliament, when at length reassembled, proved not more tractable than before. In December, 1771, the Commons rejected a money bill because it had been altered in England;[3] and again in 1773, pursued the same course, for the like reason, in regard to two other money bills.[4] In 1775, having consented to the withdrawal of four thousand troops from the Irish establishment, it refused to allow them to be replaced by Protestant troops from England,[5]—a resolution which evinced the growing spirit of national independence. And in the same year, having agreed upon the heads of two money bills,[6] which were returned by the British cabinet with amendments, they resented this interference by rejecting the bills and initiating others, not without public inconvenience and loss to the revenue.[7] This first octennial Parliament exhibited other signs of an intractable temper, and was dissolved in 1776.[8] Nor did government venture to meet the new Parliament for nearly eighteen months.[9]

Marginal dates: Dec. 21, 1771. Oct. and Nov. 1775.

---

[1] From Dec. 26th, 1769, till Feb. 26th, 1771; Comm. Journ. (Ireland), viii. 354; Plowden's Hist., i. 401.

[2] Mr. G. M. Walsingham, May 3rd, 1770; Parl. Hist., v. 309.

[3] Comm. Journ. (Ireland), viii. 467; Adolphus, ii. 14; Life of Grattan, i. 174–185.

[4] Dec. 27th, 1773: Comm. Journ. (Ireland), ix. 74.

[5] Comm. Journ. (Ireland), ix. 223; Grattan's Life, i. 268.

[6] Viz. a Bill for additional duties on beer, tobacco, &c.; and another, imposing stamp duties.

[7] Dec. 21, 1775; Comm. Journ., Ireland, ix. 244; Plowden's Hist., i. 435.

[8] Plowden's Hist., i. 441.

[9] The old Parliament was prorogued in June 1776, and after-

In the meantime, causes superior to the acts of a government, the efforts of patriots, and the combinations of parties, were rapidly advancing the independence of Ireland. The American colonies had resented restrictions upon their trade, and the imposition of taxes by the mother country; and were now in revolt against the rule of England. Who could fail to detect the parallel between the cases of Ireland and America? The patriots accepted it as an encouragement, and their rulers as a warning. The painful condition of the people was also betraying the consequences of a selfish and illiberal policy. The population had increased with astonishing fecundity. Their cheap and ready food, the potato,—and their simple wants, below the standard of civilised life,—removed all restraints upon the multiplication of a vigorous and hardy race. Wars, famine, and emigration had failed to arrest their progress: but misgovernment had deprived them of the means of employment. Their country was rich in all the gifts of God,—fertile, abounding with rivers and harbours, and adapted alike for agriculture, manufactures, and commerce. But her agriculture was ruined by absentee landlords, negligent and unskilful tenants, half-civilised cottiers; and by restraints upon the free export of her produce. Her manufactures and commerce,—the natural resources of a growing population,—were crushed by the jealousy of English rivals. To the

Effect of the American war.

Condition of the people.

---

wards dissolved: the new Parliament did not meet till October 14th, 1777.—Comm. Journ., ix. 289, &c. Plowden's Hist., i. 441.

ordinary restraints upon her industry was added, in 1776, an embargo on the export of provisions.[1] And while the industry of the people was repressed by bad laws, it was burthened by the profusion and venality of a corrupt government. What could be expected in such a country, but a wretched, ignorant, and turbulent peasantry, and agrarian outrage? These evils were aggravated by the pressure of the American war, followed by hostilities with France.[2] The English ministers and Parliament were awakened by the dangers which threatened the state, to the condition of the sister country; and England's peril became Ireland's opportunity.

Commercial restrictions removed, 1778. Encouragement had already been given to the Irish fisheries in 1775;[3] and in 1778, Lord Nugent, supported by Mr. Burke, and favoured by Lord North, obtained from the Parliament of England a partial relaxation of the restrictions upon Irish trade. The legislature was prepared to make far more liberal concessions: but, overborne by the clamours of English traders, withheld the most important, which statesmen of all parties concurred in pronouncing to be just.[4] The Irish, confirmed in the justice of their cause by these opinions, resented the undue influence of their jealous rivals; and believed that commercial freedom was only to be won by national equality.

[1] Grattan's Life, i. 283.
[2] *Ibid.*, 283–289, 298, &c.; Hardy's Life of Lord Charlemont, i. 363–379.
[3] 15 Geo. III. c. 31; Plowden's Hist., i. 430.
[4] Parl. Hist., xix. 1100–1126; Plowden's Hist., i. 459–466; 18 Geo. III. c. 45 (flax seed); c. 55 (Irish shipping); Adolphus' Hist., ii. 551–554; Grattan's Life, i. 330.

The distresses and failing revenue of Ireland again attracted the attention of the British Parliament, in the ensuing session.[1] England undertook the payment of the troops on the Irish establishment serving abroad;[2] and relieved some branches of her industry:[3] but still denied substantial freedom to her commerce. Meanwhile, the Irish were inflamed by stirring oratory, by continued suffering, and by the successes of the Americans in a' like cause. Disappointed in their expectations of relief from the British Parliament, they formed associations for the exclusion of British commodities, and the encouragement of native manufactures.[4]

Further restrictions removed, 1779.

Another decisive movement precipitated the crisis of Irish affairs. The French war had encouraged the formation of several corps of volunteers for the defence of the country. The most active promoters of this array of military force, were members of the country party; and their political sentiments were speedily caught up by the volunteers. At first the different corps were without concert or communication:[5] but in the autumn of 1779, they received a great accession of strength, and were brought into united action. The country had been drained of its regular army, for the American war; and its coasts were threatened by the enemy. The government, in its extremity,

The volunteers, 1779.

[1] Parl. Hist., xx. 111, 136, 248, 635, 663.
[2] King's Message, March 18th, 1779; Parl. Hist., xx. 327.
[3] *E.g.* hemp and tobacco.—19 Geo. III. c. 37, 83.
[4] Plowden's Hist., i. 485; Grattan's Life, i. 362-364; Hardy's Life of Lord Charlemont, i. 389.
[5] Plowden's Hist., i. 487; Grattan's Life, i. 343.

threw itself upon the volunteers,—distributed 16,000 stand of arms,—and invited the people to arm themselves, without any securities for their obedience. The volunteers soon numbered 42,000 men, chose their own officers,—chiefly from the country party,—made common cause with the people against the government, shouted for free trade; and received the thanks of Parliament for their patriotism.[1] Power had been suffered to pass from the executive and the legislature, into the hands of armed associations of men, holding no commissions from the crown, and independent alike of civil and military authority. The government was filled with alarm and perplexity; and the British Parliament resounded with remonstrances against the conduct of ministers, and arguments for the prompt redress of Irish grievances.[2] The Parliament of Ireland showed its determination, by voting supplies for six months only;[3] and the British Parliament, setting itself earnestly to work, passed some important measures for the relief of Irish commerce.[4]

The volunteers demand legislative independence, 1780.

Meanwhile the volunteers, daily increasing in discipline and military organisation, were assuming, more and more, the character of an armed political association. The different corps assembled for drill, and for

---

[1] Plowden's Hist., i. 493; Lord Sheffield's Observations on State of Ireland, 1785.

[2] Debate on Lord Shelburne's motion in the Lords, Dec. 1st, 1779.—Parl. Hist., xx. 1156; Debate on Lord Upper-Ossory's motion in the Commons, Dec. 6th, 1779; *Ibid.*, 1197; Hardy's Life of Lord Charlemont, i. 380-382; Grattan's Life, i. 368, 389, 397-400; Moore's Life of Lord E. Fitzgerald, i. 187.

[3] Nov., 1779; Plowden's Hist., i. 506.

[4] Lord North's Propositions, Dec. 13th, 1779; Parl. Hist., xx. 1272; 20 Geo. III. c. 6, 10, 18.

discussion, agreed to resolutions, and opened an extensive communication with one another. Early in 1780, the volunteers demanded, with one voice, the legislative independence of Ireland, and liberation from the sovereignty of the British Parliament.[1] And Mr. Grattan, the ablest and most temperate of the Irish patriots, gave eloquent expression to these claims in the Irish House of Commons.[2]

In this critical conjuncture, the public mind was further inflamed by another interference of the government, in England. Hitherto, Ireland had been embraced in the annual Mutiny Act of the British Parliament. In this year, however, the general sentiment of magistrates and the people being adverse to the operation of such an Act, without the sanction of the Irish legislature, Ireland was omitted from the English mutiny bill; and the heads of a separate mutiny bill were transmitted from Ireland. This bill was altered by the English cabinet into a permanent Act. Material amendments were also made in a bill for opening the sugar trade to Ireland.[3] No constitutional security had been more cherished than that of an annual mutiny bill, by which the crown is effectually prevented from maintaining a standing army, without the consent of Parliament. This security was now denied to Ireland, just when she was most sensitive to her rights, and jealous of the sovereignty

The Mutiny Bill made permanent.

---

[1] Plowden's Hist., i. 513.
[2] April 19th, 1780; Grattan's Life, ii. 39-55.
[3] Parl. Hist., xxi. 1293; Plowden's Hist., i. 515, &c.; Grattan's Life, ii. 60, 71, 85-100, *et seq.*

of England. The Irish Parliament submitted to the will of its English rulers: but the volunteers assembled to denounce them. They declared that their own Parliament had been bought with the wealth of Ireland herself, and clamoured more loudly than ever for legislative independence.[1] Nor was such an innovation without effect upon the constitutional rights of England, as it sanctioned, for the first time, the maintenance of a military force within the realm, without limitation as to numbers or duration. Troops raised in England might be transferred to Ireland, and there maintained under military law, independent of the Parliaments of either country. The anomaly of this measure was forcibly exposed by Mr. Fox and the leaders of Opposition, in the British Parliament.[2]

The volunteers, 1780-1. The volunteers continued their reviews and political demonstrations, under the Earl of Charlemont, with increased numbers and improved organisation; and again received the thanks of the Irish Parliament.[3] But while they were acting in cordial union with the leaders of the country party, in the House of Commons, the government had secured,—by means too familiar at the Castle,—a majority of that assembly, which steadily resisted further concessions.[4] In *The convention of Dungannon.* these circumstances, delegates from all the

---

[1] Grattan's Life, ii. 127, *et seq.*
[2] Feb. 20th, 23rd, 1781; Parl. Hist., xxi. 1292.
[3] Plowden's Hist., i. 529; Grattan's Life, ii. 103.
[4] Plowden's Hist., i. 535–555. Mr. Eden, writing to Lord North, Nov. 10th, 1781, informs him that the Opposition had been gained over, and adds: 'Indeed, I have had a fatiguing week of it in every respect. On Thursday I was obliged to see fifty-three gentlemen

volunteers in Ulster were invited to assemble at Dungannon on the 15th February 1782, 'to root out corruption and court influence from the legislative body,' and 'to deliberate on the present alarming situation of public affairs.' The meeting was held in the church: its proceedings were conducted with the utmost propriety and moderation; and it agreed, almost unanimously, to resolutions declaring the right of Ireland to legislative and judicial independence, and free trade.[1] On the 22nd, Mr. Grattan, in a noble speech, moved an address of the Commons to His Majesty, asserting the same principles.[2] His motion was defeated, as well as another by Mr. Flood, declaring the legislative independence of the Irish Parliament.[3]

Mr. Grattan's motion, Feb. 22nd, 1782.

Mr. Flood's motion, Feb. 26th, 1782.

In the midst of these contentions, Lord Rockingham's liberal administration was formed, who recalled Lord Carlisle, and appointed the Duke of Portland as lord-lieutenant. While the new ministers were concerting measures for the government of Ireland, Mr. Eden, secretary to Lord Carlisle,—who had resisted all the demands of the patriots in the Irish Parliament,—hastened to England; and startled the House of Commons with a glowing statement of the dangers he had left behind him, and a motion to secure the legislative

Measures of the Rockingham ministry, April, 1782.

---

separately in the course of the morning, from eight till two o'clock.' *Beresford Corr.*, i. 188; Correspondence of Lord Lieutenant, Grattan's Life, ii. 153-177.

[1] Plowden's Hist., i. 564-569; Hardy's Life of Lord Charlemont, ii. 1, *et seq.*; Life of Grattan, ii. 203, *et seq.*

[2] Irish Parl. Deb., i. 266.   [3] *Ibid.*, 279.

independence of Ireland. His motion was withdrawn, amidst general indignation at the factious motives by which it had been prompted.[1] On the following day, the king sent a message to both houses, recommending the state of Ireland to their serious consideration: to which a general answer was returned, with a view to the co-operation of the Irish Parliament. In Dublin, the Duke of Portland communicated a similar message, which was responded to by an address of singular temper and dignity,—justly called the Irish Declaration of Rights.[2] The Irish Parliament unanimously claimed for itself the sole authority to make laws for Ireland, and the repeal of the permanent Mutiny Act. These claims the British Parliament, animated by a spirit of wisdom and liberality, conceded without reluctance or hesitation.[3] The sixth Geo. I. was repealed; and the legislative and judicial authority of the British Parliament renounced. The right of the Privy Council to alter bills transmitted from Ireland was abandoned, and the perpetual Mutiny Act repealed. The concession was gracefully and honourably made; and the statesmen who had consistently advocated the rights of Ireland, while in opposition, could proudly disclaim the influence of

April 16th, 1782.

Legislative and judicial independence granted, 1782.

---

[1] April 8th, 1782: Parl. Hist., xxii. 1241–1264; Wraxall's Mem., iii. 29, 92; Fox's Mem., i. 313; Lord J. Russell's Life of Fox, i. 287–289; Grattan's Life, ii. 208; Walpole's Journ., ii. 538.
[2] Plowden's Hist., i. 595–599; Irish Debates, i. 332–346; Grattan's Life, ii. 230, *et seq.*
[3] Debates in Lords and Commons, May 17th, 1782; Parl. Hist., xxiii. 16–48; Rockingham Mem., ii. 469–476.

intimidation.[1] The magnanimity of the act was acknowledged with gratitude and rejoicings, by the Parliament and people of Ireland.

But English statesmen, in granting Ireland her independence, were not insensible to the difficulties of her future government; and endeavoured to concert some plan of union, by which the interests of the two countries could be secured.[2] No such plan, however, could be devised; and for nearly twenty years the British ministers were left to solve the strange problem of governing a divided state, and bringing into harmony the councils of two independent legislatures. Its solution was naturally found in the continuance of corruption; and the Parliament of Ireland,—having gained its freedom, sold it, without compunction, to the Castle.[3] Ireland was governed by her native legislature, but was not the less under the dominion of a close oligarchy,—factious, turbulent, exclusive

Difficulties of Irish independence.

---

[1] Fox's Mem., i. 393, 403, 404, 418; Lord J. Russell's Life of Fox, i. 290-295; Grattan's Life, ii. 289, *et seq.*; Court and Cabinets of Geo. III., i. 65.

[2] Address of both Houses to the king, May 17th, 1782; Correspondence of Duke of Portland and Marquess of Rockingham; Plowden's Hist., i. 605. The scheme of a union appears to have been discussed as early as 1757.—Hardy's Life of Lord Charlemont, i. 107. And again in 1776; Cornwallis Corr., iii. 129.

[3] See a curious analysis of the ministerial majority, in 1784, on the authority of the Bolton MSS. Massey's Hist., iii. 264; and Speech of Mr. Grattan on the Address, Jan. 19th, 1792; Irish Deb., xii. 6-8; and Speech of Mr. Fox, March 23rd, 1797. He stated that 'a person of high consideration was known to say that 500,000*l.* had been expended to quell an opposition in Ireland, and that as much more must be expended in order to bring the legislature of that country to a proper temper.'—Parl. Hist., xxxiii. 143; Speech of Mr. Spring Rice, April 23rd, 1834; Hans. Deb., 3rd Ser., xxii. 1189; Plowden's Hist., ii. 346, 609.

and corrupt. And how could it be otherwise? The people, with arms in their hands, had achieved a triumph. 'Magna Charta,' said Grattan, 'was not attained in Parliament: but by the barons, armed in the field.'[1] But what influence had the people at elections? Disfranchised and incapacitated, they could pretend to none! The anomalous condition of the Parliament and people of Ireland became the more conspicuous, as they proceeded in their new functions of self-government. The volunteers, not satisfied with the achievement of national independence, now confronted their native Parliament with demands for Parliamentary reform.[2] That cause being discussed in the English Parliament, was eagerly caught up in Ireland. Armed men organised a wide-spread political agitation, sent delegates to a national convention,[3] and seemed prepared to enforce their arguments at the point of the bayonet. Their attitude was threatening: but their cause a hollow pretence. The enfranchisement of Catholics formed no part of their scheme. In order to secure their assistance, in the recent struggle for independence, they had, indeed, recommended a relaxation of the penal laws: a common cause had softened the intolerance of Protestants; and some of the most oppressive disabilities of their Catholic brethren had been removed:[4]

The volunteers demand Parliamentary reform.

---

[1] Irish Debates, April 16th, 1782, i. 335.
[2] Plowden's Hist., ii. 28; Hardy's Life of Lord Charlemont, ii. 93–134; Grattan's Life, iii. 102–146.
[3] Plowden, ii. 56.
[4] Viz. in 1778 (17 & 18 Geo. III. c. 49, Ireland), and in 1782; Plowden's Hist., i. 555, 559, 564, 579; and *supra*, p. 110.

but as yet the patriots and volunteers had no intention of extending to them the least share of civil or political power.

Mr. Flood was the organ of the volunteers in the House of Commons,—a patriot second only to Mr. Grattan in influence and ability,— and jealous of the popularity and preeminence of his great rival. In November 1783, he moved for leave to bring in a bill, for the more equal representation of the people. He was met at once with the objection that his proposal originated with an armed association, whose pretensions were incompatible with freedom of debate; and it was rejected by a large majority.[1] *Mr. Flood's motion for reform, Nov. 29th, 1783.*

Mr. Flood renewed his efforts in the following year: but the country party were disunited; the owners of boroughs were determined not to surrender their power; the dictation of the volunteers gave just offence; and the division of opinion on the admission of Catholics to the franchise was becoming more pronounced. Again his measure was rejected.[2] The mob resented its rejection with violence and fury: but the great body of the people, whose rights were ignored by the patriots and agitators, regarded it with indifference. The armed agitation proceeded: but the volunteers continued to be divided upon the claims of the Catholics,—to *Renewed, March 13th, 20th, 1784.* *Failure of the cause of reform.*

[1] Ayes, 49; Noes, 158. Irish Debates, ii. 353; Fox's Mem., ii. 165, 186; Grattan's Life, iii. 146, *et seq.*; Hardy's Life of Lord Charlemont, ii. 135.

[2] March 13th, 20th, 1784; Irish Deb., iii. 13; Plowden's Hist., ii. 80. Ayes, 85; Noes, 159.

which their leader Lord Charlemont was himself opposed.[1] An armed Protestant agitation, and a packed council of borough proprietors, were unpromising instruments for reforming the representation of the people.[2]

A close and corrupt Parliament was left in full possession of its power; and Ireland, exulting in recent emancipation from British rule, was soon made sensible that neither was her commerce free, nor her independence assured. The regulation of her commerce was beyond the power of the Irish legislature: the restrictions under which it laboured concerned both countries, and needed the concert of the two Parliaments. Mr. Pitt, wise and liberal in his policy concerning Ireland, regarded commercial freedom as essential to her prosperity and contentment; and in 1785, he prepared a comprehensive scheme to attain that object. Ireland had recently acquired the right of trading with Europe and the West Indies: but was nearly cut off from trade with England herself, and with America and Africa. Mr. Pitt offered liberal concessions on all these points, which were first submitted to the Parliament of Ireland in the form of eleven resolutions.[3] They were gratefully accepted and acknowledged: but when the minister introduced them to the British Parliament, he was unable,

Mr. Pitt's commercial measures, 1785.

---

[1] Plowden's History, ii. 105; Moore's Life of Lord E. Fitzgerald, i. 189, 198; Hardy's Life of Lord Charlemont, ii. 129.
[2] For a list of the proprietors of Irish nomination boroughs, see Plowden's Hist., ii. *App.* No. 96.
[3] Feb. 7th, 1785; Irish Deb., iv. 116; Plowden's Hist., ii. 113, *n.*

in the plenitude of his power, to overcome the interests and jealousy of traders, and the ignorance, prejudices, and faction of his opponents in the House of Commons. He was obliged to withdraw many of the concessions he had offered,—including the right of trading with India and the foreign West Indies; and he introduced a new proposition, requiring the English navigation laws to be enacted by the Parliament of Ireland. The measure, thus changed, was received with chagrin and resentment by the Parliament and people of Ireland, as at once a mark of English jealousy and injustice, and a badge of Irish dependence.[1] The resolutions of the Irish Parliament had been set aside,—the interests of the country sacrificed to those of English traders, —and the legislature was called upon to register the injurious edicts of the British Parliament. A measure, conceived in the highest spirit of statesmanship, served but to aggravate the ill-feelings which it had been designed to allay; and was abandoned, in disappointment and disgust.[2] Its failure, however, illustrated the difficulties of governing the realm through the agency of two independent Parliaments, and foreshadowed the necessity of a legislative union. Another illustration of the danger of divided councils was afforded, four years afterwards, by the proceedings of the Irish Parliament on the regency.[3]

[1] Debates, Feb. 22nd, and May 12th, in Commons; Parl. Hist., xxv. 311, 575. In Lords, June 7th; *Ibid.*, 820.
[2] Irish Debates, v. 329, &c.; Plowden's Hist., ii. 120-136; Tomline's Life of Pitt, ii. 69-92; Lord Stanhope's Life of Pitt, i. 263-273; Beresford Corr., i. 265.
[3] *Supra*, Vol. I. 194; Hardy's Life of Lord Charlemont, ii. 168-183; Grattan's Life, iii. 341, *et seq.*

A few years later, at a time of peril and apprehension in England, a policy of conciliation was again adopted in Ireland. The years 1792 and 1793 were signalised by the admission of Catholics to the elective franchise, and to civil and military offices,[1] the limitation of the Irish pension list,[2] the settlement of a fixed civil list upon the crown, in lieu of its hereditary revenues, the exclusion of some of the swarm of placemen and pensioners from the House of Commons, and the adoption of Mr. Fox's protective law of libel.[3] Ireland, however, owed these promising concessions to the wise policy of Mr. Pitt and other English statesmen, rather than to her native Parliament. They were not yielded gracefully by the Irish cabinet, and they were accompanied by rigorous measures of coercion.[4] This was the last hopeful period in the separate history of Ireland, which was soon to close in tumults, rebellion, and civil war. To the seething elements of discord,—social, religious, and political,—were now added the perilous ingredients of revolutionary sentiments and sympathies.

Liberal measures of 1792-3.

The volunteers had aimed at worthy objects; yet their association was founded upon revolutionary principles, incompatible with constitutional government. Clamour and complaint

The United Irishmen, 1791.

---

[1] *Supra*, p. 110; Plowden's Hist., ii. 407; Moore's Life of Lord E. Fitzgerald, i. 205, 216, 217.
[2] *Supra*, Vol. I. 259; Plowden's Hist., ii. 146, 188, 279.
[3] *Supra*, p. 262.
[4] Plowden's Hist., ii. 471. In 1805 Mr. Grattan stated that this policy of conciliation originated with ministers in England; but being opposed by the ministry in Ireland, its grace and popularity were lost.—Hans. Deb., 1st Ser., iv. 926; Moore's Life of Lord E. Fitzgerald, i. 218; Hardy's Life of Lord Charlemont, ii. 294-300; Grattan's Life, iv. 53-114.

are lawful in a free state: but the agitation of armed men assumes the shape of rebellion. Their example was followed, in 1791, by the United Irishmen, whose original design was no less worthy. This association originated with the Protestants of Belfast; and sought 'a complete reform of the legislature, founded on the principles of civil, political, and religious liberty.'[1] These reasonable objects were pursued, for a time, earnestly and in good faith; and motions for reform, on the broad basis of religious equality, were submitted to the legislature by Mr. Ponsonby, where they received ample discussion.[2] But the association was soon to be compromised by republican leaders; and seduced into an alliance with French Jacobins, and a treasonable correspondence with the enemies of their country, in aid of Irish disaffection.[3] Treason took the place of patriotism. This unhappy land was also disturbed by armed and hostile associations of peasants, known as 'defenders' and 'peep-of-day boys.'[4] Society was convulsed with violence, agrarian outrage, and covert treason.

[1] Plowden's Hist., ii. 330–334, and App., No. 84; Report of Secret Committee of Lords; Lords' Journ., Ireland, vii. 580; Madden's United Irishmen; Moore's Life of Lord E. Fitzgerald, i. 197.

[2] March 4th, 1794; May 15th, 1797. Plowden's Hist., ii. 452, &c.

[3] In 1795, the Irish Union Societies were formed out of the United Irishmen. The correspondence appears to have commenced in 1795.—Plowden's Hist., ii. 567; Report of Secret Committee of Commons, 1797; Irish Debates, xvii. 522; Grattan's Life, iv. 259, &c.; Moore's Life of Lord E. Fitzgerald, i. 164–166, 256–260, 273, et seq., 296; ii. 9, et seq.; Life of Wolfe Tone, i. 132–136; ii. 14, et seq.; Report of Secret Committee of Commons, Ireland, 1797; Comm. Journ., Ireland, xvii. App. 829; Castlereagh Corr., i. 189, 296, 366, &c.; Cornwallis Corr., ii. 338.

[4] Plowden's Hist., ii. 335; Moore's Life of Lord E. Fitzgerald, ii. 6.

Meanwhile, religious animosities, which had been partially allayed by the liberal policy of the government, and by the union of Protestants and Catholics in the volunteer forces, were revived with increased intensity. In 1795, Lord Fitzwilliam's brief rule,—designed for conciliation,—merely raised the hopes of Catholics, and the fears of Protestants.[1] The peasantry, by whom the peace of the country was disturbed, generally professed one faith: the gentry, another. Traditional hatred of the Romish faith was readily associated, in the minds of the latter, with loyalty and the protection of life and property. To them papist and 'defender' were the same. Every social disorder was ascribed to the hated religion. Papist enemies of order, and conspirators against their country, were banded together; and loyal Protestants were invited to associate in defence of life, property, and religion. With this object, Orange societies were rapidly formed; which, animated by fear, zeal, and party spirit, further inflamed the minds of Protestants against Catholics. Nor was their hostility passive. In September 1795, a fierce conflict arose between the Orangemen and defenders,—since known as the battle of the Diamond,—which increased the inveteracy of the two parties. Orangemen endeavoured, by the eviction of tenants, the dismissal of servants, and worse forms of persecution, to drive every Catholic out of the county of Armagh;[2]

Feuds between Protestants and Catholics.

Orange societies.

[1] Moore's Life of Lord E. Fitzgerald, i. 260; Grattan's Life, iv. 182; Castlereagh Corr., i. 10.
[2] Speech of Mr. Grattan, Feb. 22nd, 1796; Irish Parl. Deb., xvi. 107.

and defenders retaliated with murderous outrages.[1] In 1796, the disturbed state of the country was met by further measures of repression, which were executed by the magistrates and military with merciless severity,—too often unwarranted by law.[2] To other causes of discontent, was added resentment of oppression and injustice. The country was rent asunder by hatreds, strifes, and disaffection, and threatened, from without, by hostile invasion, which Irish traitors had encouraged.[3] At length these evil passions, fomented by treason on one side, and by cruelty on the other, exploded in the rebellion of 1798.

The leaders of this rebellion were Protestants.[4] The Catholic gentry and priesthood recoiled from any contact with French atheists and Jacobins: they were without republican sympathies; but could not fail to deplore the sufferings and oppression of the wretched peasantry who professed their faith. The Protestant party, however,—frantic with fear, bigotry, and party spirit,—denounced the whole Catholic body as rebels and public enemies. The hideous scenes of this rebellion are only to be paralleled by the enormities of the French Revolution. The rebels were unloosed savages,—mad with hatred and revenge,—burning, destroying and slaying: the loyalists and military were ferocious and cruel beyond belief.

The rebellion of 1798.

[1] Speech of attorney-general, Feb. 20th, 1796; *Ibid.*, xvi. 102.
[2] Plowden's Hist., ii. 544–567, 573, 582, 624; Lord Moira's Speech, Nov. 22nd, 1797; Parl. Hist., xxxiii. 1058.
[3] Report of Secret Committee of Lords, 1798; Lords' Journ., Ireland, viii. 588; Moore's Life of Lord E. Fitzgerald, i. 282.
[4] Plowden's Hist., ii. 700.

Not only were armed peasants hunted down like wild beasts: but the disturbed districts were abandoned to the license of a brutal soldiery. The wretched 'croppies' were scourged, pitch-capped, picketed, half-hung, tortured, mutilated, and shot: their homes rifled and burned: their wives and daughters violated with revolting barbarity.[1] Before the outbreak of the rebellion, the soldiers had been utterly demoralised by license and cruelty, unchecked by the civil power.[2] Sir Ralph Abercromby, in a general order, had declared 'the army to be in a state of licentiousness, which must render it formidable to every one but the enemy.'[3] In vain had that humane and enlightened soldier attempted to restrain military excesses. Thwarted by the weakness of Lord Camden, and the bigotry and fierce party zeal of his cabinet, he retired in disgust from the command of an army, which had been degraded into bands of ruffians and bandits.[4] The troops, hounded on to renewed license, were fit instruments of the infuriated vengeance of the ruling faction.

In the midst of these frightful scenes, Lord Cornwallis assumed the civil and military government of Ireland. Temperate, sensible, and humane, he was horrified not less by the

Lord Cornwallis lord-lieutenant.

---

[1] Plowden's Hist., ii. 701, 705 and *note,* 712–714. It was a favourite sport to fasten caps filled with hot pitch on to the heads of the peasants, or to make them stand upon a sharp stake or picket.—*Ibid.,* 713; Moore's Life of Lord E. Fitzgerald, ii. 74, 203.

[2] The military had been enjoined by proclamation to act without being called upon by the civil magistrates.—Plowden's Hist., ii. 622, App. civ. cv.; Lord Dunfermline's Memoir of Sir Ralph Abercromby, 69.

[3] Memoir of Sir Ralph Abercromby, 93.   [4] *Ibid.,* 89–138.

atrocities of the rebels, than by the revolting cruelty and lawlessness of the troops, and the vindictive passions of all concerned in the administration of affairs.[1] Moderation and humanity were to be found in none but English regiments.[2] With native officers, rapine and murder were no crimes.[3]

. The rebellion was crushed : but how was a country so convulsed with evil passions to be governed? Lord Cornwallis found his council, or junto, at the Castle, by whom it had long been ruled, 'blinded by their passions and prejudices.' Persuaded that the policy of this party had aggravated the political evils of their wretched country, he endeavoured to save the Irish from

[1] Writing June 28th, 1798, he said : 'I am much afraid that any man in a brown coat, who is found within several miles of the field of action, is butchered without discrimination.'—'It shall be one of my first objects to soften the ferocity of our troops, which I am afraid, in the Irish corps at least, is not confined to the private soldiers.'—*Cornwallis Corr.*, ii. 355. Of the militia he said : 'They are ferocious and cruel in the extreme, when any poor wretches, either with or without arms, come within their power : in short, murder appears to be their favourite pastime.'—*Ibid.*, 358. 'The principal persons of this country, and the members of both Houses of Parliament, are, in general, averse to all acts of clemency . . . . and would pursue measures that could only terminate in the extirpation of the greater number of the inhabitants, and in the utter destruction of the country.'—*Ibid.*, 358. Again, he deplores 'the numberless murders that are hourly committed by our people without any process or examination whatever.' 'The conversation of the principal persons of the country tends to encourage this system of blood ; and the conversation, even at my table, where you may well suppose I do all I can to prevent it, always turns on hanging, shooting, burning, &c. &c. ; and if a priest has been put to death, the greatest joy is expressed by the whole company.'—*Ibid.*, 369.

[2] In sending the 100th Regiment and 'some troops that can be depended upon,' he wrote : 'The shocking barbarities of our national troops would be more likely to provoke rebellion than to suppress it.'—*Ibid.*, 377. See also his General Order, Aug. 31st, 1798.—*Ibid.*, 395.

[3] *E.g.* the murder of Dogherty.—*Ibid.*, 420. See also Lord Holland's *Mem.*, i. 105–114.

themselves, by that scheme of union which a greater statesman than himself had long since conceived.[1] Under the old system of government, concessions, conciliation, and justice were impracticable.[2] The only hope of toleration and equity was to be found in the mild and impartial rule of British statesmen, and an united Parliament. In this spirit was the union sought by Mr. Pitt, who ' resented and spurned the bigoted fury of Irish Protestants:'[3] in this spirit was it promoted by Lord Cornwallis.[4] Self-government had become impossible. 'If ever there was a country,' said Lord Hutchinson, 'unfit to govern itself, it is Ireland; a corrupt aristocracy, a ferocious commonalty, a distracted government, a divided people.'[5] Imperial considerations, no less paramount, also pointed to the union. Not only had the divisions of the Irish people rendered the difficulties of internal administration insuperable: but they had proved a source of weakness and danger from without. Ireland could no longer be suffered to continue a separate realm: but must be fused and welded into one state, with Great Britain.

But the difficulties of this great scheme were not easily to be overcome. However desirable, and even necessary, for the interests of Ireland herself, an invitation to surrender her independence,—so recently acquired,—deeply affected her national sensibilities. To be merged

Difficulties in effecting the Union.

---

[1] Cornwallis Corr., ii. 404, 405.   [2] Ibid., 414, 415, 416.
[3] Wilberforce's Diary, July 16th, 1798.
[4] Cornwallis Corr., ii. 418. 419, &c.; Castlereagh Corr., i. 442.
[5] Memoir of Sir Ralph Abercromby, 136.

in the greater and more powerful kingdom, was to lose her distinct nationality. And how could she be assured against neglect and oppression, when wholly at the mercy of the Parliament of Great Britain, whose sovereignty she had lately renounced? The liberties she had won in 1782, were all to be forfeited and abandoned. At any other time, these national feelings alone would have made an union impossible. But the country, desolated by a war of classes and religions, had not yet recovered the united sentiments of a nation.

Objections of the ruling party.

But other difficulties, no less formidable, were to be encountered. The Irish party were invited to yield up the power and patronage of the Castle: the peers to surrender their proud position as hereditary councillors, in Parliament: the great families to abandon their boroughs. The compact confederacy of interests and corruption was to be broken up.[1] But the government, convinced of the necessity of the Union, was prepared to overcome every obstacle.

The Parliament of Great Britain recognised the

[1] There are two classes of men in Parliament, whom the disasters and sufferings of the country have but very imperfectly awakened to the necessity of a change, viz. the borough proprietors, and the immediate agents of government.'—*Lord Cornwallis to Duke of Portland*, Jan. 5th, 1799; Corr., iii. 31. Again: 'There certainly is a very strong disinclination to the measure in many of the borough proprietors, and a not less marked repugnance in many of the official people, particularly in those who have been longest in the habits of the current system.'—*Same to same*, Jan. 11th, 1799; *Ibid.*, 34. And much later in the struggle, his lordship wrote: 'The nearer the great event approaches, the more are the needy and interested senators alarmed at the effects it may possibly have on their interests, and the provision for their families; and I believe that half of our majority would be at least as much delighted as any of our opponents, if the measure could be defeated.'—*Ibid.*, 228.

Union as a necessary measure of state policy; and the masterly arguments of Mr. Pitt[1] admitted of little resistance.[2] But the first proposal to the Irish Parliament miscarried; an amendment in favour of maintaining an independent legislature being lost by a single vote.[3] It was plain that corrupt interests could only be overcome by corruption. Nomination boroughs must be bought, and their members indemnified,—county interests conciliated,—officers and expectant lawyers compensated,—opponents bribed. Lord Castlereagh estimated the cost of these expedients at a million and a half; and the price was forthcoming.[4] The purchase of boroughs was no new scheme, having been proposed by Mr. Pitt himself, as the basis of his measure of Parliamentary reform in 1785;[5] and now it was systematically carried out in Ireland. The patrons of boroughs received 7,500*l.* for each seat; and eighty-four boroughs were disfranchised.[6] Lord Down-

Means by which the Union was accomplished.

---

[1] Jan. 23rd and 31st, 1799.

[2] In the Commons, his resolutions were carried by 149 votes against 24, and in the Lords without a division.—Plowden's Hist., ii. 896.

[3] Jan. 22nd, 1799. Ayes, 106; Noes, 105.—Cornwallis Corr., iii. 40-51.

[4] Castlereagh Corr., ii. 151. His lordship divided the cost as follows:—Boroughs, 756,000*l.*; county interests, 224,000*l.*; barristers, 200,000*l.*; purchasers of seats, 75,000*l.*; Dublin, 200,000*l.*: total, 1,433,000*l.*—Cornwallis Corr., iii. 81; Stanhope's Life of Pitt, iii. 180. Lord Cornwallis wrote, July 1st, 1799: 'There cannot be a stronger argument for the measure than the overgrown Parliamentary power of five or six of our pampered borough-mongers, who are become most formidable to government, by their long possession of the entire patronage of the crown, in their respective districts.'—*Corr.*, iii. 110.

[5] *Supra*, Vol. I., 400.

[6] Of the 34 boroughs retained, nine only were open.—Cornwallis Corr., iii. 234, 324. See list of boroughs disfranchised and sums paid to proprietors.—*Ibid.*, 321-324. The Ponsonbys exercised in-

shire was paid 52,500*l.* for seven seats; Lord Ely, 45,000*l.* for six.[1] The total compensation amounted to 1,260,000*l.*[2] Peers were further compensated for the loss of their privileges in the national council, by profuse promises of English peerages, or promotion in the peerage of Ireland: commoners were conciliated by new honours,[3] and by the *largesses* of the British government. Places were given or promised,—pensions multiplied,—secret-service money exhausted.[4] In vain Lord Cornwallis complained of the 'political jobbing' and 'dirty business' in which he was 'involved beyond all bearing,' and 'longed to kick those whom his public duty obliged him to court.' In vain he 'despised and hated himself,' while 'negotiating and jobbing with the most corrupt people under heaven.'[5] British gold was sent for and distri-

fluence over 22 seats; Lord Downshire and the Beresfords, respectively, over nearly as many. 23 of the 34 boroughs remained close until the Reform Act of 1832.—*Ibid.*, 324. Many of the counties also continued in the hands of the great families.—*Ibid.*; and see *supra*, Vol. I. 360.

[1] Plowden's Hist., ii. 1018, 1067; Castlereagh Corr., iii. 56-67; Cornwallis Corr., iii. 324; Stanhope's Life of Pitt, iii. 227.

[2] Cornwallis Corr., iii. 323.

[3] Castlereagh Corr., iii. 330; Cornwallis Corr., iii. 244, 252, 257, 262. 29 Irish peerages were created, of which seven were unconnected with the Union; 20 Irish peers were promoted, and 6 English peerages granted for Irish services.—*Ibid.*, 318. See also Lord Stanhope's Life of Pitt, iii. 180.

[4] Cornwallis Corr., iii. 278, 340; Grattan's Life, v. iii.

[5] Cornwallis Corr., iii. 102. The luckless viceroy applied to himself the appropriate lines of Swift:—

'So to effect his monarch's ends,
From hell a viceroy devil ascends:
His budget with corruption cramm'd—
The contributions of the damn'd—
Which with unsparing hand he strows
Through courts and senates, as he goes;
And then, at Beelzebub's black hall,
Complains his budget is too small.'

buted;[1] and, at length,—in defiance of threats of armed resistance,[2]—in spite of insidious promises of relief to Catholics,[3]—and corrupt defection among the supporters of government,[4]—the cause was won. A great end was compassed by means the most base and shameless. Grattan, Lord Charlemont, Ponsonby, Plunket, and a few patriots continued to protest against the sale of the liberties and free constitution of Ireland. Their eloquence and public virtue command the respect of posterity: but the wretched history of their country denies them its sympathy.[5]

The terms of the Union were now speedily adjusted and ratified by the Parliaments of both countries.[6] Ireland was to be represented, in the Parliament of the United Kingdom, by four spiritual lords, sitting by rotation of sessions; by twenty-eight temporal peers, elected for life by the Irish peerage; and by a hundred members of the House of Commons. Her commerce was at

Terms of the Union.

[1] Cornwallis Corr., iii. 151, 156, 201, 202, 226, 309; Coote's Hist. of the Union.
[2] *Ibid.*, 167, 180.
[3] *Ibid.*, 51, 55, 63, 149; Castlereagh Corr., ii. 45, *et supra*, p. 116.
[4] 'Sir R. Butler, Mahon, and Fetherstone were taken off by county cabals during the recess, and Whaley absolutely bought by the Opposition stock purse. He received, I understand, 2,000*l.* down, and is to receive as much more after the service is performed. We have undoubted proofs, though not such as we can disclose, that they are enabled to offer as high as 5,000*l.* for an individual vote, and I lament to state that there are individuals remaining amongst us that are likely to yield to this temptation.'—*Lord Castlereagh to Duke of Portland,* Feb. 7th, 1800; Cornwallis Corr., iii. 182. 'The enemy, to my certain knowledge, offer 5,000*l.* ready money for a vote.'—*Lord Cornwallis to Bishop of Lichfield; Ibid.*, 184.
[5] Grattan's Life, v. 17, *et seq.*; 75-180.
[6] 39 & 40 Geo. III. c. 67; 40 Geo. III. c. 38. (Ireland.)

length admitted to a freedom which, under other conditions, could not have been attained.[1]

Such was the incorporation of the two countries; and henceforth the history of Ireland became the history of England. Had Mr. Pitt's liberal and enlightened policy been carried out, the Catholics of Ireland would have been at once admitted to a participation in the privileges of the constitution: provision would have been made for their clergy; and the grievances of the tithe system would have been redressed.[2] But we have seen how his statesmanship was overborne by the scruples of the king;[3] and how long and arduous was the struggle by which religious liberty was won. The Irish were denied those rights which English statesmen had designed for them. Nor was this the worst evil which followed the fall of Mr. Pitt, and the reversal of his policy. So long as narrow Tory principles prevailed in the councils of England, the government of Ireland was confided to the kindred party at the Castle. Protestant ascendency was maintained as rigorously as ever: Catholics were governed by Orangemen: the close oligarchy which had ruled Ireland before the Union was still absolute. Repression and coercion continued to be the principles of its harsh domination.[4] The represen-

---

[1] 39 & 40 Geo. III. c. 67.
[2] Letter of Mr. Pitt, Nov. 17th, 1798; Cornwallis Corr., ii. 440; Lord Stanhope's Life of Pitt, iii. 160.
[3] Vol. I. 92; and *supra*, p. 118.
[4] Lord Cornwallis had foreseen this evil. He wrote, May 1st, 1800: 'If a successor were to be appointed who should, as almost all former lords-lieutenants have done, throw himself into the hands of this party, no advantage would be derived from the Union.'—

tation of Ireland, in the United Parliament, continued in the hands of the same party, who supported Tory ministers, and encouraged them to resist every concession which more liberal statesmen proposed. Potitical liberties and equality were withheld; yet the superior moderation and enlightenment of British statesmen secured a more equitable administration of the laws, and much remedial legislation,—designed for the improvement of the social and material condition of the people. These men earnestly strove to govern Ireland well, within the range of their narrow principles. The few restrictions which the Union had still left upon her commerce were removed;[1] her laws were reviewed, and their administration amended; her taxation was lightened; the education of her people encouraged; her prosperity stimulated by public works. Despite of insufficient capital and social disturbance, her trade, shipping, and manufactures expanded with her freedom.[2]

At length, after thirty years, the people of Ireland

Corr., iii. 237. Again, Dec. 1st, 1800: 'They assert that the Catholics of Ireland (seven-tenths of the population of the country) never can be good subjects to a Protestant government. What then have we done, if this position be true? We have united ourselves to a people whom we ought, in policy, to have destroyed.'—*Ibid.*, 307. Again, Feb. 15th, 1801: 'No consideration could induce me to take a responsible part with any administration who can be so blind to the interest, and indeed to the immediate security, of their country, as to persevere in the old system of proscription and exclusion in Ireland.'—*Ibid.*, 337.

[1] Corn trade, 46 Geo. III. c. 97; Countervailing Duties, 4 Geo. IV. c. 72; Butter trade, 8 Geo. IV. c. 61; 9 Geo. IV. c. 88.

[2] See Debate on Repeal of the Union, April 1834, and especially Mr. Spring Rice's able and elaborate speech.—Hans. Deb., 3rd Ser., xxii. 1092, *et seq.* Martin's Ireland before and after the Union, 3rd ed., pref., and chap. ii. iii. &c.

were admitted to the rights of citizens. The Catholic Relief Act was speedily followed by an amendment of the representation; and from that time, the spirit of freedom and equality has animated the administration of Irish affairs. *Irish liberties secured by Relief Act and reform.* The party of Protestant ascendency was finally overthrown; and rulers pledged to a more liberal policy, guided the councils of the state. Ireland shared with England every extension of popular rights. The full development of her liberties, however, was retarded by the factious violence of parties,—by the divisions of Orangemen and repealers,—by old religious hatreds,—by social feuds and agrarian outrages; and by the wretchedness of a population constantly in excess of the means of employment. The frightful visitation of famine in 1846, succeeded by an *The Irish famine.* unparalleled emigration, swept from the Irish soil more than a fourth of its people.[1] Their sufferings were generously relieved by England; and, grievous as they were, the hand of God wrought greater blessings for the survivors, than any legislation of man could have accomplished.

In the midst of all discouragements,—in spite of clamours and misrepresentation,—in defiance of hostile factions,—the executive *Freedom and equality of Ireland.* and the legislature have nobly striven to effect the political and social regeneration of Ireland. The great English parties have honourably vied with one

---

[1] In the ten years, from 1841 to 1851, it had decreased from 8,175,124 to 6,552,385, or 19·85 per cent. The total loss, however, was computed at 2,466,414. The decrease amounted to 49 persons to every square mile.—Census Report, 1851.

another, in carrying out this policy. Remedial legislation for Ireland, and the administration of her affairs, have, at some periods, engrossed more attention than the whole British Empire. Ancient feuds have yet to be extinguished, and religious divisions healed: but nothing has been wanting that the wisdom and beneficence of the state could devise for insuring freedom, equal justice, and the privileges of the constitution, to every class of the Irish people. Good laws have been well administered: franchises have been recognised as rights,— not admitted as pretences. Equality has been not a legal theory, but an unquestioned fact. We have seen how Catholics were excluded from all the rights of citizens. What is now their position? In 1860, of the twelve judges on the Irish bench, eight were Catholics.[1] In the southern counties of Ireland, Catholic gentlemen have been selected, in preference to Protestants, to serve the office of sheriff, in order to insure confidence in the administration of justice. England has also freely opened to the sons of Ireland the glittering ambition of arms, of statesmanship, of diplomacy, of forensic honour. The names of Wellington, Castlereagh, and Palmerston attest that the highest places in the state may be won by Irish genius.

The number of distinguished Irishmen who have been added to the roll of British peers, proves with what welcome the incorporation of the sister kingdom has been accepted. Nor have other dignities

[1] Sir Michael O'Loghlen was the first Catholic promoted to the bench, as Master of the Rolls.—Grattan's Life, i. 66.

been less freely dispensed to the honourable ambition of their countrymen. One illustration will suffice. In 1860, of the fifteen judges on the English bench, no less than four were Irishmen.[1] Freedom, equality, and honour have been the fruits of the Union; and Ireland has exchanged an enslaved nationality, for a glorious incorporation with the first empire of the world.

[1] Viz., Mr. Justice Willes, Mr. Justice Keating, Mr. Justice Hill, and Baron Martin; to whom has since been added Mr. Justice Shee an Irishman and a Catholic.

CHAPTER XVII.

FREE CONSTITUTIONS OF BRITISH COLONIES :—SOVEREIGNTY OF ENGLAND :—COMMERCIAL RESTRICTIONS :—TAXATION OF THE AMERICAN COLONIES :—THEIR RESISTANCE AND SEPARATION :—CROWN COLONIES :—CANADA :—AUSTRALIA :—COLONIAL ADMINISTRATION AFTER THE AMERICAN WAR :—NEW COMMERCIAL POLICY AFFECTING THE COLONIES :—RESPONSIBLE GOVERNMENT :—DEMOCRATIC COLONIAL CONSTITUTIONS :—INDIA.

Colonists have borne with them the laws of England.

It has been the destiny of the Anglo-Saxon race to spread through every quarter of the globe their courage and endurance, their vigorous industry, and their love of freedom. Wherever they have founded colonies they have borne with them the laws and institutions of England, as their birthright, so far as they were applicable to an infant settlement.[1] In territories acquired by conquest or cession, the existing laws and customs of the people were respected, until they were qualified to share the franchises of Englishmen. Some of these,—held only as garrisons,—others peopled with races hostile to our rule, or unfitted for freedom, —were necessarily governed upon different principles. But in quitting the soil of England to settle new colonies, Englishmen never renounced her freedom. Such being the noble principle of English

---

[1] Blackstone's Comm., i. 107; Lord Mansfield's Judgment in Campbell *v.* Hall; Howell's St. Tr., xx. 289; Clark's Colonial Law, 9, 139. 181, &c.; Sir G. C. Lewis on the Government of Dependencies, 189–203, 308; Mills' Colonial Constitutions, 18.

colonisation, circumstances favoured the early development of colonial liberties. The Puritans, who founded the New England colonies, having fled from the oppression of Charles I., carried with them a stern love of civil liberty, and established republican institutions.[1] The persecuted Catholics who settled Maryland, and the proscribed Quakers who took refuge in Pennsylvania, were little less democratic.[2] Other colonies founded in America and the West Indies, in the seventeenth century, merely for the purposes of trade and cultivation, adopted institutions,—less democratic, indeed, but founded on principles of freedom and self-government.[3] Whether established as proprietary colonies, or under charters held direct from the crown, the colonists were equally free.

The English constitution was generally the type of these colonial governments. The governor was the viceroy of the crown: the legislative council, or upper chamber, appointed by the governor, assumed the place of the House of Lords; and the representative assembly, chosen by the people, was the express image of the House of Commons. This miniature Parliament, complete in all its parts, made laws for the internal government of the colony. The governor assembled, prorogued, and dissolved it; and signified his assent *Ordinary form of colonial constitutions.*

---

[1] In three of their colonies the council was elective; in Connecticut and Rhode Island the colonists also chose their governor.—Adam Smith, book iv. ch. 7. But the king's approval of the governor was reserved by 7 & 8 Will. III. c. 22.

[2] Bancroft's Hist. of the Colonisation of the United States, i. 264; iii. 394.

[3] Merivale's Colonisation, ed. 1861, 95, 103.

or dissent to every act agreed to by the chambers: the Upper House mimicked the dignity of the House of Peers;[1] and the Lower House insisted on the privileges of the Commons, especially that of originating all taxes and grants of money, for the public service.[2] The elections were also conducted after the fashion of the mother country.[3] Other laws and institutions were imitated not less faithfully. Jamaica, for example, maintained a court of king's bench, a court of common pleas, a court of exchequer, a court of chancery, a court of admiralty, and a court of probate. It had grand and petty juries, justices of the peace, courts of quarter-sessions, vestries, a coroner, and constables.[4]

Every colony was a little state, complete in its legislature, its judicature, and its executive administration. But, at the same time, it acknowledged the sovereignty of the mother country, the prerogatives of the crown, and the legislative supremacy of Parliament. The assent of the king, or his representative, was required to give validity to acts of the colonial legislature: his *veto* annulled them;[5] while the Imperial Parliament was able to

The sovereignty of England.

[1] In 1858 a quarrel arose between the two Houses in Newfoundland, in consequence of the Upper House insisting upon receiving the Lower House at a conference, sitting and covered,—an assumption of dignity which was resented by the latter. The governor having failed to accommodate the difference, prorogued the Parliament before the supplies were granted. In the next session these disputes were amicably arranged. Message of Council, April 23rd, 1858, and reply of House of Assembly; Private Correspondence of Sir A. Bannerman.

[2] Stokes' British Colonies, 241; Edwards' Hist. of the West Indies, ii. 419; Long's Hist. of Jamaica, i. 56.

[3] Edwards, ii. 419; Haliburton's Nova Scotia, ii. 319.

[4] Long's Hist. of Jamaica, i. 9.

[5] In Connecticut and Rhode Island, neither the crown nor the governor were able to negative laws passed by the Assemblies.

bind the colony by its acts, and to supersede all local legislation. Every colonial judicature was also subject to an appeal to the king in council, at Westminster. The dependence of the colonies, however, was little felt in their internal government. They were secured from interference by the remoteness of the mother country,[1] and the ignorance, indifference, and preoccupation of her rulers. In matters of imperial concern, England imposed her own policy: but otherwise left them free. Asking no aid of her, they escaped her domination. All their expenditure, civil and military, was defrayed by taxes raised by themselves. They provided for their own defence against the Indians, and the enemies of England. During the seven years' war, the American colonies maintained a force of 25,000 men, at a cost of several millions. In the words of Franklin, 'they were governed, at the expense to Great Britain, of only a little pen, ink and paper: they were led by a thread.'[2]

But little as the mother country concerned herself in the political government of her colonies, she evinced a jealous vigilance in regard to their commerce. Commercial monopoly, indeed, was the first principle in the colonial policy of England, as well as of the other maritime states of Europe. She suffered no other country but herself to supply their wants: she appropriated many of their exports;

Commercial restrictions.

---

[1] 'Three thousand miles of ocean lie between you and them,' said Mr. Burke. 'No contrivance can prevent the effect of this distance in weakening government.' Adam Smith observed: 'Their situation has placed them less in the view and less in the power of the mother country.'—Book iv. ch. 7.

[2] Evidence before the Commons, 1766; Parl. Hist., xvi. 139–141.

and, for the sake of her own manufacturers, insisted that their produce should be sent to her in a raw, or unmanufactured state. By the Navigation Acts, their produce could only be exported to England in English ships.[1] This policy was avowedly maintained for the benefit of the mother country,—for the encouragement of her commerce, her shipping, and manufactures,—to which the interests of the colonies were sacrificed.[2] But, in compensation for this monopoly, she gave a preference to the produce of her own colonies, by protective and prohibitory duties upon foreign commodities. In claiming a monopoly of their markets, she, at the same time, gave them a reciprocal monopoly of her own. In some cases she encouraged the production of their staples by bounties. A commercial policy so artificial as this,—the creature of laws striving against nature,—marked the dependence of the colonies, crippled their industry, fomented discontents, and even provoked war with foreign states.[3] But it was a policy common to every European government, until enlightened by economical science; and commercial advantages were, for upwards of a century, nearly the sole benefit which England recognised in the possession of her colonies.[4]

In all ages, taxes and tribute had been characteristic incidents of a dependency. The subject provinces of Asiatic monarchies, in ancient and modern times, had been des-

Taxes and tribute common to dependencies.

---

[1] The first Navigation Act was passed in 1651, during the Commonwealth; Merivale, 75, 84, 89; Adam Smith, book iv. ch. 7.
[2] Ibid.
[3] Adam Smith's Wealth of Nations, book iv. ch. 7.   [4] Ibid.

poiled by the rapacity of satraps and pashas, and the greed of the central government. The Greek colonies, which resembled those of England more than any other dependencies of antiquity, were forced to send contributions to the treasury of the parent state. Carthage exacted tribute from her subject towns and territories. The Roman provinces 'paid tribute unto Cæsar.' In modern times, Spain received tribute from her European dependencies, and a revenue from the gold and silver mines of her American colonies. It was also the policy of France, Holland, and Portugal to derive a revenue from their settlements.[1]

But England, satisfied with the colonial trade, by which her subjects, at home, were enriched, imposed upon them alone all the burthens of the state.[2] Her costly wars, the interest of her increasing debt, her naval and military establishments,—adequate for the defence of a widespread empire,—were all maintained by the dominant country herself. James II. would have levied taxes upon the colonists of Massachusetts: but was assured by Sir William Jones that he could no more 'levy money without their consent in an assembly, than they could discharge themselves from their allegiance.'[3] Fifty years later, the shrewd instinct of Sir Robert Walpole revolted against a

English colonies free from imperial taxation.

Arguments in favour of taxation.

---

[1] Sir G. C. Lewis on the Government of Dependencies, 99, 101, 106, 112, 124, 139, 149, 211, *et seq.*; Adam Smith, book iv. ch. 7· Raynal, Livres i. ii. vi.–ix. xii. xiii.

[2] 'The English colonists have never yet contributed anything towards the defence of the mother country, or towards the support of its civil government.'—*Adam Smith*, book iv. ch. 7.

[3] Grahame's Hist. of the United States, i. 366.

similar attempt.[1] But at length, in an evil hour, it was resolved by George III. and his minister Mr. Grenville,[2] that the American colonies should be required to contribute to the general revenues of the government. This new principle was apparently recommended by many considerations of justice and expediency. Much of the national debt had been incurred in defence of the colonies, and in wars for the common cause of the whole empire.[3] Other states had been accustomed to enrich themselves by the taxation of their dependencies; and why was England alone to abstain from so natural a source of revenue? If the colonies were to be exempt from the common burthens of the empire, why should England care to defend them in war, or incur charges for them in time of peace? The benefits of the connexion were reciprocal; why, then, should the burthens be all on one side? Nor, assuming the equity of imperial taxation, did it seem beyond the competence of Parliament to establish it. The omnipotence of Parliament was a favourite theory of lawyers; and for a century and a half, the force of British statutes had been acknowledged without question, in every matter concerning the government of the colonies.

No charters exempted colonists from the sovereignty of the parent state, in matters of taxation;

---

[1] Walpole's Mem., ii. 70. 'I have Old England set against me,' he said,—by the excise scheme,—'do you think I will have New England likewise?'—*Coxe's Life*, i. 123.

[2] Wraxall's Mem., ii. 111; Nichols' Recoll., i. 205; Bancroft's Amer. Rev., iii. 307.

[3] Adam Smith, book iv. ch. 7; Walpole's Mem., ii. 71.

nor were there wanting precedents, in which they had submitted to imperial imposts without remonstrance. In carrying out a restrictive commercial policy, Parliament had passed numerous acts providing for the levy of colonial import and export duties. Such duties, from their very nature, were unproductive,—imposing restraints upon trade, and offering encouragements to smuggling. They were designed for commercial regulation rather than revenue: but were collected by the king's officers, and payable into the exchequer. The state had further levied postage duties within the colonies.[1]

Arguments on the other side.

But these considerations were outweighed by reasons on the other side. Granting that the war expenditure of the mother country had been increased by reason of her colonies, who was responsible for European wars and costly armaments? Not the colonies, which had no voice in the government: but their English rulers, who held in their hands the destinies of the empire. And if the English treasury had suffered, in defence of the colonies, —the colonists had taxed themselves heavily for protection against the foes of the mother country, with whom they had no quarrel.[2] But, apart from the equity of the claim, was it properly within the jurisdiction of Parliament to enforce it? The

[1] Evidence of Dr. Franklin, 1766; Parl. Hist., xvi. 143; Stedman's Hist. of the American War, i. 10, 44; Rights of Great Britain Asserted, 102; Adolphus's Hist., i. 145; Bancroft's Hist. of the American Revolution, ii. 260, *et seq.*; Dr. Johnson's Taxation no Tyranny, Works, xii. 177; Speech of Lord Mansfield, Jan. 1766; Parl. Hist., xvi. 166; Burke's Speech on American Taxation, 1774, Works, ii. 380; Speech of Governor Pownall, Nov. 16th, 1775; Parl. Hist., xviii. 984.

[2] Dr. Franklin's Ev., Parl. Hist., xvi. 139.

colonists might be induced to grant a contribution: but could Parliament constitutionally impose a tax, without their consent? True, that this imperial legislature could make laws for the government of the colonies: but taxation formed a marked exception to general legislation. According to the principles, traditions, and usage of the constitution, taxes were granted by the people, through their representatives. This privilege had been recognised for centuries, in the parent state; and the colonists had cherished it with traditional veneration, in the country of their adoption. They had taxed themselves, for local objects, through their own representatives: they had responded to requisitions from the crown for money: but never until now, had it been sought to tax them directly, for imperial purposes, by the authority of Parliament.

A statesman imbued with the free spirit of our constitution could not have failed to recognise these overruling principles. He would have seen, that if it were fit that the colonies should contribute to the imperial treasury, it was for the crown to demand their contributions through the governors; and for the colonial legislatures to grant them. But neither the king nor his minister were alive to these principles. The one was too conscious of kingly power, to measure nicely the rights of his subjects; and the other was blinded by a pedantic reverence for the authority of Parliament.[1]

In 1764, an act was passed, with little discussion,

---

[1] Walpole's Mem., ii. 70, 220; Bancroft's Hist. of the American Revolution, ii. 88.

imposing customs' duties upon several articles imported into the American colonies,—the produce of these duties being reserved for the defence of the colonies themselves.[1] At the same time, the Commons passed a resolution, that 'it may be proper to charge certain stamp duties' in America,[2] as the foundation of future legislation. The colonists, accustomed to perpetual interference with their trade, did not dispute the right of the mother country to tax their imports: but they resolved to evade the impost, as far as possible, by the encouragement of native manufactures. The threatened Stamp Act, however, they immediately denounced as an invasion of the rights of Englishmen, who could not be taxed otherwise than by their representatives. But, deaf to their remonstrances, Mr. Grenville, in the next session, persisted in his stamp bill. It attracted little notice in this country: the people could bear with complacency the taxation of others; and never was there a Parliament more indifferent to constitutional principles, and popular rights. The colonists, however, and their agents in this country, remonstrated against the proposal.

Their opinion had been invited by ministers; and that it might be expressed, a year's delay had been agreed upon. Yet when they petitioned against

[1] 4 Geo. III. c. 15. Mr. Bancroft regards a measure, introduced by Mr. Townshend in the previous session for lowering some of the prohibitory duties, and making them productive, as the commencement of the plan for the taxation of America; but that measure merely dealt with existing duties. It was not until 1764 that any new issue was raised with the colonies.—Hist. of American Revolution, ii. 102.

[2] March 10th, 1764. Parl. Hist., xv. 1427; Grahame's Hist., iv. 179.

the bill, the Commons refused to entertain their petitions, under a rule, by no means binding on their discretion, which excluded petitions against a tax proposed for the service of the year.[1] An arbitrary temper and narrow pedantry prevailed over justice and sound policy. Unrepresented communities were to be taxed,—even without a hearing. The bill was passed with little opposition:[2] but the colonists combined to resist its execution. Mr. Pitt had been ill in bed when the Stamp Act was passed: but no sooner were the discontents in America brought into discussion, than he condemned taxation without representation; and counselled the immediate repeal of the obnoxious Act. 'When in this House,' he said, 'we give and grant, we grant what is our own. But in an American tax, what do we do? We, Your Majesty's Commons for Great Britain, give and grant to Your Majesty—what? Our own property? No: we give and grant to Your Majesty the property of Your Majesty's Commons of America.' At the same time, he proposed to save the honour of England by an act declaratory of the general legislative authority of Parliament over the colonies.[3] Lord Rockingham, who had succeeded Mr. Grenville, alarmed by the unanimity and violence of the colonists, readily caught at Mr. Pitt's

---

[1] This monstrous rule, or usage, which set at naught the right of petition on the most important matters of public concern, dates from the Revolution; and was not relinquished until 1842.—Hatsell, Prec., iii. 226; May's Proceedings and Usage of Parliament, 6th ed., 516.
[2] Parl. Hist., xvi. 34. 'We might as well have hindered the sun's setting,' wrote Franklin.—*Bancroft*, ii. 281.
[3] Parl. Hist., xvi. 93; Life of Lord Chatham, i. 427.

suggestion. The Stamp Act was repealed, notwithstanding the obstinate resistance of the king and his friends, and of Mr. Grenville and the supporters of the late ministry.[1] Mr. Pitt had desired expressly to except from the declaratory act the right of taxation, without the consent of the colonists: but the crown lawyers and Lord Mansfield denied the distinction between legislation and the imposition of taxes, which that great constitutional statesman had forcibly pointed out; and the bill was introduced without that exception. In the House of Lords, Lord Camden, the only sound constitutional lawyer of his age, supported with remarkable power the views of Mr. Pitt: but the bill was passed in its original shape, and maintained the unqualified right of England to make laws for the colonies.[2] In the same session some of the import duties imposed in 1764 were also repealed, and others modified.[3] The colonists were appeased by these concessions; and little regarded the abstract terms of the declaratory act. They were, indeed, encouraged in a spirit of independence, by their triumph over the English Parliament: but their loyalty was as yet unshaken.[4]

The error of Mr. Grenville had scarcely been re-

[1] Walpole's Mem., ii. 258, 285, &c.; Rockingham Mem., i. 291-295; ii. 250, 294.
[2] 6 Geo. III. c. 11, 12; Parl. Hist., xvi. 163, 177, &c.; Walpole's Mem., ii. 277-298, 304-307, &c.; Rockingham Mem., i. 282-293; Bancroft, ii. 459-473; Chatham Corr., ii. 375.
[3] 6 Geo. III. c. 52.
[4] Stedman's Hist., i. 48, *et seq.*; Bancroft's Hist. of the American Revolution, ii. 523; Burke's Speech on American Taxation: see also Lord Macaulay's Life of Lord Chatham, Essays; Lord Campbell's Lives of the Chief Justices (Lord Camden).

paired, when an act of political fatuity caused an irreparable breach between the mother country and her colonies. Lord Chatham, by his timely intervention, had saved England her colonies; and now his ill-omened administration was destined to lose them. His witty and accomplished, but volatile and incapable Chancellor of the Exchequer, Mr. Charles Townshend, having lost half a million of his ways and means, by an adverse vote of the Commons on the land tax,[1] ventured, with incredible levity, to repeat the disastrous experiment of colonial taxation. The Americans, to strengthen their own case against the Stamp Act, had drawn a distinction between internal and external taxation,—a distinction plausible and ingenious, in the hands of so dexterous a master of political fence as Dr. Franklin,[2] but substantially without foundation. Both kinds of taxes were equally paid by the colonists themselves; and if it was their birthright to be taxed by none but representatives of their own, this doctrine clearly comprehended customs, no less than excise. But, misled by the supposed distinction which the Americans themselves had raised, Mr. Townshend proposed a variety of small colonial customs' duties, —on glass, on paper, on painters' colours, and lastly, on tea. The estimated produce of these paltry taxes amounted to no more than 40,000*l*. Lord Chatham would have scornfully put aside a scheme, at once so contemptible and impolitic, and so plainly in violation of the principles for which he had him-

Mr. Charles Townshend's colonial taxes, 1767.

---

[1] *Supra*, Vol. II. 101.   [2] Parl. Hist., xvi. 144.

self recently contended: but he lay stricken and helpless, while his rash lieutenant was rushing headlong into danger. Lord Camden would have arrested the measure in the Cabinet; but standing alone, in a disorganised ministry, he accepted under protest a scheme, which none of his colleagues approved.[1] However rash the financier, however weak the compliance of ministers, Parliament fully shared the fatal responsibility of this measure. It was passed with approbation, and nearly in silence.[2] Mr. Townshend did not survive to see the mischief he had done: but his colleagues had soon to deplore their error. The colonists resisted the import duties, as they had resisted the Stamp Act; and, a second time, ministers were forced to recede from their false position. But their retreat was effected awkwardly, and with a bad grace. They yielded to the colonists, so far as to give up the general scheme of import duties: but persisted in continuing the duties upon tea.[3]

All repealed but the tea duties.

This miserable remnant of the import duties was not calculated to afford a revenue exceeding 12,000*l*.; and its actual proceeds were reduced to 300*l*. by smuggling, and the determination of the colonists not to consume an article to which the obnoxious impost was attached. The insignificance of the tax, while it left ministers without justification for continuing such a cause of irri-

Insignificance of the tea duties.

---

[1] See Lord Camden's Statement.—Parl. Hist., xviii. 1222.
[2] 7 Geo. III. c. 46; Rockingham Mem., ii. 75; Bancroft's Hist. of the American Revolution, iii. 83, *et seq.*
[3] 10 Geo. III. c. 17; Parl. Hist., xvi. 853; Cavendish Deb., ii. 484.

tation, went far to secure the acquiescence of the colonists. But their discontents,—met without temper or moderation,—were suddenly inflamed by a new measure, which only indirectly concerned them. To assist the half-bankrupt East India Company, in the sale of their teas, a drawback was given them, of the whole English duty, on shipments to the American plantations.[1] By this concession to the East India Company, the colonists, exempted from the English duty, in fact received their teas at a lower rate than when there was no colonial tax. The Company were also empowered to ship their teas direct from their own warehouses. A sudden stimulus was thus given to the export of the very article, which alone caused irritation and dissension. The colonists saw, or affected to see, in this measure, an artful contrivance for encouraging the consumption of taxed tea, and facilitating the further extension of colonial taxation. It was met by a daring outrage. The first tea-ships which reached Boston were boarded by men disguised as Mohawk Indians, and their cargoes cast into the sea.[2] This being the crowning act of a series of provocations and insults, by which the colonists, and especially the people of Boston, had testified their resentment against the Stamp Act, the import duties, and other recent measures, the government at home regarded it with just indignation. Every one agreed

Sidenote: Drawbacks granted on tea.

Sidenote: Attack upon the tea-ships at Boston, 1773.

---

[1] 12 Geo. III. c. 60; 13 Geo. III. c. 44. The former of these Acts granted a drawback of three-fifths only.

[2] Adams' Works, ii. 322; Bancroft's Hist. of the American Rev., iii. 514-541, &c.

that the rioters deserved punishment; and that reparation was due to the East India Company. But the punishment inflicted by Parliament, at the instance of Lord North, was such as to provoke revolt. Instead of demanding compensation, and attaching penalties to its refusal, the flourishing port of Boston was summarily closed: no ship could lade or unlade at its quays: the trade and industry of its inhabitants were placed under an interdict. The ruin of the city was decreed: no penitence could avert its doom: but when the punishment had been suffered, and the atonement made: when Boston, humbled and contrite, had kissed the rod; and when reparation had been made to the East India Company, the king in council might, as an act of grace, remove the fatal ban.[1] It was a deed of vengeance, fitter for the rude arbitrament of an eastern prince, than for the temperate equity of a free state.

Boston Port Act, 1774.

Nor was this the only act of repression. The republican constitution of Massachusetts, cherished by the descendants of the pilgrim fathers, was superseded. The council, hitherto elective, was to be nominated by the crown; and the appointment of judges, magistrates, and sheriffs, was transferred from the council to the governor.[2] And so much was the administration of justice suspected, that by another act, accused persons

Constitution of Massachusetts superseded.

---

[1] Boston Port Act, 14 Geo. III. c. 19; Parl. Hist., xvii. 1159-1189; Chatham Corr., iv. 342; Rockingham Mem., ii. 238-243; Bancroft's Hist., iii. 565, *et seq.*

[2] 14 Geo. III. c. 45; Parl. Hist., xvii. 1192, 1277, &c.

might be sent for trial to any other colony, or even to England.¹ Troops were also despatched to overawe the turbulent people of Massachusetts.

The colonists, however, far from being intimidated by the rigours of the mother country, associated to resist them. Nor was Massachusetts left alone in its troubles. A congress of delegates from twelve of the colonies was assembled at Philadelphia, by whom the recent measures were condemned, as a violation of the rights of Englishmen. It was further agreed to suspend all imports from, and all exports to, Great Britain and her dependencies, unless the grievances of the colonies were redressed. Other threatening measures were adopted, which proved too plainly that the stubborn spirit of the colonists was not to be overcome. In the words of Lord Chatham, 'the spirit which now resisted taxation in America, was the same spirit which formerly opposed loans, benevolences, and ship-money in England.'²

Resistance of the colonists.

In vain Lord Chatham,—appearing after his long prostration,—proffered a measure of conciliation, repealing the obnoxious acts, and explicitly renouncing imperial taxation: but requiring from the colonies the grant of a revenue to the king. Such a measure might even yet have saved the colonies:³ but it was contemptuously rejected by the Lords, on the first reading.⁴

Lord Chatham's conciliatory proposition, Feb. 1st, 1775.

[1] 14 Geo. III. c. 39; Parl. Hist., xvii. 1199, &c.
[2] Speech, Jan. 20th, 1777.—Parl. Hist., xviii. 154, n.
[3] See Lord Mahon's Hist., vi. 43.
[4] Feb. 1st, 1775.—Parl. Hist., xviii. 198.

Lord North himself soon afterwards framed a conciliatory proposition, promising that, if the colonists should make provision for their own defence, and for the civil government, no imperial tax should be levied. His resolution was agreed to: but, in the present temper of the colonists, its conditions were impracticable.[1] Mr. Burke also proposed other resolutions, similar to the scheme of Lord Chatham, which were rejected by a large majority.[2]

Propositions of Lord North and Mr. Burke, Feb. 20th, 1775.

March 22nd, 1775.

The Americans were already ripe for rebellion, when an unhappy collision occurred at Lexington, between the royal troops and the colonial militia. Blood was shed; and the people flew to arms. The war of independence was commenced. Its sad history and issue are but too well known. In vain Congress addressed a petition to the king, for redress and conciliation. It received no answer. In vain Lord Chatham devoted the last energies of his wasting life[3] to effect a reconciliation, without renouncing the sovereignty of England. In vain the British Parliament,—humbling itself before its rebellious subjects,—repealed the American tea duty, and renounced its claims to im-

Outbreak of the civil war, April 19th, 1775.

Petition to the king, Sept. 1st, 1775.

Overtures for peace, 1778.

---

[1] Parl. Hist., xviii. 319; Chatham Corr., iv. 403; Gibbon's Posthumous Works, i. 490.

[2] Parl. Hist., xviii. 478; Burke's Works, iii. 23.

[3] Lord Chatham was completely secluded from political and social life, from the spring of 1767 to the spring of 1769; and again, from the spring of 1775 to the spring of 1777.

perial taxation.[1] In vain were parliamentary commissioners empowered to suspend the acts of which the colonists complained,—to concede every demand but that of independence,—and almost to sue for peace.[2] It was too late to stay the civil war. Disasters and defeat befell the British arms, on American soil; and, at length, the independence of the colonies was recognised.[3]

Such were the disastrous consequences of a misunderstanding of the rights and pretensions of colonial communities, who had carried with them the laws and franchises of Englishmen. And here closes the first period in the constitutional history of the colonies.

We must now turn to another class of dependencies, not originally settled by English subjects, but acquired from other states by conquest or cession. To these a different rule of public law was held to apply. They were dominions of the crown, and governed, according to the laws prevailing at the time of their acquisition, by the king in council.[4] They were distinguished from other settlements as crown colonies. Some of them, however, like Jamaica

Crown colonies.

Free constitutions to crown colonies.

---

[1] 28 Geo. III. c. 12; Parl. Hist., xix. 762; Ann. Reg., 1778, 133.

[2] 28 Geo. III. c. 13.

[3] No part of English history has received more copious illustration than the revolt of the American colonies. In addition to the general histories of England, the following may be consulted: Franklin's Works, Sparks' Life of Washington, Marshall's Life of Washington, Randolph's Mem. of Jefferson, Chalmers' Political Annals, Dr. Gordon's History of the American Revolution, Grahame's History of the United States, Stedman's History, Bancroft's History of the American Revolution.

[4] Clark's Colonial Law, 4; Mills' Colonial Constitutions, 19, &c.

and Nova Scotia, had received the free institutions of England, and were practically self-governed, like other English colonies. Canada, the most important of this class, was conquered from the French, in 1759, by General Wolfe, and ceded to England in 1763, by the treaty of Paris. In 1774, the administration of its affairs was intrusted to a council appointed by the crown:[1] but in 1791, it was divided into two provinces, to each of which representative institutions were granted.[2] It was no easy problem to provide for the government of such a colony. It comprised a large and ignorant population of French colonists, having sympathies with the country whence they sprang, accustomed to absolute government and feudal institutions, and under the influence of a Catholic priesthood. It further comprised an active race of British settlers, speaking another language, professing a different religion, and craving the liberties of their own free land. The division of the provinces was also a separation of races; and freedom was granted to both alike.[3] The immediate objects of this measure were to secure the attachment of Canada, and to exempt the British colonists from the French laws: but it marked the continued adhesion of Parliament to the principles of self-government. In discussing its policy, Mr. Fox laid down a principle, which was destined, after half a century, to become the rule of colonial administration. 'I am convinced,' said he,

[1] 14 Geo. III. c. 83.
[2] 31 Geo. III. c. 31; Parl. Hist., xxviii. 1377.
[3] See Lord Durham's description of the two races.—Report, 1839, p. 8–18.

"that the only means of retaining distant colonies with advantage, is to enable them to govern themselves."[1] In 1785, representative institutions were given to New Brunswick, and, so late as 1832, to Newfoundland; and thus, eventually, all the British American colonies were as free, in their forms of government, as the colonies which had gained their independence. But the mother country, in granting these constitutions, exercised, in a marked form, the powers of a dominant state. She provided for the sale of waste lands, for the maintenance of the church establishment, and for other matters of internal polity.

England was soon compensated for the loss of her colonies in America by vast possessions in another hemisphere. But the circumstances under which Australia was settled were unfavourable to free institutions. Transportation to the American plantations, commenced in the reign of Charles II., had long been an established punishment for criminals.[2] The revolt of these colonies led to the establishment of penal settlements in Australia. New South Wales was founded in 1788,[3] and Van Diemen's Land in 1825.[4] Penal settlements were necessarily without a constitution, being little more than state prisons. These fair countries,

Australian colonies.

---

[1] March 6th, 1791; Parl. Hist., xxviii. 1379; Lord J. Russell's Life of Fox, ii. 259; Lord Stanhope's Life of Pitt, ii. 89.

[2] 4 Geo. I. c. 2; 6 Geo. I. c. 23. Banishment was made a punishment, in 1597, by 39 Elizabeth, c. 4; and transportation, by orders in council, in 1614, 1615, and 1617.—Mills' Colonial Constitutions, 344.

[3] 24 Geo. III. c. 56; Orders in Council, Dec. 6th, 1786.

[4] Mills' Colonial Const., 325.

instead of being the homes of free Englishmen, were peopled by criminals sentenced to long terms of punishment and servitude. Such an origin was not promising to the moral or political destinies of Australia: but the attractions which it offered to free emigrants gave early tokens of its future greatness. South Australia and New Zealand, whence convicts were excluded, were afterwards founded, in the same region, without free constitutions. The early political condition of the Australian colonies forms, indeed, a striking contrast to that of the older settlements, to which Englishmen had taken their birthrights. But free emigration developed their resources, and quickly reduced the criminal population to a subordinate element in the society; and, in 1828, legislative councils nominated by the Crown, were granted to New South Wales and Van Diemen's Land.[1]

While these colonies were without an adequate population, transportation was esteemed by the settlers, as the means of affording a steady supply of labour: but as free emigration advanced, the services of convicts became less essential to colonial prosperity; and the moral taint of the criminal class was felt more sensibly. In 1838, Sir William Molesworth's committee exposed the enormities of transportation as part of a scheme of colonisation; and in 1840, the sending of convicts to New South Wales was discontinued. In Van Diemen's Land, after various attempts to improve the system of convict labour and discipline, trans-

Transportation discontinued.

[1] 9 Geo. IV. c. 83.

portation was finally abolished in 1854. Meanwhile, an attempt to send convicts to the Cape of Good Hope in 1848, had been resisted by the colonists, and abandoned. In the following year, a new penal settlement was founded in Western Australia.

The discontinuance of transportation to the free colonies of Australia, and a prodigious increase of emigration and productive industry, were preparing them for a further development of freedom, at no distant period.

<small>Free constitutions to Australian colonies.</small>

From the period of the American war the home government, awakened to the importance of colonial administration, displayed greater activity, and a more ostensible disposition to interfere in the affairs of the colonies. Until the commencement of the difficulties with America, there had not even been a separate department for the government of the colonies: but the board of trade exercised a supervision, little more than nominal, over colonial affairs. In 1768, however, a third secretary of state was appointed, to whose care the colonies were intrusted. In 1782, the office was discontinued by Lord Rockingham, after the loss of the American provinces: but was revived in 1794, and became an active and important department of the state.[1] Its influence was felt throughout the British colonies. However popular the form of their institutions, they were steadily governed by British ministers in Downing Street.

<small>Colonial administration after the American war.</small>

In crown colonies,—acquired by conquest or ces-

[1] Mills' Colonial Const., 2-13.

sion,—the dominion of the crown was absolute; and the authority of the colonial office was exercised directly, by instructions to the governors. In free colonies it was exercised, for the most part, indirectly, through the influence of the governors and their councils. Self-government was there the theory: but in practice, the governors, aided by dominant interests in the several colonies, contrived to govern according to the policy dictated from Downing Street. Just as at home, the crown, the nobles, and an ascendant party were supreme in the national councils,—so in the colonies, the governors and their official aristocracy were generally able to command the adhesion of the local legislatures. *Colonies governed in Downing Street.*

A more direct interference, however, was often exercised. Ministers had no hesitation in disallowing any colonial acts of which they disapproved, even when they concerned the internal affairs of the colony only. They dealt freely with the public lands, as the property of the crown: often making grants obnoxious to the colonists; and peremptorily insisting upon the conditions under which they should be sold and settled. Their interference was also frequent, regarding church establishments and endowments, official salaries and the colonial civil lists. Misunderstandings and disputes were constant, but the policy and will of the home government usually prevailed.

Another incident of colonial administration was that of patronage. The colonies offered a wide field of employment for the friends, connexions, *Patronage.*

and political partisans of the home government. The offices in England, available for securing parliamentary support, fell short of the demand; and appointments were accordingly multiplied abroad. Of these, many of the most lucrative were executed by deputy. The favoured friends of ministers, who were gratified by the emoluments of office, were little disposed to suffer banishment in a distant dependency. Infants in the cradle were endowed with colonial appointments, to be executed through life by convenient deputies. Extravagant fees or salaries were granted in Downing Street, and spent in England; but paid out of colonial revenues. Other offices again, to which residence was attached, were too frequently given to men wholly unfit for employment at home, but who were supposed to be equal to colonial service, where indolence, incapacity, or doubtful character might escape exposure.[1] Such men as these, however, were more mischievous in a colony than at home. The higher officers were associated with the governor, in the administration of affairs: the subordinate officers were subject to less control and discipline. In both, negligence and unfitness were injurious to the colonies. As colonial societies expanded, these appointments from home further excited the jealousy of colonists, many of whom were better qualified for office than

[1] 'As to civil officers appointed for America, most of the places in the gift of the crown have been filled with broken members of Parliament, of bad, if any, principles,—*valets de chambre*, electioneering scoundrels, and even livery servants. In one word, America has been, for many years, made the hospital of England.'—*Letter of General Huske, in* 1758; Phillimore's Life of Lord Lyttelton, ii. 604, cited by Lord Mahon.

the strangers who came amongst them to enjoy power, wealth, and distinction, which were denied to themselves.[1] This jealousy and the natural ambition of the colonists, were among the principal causes which led to demands for more complete self-government. As this feeling was increasing in colonial society, the home government were occupied with arrangements for insuring the permanent maintenance of the civil establishment out of the colonial revenues. To continue to fill all the offices with Englishmen, and at the same time to call upon the jealous colonists to pay them, was not to be attempted. And accordingly the home government surrendered to the governors all appointments under 200*l.* a year; and to the greater number of other offices, appointed colonists recommended by the governors.[2] A colonial grievance was thus redressed, and increased influence given to the colonists; while one of the advantages of the connexion was renounced by the parent state.

While England was entering upon a new period of extended liberties, after the Reform Act, circumstances materially affected her relations with the colonies; and this may be termed the third and last period of colonial history. First, the abolition of slavery, in 1833, loosened the ties by which the sugar colonies had been bound to the mother country. This was fol-

New commercial policy affecting the colonies.

---

[1] Long's Hist. of Jamaica, i. 27, 79; Edwards' Hist. of the West Indies, ii. 390; Sir G. C. Lewis on Dependencies, 278-284; MS. Memorandum by the Right Hon. Edw. Ellice, M.P.

[2] Earl Grey's Colonial Policy, i. 37-41; Rules and Regulations for Her Majesty's Colonial Service, ch. iii.; Mills' Colonial Constitutions, App. 378.

lowed by the gradual adoption of a new commercial policy, which overthrew the long-established protections and monopolies of colonial trade. The main purpose for which both parties had cherished the connexion was lost. Colonists found their produce exposed to the competition of the world; and, in the sugar colonies, with restricted labour. The home consumer, independent of colonial supplies, was free to choose his own market, wherever commodities were best and cheapest. The sugars of Jamaica competed with the slave-grown sugars of Cuba: the woods of Canada with the timber of Norway and the Baltic.

These new conditions of colonial policy seriously *Its effect upon the political relations of colonies.* affected the political relations of the mother country with her dependencies. Her interference in their internal affairs having generally been connected with commercial regulations, she had now less interest in continuing it; and they, having submitted to it for the sake of benefits with which it was associated, were less disposed to tolerate its exercise. Meanwhile the growing population, wealth, and intelligence of many of the colonies, closer communications with England, and the example of English liberties, were developing the political aspirations of colonial societies, and their capacity for self-government.

Early in this period of transition, England twice *Contumacy of Jamaica repressed.* had occasion to assert her paramount authority: but learned at the same time to estimate the force of local opinion, and to seek in the further development of free institutions, the problem of colonial government. Jamaica, discontented after the abolition of slavery, neglected to make adequate provision for her prisons, which that measure had rendered necessary. In 1838, the Imperial Parliament interposed, and promptly supplied this defect in colonial legislation.[1] The local assembly, resenting this act of authority, was contumacious, stopped the supplies, and refused to exercise the proper functions of a legislature. Again Parliament asserted its supremacy. The sullen legislature was commanded to resume its duties; and submitted in time to save the ancient constitution of Jamaica from suspension.[2]

At the same period, the perilous state of Canada called forth all the authority of England. In 1837 and 1838, the discontents of Lower Canada exploded in insurrection. The constitution of that province was immediately suspended by the British Parliament; and a provisional government was established, with large legislative and executive powers.[3] This necessary act of authority was followed by the reunion of the provinces of Upper and Lower Canada into a single colony, under a governor-general.[4]

Insurrection in Canada.

Reunion of the provinces.

But while these strong measures were resorted to, the British Government carefully defined the principles upon which parliamentary interposition was justified. 'Parliamentary legislation,' wrote Lord Glenelg, the colonial minister, 'on any subject of exclusively internal concern to any British colony possessing a representative

Right of colonial self-government admitted.

---

[1] 1 & 2 Vict. c. 67.
[2] 2 & 3 Vict. c. 26; Hans. Deb., 3rd Ser., xlvi. 1243; xlvii. 459, &c.
[3] 1 & 2 Vict. c. 9; 2 & 3 Vict. c. 53.   [4] 3 & 4 Vict. c. 35.

assembly is, as a general rule, unconstitutional. It is a right of which the exercise is reserved for extreme cases, in which necessity at once creates and justifies the exception.'[1] Never before had the rights of colonial self-government been so plainly acknowledged.

But another principle was about to be established in Canada, which still further enlarged the powers of colonial assemblies, and diminished the influence of the mother country. This principle is known as the doctrine of responsible government. Hitherto the advisers of the governor in this, as in every other colony, were the principal officers appointed by the crown, and generally holding permanent offices. Whatever the fluctuations of opinion in the legislature, or in the colony,—whatever the unpopularity of the measures or persons of the executive officers, they continued to direct the councils of the colony. For many years, they had contrived, by concessions, by management and influence, to avoid frequent collisions with the assemblies: but as the principles of representative government were developed, irresponsible rulers were necessarily brought into conflict with the popular assembly. The advisers of the governor pursued one policy, the assembly another. Measures prepared by the executive were rejected by the assembly: measures passed by the assembly were refused by the council, or vetoed by the governor. And whenever such collisions arose, the constitutional means were wanting, for restoring

Principle of responsible government.

---

[1] Parl. Paper, 1839, No. 118, p. 7.

confidence between the contending powers.[1] Frequent dissolutions exasperated the popular party, and generally resulted in their ultimate triumph. The hostility between the assembly and permanent and unpopular officers became chronic. They were constantly at issue; and representative institutions, in collision with irresponsible power, were threatening anarchy. These difficulties were not confined to Canada: but were common to all the North American colonies; and proved the incompatibility of two antagonistic principles of government.[2]

After the reunion of the Canadian provinces, a remedy was sought for disagreements between the executive and the legislature in that principle of ministerial responsibility, which had long been accepted as the basis of constitutional government in England. At first, ministers at home were apprehensive lest the application of that principle to a dependency should lead to a virtual renunciation of control by the mother country.[3] Nor had Canada yet sufficiently recovered from the passions of the recent rebellion, to favour the experiment. But arrangements were immediately made for altering the tenure of the principal colonial offices; and in 1847, responsible government was fully established under Lord Elgin.[4] From that time, the governor-general selected his

Introduction of responsible government into Canada,

---

[1] See Lord Durham's Report on Canada, 1839, p. 27–39.
[2] *Ibid.*
[3] Despatches of Lord J. Russell to Mr. Poulett Thomson, governor-general of Canada, Oct. 14th and 16th, 1939; Parl. Papers, 1848, No. 621.
[4] Earl Grey's Colonial Policy, i. 200–234, 269; Despatches of Lord Elgin; Parl. Papers, 1848.

advisers from that party which was able to command a majority in the legislative assembly; and accepted the policy recommended by them.[1] The same principle was adopted, about the same time, in Nova Scotia;[2] and has since become the rule of administration in other free colonies.[3]

and other colonies.

By the adoption of this principle, a colonial constitution has become the very image and reflection of parliamentary government in England. The governor, like the sovereign whom he represents, holds himself aloof from, and superior to parties; and governs through constitutional advisers, who have acquired an ascendency in the legislature. He leaves contending parties to fight out their own battles; and by admitting the stronger party to his councils, brings the executive authority into harmony with popular sentiments.[4] And as the recognition of this doctrine, in England, has practically transferred the supreme authority of the state, from the crown, to Parliament and the people,—so in the colonies has it wrested from the governor and from the parent state, the direction of colonial affairs. And again, as the crown has gained in ease and popularity what it has lost in power,—so has the

Its results.

---

[1] See Resolutions of the Canadian Parliament, Sept. 3rd, 1841; Parl. Paper, 1848, No. 621.

[2] Despatch of Earl Grey to Sir John Harvey, Nov. 3rd, 1846; Parl. Paper, 1848, No. 621, p. 8.

[3] Mills' Colonial Constitutions, 201, 205, 209, &c. The only free colonies to which responsible government has not been extended are the Cape of Good Hope and Western Australia.

[4] 'The executive council is a removable body, in analogy to the usage prevailing in the British constitution' . . . 'it being understood that councillors who have lost the confidence of the local legislature will tender their resignations to the governors.'—*Rules and Regulations for the Colonial Service*, ch. ii.

mother country, in accepting, to the full, the principles of local self-government, established the closest relations of amity and confidence between herself and her colonies.

There are circumstances, however, in which the parallel is not maintained. The Crown and Parliament have a common interest in the welfare of their country: but England and her colonies may have conflicting interests, or an irreconcilable policy. The crown has, indeed, reserved its veto upon the acts of the colonial legislatures: but its practical exercise has been found scarcely more compatible with responsible government in the colonies, than in England. Hence colonies have been able to adopt principles of legislation inconsistent with the policy and interests of the mother country. For example, after England had accepted free trade as the basis of her commercial policy, Canada adhered to protection; and established a tariff injurious to English commerce.[1] Such laws could not have been disallowed by the home government without a revival of the conflicts and discontents of a former period; and in deference to the principles of self-government, they were reluctantly confirmed. *Conflicting interests of England and colonies.*

But popular principles, in colonial government, have not rested here. While enlarged powers have been intrusted to the local *Democratic constitutions.*

---

[1] Report on Colonial Military Expenditure, 1861. Ev. of Mr. Gladstone, 3785; MS. Paper by the Right Hon. Edw. Ellice, M.P.; and see a statement of difficulties experienced by the home government in endeavouring to restrain New Brunswick in the granting of bounties.—Earl Grey's Colonial Policy, i. 279.

legislatures, those institutions again have been reconstituted upon a more democratic basis. The constitution granted to Canada in 1840, on the reunion of the provinces, was popular, but not democratic.[1] It was composed of a legislative council, nominated by the crown, and of a representative assembly, to which freeholders or roturiers to the amount of 500*l.* were eligible as members. The franchise comprised 40*s.* freeholders, 5*l.* houseowners, and 10*l.* occupiers: but has since been placed upon a more popular basis by provincial acts.[2]

Franchise in Canada.

Democracy made more rapid progress in the Australian colonies. In 1842, a new constitution was granted to New South Wales, which, departing from the accustomed model of colonial constitutions in other parts of the Empire, provided for the legislation of the colony by a single chamber.

Australian constitutions.

The constitution of an upper chamber in a colonial society, without an aristocracy, and with few persons of high attainments, and adequate leisure, had ever been a difficult problem. Nominated by the governor, aud consisting mainly of his executive officers, it had failed to exercise a material influence over public opinion; and had been readily overborne by the more popular assembly. The experiment was, therefore, tried of bringing into a single chamber the aristocratic and democratic elements of colonial government. It was hoped that

Policy of a single chamber.

---

[1] 3 & 4 Vict. c. 35; Mills' Colonial Const., 184.
[2] Canadian Acts, 16 Vict. c. 153; 22 Vict. c. 82.

eminent men would have more weight in the deliberations of the popular assembly, than sitting apart and exercising an impotent veto. The experiment found favour with experienced statesmen: yet it can scarcely be doubted that it was a concession to democracy. Timely delays in legislation,—a cautious review of public measures,—resistance to the tyranny of a majority, and the violence of a faction,—the means of judicious compromise,—were wanting in such a constitution. The majority of a single chamber was absolute.[1]

In 1850, it became expedient to divide the vast territories of New South Wales into two, and the southern portion was erected into the new colony of Victoria. *Constitutions of 1850.* This opportunity was taken of revising the constitutions of these colonies, and of South Australia and Van Diemen's Land.[2] The New South Wales model was adhered to by Parliament; and a single chamber was constituted in each of these colonies, of which one-third were nominated by the crown, and two-thirds elected under a franchise, restricted to persons holding freehold property worth 100*l.* and 10*l.* householders or leaseholders. A fixed charge was also imposed upon the colonial revenues for the civil and judicial establishments, and for religious worship. At the same time, powers were conceded to the governor and legislative council of each colony, with the assent

---

[1] The relative advantages of a single and double chamber are fully argued by Earl Grey, Colonial Policy, ii. 96, and by Mr. Mills, Colonial Const., Introd., 57.

[2] This constitution was postponed, as regards Western Australia, until the colony should undertake to pay the charges of its civil government.

of the queen in council, to alter every part of the constitution so granted.[1] The experiment of a single chamber was soon abandoned by those colonies themselves; while the principle of election was introduced into the legislative councils.[2] But otherwise the tendency of such societies was naturally favourable to democracy; and in a few years the limited franchise was changed, in nearly all of these colonies, for universal or manhood suffrage and vote by ballot.[3] It was open to the queen in council to disallow these laws, or for Parliament itself to interpose and suspend them:[4] but in deference to the principle of self-government, these critical changes were allowed to come into operation.

In 1852, a representative constitution, with two chambers, was introduced, after some delay, into New Zealand;[5] and, about the same period, into the Cape of Good Hope.[6]

New Zealand and Cape of Good Hope.

To conclude this rapid summary of colonial liber-

---

[1] 13 & 14 Vict. c. 59; Earl Grey's Colonial Policy, i. App. 422; ii. 88–111; Mills, 291; Hans. Deb., 3rd Ser., cviii. 634; cix. 1384, &c.

[2] New South Wales Colonial Act, 17 Vict. c. 41; Mills, 296; Victoria Colonial Act, March 25, 1854; Mills, 309; South Australia, 1854; Mills, 316; Van Diemen's Land Colonial Act, 18 Vict. c. 18; Mills, 326. Western Australia is the only colony now having a single chamber.

[3] Colonial Acts, Victoria, Nov. 24th, 1857, 21 Vict. No. 33; South Australia, Jan. 27th, 1858, 21 Vict. No. 12; New South Wales, Nov. 24th, 1858, 22 Vict. No. 22. In New Zealand the franchise has been given to the gold-miners.

[4] Colonial Acts for such purposes were required to be laid before Parliament, for thirty days, before her Majesty's pleasure should be signified in regard to them.

[5] 15 & 16 Vict. c. 72. A previous Act had been passed with this object in 1846, but its operation was suspended in the following year.—Earl Grey's Colonial Policy, ii. 153–158; Mills, 335; Hans. Deb., 3rd Ser., cxxi. 922.

[6] Earl Grey, ii. 226–234, App. C. and D.; Cape of Good Hope Papers, presented by command, Feb. 5th, 1850; Mills, 151.

ties,—it must be added that the colonies have further enjoyed municipal institutions,[1] a free press,[2] and religious freedom and equality. No liberty or franchise prized by Englishmen at home, has been withheld from their fellow-countrymen in distant lands. *Other colonial liberties.*

Thus, by rapid strides, have the most considerable dependencies of the British crown advanced, through successive stages of political liberty, until an ancient monarchy has become the parent of democratic republics, in all parts of the globe. The constitution of the United States is scarcely so democratic as that of Canada, or the Australian colonies. The president's fixed tenure of office, and large executive powers,—the independent position and authority of the Senate,—and the control of the supreme court,—are checks upon the democracy of congress.[3] But in these colonies the majority of the democratic assembly, for the time being, are absolute masters of the colonial government: they can overcome the resistance of the legislative council, and dictate conditions to the governor, and indirectly to the parent state. This transition from a state of control and pupilage, to that of unrestrained freedom, may have been too precipitate. Society,—particularly in Australia,—had scarcely had time to prepare itself for the successful trial of so free a representation. The settlers of a new country were suddenly *Colonial democracy.*

[1] Earl Grey's Colonial Policy, i. 32, 235, 437; ii. 327; Mills 185, &c.; Merivale, Colonisation, 1861, 651-656.
[2] Earl Grey's Colonial Policy, i. 29.
[3] De Tocqueville, i. p. 143, 151, 179.

intrusted with uncontrolled power, before education, property, traditions and usage had given stability to public opinion. Nor were they trained to freedom, like their English brethren, by many ennobling struggles, and the patient exercise of public virtues. But such a transition, more or less rapid, was the inevitable consequence of responsible government, coupled with the power given to colonial assemblies, of reforming their own constitutions. The principle of self-government once recognised, has been carried out without reserve or hesitation. Hitherto there have been many failures and discouragements in the experiment of colonial democracy: yet the political future of these thriving communities affords far more ground for hope than for despondency.

England ventured to tax her colonies, and lost them: she endeavoured to rule them from Downing Street, and provoked disaffection and revolt. At last, she gave freedom, and found national sympathy and contentment. But in the meantime, her colonial dependencies have grown into affiliated states. The tie which binds them to her, is one of sentiment rather than authority. Commercial privileges, on either side, have been abandoned: transportation,—for which some of the colonies were founded,—has been given up: patronage has been surrendered, the disposal of public lands waived by the crown, and political dominion virtually renounced. In short, their dependence has become little more than nominal, except for purposes of military defence.

Colonies have become affiliated states.

We have seen how, in the earlier history of the colonies, they strove to defend themselves. But during the prolonged hostilities of the French revolutionary war, assaults upon our colonies naturally formed part of the tactics of the enemy, which were met, on our part, by costly naval and military armaments. And after the peace, England continued to garrison her colonies with large military forces,—wholly paid by herself,—and to construct fortifications, requiring still larger garrisons. Wars were undertaken against the natives, as in the Cape of Good Hope and New Zealand,—of which England bore all the cost, and the colonies gained all the profit. English soldiers have further performed the services of colonial police. Instead of taxing her colonies, England has suffered herself to be taxed heavily on their account. The annual military expenditure, on account of the colonies, ultimately reached 3,225,081*l*., of which 1,715,246*l*. was incurred for free colonies, and 1,509,835*l*. for military garrisons and dependencies, maintained chiefly for imperial purposes.[1] Many of the colonies have already contributed towards the maintenance of British troops, and have further raised considerable bodies of militia and volunteers: but Parliament has recently pronounced it to be just that the colonies which enjoy self-government, should undertake the responsibility and cost of their own military defence.[2] To carry this

Military defence of colonies.

---

[1] Report of Committee on Colonial Military Expenditure, 1861.
[2] Report of Committee on Colonial Military Expenditure, 1861, and Evidence; Resolution of Commons, March 4, 1862.—Hans.

policy into effect must be the work of time. But whenever it may be effected, the last material bond of connection with the colonies will have been severed; and colonial states, acknowledging the honorary sovereignty of England, and fully armed for self-defence,—as well against herself as others,—will have grown out of the dependencies of the British Empire. They will still look to her, in time of war, for at least naval protection; and, in peace, they will continue to imitate her laws and institutions, and to glory in the proud distinction of British citizenship. On her part, England may well be prouder of the vigorous freedom of her prosperous sons, than of a hundred provinces subject to the iron rule of British pro-consuls. And, should the sole remaining ties of kindred, affection, and honour be severed, she will reflect, with just exultation, that her dominion ceased, not in oppression and bloodshed, but in the expansive energies of freedom, and the hereditary capacity of her manly offspring for the privileges of self-government.

Dependencies unfitted for self-government. Other parts of the British Empire have,—from the conditions of their occupation, the relations of the state to the native population, and other circumstances,—been unable to participate in the free institutions of the more favoured colonies;[1] but they have largely shared in that spirit of enlightened liberality, which, during the last

Deb., 3rd Ser., clxxv. 1032; Earl Grey's Colonial Policy, i. 265; Mr. Adderley's Letter to Mr. Disraeli on the Relations of England with the Colonies, 1861.

[1] Viz., India, Malta, Gibraltar, Ceylon, Hong Kong, St. Helena, Falklands, Labuan, Sierra Leone, Gambia, Gold Coast.

twenty years, has distinguished the administration of colonial affairs.

Of all the dependencies of the British crown, India is the most considerable in territory, in population, in revenue, and in military resources. It is itself a great empire. Originally acquired and governed by a trading company, England was responsible for its administration no further than was implied in the charters and Acts of Parliament, by which British subjects were invested with sovereignty over distant regions.[1] Trade was the first, —dominion the secondary object of the company. Early in the reign of George III. their territories had become so extended, that Lord Chatham conceived the scheme of claiming them as dominions of the crown.[2] This great scheme, however, dwindled, in the hands of his colleagues, into an agreement that the company should pay 400;000*l.* a year, as the price of their privileges.[3] This tribute was not long enjoyed, for the company, impoverished by perpetual wars, and mal-administration, fell into financial difficulties; and in 1773, were released from this obligation.[4] And in this year, Parliament, for the first time, undertook to regulate the constitution of the government of India.[5] The court of directors, consisting of twenty-four members,

India.

The East India Company.

---

[1] The first charter was granted in 1600; the first Act concerning the East India Company was passed in 1698, 9 & 10 Will. III. c. 44.

[2] Lord Mahon's Hist,, v. 262; Chatham Corr., iv. 264.

[3] 7 Geo. III. c. 57; 9 Geo. III. c. 24; Parl. Hist., xvi. 350; Walp. Mem., ii. 394, 427, 449; iii. 39–57.

[4] 13 Geo. III. c. 63.   [5] *Ibid.* c. 64.

elected by the proprietors of India stock, and virtually independent of the government, became the home authority, by whom the governor-general was appointed, and to whom alone he was responsible. An Asiatic empire was still intrusted to a company, having an extensive civil and military organisation, making wars and conquests, negotiating treaties, and exercising uncontrolled dominion. A trading company had grown into a corporate emperor. The genius of Clive and Warren Hastings had acquired the empire of the Great Mogul.

Abuses of Indian administration, 1781-82. But power exercised by irresponsible and despotic rulers was naturally abused; and in 1773, and again in 1780, the directors were placed under the partial control of a secretary of state.[1] Soon afterwards some of the most glaring excesses of Indian misrule were forced upon the notice of Parliament.[2] English statesmen became sensible that the anomalies of a government, so constituted, could no longer be endured. It was not fit that England should suffer her subjects to practise the iniquities of Asiatic rule, without effective responsibility and control. On Mr. Fox and the coalition ministry first devolved the task of Mr. Fox's India Bill, 1783. providing against the continued oppression and misrule, which recent inquiries had exposed. They grappled boldly with the evils which demanded a remedy. Satisfied that the government of an empire could not be confided with safety or

---

[1] Burke's Speech, Works, iv. 115.
[2] See Debates Feb. 1st and 12th, and May 8th, 1781; April 15th, 1782; Parl. Hist. xxi. 1162, 1182; xxii. 200, 1275; Reports of Secret and Select Committees, 1782 and 1783.

honour to a commercial company, they proposed at once to transfer it to another body. But to whom could such a power be intrusted? Not to the crown, whose influence they had already denounced as exorbitant: not to any department of the executive government, which could become accessory to Parliamentary corruption. The company had been, in great measure, independent of the crown and of the ministers of the day; and the power which had been abused, they now proposed to vest in an independent board. This important body was to consist of seven commissioners appointed, in the first instance, by Parliament, for a term of four years, and ultimately by the crown. The leading concerns of the company were to be managed by eight assistants, appointed first by Parliament, and afterwards by the proprietors of East India stock.[1] It was a bold and hazardous measure, on which Mr. Fox and his colleagues staked their power. Conceived in a spirit of wisdom and humanity, it recognised the duty of the state to redress the wrongs, and secure the future welfare of a distant empire; yet was it open to objections which a fierce party contest discoloured with exaggeration. The main objections urged against the bill were these: that it violated the chartered rights of the company,—that it increased the influence of the crown—and that it invested the coalition party, then having a Parliamentary majority, with a power superior to the crown itself. As regards the first objection, it was vain to contend that Parliament might not lawfully

[1] Mr. Fox's Speech, Nov. 18th, 1783; Parl. Hist., xxiii. 1187.

dispossess the company of their dominion over millions of men, which they had disgraced by fraud, rapine, oppression, cruelty, and bloodshed. They had clearly forfeited the political powers intrusted to them for the public good. A solemn trust, having been flagrantly violated, might justly be revoked. But had they forfeited their commercial privileges? They were in difficulties and debt: their affairs were in the utmost confusion: the grossest mismanagement was but too certainly proved. But such evils in a commercial company, however urgently needing correction, scarcely justified the forfeiture of established rights. The two last objections were plainly contradictory. The measure could not increase the influence of the crown, and at the same time exalt a party above it. The former was, in truth, wholly untenable, and was relinquished; while the king, the opposition, the friends of the company, and the country, made common cause in maintaining the latter. And assuredly the weakest point was chosen for attack. The bill nominated the commissioners, exclusively from the ministerial party; and intrusted them with all the power and patronage of India, for a term of four years. At a time when corrupt influence was so potent, in the councils of the state, it cannot be doubted that the commissioners would have been able to promote the political interests of their own party. To add to their weight, they were entitled to sit in Parliament. Already the parliamentary influence of the company had aroused jealousy; and its concentration in a powerful and organised party naturally excited alarm. However exaggerated by party violence, it was unquestionably a well-founded objection, which ought to have been met and counteracted. It is true that vacancies were to be filled up by the crown, and that the appointment of the commissioners was during good behaviour; but, practically, they would have enjoyed an independent authority for four years. It was right to wrest power from a body which should never have been permitted to exercise it, and by whom it had been flagrantly abused: but it was wrong to constitute the new government an instrument of party, uncontrolled by the crown, and beyond the immediate reach of that parliamentary responsibility which our free constitution recognises as necessary for the proper exercise of authority. The error was fatal to the measure itself, and to the party by whom it was committed.[1]

Mr. Fox's scheme having been overthrown, Mr. Pitt proceeded to frame a measure, in which he dexterously evaded all the difficulties under which his rival had fallen. He left the company in possession of their large powers: but subjected them to a board of control representing the crown.[2] The company were now accountable to ministers, in their rule; and ministers, if they suffered wrong to be done, were responsible to Parliament. So far the theory of this measure was good: but power and responsibility

Mr. Pitt's India Bill, 1784.

The double government.

---

[1] *Supra*, Vol. I. 67; Parl. Hist., xxiii. 1224, 1255, &c.; Burke's Works, iv. 1; Adolphus' Hist., iv. 34–65; Massey's Hist., iii. 196–218; Fox, Mem., ii. 212–221; Lord J. Russell's Life of Fox, ii. 24–48; Lord Stanhope's Life of Pitt, i. 138.
[2] 24 Geo. III. c. 25.

were divided; and distracted councils, an infirm executive, and a cumbrous and perplexed administration, were scarcely to be avoided in a double government.[1] The administration of Indian affairs came frequently under the review of Parliament:[2] but the system of double or divided government was continued, on each successive renewal of the privileges of the company. In 1833, the first great change was effected in the position of the company. Up to this time, they had enjoyed the exclusive trade with China, and other commercial privileges. This monopoly was now discontinued; and they ceased to be a trading company; but their dominion over India was confirmed for a further period of twenty years.[3] The right of Parliament, however, to legislate for India was then reserved. It was the last periodical renewal of the powers of the company. In 1853, significant changes were made: their powers being merely continued until Parliament should otherwise provide; and their territories being held in trust for the crown. The Court of Directors was reconstituted, being henceforth composed of twelve elected members, and six nominees of the crown. At the same time, the council of the Governor-General, in India, was enlarged, and invested with a more legislative character. The government of India being thus drawn into closer connection with ministers, they met objections to the increase of patronage, which

Later measures.

India Bill, 1853.

---

[1] Mr. Fox's Speech, Parl. Hist., xxiv. 1122; Fox, Mem., ii. 254; Debates on India bill of 1858, *passim.*
[2] 28 Geo. III, c. 8; 33 Geo. III. c. 52; 53 Geo. III. c. 155.
[3] 3 & 4 Will. IV. c. 85.

had been fatal to Mr. Fox's scheme, by opening the civil and medical services to competition.[1] This measure prepared the way for a more complete identity between the executive administration of England and of India. It had a short and painful trial. The mutiny of the native army, in 1857, disclosed the perils and responsibilities of England, and the necessity of establishing a single and supreme authority.

The double government of Mr. Pitt was at length condemned: the powers and territories of the company were transferred to the Queen; and the administration of India was intrusted to a Secretary of State, and Council. But this great change could not be accomplished without a compromise; and of the fifteen members of the council, seven were elected by the Board of Directors, and eight appointed by the crown. And again, with a view to restrict the state patronage, cadetships in the engineers and artillery were thrown open to competition.[2] *Government of India transferred to the crown, 1858.*

The transfer of India to the crown was followed by a vigorous administration of its vast dominions. Its army was amalgamated with that of England:[3] the constitution of the council in India was placed upon a wider basis:[4] the courts of judicature were remodelled;[5] the civil service enlarged;[6] and the exhausted revenues *Subsequent Indian administration.*

---

[1] 16 & 17 Vict. c. 95. [2] 21 & 22 Vict. c. 106.
[3] 23 & 24 Vict. c. 100 (discontinuing a separate European force in India); 24 & 25 Vict. c. 74; and Parl. Papers, 1860, Nos. 364, 471, &c.
[4] 24 & 25 Vict. c. 67. [5] *Ibid.*, c. 104. [6] *Ibid.*, c. 54.

of the country regenerated. To an empire of subjugated states, and Asiatic races, self-government was plainly impossible. But it has already profited by European civilisation and statesmanship; and while necessarily denied freedom, its rulers are guided by the principles upon which free states are governed; and its interests are protected by a free English Parliament, a vigilant press, and an enlightened and humane people.

Beyond these narrow isles, England has won, indeed, a vast and glorious empire. In the history of the world, no other state has known how to govern territories so extended and remote,—and races of men so diverse: giving to her own kindred colonies the widest liberty,—and ruling, with enlightened equity, dependencies unqualified for freedom. To the Roman, Virgil proudly sang,

Freedom of the British empire.

> 'Tu regere imperio populos, Romane, memento:
> Hæ tibi erunt artes.'

To the Englishman may it not be said with even juster pride, 'having won freedom for thyself, and used it wisely, thou hast given it to thy children, who have peopled the earth; and thou hast exercised dominion with justice and humanity!'

CHAPTER XVIII.

IMPROVED SPIRIT OF LEGISLATION COINCIDENT WITH LIBERTY:—ADMINISTRATION OF JUSTICE:—MITIGATION OF THE CRIMINAL CODE:—CAPITAL AND SECONDARY PUNISHMENTS:—PRISONS:—POLICE:—THE POOR LAWS:—LUNATICS:—PROVISIONS FOR THE SOCIAL WELFARE OF THE PEOPLE:—POPULAR EDUCATION:—COMMERCIAL AND FINANCIAL POLICY:—ACTIVITY OF PARLIAMENT SINCE THE REFORM ACT:—CONCLUSION.

WE have now surveyed the progress of freedom and popular influence, in all the institutions of England. Everywhere we have seen the rights and liberties of the people assured; and closer relations established between the state and the community. The liberal spirit of general legislation has kept pace with this remarkable development of constitutional liberty. While the basis of power was narrow, rulers had little sympathy with the people. The spirit of their rule was hard and selfish: favouring the few at the expense of the many: protecting privileges and abuses by which the governing classes profited: but careless of the welfare of the governed. Responsibility and popular control gradually forced upon them larger views of the public interests; and more consideration for the claims of all classes to participate in the benefits of enlightened government. With freedom there grew a stronger sense of duty in rulers—more enlighten-

Improved spirit of modern legislation.

ment and humanity among the people : wiser laws, and a milder policy. The asperities of power were tempered; and the state was governed in the spirit which society approved.

This improved spirit has displayed itself throughout the wide range of modern legislation : but, in passing beyond the strict limits of constitutional history, we must content ourselves with a rapid glance at some of its more remarkable illustrations.

No example more aptly illustrates the altered relations of rulers to the people, than the revision of official emoluments. Ministers once grew rich upon the gains of office; and provided for their relatives by monstrous sinecures, and appointments egregiously overpaid. To grasp a great estate out of the public service, was too often their first thought. Families were founded, titles endowed, and broken fortunes repaired, at the public expense. It was asked what an office was worth: not what services were to be rendered. This selfish and dishonest system perished under exposure : but it proved a tedious and unthankful labour to bring its abuses to the light of day. Inquiries were commenced early in the present century; but were followed by few practical results. At that time, 'all abuses were freeholds,'[1] which the government did not venture to invade. Mr. Joseph Hume, foremost among the guardians of public interests, afterwards applied his patient industry and fearless public spirit to this work; and,

Emoluments of office.

---

[1] This happy phrase is assigned to Richard Bentley, son of Dr. Bentley.—Walpole's Mem., ii. 391.

unruffled by discouragements and ridicule, he lived to see its accomplishment. Soon after the Reform Act, ministers of state accepted salaries scarcely equal to the charges of office:[1] sinecures and reversions were abolished: offices discontinued or consolidated; and the scale of official emoluments revised, and apportioned to the duties performed, throughout the public service. The change attested a higher sense of duty in ministers, and increased responsibility to public opinion.

The abuses in the administration of justice, which had been suffered to grow and flourish without a check, illustrate the inert and stagnant spirit of the eighteenth century. The noble principles of English law had been expounded by eminent judges, and applied to the varying circumstances of society, until they had expanded into a comprehensive system of jurisprudence, entitled to respect and veneration. But however admirable its principles, its practice had departed from the simplicity of former times, and, by manifold defects, went far to defeat the ends of justice. Lawyers, ever following precedents, were blind to principles. Legal fictions, technicalities, obsolete forms, intricate rules of procedure, accumulated. Fine intellects were wasted on the narrow subtilties of special pleading; and clients won or lost causes,—like a

Administration of justice.

---

[1] Reports on Sinecure Offices, 1807, 1810–12, and 1834; Debates on Offices in Reversion Bill, 1807, 1808; Hans. Deb., 1st Ser., ix. 178, 1073, &c.; x. 194, 870, &c.; Romilly's Life, ii. 219, 302; iii. 9; Twiss's Life of Lord Eldon, ii. 116, 225; Reports of Commons on offices held by Members, 1830–31, No. 322; 1833, No. 671; Report on Miscellaneous Expenditure, 1847–48, No. 643; and on Public Offices, 1856, No. 368.

game of chess,—not by the force of truth and right, but by the skill and cunning of the players. Heartbreaking delays and ruinous costs were the lot of suitors. Justice was dilatory, expensive, uncertain, and remote. To the rich it was a costly lottery: to the poor a denial of right, or certain ruin. The class who profited most by its dark mysteries, were the lawyers themselves. A suitor might be reduced to beggary or madness: but his advisers revelled in the chicane and artifices of a life-long suit, and grew rich. Out of a multiplicity of forms and processes arose numberless fees and well-paid offices. Many subordinate functionaries, holding sinecure or superfluous appointments, enjoyed greater emoluments than the judges of the court; and upon the luckless suitors, again, fell the charge of these egregious establishments. If complaints were made, they were repelled as the promptings of ignorance: if amendments of the law were proposed, they were resisted as innovations. To question the perfection of English jurisprudence was to doubt the wisdom of our ancestors,—a political heresy, which could expect no toleration.

Delays of the Court of Chancery. The delays of the Court of Chancery, in the time of Lord Eldon, were a frequent cause of complaint; and formed the subject of parliamentary inquiry in both Houses.[1] In 1813, a vice-chancellor was appointed, to expedite the business of the court: but its complex and dilatory procedure remained without improvement. Complaints continued to be made, by Mr. Michael

---

[1] Romilly's Life, ii. 368, 386, 392; iii. 13, &c.; Twiss's Life of Lord Eldon, ii. 167, 199.

Angelo Taylor, Mr. Williams, and others, until, in 1825, a commission was appointed to inquire into the administration of justice in that court.[1]

In 1828, Mr. Brougham exposed the complicated abuses of the courts of common law, and the law of real property. His masterly speech, of six hours, displayed the combined powers of the philosophic jurist, the practised lawyer, the statesman, and the orator.[2] Suggesting most of the law reforms which have since been carried into effect, and some not yet accomplished, it stands a monument to his fame as a lawgiver.[3] Commissions of inquiry were immediately appointed; and, when their investigations were completed, a new era of reform and renovation was commenced. Thenceforth, the amendment of the law was pursued in a spirit of earnestness and vigour. Judges and law officers no longer discountenanced it: but were themselves foremost in the cause of law reform. Lord Brougham, on the woolsack, was able to give effect to some of his own cherished schemes; and never afterwards faltered in the work. Succeeding chancellors followed in his footsteps; and Lord Denman, Lord Campbell, Sir Richard Bethell, and other eminent jurists, laboured successfully in the same honourable field of legislation. The work was slow and toilsome,—beset with many difficulties,—and generally unthankful: but

Defects of the Common Law Courts.

Law reforms.

[1] Romilly's Life, ii. 474, 486, 567; iii. 321, *et seq.*
[2] Feb. 7th, 1828, Hans. Deb., 2nd Ser., xviii. 127; Lord Brougham's Speeches, ii. 311.
[3] Acts and Bills of Lord Brougham, by Sir Eardley Wilmot, Intr. xv., *et seq.*; lvi. *et seq.*; lxxx.; Speech of Lord Brougham on Law Reform, May 12th, 1848, Hans. Deb., 3rd Ser., xcviii. 877.

it was accomplished. The procedure of the court of Chancery was simplified: its judicial establishment enlarged and remodelled: its offices regulated. Its delays were in great measure averted; and its costs diminished. The courts of common law underwent a like revision. The effete Welsh judicature was abolished: the bench of English judges enlarged from twelve to fifteen: the equitable jurisdiction of the court of Exchequer superseded: the procedure of the courts freed from fiction and artifice: the false system of pleading swept away: the law of evidence amended; and justice restored to its natural simplicity. The law of bankruptcy and insolvency was reviewed; and a court established for its administration, with wide general and local jurisdiction. Justice was brought home to every man's door, by the constitution of county courts. Divorce, which the law had reserved as the peculiar privilege of the rich, was made the equal right of all. The ecclesiastical courts were reconstituted; and their procedure and jurisdiction reviewed. A new court of appeal,—of eminent learning and authority,—was found in a judicial committee of the Privy Council,—which, as the court of last resort from India and the colonies, from the ecclesiastical courts and the court of Admiralty, is second only to the House of Lords in the amplitude of its jurisdiction. The antiquated law of real property was recast; and provision made for simplifying titles, and facilitating the transfer of land. Much was done, and more attempted, for the consolidation of the statutes. Nor have these remarkable amendments of the law been confined to England. Scotland and

Ireland, and especially the latter, have shared largely in the work of reformation. Of all the law reforms of this period, indeed, none was so signal as the constitution of the Irish encumbered estates court.

Such were the more conspicuous improvements of the law, during the thirty years preceding 1860. Before they had yet been commenced, Lord Brougham eloquently foreshadowed the boast of that sovereign who should have it to say 'that he found law dear, and left it cheap: found it a sealed book,—left it a living letter: found it the patrimony of the rich,—left it the inheritance of the poor: found it the two-edged sword of craft and oppression,—left it the staff of honesty, and the shield of innocence.' The whole scheme of renovation is not yet complete: but already may this proud boast be justly uttered by Queen Victoria.

In reviewing the administration of justice, the spirit and temper of the judges themselves, at different periods, must not be overlooked. One of the first acts of George III. was to complete the independence of the judges by providing that their commissions should not expire with the demise of the crown. It was a necessary measure, in consummation of the policy of the Revolution; and,—if unworthy of the courtly adulations with which it was then received,—it was, at least, entitled to approval and respect.[1]

Spirit and temper of the judges.

---

[1] King's Message, March 3rd, 1761; 1 Geo. III. c. 23; Walpole Mem., i. 41; Cooke's Hist. of Party, ii. 400. In 1767 the same law was extended to Ireland, on the recommendation of Lord Townshend, the lord-lieutenant.—Walpole Mem., iii. 109.

The tenure of the judges was now assured; and their salaries were charged permanently on the civil list.

The law had secured their independence of the crown: but the spirit of the times leagued them closely with its authority. No reign was more graced by the learning and accomplishments of its judges. They were superior to every corrupt influence: but all their sympathies and predilections were with power. The enemies of Lord Mansfield asserted 'that he was better calculated to fill the office of prætor under Justinian, than to preside as chief criminal judge of this kingdom, in the reign of George III.'[1] Neither Lord Mansfield himself, nor any other judge, deserved so grave a censure: but, with the illustrious exception of Lord Camden, the most eminent magistrates of that reign were unfriendly to liberty. Who so allied to the court,— so stanch to arbitrary principles of government,—so hostile to popular rights and remedial laws, as Lord Mansfield, Lord Thurlow, Lord Loughborough, Lord Eldon, and Lord Ellenborough? The first and last of these so little regarded their independence, in the exercise of the chief criminal judicature of the realm, that they entered the cabinet, as ministers of the crown; and identified themselves with the executive government of the day. What further illustration is needed of the close relations of the judgment-seat with power? But no sooner had principles of freedom and responsible government gained ascendency, than judges were animated by in-

---

[1] Wraxall Mem., ii. 307.

dependence and liberality. Henceforward they administered justice in the spirit of Lord Camden; and promoted the amendment of the laws, with the enlightenment of statesmen.

The deepest stain upon the policy of irresponsible government, is to be found in the history of the criminal law. The lives of men were sacrificed with a reckless barbarity, worthier of an Eastern despot, or African chief, than of a Christian state. The common law was guiltless of this severity: but as the country advanced in wealth, lawgivers grew merciless to criminals. Life was held cheap, compared with property.[1] To hang men was the ready expedient of thoughtless power. From the Restoration to the death of George III.,—a period of 160 years,—no less than 187 capital offences were added to the criminal code. The legislature was able, every year, to discover more than one heinous crime deserving of death. In the reign of George II., thirty-three Acts were passed creating capital offences:[2] in the first fifty years of George III., no less than sixty-three.[3] In such a multiplication of offences all principle was ignored: offences wholly different in character and degree, were confounded in the indiscriminating penalty of death. Whenever an

The criminal code.

Capital punishments.

---

[1] 'Penal laws, which are in the hands of the rich, are laid upon the poor; and all our paltriest possessions are hung round with gibbets.'—*Goldsmith's Vicar of Wakefield.*
[2] Speech of Sir W. Meredith, 1777; Parl. Hist., xix. 237.
[3] Lord Grenville's Speech, April 2nd, 1813, on Sir S. Romilly's Shoplifting Bill; Hans. Deb., 1st Ser., xxv. 535. This excellent speech, however, is scarcely reported in Hansard, but was printed separately by the Capital Punishments Society.

offence was found to be increasing, some busy senator called for new rigour,[1] until murder became, in the eye of the law, no greater crime than picking a pocket, purloining a ribbon from a shop, or pilfering a pewter-pot. Such law-makers were as ignorant as they were cruel. Obstinately blind to the failure of their blood-stained laws, they persisted in maintaining them long after they had been condemned by philosophers, by jurists, and by the common sense and humanity of the people. Dr. Johnson,—no squeamish moralist,—exposed them:[2] Sir W. Blackstone, in whom admiration of our jurisprudence was almost a foible, denounced them.[3] Beccaria, Montesquieu, and Bentham[4] demonstrated that certainty of punishment was more effectual in the repression of crime, than severity: but lawgivers were still inexorable. Nor within the walls of Parliament itself, were there wanting humane and enlightened men to protest against the barbarity of our laws. In 1752, the Commons passed a bill to

[1] Mr. Burke sarcastically observed, that if a country gentleman could obtain no other favour from the government, he was sure to be accommodated with a new felony, without benefit of clergy. Paley justified the same severity to unequal degrees of guilt, on the ground of 'the necessity of preventing the repetition of the offence.'—*Moral and Political Philosophy*, Book vi. ch. ix.

[2] 'Whatever may be urged by casuists or politicians, the greater part of mankind, as they can never think that to pick a pocket and to pierce the heart are equally criminal, will scarcely believe that two malefactors, so different in guilt, can be justly doomed to the same punishment.'—*Rambler*, i. 114; Works, iii. 275. In this admirable essay, published in 1751, the restriction of death to cases of murder was advocated.

[3] 'It is a kind of quackery in government; and argues a want of solid skill, to apply the same universal remedy, the *ultimum supplicium*, to every case of difficulty.'—Comm., iv. 15.

[4] Bentham's work, 'Théorie des Peines et des Récompenses,' appeared in 1811.

commute the punishment of felony, in certain cases, to hard labour in the dockyards: but it was not agreed to by the Lords.[1] In 1772, Sir Charles Bunbury passed a bill through the Commons, to repeal some of the least defensible of the criminal statutes: but the Lords refused to entertain it, as an innovation.[2] In 1777, Sir W. Meredith, in resisting one of the numerous bills of extermination, made a memorable speech which still stands out in judgment against his contemporaries. Having touchingly described the execution of a young woman for shop-lifting, who had been reduced to want by her husband's impressment, he proceeded: 'I do not believe that a fouler murder was ever committed against law, than the murder of this woman, by law;' and again: 'the true hangman is the member of Parliament: he who frames the bloody law, is answerable for the blood that is shed under it.'[3] But such words fell unheeded on the callous ears of men intent on offering new victims to the hangman.[4]

Warnings more significant than these were equally neglected. The terrors of the law, far from preventing crime, interfered with its just punishment. Society revolted against barbarities which the law prescribed. Men wronged

Uncertainty of punishment.

---

[1] Comm. Journ., xxvi. 345; Lords' Journ., xxvii. 661.

[2] Parl. Hist., xvii. 448; Comm. Journ., xxxiii. 695, &c.; Speech of Sir W. Meredith, 1777.

[3] Parl. Hist., xix. 237.

[4] Sir William Meredith said: 'When a member of Parliament brings in a new hanging Bill, he begins with mentioning some injury that may be done to private property, for which a man is not yet liable to be hanged; and then proposes the gallows as the specific and infallible means of cure and prevention.'

by crimes, shrank from the shedding of blood, and forbore to prosecute: juries forgot their oaths and acquitted prisoners, against evidence: judges recommended the guilty to mercy.[1] Not one in twenty of the sentences was carried into execution. Hence arose uncertainty,—one of the worst defects in criminal jurisprudence. Punishment lost at once its terrors, and its example. Criminals were not deterred from crime, when its consequences were a lottery: society could not profit by the sufferings of guilt, when none could comprehend why one man was hung, and another saved from the gallows. The law was in the breast of the judge; the lives of men were at the mercy of his temper or caprice.[2] At one assize town, a 'hanging judge' left a score of victims for execution: at another, a milder magistrate reprieved the wretches whom the law condemned. Crime was not checked: but, in the words of Horace Walpole, the country became 'one great shambles;' and the people were brutalised by the hideous spectacle of public executions.

Such was the state of the criminal law, when Sir Samuel Romilly commenced his generous labours. He entered upon them cautiously. In 1808, he obtained the remission of capital punishment for picking pockets. In 1810, he vainly sought to extend the same clemency to other

Sir Samuel Romilly's bills, 1808–1818.

---

[1] Blackstone Comm., iv. 15.
[2] Lord Camden said: 'The discretion of the judge is the law of tyrants. It is always unknown: it is different in different men: it is casual, and depends upon constitution, temper, and passion. In the best, it is oftentimes caprice; in the worst, it is every vice, folly, and passion to which human nature is liable.'—*St. Tr.,* viii. 58.

trifling thefts. In the following year, he succeeded in passing four bills through the Commons. One only,—concerning thefts in bleaching grounds,—obtained the concurrence of the Lords. He ventured to deal with no crimes but those in which the sentence was rarely carried into execution: but his innovations on the sacred code were sternly resisted by Lord Eldon, Lord Ellenborough, and the first lawyers of his time. Year after year, until his untimely death, he struggled to overcome the obduracy of men in power. The Commons were on his side: Lord Grenville, Lord Lansdowne, Lord Grey, Lord Holland, and other enlightened peers supported him: but the Lords, under the guidance of their judicial leaders, were not to be convinced. He did much to stir the public sentiment in his cause: but little, indeed, for the amendment of the law.[1]

His labours were continued, under equal discouragement, by Sir James Mackintosh.[2] In 1819, he obtained a Committee, in opposition to the government; and in the following year, succeeded in passing three out of the six measures which they recommended. This was all that his continued efforts could accomplish. But his philosophy and earnest reasoning were not lost upon the more enlightened of contemporary statesmen. He lived to see many of his own measures carried out; and to mark so great a change of

Sir James Mackintosh, 1819–1823.

---

[1] Romilly's Life, ii. 303, 315, 325, 333, 383; iii. 95, 233, 331, 337; Twiss's Life of Lord Eldon, ii. 119.
[2] Hans. Deb., 1st Ser., xxxix. 784, &c.

opinion 'that he should almost think that he had lived in two different countries, and conversed with people who spoke two different languages.'[1]

Sir Robert Peel was the first minister of the crown who ventured upon a revision of the criminal code. He brought together, within the narrow compass of a few statutes, the accumulated penalties of centuries. He swept away several capital punishments that were practically obsolete: but left the effective severity of the law with little mitigation. Under his revised code upwards of forty kinds of forgery alone, were punishable with death.[2] But public sentiment was beginning to prevail over the tardy deliberations of lawyers and statesmen. A thousand bankers, in all parts of the country, petitioned against the extreme penalty of death, in cases of forgery:[3] the Commons struck it out of the government bill; but the Lords restored it.[4]

Sir Robert Peel's criminal law bills, 1824–1830.

With the reform period, commenced a new era in criminal legislation. Ministers and law officers now vied with philanthropists in undoing the unhallowed work of many generations. In 1832, Lord Auckland, Master of the Mint, secured the abolition of capital punishment for offences connected with coinage: Mr. attorney-general Denman exempted forgery from the same penalty,—in all but two cases, to which the Lords would not assent; and Mr. Ewart ob-

Revision of criminal code, 1832–1860.

[1] Mackintosh's Life, ii. 387–396.
[2] 11 Geo. IV. and 1 Will. IV. c. 66.
[3] Presented by Mr. Brougham, May 24th, 1830; Hans. Deb., 2nd Ser., xxiv. 1014.   [4] *Ibid.*, xxv. 838.

tained the like remission for sheep-stealing, and other similar offences. In 1833, the Criminal Law Commission was appointed, to revise the entire code. While its labours were yet in progress, Mr. Ewart, ever foremost in this work of mercy,—and Mr. Lennard carried several important amendments of the law.[1] The commissioners recommended numerous other remissions,[2] which were promptly carried into effect by Lord John Russell, in 1837. Even these remissions, however, fell short of public opinion, which found expression in an amendment of Mr. Ewart, for limiting the punishment of death to the single crime of murder. This proposal was then lost by a majority of one:[3] but has since, by successive measures, been accepted by the legislature,—murder alone, and the exceptional crime of treason, having been reserved for the last penalty of the law.[4] Great indeed, and rapid, was this reformation of the criminal code. It was computed that from 1810 to 1845, upwards of 1,400 persons had suffered death for crimes which had since ceased to be capital.[5]

While these amendments were proceeding, other wise provisions were introduced into the criminal law. In 1834, the barbarous custom of hanging in chains was abolished. In 1836, Mr. Ewart, after a contention of many years, secured to prisoners, on trial for felony, the just privilege of being heard by counsel, which the cold cruelty of our criminal

[1] In 1833, 1834, and 1835. [2] Second Report, p. 33.
[3] Hans. Deb., 3rd Ser., xxxviii. 908-922.
[4] 24 & 25 Vict. c. 100.
[5] Report of Capital Punishments Society, 1845.

jurisprudence had hitherto denied them.[1] In the same year, Mr. Aglionby broke down the rigorous usage which had allowed but forty-eight hours to criminals under sentence of death, for repentance or proof of innocence. Nor did the efforts of philanthropists rest here. From 1840, Mr. Ewart, supported by many followers, pressed upon the Commons, again and again, the total abolition of capital punishment. This last movement failed, indeed; and the law still demands life for life. But such has been the sensitive,—not to say morbid,—tenderness of society, that many heinous crimes have since escaped this extreme penalty: while uncertainty has been suffered to impair the moral influence of justice.

While lives were spared, secondary punishments were no less tempered by humanity and Christian feeling. In 1816, the degrading and unequal punishment of the pillory was confined to perjury; and was, at length, wholly condemned in 1837.[2]

Secondary punishments.

In 1838, serious evils were disclosed in the system of transportation: the penal colonies protested against its continuance; and it was afterwards, in great measure, abandoned. Whatever the objections to its principle: however grave the faults of its administration,—it was, at least in two particulars, the most effective secondary punish-

Transportation.

---

[1] This measure had first been proposed in 1824 by Mr. George Lamb. See Sydney Smith's admirable articles upon this subject.—*Works,* ii. 259, iii. 1.

[2] 56 Geo. III. c. 138; 1 Vict. c. 23. In 1815 the Lords rejected a Bill for its total abolition.—Romilly's Life, iii. 144, 166, 189.

ment hitherto discovered. It cleansed our society of criminals; and afforded them the best opportunity of future employment and reformation. For such a punishment no equivalent could readily be found.[1] Imprisonment became nearly the sole resource of the state; and how to punish and reform criminals, by prison discipline, was one of the most critical problems of the time.

The condition of the prisons, in the last century, was a reproach to the state, and to society. *Prisons.* They were damp, dark, and noisome: prisoners were half-starved on bread and water,—clad in foul rags,—and suffered to perish of want, wretchedness, and gaol fever. Their sufferings were aggravated by the brutality of tyrannous gaolers and turnkeys,—absolute masters of their fate. Such punishment was scarcely less awful than the gallows, and was inflicted in the same merciless spirit. Vengeance and cruelty were its only principles: charity and reformation formed no part of its scheme. Prisons without separation of sexes,—without classification of age or character,—were schools of crime and iniquity. The convicted felon corrupted the untried, and perhaps innocent prisoner; and confirmed the penitent novice in crime. The unfortunate who entered prison capable of moral improvement, went forth impure, hardened, and irreclaimable.

Such were the prisons which Howard visited; and such the evils he exposed. However inert the legis-

---

[1] Reports of Sir W. Molesworth's Committee, 1837, No. 518; 1838, No. 669. Bentham's 'Théorie des Peines,' &c.; Dr. Whately's Letters to Earl Grey; Reply of Colonel Arthur; Innes on Home and Colonial Convict Management, 1842.

lature, it was not indifferent to these disclosures, and attempts were immediately made to improve the regulation and discipline of prisons.[1] The cruelty and worst evils of prison life were gradually abated. Philanthropists penetrated the abodes of guilt; and prisons came to be governed in the spirit of Howard and Mrs. Fry. But, after the lapse of half a century, it was shown that no enlarged system had yet been devised to unite condign punishment with reformation; adequate classification, judicious employment, and instruction were still wanting.[2] The legislature, at length, applied itself to the systematic improvement of prisons. In 1835, inspectors were appointed to correct abuses, and insure uniformity of management.[3] Science and humanity laboured together to devise a punishment, calculated at once to deter from crime, and to reform criminals. The magistracy, throughout the country, devoted themselves to this great social experiment. Vast model prisons were erected by the state: costly gaols by counties,—light, airy, spacious and healthful. Physical suffering formed no part of the scheme. Prisoners were comfortably lodged, well fed and clothed, and carefully tended. But a strict classification was enforced: every system of confinement, —solitary, separate, and silent,—was tried: every variety of employment devised. While reformation was sought in restraints and discipline,—in industrial

[1] Two bills were passed in 1774, and others at later periods; and see Reports of Commons' Committees on gaols, 1819, 1822; Sydney Smith's Works, ii. 196, 244.
[2] Five Reports of Lords' Committee, 1835 (Duke of Richmond), on Gaols and Houses of Correction.   [3] 5 & 6 Will. IV. c. 38.

training,—in education and spiritual instruction,—good conduct was encouraged by hopes of release from confinement, under tickets-of-leave, before the expiration of the sentence. In some cases penal servitude was followed by transportation,—in others it formed the only punishment. Meanwhile, punishment was passing from one extreme to another. It was becoming too mild and gentle to deter from crime: while hopes of reformation were too generally disappointed. Further experiments may be more complete: but crime is an intractable ill, which has baffled the wisdom of all ages. Men born of the felon type, and bred to crime, will ever defy rigour and frustrate mercy. If the present generation have erred, its errors have been due to humanity, and Christian hopefulness of good. May we not contrast them proudly with the wilful errors of past times,—neglect, moral indifference, and cruelty?

Nor did the state rest satisfied with the improvement of prisons: but alive to the peculiar needs and dangers of juvenile delinquents, and the classes whence they sprang, it provided for the establishment of reformatory and industrial schools, in which the young might be spared the contamination and infamy of a gaol, and trained, if possible, to virtue.[1] *Reformatories.*

Our ancestors, trusting to the severity of their punishments, for the protection of life and property, took little pains in the prevention of crime. The metropolis was left to the care of drunken and decrepid watchmen, and scoundrel thief-takers,— *Police.*

[1] 17 & 18 Vict. c. 86, &c.

companions and confederates of thieves.[1] The abuses of such a police had long been notorious, and a constant theme of obloquy and ridicule. They had frequently been exposed by parliamentary committees; but it was not until 1829, that Mr. Peel had the courage to propose his new metropolitan police. This effective and admirable force has since done more for the order and safety of the metropolis, than a hundred executions, every year, at the Old Bailey. A similar force was afterwards organised in the city of London; and every considerable town throughout the realm, was prompt to follow a successful example. The rural districts, however, and smaller boroughs, were still without protection. Already, in 1836, a constabulary of rare efficiency had been organised in Ireland: but it was not until 1839 that provision was made for the voluntary establishment of a police in English counties and boroughs. A rural police was rendered the more necessary by the efficient watching of large towns; and at length, in 1856, the support of an adequate constabulary force was required of every county and borough.

And further, criminals have been brought more readily to justice, by enlargements of the summary jurisdiction of magistrates. A principle of criminal jurisprudence which excludes trial by jury, is to be accepted with caution: but its practical administration has been unquestionably beneficial. Justice has been administered well and

Summary jurisdiction.

---

[1] Wraxall's Mem., i. 329; Reports of Commons' Comm., 1812, 1816, 1817, 1822, and 1828.

speedily; while offenders have been spared a long confinement prior to trial; and the innocent have had a prompt acquittal. The like results have also been attained by an increase of stipendiary magistrates, in the metropolis and elsewhere,—by the institution of the Central Criminal Court,—and by more frequent assizes.

The stern and unfeeling temper which had dictated the penal code, directed the discipline of fleets and armies. Life was sacrificed with the same cruel levity; and the lash was made an instrument of torture. *Flogging in the navy and army.* This barbarous rigour was also gradually relaxed, under the combined influence of humanity and freedom.

Equally wise and humane were numerous measures for raising the moral and social condition of the people. And first in importance *The poor laws.* was an improved administration of relief to the poor. Since the reign of Elizabeth, the law had provided for the relief of the destitute poor of England. This wise and simple provision, however, had been so perverted by ignorant administration that, in relieving the poor, the industrial population of the whole country was being rapidly reduced to pauperism, while property was threatened with no distant ruin. The system which was working this mischief assumed to be founded upon benevolence: but no evil genius could have designed a scheme of greater malignity for the corruption of the human race. The fund intended for the relief of want and sickness,—of age and impotence,—was recklessly distributed to all who begged a share. Everyone was taught to look to the parish, and not to his own honest industry, for support. The idle clown, without work, fared as well as the industrious labourer who toiled from morn till night. The shameless slut, with half a dozen children,—the progeny of many fathers,—was provided for as liberally as the destitute widow and her orphans. But worse than this,—independent labourers were tempted and seduced into the degraded ranks of pauperism, by payments freely made in aid of wages. Cottage rents were paid, and allowances given according to the number of a family. Hence thrift, self-denial, and honest independence were discouraged. The manly farm labourer, who scorned to ask for alms, found his own wages artificially lowered, while improvidence was cherished and rewarded by the parish. He could barely live, without incumbrance: but boys and girls were hastening to church,—without a thought of the morrow,—and rearing new broods of paupers, to be maintained by the overseer. Who can wonder that labourers were rapidly sinking into pauperism, without pride or self-respect? But the evil did not even rest here. Paupers were actually driving other labourers out of employment,—that labour being preferred which was partly paid out of rates, to which employers were forced to contribute. As the cost of pauperism, thus encouraged, was increasing, the poorer ratepayers were themselves reduced to poverty. The soil was ill-cultivated by pauper labour, and its rental consumed by parish rates. In a period of fifty years, the poor-rates were quadrupled; and had reached, in 1833, the enormous amount of 8,600,000*l*. In many parishes they were approaching the annual value of the land itself.

Such evils as these demanded a bold and thorough remedy; and the recommendations of a masterly commission of inquiry were accept- *The new poor law, 1834.* ed by the first reformed Parliament in 1834, as the basis of a new poor law. The principle was that of the Act of Elizabeth,—to confine relief to destitution; and its object, to distinguish between want and imposture. This test was to be found in the workhouse. Hitherto pauperism had been generally relieved at home, the parish workhouse being the refuge for the aged, for orphans, and others, whom it suited better than out-door relief. Now out-door relief was to be withdrawn altogether from the able-bodied, whose wants were to be tested by their willingness to enter the workhouse. This experiment had already been successfully tried in a few well-ordered parishes, and was now generally adopted. But instead of continuing ill-regulated parish workhouses, several parishes were united, and union workhouses established, common to them all. The local administration of the poor was placed under elected boards of guardians; and its general superintendence under a central board of commissioners in London. A change so sudden in all the habits of the labouring classes could not be introduced without discontents and misconception. Some of the provisions of the new law were afterwards partially relaxed: but its main principles were carried into successful operation. Within three years the annual expenditure for the relief of the poor was reduced to the extent of three millions. The plague of pauperism was stayed; and the English peasantry rescued from irretrievable corruption. The full benefits of the new poor law have not yet been realised: but a generation of labourers has already grown up in independence and self-respect; and the education and industrial training of children, in the workhouses, have elevated a helpless class, formerly neglected and demoralised.[1]

While England had been threatened with ruin, from a reckless encouragement of pauperism, the law of Scotland had made no adequate provision for the support of the destitute poor. This error, scarcely more defensible, was corrected in 1845. But worst of all was the case of Ireland, where there was absolutely no legal provision for the destitute.[2] The wants of the peasantry were appalling: two millions and a half were subsisting, for a part of every year, on charity. The poor man shared his meal with his poorer neighbour; and everywhere the vagrant found a home. To approach so vast a mass of destitution, and so peculiar a condition of society, was a hazardous experiment. Could property bear the burden of providing for such multitudes? could the ordinary machinery of poor-law administration safely deal with them? The experiment was tried in 1838,—

Poor laws of Scotland.
Of Ireland.

---

[1] Extracts of information collected, 1833; Report of Commissioners of Inquiry, 1834; Debates in Lords and Commons, April 17th and July 21st, 1834; Nicholls' Hist. of the Poor Law, &c.

[2] 3rd Report of Commissioners on the Poorer Classes in Ireland, 1836, p. 25, &c.

not without serious misgivings,—and it succeeded. The burden, indeed, was often ruinous to the land; and the workhouse was peculiarly repugnant to the Irish peasantry: but the operation of the new law was facilitated by the fearful famine of 1846; and has since contributed, with other causes, to the advancing prosperity of Ireland. The poor-law legislation of this period was conceived in a spirit of enlightened charity: it saved England from pauperism, and the poor of Scotland and Ireland from destitution.

The same beneficence has marked recent legislation for the care of lunatics. Within the wide range of human suffering, no affliction so much claims pity and protection as insanity. Rich and poor are stricken alike; and both are equally defenceless. Treated with care and tenderness, it is sad enough: aggravated by neglect and cruelty, it is unspeakably awful. To watch over such affliction, —to guard it from wrong and oppression,—to mitigate its sufferings, and, if possible, to heal it,—is the sacred office of the state. But until a period, comparatively recent, this office was grievously neglected. Rich patients were left in charge of keepers, in their own homes, or in private asylums, without control or supervision: the poor were trusted to the rude charge of their own families, or received into the workhouse, with other paupers. Neglect, and too often barbarity, were the natural results. The strong may not be safely trusted with unrestrained power over the weak. The well-paid keeper, the pauper family, the workhouse matron, could all tyrannise over helpless beings, bereft of reason. Sad tales were heard of cruelty committed within walls, to which no watchful guardian was admitted; and idiots were suffered to roam at large, the sport of idle jests, or worse brutality.

A few charitable asylums had been founded, by private or local munificence, for the treatment of the insane;[1] but it was not until the present century that county and borough lunatic asylums began to be established; nor until after the operation of the new poor law, that their erection was rendered compulsory.[2] At the same time, provision was made for the inspection of asylums; and securities were taken against the wrongful detention or mismanagement of lunatics. Private asylums are licensed: every house tenanted by the insane is subjected to visitation; and the care of all lunatics is intrusted to commissioners.[3] The like provision has also been made for the care of lunatics in Scotland and Ireland.[4] Two principles were here carried out,—the guardianship of the state, and the obligation of property to bear the burden of a liberal treatment of the lunatic poor. Both are no less generous than just; and the resources of medical science, and private charity, have more than kept pace with the watchfulness of the state, in alleviating the sufferings of the insane.

In other cases, the state has also extended its

[1] E.g. Bethlehem Hospital, in 1547; St. Peter's Hospital, Bristol, in 1697; Bethel Hospital, Norwich, in 1713; St. Luke's Hospital, in 1751.
[2] In 1845; 8 & 9 Vict. c. 126.   [3] 8 & 9 Vict. c. 100, &c.
[4] 9 and 10 Vict. c. 115, &c.; 20 & 21 Vict. c. 71.

generous protection to the weak,—even where its duty was not so clear. To protect women and children from excessive, or unsuitable labour, it has ventured to interfere with husband and wife, parent and child, labourer and employer, —with free labour, and wages, production and profits. The first Sir Robert Peel had induced the legislature to interfere for the preservation of the health and morals of factory children.[1] But to the earnest philanthropy of Mr. Sadler and Lord Ashley (now Earl of Shaftesbury) is due their first protection from excessive labour. It was found that children were doomed to immoderate toil in factories, by the cupidity of parents; and young persons and females accustomed to hours of labour, injurious to health and character. The state stretched forth its arm to succour them. The employment of children of tender years in factories was prohibited: the labour of the young, of both sexes under eighteen, and of all women, was subjected to regulation: an inspection of factories was instituted; and provision made for the education of factory children.[2] The like parental care was extended to other departments of labour,—to mines,[3] and bleaching works,[4] and even to the sweeping of chimneys.[5]

<small>Labour in factories, mines, &c.</small>

The state has further endeavoured to improve the social condition of the working classes, by providing for the establishment of savings' banks, and provident societies,—of schools

<small>Measures for the improvement of the working classes.</small>

---

[1] In 1802 and 1819; Acts 42 Geo. III. c. 73; 59 Geo. III. c. 66, &c.   [2] 3 & 4 Will. IV. c. 103; 7 Vict. c. 15, &c.
[3] 5 & 6 Vict. c. 99.   [4] 23 & 24 Vict. c. 78.
[5] 4 & 5 Will. IV. c. 35, &c.

of design, of baths and washhouses, of parks and places of recreation; by encouraging the construction of more suitable dwellings, by the supervision of common lodging houses,—and by measures of sanitary improvement; the benefits of which, though common to all classes, more immediately affect the health and welfare of the labouring multitudes. In this field, however, the state can do comparatively little: it is from society,—from private benevolence and local activity, that effectual aid must be sought for the regeneration of the poorer classes. And this great social duty has fallen upon a generation already awakened to its urgency.

Among the measures most conducive to the moral and social improvement of the people, has been the promotion of popular education. That our ancestors were not insensible to the value of extended education, is attested by the grammar-schools and free or charity-schools in England, and by the parochial schools of Scotland. The state, however,—inert and indifferent,—permitted endowments for the good of society to be wasted and misapplied. From the latter end of last century much was done, by private zeal and liberality, for the education of the poor: but the state stirred not.[1] It was reserved for Mr. Brougham, in 1816, to awaken Parliament to the ignorance of the poor; and to his vigilance was it due, that many educational endowments were restored to the uses for which they were designed. Again, in 1820, he proposed a scheme

Popular education.

---

[1] See Porter's Progress of the Nation, pp. 690-699.

for the systematic education of the poor.[1] To the general education of the people, however, there was not only indifference, but repugnance. The elevation of the lower grades of society was dreaded, as dangerous to the state. Such instruction as impressed them with the duty of contentment and obedience might be well: but education which should raise their intelligence and encourage freedom of thought, would promote democracy, if not revolution. It was right that the children of the poor should be taught the church catechism: it was wrong that they should learn to read newspapers.[2] So long as this feeling prevailed, it was vain to hope for any systematic extension of secular education: but the church and other religious bodies were exerting themselves earnestly, in their proper sphere of instruction. In their schools, religious teaching was the primary object: but great advances were also made in the general education of the poor. Meanwhile, the increasing prosperity of the country was rapidly developing the independent education of the children of other classes, who needed no encouragement or assistance. As society advanced, it became more alive to the evils of ignorance; and in a reformed Parliament, the political jealousy of popular education was speedily overcome.

In Ireland, as we have seen, a broad scheme of national education was introduced, in 1831, on the principle of 'a combined literary, and a separate religious education.'[3] In *Obstacles to any scheme of national education.*

---

[1] Hans. Deb., 2nd Ser., ii. 49; Harwood's Mem. of Lord Brougham, 124, 161.
[2] See Lord Cockburn's Life of Jeffrey, i. 68; Porter's Progress, p. 694. [3] *Supra*, p. 270.

Great Britain, however, there were obstacles to any such system of national education. In the schools of the church, and of dissenters, religious teaching was the basis of education. The patrons of both were jealous of one another, resentful of interference, and unwilling to co-operate in any combined scheme of national education. The church claimed the exclusive right of educating the people: dissenters asserted an equal title to direct the education of the children of their own sects. Both parties were equally opposed to any scheme of secular education, distinct from their own religious teaching. Hence the government was obliged to proceed with the utmost caution. Its connection with education was

Parliamentary grants in aid of education. commenced in 1834, by a small parliamentary grant, in aid of the building of schoolhouses. The administration of this fund was confided to the Treasury, by whom it was to be distributed, through the National School Society, representing the church, and the British and Foreign School Society, to whose schools children of all religious denominations were admitted. This arrangement was continued until 1839; when Lord Melbourne's government vested the management of the education funds in a Committee of Privy Council. This change was effected, in contemplation of a more comprehensive scheme, by which aid should be given directly to schools connected with the church, and other religious bodies. The church was alarmed, lest her own privileges should be disturbed: many of the conservative party were still adverse, on political grounds, to the extension of education; and the government scheme was nearly overthrown. The annual grant met with strenuous resistance; and was voted in the Commons by a bare majority of two.[1] The Lords, coming to the aid of the church and their own party, hastened to condemn the new scheme, in an address to the Crown.[2] Their lordships, however, received a courteous rebuke from the throne;[3] and the scheme was vigorously carried out. Despite of jealousies and distrust, the operations of the Committee of the Privy Council were speedily extended. Society was awakened to the duty of educating the people: local liberality abounded: the rivalry of the church and dissenters prompted them to increased exertions; and every year, larger demands were made upon the public fund, until, in 1860, the annual grant amounted to nearly 700,000*l.*

However such a system may have fallen short of a complete scheme of national education, embracing the poorest and most neglected classes, it gave an extraordinary impulse to popular education; and bore ample testimony to the earnestness of the state, in promoting the social improvement of the people.

Let us now turn to the material interests of the country,—its commerce, its industry, its productive energies. How were these treated by a close and irresponsible government? and how by a government based upon public opinion, and striving to promote the general welfare and happiness of the people? Our former commercial policy

Commercial policy.

---

[1] Hans. Deb., 3rd Ser., xlviii. 229, *et seq.* [2] *Ibid.*, 1332.
[3] *Ibid.*, xlix. 128 ; Ann. Reg., 1839, 171.

was founded on monopolies, and artificial protections and encouragements,—maintained for the benefit of the few, at the expense of the many. The trade of the East was monopolised by the East India Company: the trade of the Mediterranean by the Levant Company:[1] the trade of a large portion of North America by the Hudson's Bay Company.[2] The trade of Ireland and the colonies was shackled for the sake of English producers and manufacturers. Every produce and manufacture of England was protected, by high duties or prohibitions, against the competition of imported commodities of the like nature. Many exports were encouraged by bounties and drawbacks. Everyone sought protection or encouragement for himself,—utterly regardless of the welfare of others. The protected interests were favoured by the state, while the whole community suffered from prices artificially raised, and industry unnaturally disturbed. This selfish and illiberal policy found support in erroneous doctrines of political economy: but its foundation was narrow self-interest. First one monopoly was established, and then another, until protected interests dominated over a Parliament in which the whole community were unrepresented. Lord North and Mr. Pitt, generally commanding obedient majorities, were unable to do justice to the industry of Ireland, in opposition to English traders.[3] No power short of rebellion could have arrested the monstrous corn bill of 1815, which

---

[1] This Company was wound up in 1826.—6 Geo. IV. c. 33.
[2] The charter of this Company expired in 1859.
[3] *Supra*, p. 320.

landowners, with one voice, demanded. But political science and liberty advanced together: the one pointing out the true interests of the people: the other ensuring their just consideration.

It was not until fifty years after Adam Smith had exposed what he termed 'the mean and malignant expedients of the mercantile system,' that this narrow policy was disturbed. Mr. Huskisson was the first minister, after Mr. Pitt, who ventured to touch protected interests. A close representation still governed: but public opinion had already begun to exercise a powerful influence over Parliament; and he was able to remove some protections from the silk and woollen trades,—to restore the right of free emigration to artisans,—and to break in upon the close monopoly of the navigation laws. These were the beginnings of free trade: but a further development of political liberty was essential to the triumph of that generous and fruitful policy. A wider representation wrested exclusive power from the hands of the favoured classes; and monopolies fell, one after another, in quick succession. The trade of the East was thrown open to the free enterprise of our merchants: the productions of the world were admitted, for the consumption and comfort of our teeming multitudes: exclusive interests in shipping,—in the colonies,—in commerce and manufactures,—were made to yield to the public good. But above all, the most baneful of monopolies, and the most powerful of protected interests, were overborne. The lords of the soil, once dominant in Parliament, had secured to themselves a monopoly in the food

Free trade.

of the people. To ensure high rents, it had been decreed that multitudes should hunger. Such a monopoly was not to be endured; and so soon as public opinion had fully accepted the conclusions of science, it fell before enlightened statesmen and a popular Parliament.

The fruits of free trade are to be seen in the marvellous development of British industry. England will ever hold in grateful remembrance the names of the foremost promoters of this new policy,— of Huskisson, Poulett Thomson, Hume, Villiers, and Labouchere,—of Cobden and Bright,—of Peel and Gladstone: but let her not forget that their fruitful statesmanship was quickened by the life of freedom.

The financial policy of this period was conceived in the same spirit of enlightened liberality; and regarded no less the general welfare and happiness of the people. Industry, while groaning under protection, had further been burdened by oppressive taxes, imposed simply for purposes of revenue. It has been the policy of modern finance to dispense with duties on raw materials, on which the skill and labour of our industrious artisans is exercised. Free scope has been given to productive industry. The employment and comfort of the people have been further encouraged by the removal or reduction of duties on manufactured articles of universal use,—on glass, on bricks and tiles, on soap and paper, and hundreds of other articles.

Financial policy.

The luxuries of the many, as well as their food, have also been relieved from the pressure of taxation. Tea, sugar, coffee, cocoa,—nay, nearly all articles which contribute to the comfort and enjoyment of daily life,—have been placed within reach of the poorest.[1] And among financial changes conceived in the interest of the whole community, the remarkable penny postage of Sir Rowland Hill deserves an honourable place. Notwithstanding extraordinary reductions of taxation, the productive energies of the country, encouraged by so liberal a policy, have more than made good the amount of these remissions. Tax after tax has been removed; yet the revenue,—ever buoyant and elastic,—has been maintained by the increased productiveness of the remaining duties. This policy,—the conception of Sir Henry Parnell,—was commenced by Lord Althorp, boldly extended by Sir Robert Peel, and consummated by Mr. Gladstone.

To ensure the safe trial of this financial experiment, Sir Robert Peel proposed a property-tax, in time of peace, to fall exclusively on the higher and middle classes. It was accepted: and marks, no less than other examples, the solicitude of Parliament for the welfare of the many, and the generous spirit of those classes who have most influence over its deliberations. The succession duty, imposed some years later, affords another example of the self-denying principles of a popular Parliament. In 1796, the Commons, ever ready to mulct the people at the bidding of the minister,—yet unwilling to bear their own proper burthen, refused to grant Mr. Pitt such

---

[1] In 1842, the customs' tariff embraced 1,163 articles; in 1860, it comprised less than 50, of which 15 contributed nearly the whole revenue.

a tax upon their landed property. In 1853, the reformed Parliament, intent upon sparing industry, accepted this heavy charge from Mr. Gladstone.

The only unsatisfactory feature of modern finance has been the formidable and continuous increase of expenditure. The demands upon the Exchequer,—apart from the fixed charge of the public debt,—were nearly doubled during the last ten years of this period.[1] Much of this serious increase was due to the Russian, Chinese, and Persian wars,—to the vast armaments and unsettled policy of foreign states,—to the proved deficiencies of our military organisation,—to the reconstruction of the navy,—and to the greater costliness of all the equipments of modern warfare. Much, however, was caused by the liberal and humane spirit of modern administration. While the utmost efficiency was sought in fleets and armies, the comforts and moral welfare of our seamen and soldiers were promoted, at great cost to the state. So, again, large permanent additions were made to the civil expenditure, by an improved administration of justice,—a more effective police,—extended postal communications,—the public education of the people,—and the growing needs of civilisation, throughout a powerful and wide-spread empire. This augmented expenditure, however, deprived the

Vast increase of expenditure.

---

[1] In 1850, the estimated expenditure was 50,763,583*l.*; in 1860, it amounted to 73,534,000*l.* The latter amount, however, comprised 4,700,000*l.* for the collection of the revenue, which had not been brought into the account until 1856. In the former year the charge of the public debt was 28,105,000*l.*; in the latter, 26,200,000*l.* Hence an expenditure of 22,658,583*l.* at one period, is to be compared with 42,634,000*l.* at the other.

people of the full benefits of a judicious scheme of taxation. The property tax, intended only as a temporary expedient, was continued; and, however light and equal the general incidence of other taxes,—enormous contributions to the state were necessarily a heavy burden upon the industry, the resources, and the comforts of the people.

Such have been the legislative fruits of extended liberty: wise laws, justly administered: a beneficent care for the moral and social welfare of the people: freedom of trade and industry: lighter and more equitable taxation. Nor were these great changes in our laws and policy effected in the spirit of democracy. They were made slowly, temperately, and with caution. They were preceded by laborious inquiries, by discussion, experiments, and public conviction. Delays and opposition were borne patiently, until truth steadily prevailed; and when a sound policy was at length recognised, it was adopted and carried out, even by former opponents.[1] *These changes carefully made.*

Freedom, and good government, a generous policy, and the devotion of rulers to the welfare of the people, have been met with general confidence, loyalty, and contentment. The great ends of freedom have been attained, *Good government promotes content and discourages democracy.*

---

[1] M. Guizot, who never conceals his distrust of democracy, says: 'In the legislation of the country, the progress is immense: justice, disinterested good sense, respect for all rights, consideration for all interests, the conscientious and searching study of social facts and wants, exercises a far greater sway than they formerly did, in the government of England: in its domestic matters, and as regards its daily affairs, England is assuredly governed much more equitably and wisely.'—*Life of Sir R. Peel,* p. 373.

in an enlightened and responsible rule, approved by the judgment of the governed. The constitution, having worked out the aims, and promoted the just interests of society, has gained upon democracy; while growing wealth and prosperity have been powerful auxiliaries of constitutional government.

To achieve these great objects, ministers and Parliaments have laboured, since the Reform Act, with unceasing energy and toil. In less than thirty years, the legislation of a century was accomplished. The inertness and errors of past ages had bequeathed a heavy arrear to lawgivers. Parliament had long been wanting in its duty of 'devising remedies as fast as time breedeth mischief.'[1] There were old abuses to correct,—new principles to establish,—powerful interests and confirmed prejudices to overcome,—the ignorance, neglect, and mistaken policy of centuries to review. Every department of legislation,—civil, ecclesiastical, legal, commercial, and financial,—demanded revision. And this prodigious work, when shaped and fashioned in council, had to pass through the fiery ordeal of a popular assembly,—to encounter opposition and unrestrained freedom of debate,—the conflict of parties,—popular agitation,—the turmoil of elections,—and lastly, the delays and reluctance of the House of Lords, which still cherished the spirit and sympathies of the past. And further, this work had to be slowly wrought out in a Parliament of wide remedial jurisdiction,—the Grand Inquest of the nation. Ours is not a council of

Pressure of legislation since the Reform Act.

---

[1] Lord Bacon; Pacification of the Church.

sages for framing laws, and planning amendments of the constitution: but a free and vigorous Parliament, which watches over the destinies of an empire. It arraigns ministers: directs their policy, and controls the administration of affairs: it listens to every grievance; and inquires, complains, and censures. Such are its obligations to freedom; and such its paramount trust and duty. Its first care is that the state be well governed: its second that the laws be amended. These functions of a Grand Inquest received a strong impulse from Parliamentary Reform, and were exercised with a vigour characteristic of a more popular representation. Again, there was the necessary business of every session,—provision for the public service, the scrutiny of the national expenditure, and multifarious topics of incidental discussion, ever arising in a free Parliament. Yet, notwithstanding all these obstacles, legislation marched onwards. The strain and pressure were great, but they were borne;[1] and the results may be recounted with pride. Not only was a great arrear overtaken: but the labours of another generation were, in some measure, anticipated. An exhausting harvest was gathered: but there is yet ample work for the gleaners; and a soil that claims incessant cultivation. 'A free government,' says Machiavel, 'in order to maintain itself free, hath need, every day, of some new provisions in favour of liberty.' Parliament must be watchful and earnest,

[1] The extent of these labours is shown in the reports of Committees on Public business in 1848, 1855, and 1861; in a pamphlet, by the author, on that subject, 1849; and in the Edinburgh Review, Jan. 1854, Art. vii.

lest its labours be undone. Nor will its popular constitution again suffer it to cherish the perverted optimism of the last century, which discovered perfection in everything as it was, and danger in every innovation.

Even the foreign relations of England were affected by her domestic liberty. When kings and nobles governed, their sympathies were with crowned heads: when the people were admitted to a share in the government, England favoured constitutional freedom in other states; and became the idol of every nation which cherished the same aspirations as herself.

<small>Foreign relations affected by freedom.</small>

This history is now completed. However unworthy of its great theme, it may yet serve to illustrate a remarkable period of progress and renovation, in the laws and liberties of England. Tracing the later development of the constitution, it concerns our own time, and present franchises. It shows how the encroachments of power were repelled, and popular rights acquired, without revolution: how constitutional liberty was won, and democracy reconciled with time-honoured institutions. It teaches how freedom and enlightenment, inspiring the national councils with wisdom, promoted the good government of the state, and the welfare and contentment of society. Such political examples as these claim the study of the historian and philosopher, the reflection of the statesman, and the gratulations of every free people.

<small>Conclusion.</small>

SUPPLEMENTARY CHAPTER.

1861—1871.

REVIEW OF POLITICAL PROGRESS SINCE 1860 :—TRANQUILLITY UNDER LORD PALMERSTON :—HIS DEATH :—EARL RUSSELL'S REFORM BILL, 1866 :—REFORM ACTS OF EARL OF DERBY AND MR. DISRAELI, 1867-1868 :—DISESTABLISHMENT OF THE IRISH CHURCH :—IRISH LAND ACT :—SETTLEMENT OF CHURCH-RATE QUESTION : — UNIVERSITY TESTS :—REPEAL OF ECCLESIASTICAL TITLES ACT :—EDUCATION :— THE BALLOT.

THE century comprised in this history was a period of remarkable constitutional progress. The political abuses of many ages were corrected; and our laws and institutions judiciously improved and developed. While other states were convulsed by revolutions, English liberties were steadily advancing without violence or tumult. The influence of the crown was constantly diminished, and ministerial responsibility increased. The political ascendency of the House of Peers was reduced. The House of Commons, purged of corruption, and casting off its dependence upon patrons, received a vast increase of power from a wider representation of the people, while it became more responsible to the country, and more sensitive to public opinion. *Constitutional changes, 1760-1860.*

Meanwhile, the press attained a power which had never been conceived in any constitutional system.

Irresponsible itself, but at once forming and expressing the sentiments of the people, it swayed the councils of responsible rulers. In alliance with the press, political agitation exercised a potent influence over the executive government and the legislature.

No less remarkable was the change in the relations of the church to the state, and to the community. The supremacy of the state church had been maintained by a penal code for the repression and discouragement of Roman Catholics and nonconformists. Within this period every restraint upon freedom of conscience, and every civil disability, was swept away. Religious freedom and equality had become the settled policy of the state.

Such were the changes in the laws and liberties of England, which distinguished this period of our history. Let us now approach the consideration of our political progress since 1860.

The five first years of this period were marked by unusual political tranquillity. *Political tranquillity under Lord Palmerston.* The discussions upon Parliamentary reform, in 1860, had failed to awaken any excitement, or even interest, in favour of further electoral changes. After thirty years of agitation, and legislative activity, the minds of men appeared to be at rest. The Crimean war, and the Indian mutiny, had served to divert public attention from domestic politics; and the great civil conflict in the United States engrossed the thoughts of all classes of Englishmen.

Such being the sentiments and temper of the country, the venerable statesman who directed its policy, as first minister, was little inclined to disturb them by startling experiments in legislation. No ruler was ever more impressed with the practical wisdom of the maxim '*quieta non movete*,' than Lord Palmerston, in the last years of his long political life. Originally an enlightened member of that party which had been opposed to change, he had developed into a member of the liberal administration, which had carried the Reform Act of 1832. Henceforward he frankly accepted the policy, and shared the fortunes, of the liberal party, until he became their popular leader. He had outlived some generations of his countrymen: he had borne a part in the political strifes of more than half a century: he had observed revolutions abroad, and organic changes at home: and in these, his latter days, he was disposed, as well by conviction as by temperament, to favour political tranquillity. Of rare sagacity, and ripe judgment, it had long been his habit to regard public affairs from a practical rather than a theoretical point of view; and the natural inertness of age could not fail to discourage an experimental policy.

The miscarriage of the Reform Bill of 1860 had demonstrated the composure of the public mind; and Lord Palmerston perceived that in a policy of inaction he could best satisfy the present judgment of the country, and his own matured opinions.

Such an attitude, if it alienated the more advanced section of his supporters, was congenial to the great body of the Whigs, and disarmed the opposition, who were convinced that his rule would insure the maintenance of a Conservative policy.

Hence, during his life, the condition of the country may be described as one of political repose. There was no great agitation or popular movement: no pressure from without: while within the walls of Parliament this adroit and popular minister contrived at once to attach his friends, and to conciliate his opponents.

The question of parliamentary reform, now dropped by the Government, was occasionally pressed forward by other members. In 1851, Mr. Locke King sought to lower the county franchise to 10*l*., and Mr. Baines to reduce the borough franchise to 6*l*.; but neither of these proposals found favour with the House of Commons.

<small>Attempts to disturb the franchises of 1832.</small>

Again, in 1864, these proposals were repeated, without success, though supported by strong minorities. Meanwhile, reformers were perplexed by the utterances of statesmen. The veteran reformer, Earl Russell, had lately counselled the people of Scotland to 'rest and be thankful;' while Mr. Gladstone earnestly advocated the claims of working men to the suffrage, and contended that 'every man who is not presumably incapacitated by some personal unfitness, or political danger, is morally entitled to come within the pale of the constitution.'

In 1865, Mr. Baines' bill revived the discussion of parliamentary reform. Though supported by Government, it was defeated by a considerable majority. The debate was signalised by a protest against democracy by Mr. Lowe, which foreshadowed his relations to his own party, and to the cause of reform, at no distant period.

After this session, Parliament, which had exceeded the usual span of Parliamentary life,[1] was dissolved. The elections were not marked by the excitements of a severe party conflict: no distinct issue was referred to the constituencies; and general confidence in Lord Palmerston was relied upon by candidates rather than any special policy: but the Liberal party gained a considerable accession of strength. *Dissolution of Parliament, 1865.*

There was, however, one memorable election. Mr. Gladstone, who had represented the University of Oxford for eighteen years, lost his seat, and was returned for South Lancashire. As member for the University his career was always restrained and trammelled: as member for a great manufacturing and commercial county, he was free to become the leader of the Liberal party. *Mr. Gladstone rejected by the University of Oxford.*

At length in October, 1865, the aged premier died, at the summit of his power and popularity; and at once a change came over the national councils. He was succeeded by Earl Russell, the acknowledged leader of the Whigs, and the statesman most associated with Parliamentary reform. He had felt deeply the loss of his own measure in 1860, and the subsequent relations of Lord Palmerston's government to its policy. They had fought their way into office as the champions of reform, and at the first check, had abandoned it. For five years they had been content to rule and prosper, without doing further homage to that cause; and now Earl Russell, Mr. Glad- *Death of Lord Palmerston. Earl Russell Premier.*

---

[1] Upwards of six years.

stone, and other members of the cabinet would no longer submit to the reproach of insincerity. Nor was a change of policy, at this time, dictated merely by a sense of honour and consistency. It rested upon a continued conviction of the necessity of such a measure, in the interests of the state, and in fulfilment of obligations which Parliament, no less than ministers, had assumed. And further it was deemed politic, with a view to satisfy the long-deferred hopes of the more advanced members of the Liberal party. Accordingly, in the autumn, Earl Russell announced that the consideration of reform would be renewed in the approaching session.

Revival of Parliamentary Reform.

There were, however, some considerations, not sufficiently weighed at the time, which had a disastrous influence over the fate of ministers, and of the measure to which they stood committed. Parliament had recently been dissolved, while Lord Palmerston was still minister, and reform had been treated, upon the hustings, with little more earnestness than in the House of Commons. Hence the cause was without the impulse of a popular demand. Again, a large proportion of the members, returned at the general election, sharing the sentiments of Lord Palmerston and the late Parliament, had no inclination to disturb the political calm of the past few years. But above all, in this, the first session of a new Parliament, members were invited to recast the constitution of the House of Commons, many of them to forfeit their seats, and all to return speedily to their constituents. The political

Considerations adverse to its settlement.

situation, indeed, may be compared to a feast offered to guests who had lately dined.

At the first meeting of the Cabinet after Lord Palmerston's funeral, ministers had taken means to collect ample electoral statistics:[1] and early in the session of 1866 were prepared to submit their proposals to Parliament. Warned by the obstacles which a comprehensive measure had encountered in 1860, they confined their scheme to a revision of the franchise, reserving for another session the embarrassing problem of a re-distribution of seats. It was proposed to reduce the occupation franchise in counties to 14*l.* annual value, and in boroughs to 7*l.* The addition to the voters was estimated at 400,000, of which one-half would be working men. This measure, however moderate and cautious, was at once beset with difficulties. Though falling short of the views of Mr. Bright and the radicals, it was supported by them as an 'honest measure.' But it was denounced by the Conservatives, and even by several Whigs, as democratic and revolutionary; and an alarming defection soon disclosed itself in the ministerial ranks. Comprising about forty members, it numbered among its leaders Mr. Lowe, Mr. Horsman, Mr. Laing, Lord Elcho, Earl Grosvenor, and Lord Dunkellin. This party was humorously compared by Mr. Bright with those who had gathered in the 'cave of Adullam,' by which name it was henceforth familiarly known.

Earl Russell's Reform Bill.

'The Cave.'

[1] Mr. Gladstone's speech on introducing the English Reform Bill, March 12th, 1866.

The first weak point in the scheme which was assailed, was the omission of a redistribution of seats. This was brought to an issue by an amendment of Earl Grosvenor, on the second reading of the bill, when ministers, after a spirited debate of eight nights, and in a very full house, escaped defeat by five votes only.[1] Deferring to the opinion of so large a minority, ministers promised a bill for the redistribution of seats, and reform bills for Scotland and Ireland, before they proceeded with the original measure. On the 7th May, these bills were introduced. By the redistribution of seats bill, thirty boroughs having a population under 8,000 lost one member, and nineteen other seats were obtained by the grouping of smaller boroughs,—forty-nine seats being available for larger places. Though sharply criticised, this bill was read a second time without a division: but ministers were obliged to agree to a proposal of Mr. Bouverie to refer it and the franchise bill to the same committee, with a view to their consolidation. Nor was this all: the measure was already too large to be fully discussed, when Sir R. Knightley carried an instruction to the committee, by a majority of ten, to provide for the better prevention of bribery and corruption at elections.

In committee Lord Stanley moved, without notice, the postponement of the franchise clauses; but was defeated by a majority of twenty-seven. Mr. Walpole moved that the occupation franchise in counties should be raised to 20*l*., and his

---

[1] Ayes, 318; Noes, 313.

amendment was lost by fourteen votes only. Mr. Hunt proposed that the county franchise should be based on rating instead of rental, and was resisted by a majority of seven; and lastly, Lord Dunkellin moved a similar amendment in regard to boroughs, which was carried against the government, by a majority of eleven.

Ministers now perceived that the game was lost. They had declared their resolution to stand or fall by their bill; and its fate was beyond hope of recovery. They submitted their resignation to the Queen, who hesitated to accept it; and a vote of confidence was about to be moved with a view to re-establish them, when they finally determined to resign.[1] Their defeat, indeed, had been sustained upon a question of secondary importance, and might have been repaired at a later stage of the bill: but they had been sorely pressed on other occasions: their party was disorganised and broken up: it was plainly impossible to pass the bill, and they could not abandon it without discredit. *Resignation of ministers.*

Such was the issue of this infelicitous measure. A strong ministry was ruined; a triumphant party overthrown; and the minority again placed in power, under the Earl of Derby. But events of higher importance resulted from the miscarriage of this measure. For some years, reformers had been indifferent and inert: when Earl Russell promised reform, they trusted him, *Earl of Derby Premier, 1866. Popular agitation.*

---

[1] Mr. Crawford, member for the City of London, was on the point of rising to give notice of a vote of confidence, when he received a letter from Earl Russell announcing his resignation.

and were calm and hopeful: but now that he had been driven from power, and supplanted by the opponents of reform, they became restless and turbulent. The spirit of democracy was again awakened, and the new government were soon brought into collision with it. A meeting in Hyde Park had been announced by the Reform League for July 23rd, as a demonstration in favour of an extension of the suffrage. Ministers being advised that the crown had power to prevent such a meeting in a Royal Park,[1] and fearful of a disturbance to the public peace, instructed the police to close the gates of the park, and prevent the entrance of the multitudes expected to assemble there. The gates were accordingly barred; and the leaders of the League, on being refused admittance, proceeded, according to previous arrangement, to Trafalgar Square to hold their meeting. Meanwhile, the park gates were securely held, and a considerable police force was collected inside. But the vast enclosure was without protection, and the mob, pulling down the railings, rushed through every breach, and took forcible possession of the park. Democracy had overcome the government; and the maintenance of order was afterwards due, as much to the exertions of Mr. Beales and the Reform League, as to the police.

Hyde Park riots, July 23rd, 1866.

These events increased the public excitement, and encouraged the activity of the reformers. Several important meetings and

Impulse given to reform.

---

[1] This right had been affirmed in 1855 by an opinion of the Law Officers of the Crown, Sir A. Cockburn and Sir R. Bethell, and of Mr. Willes.

popular demonstrations were held, which stirred the public mind: while political uneasiness and discontents were aggravated by commercial distress and an indifferent harvest.

Public opinion had, at length, been aroused in favour of reform: but the House of Commons had lately shown its disinclination to deal with that question; and the party of whom the new ministry was composed, aided by a strong body of Whigs, had defeated Earl Russell's moderate measure, as revolutionary. Would ministers resist reform, and count upon the support of their new allies: or venture upon another reform bill, and trust for success to adroit management, and the divisions in the Liberal party? *Position of Ministers in regard to reform.*

These questions were set at rest, at the opening of the session, by the announcement of a reform bill in the Queen's speech. No position could be more embarrassing for a government. In a minority of seventy in the House of Commons: representing a party opposed to the principles of reform: brought into power by resisting such a measure when offered by the late government: confronted by a strong party in the House pledged to reform, and by popular agitation: in what manner could they venture to approach this perilous question? At first they invited the House no longer to treat reform as a party question, but to concert a satisfactory measure in friendly consultation; and for this purpose they offered to submit resolutions as the basis of a bill. Such a course was naturally objected to, as being designed *Introduction of the question, 1867.* *Mr. Disraeli's resolutions.*

to evade ministerial responsibility; and when the resolutions appeared, they proved too vague and ambiguous for effective discussion. In explaining them, indeed, Mr. Disraeli sketched the outline of the ministerial scheme: but they were eventually withdrawn; and ministers were forced to commit themselves to more definite proposals. And here the difficulties of their position were disclosed by the resignation of three members of the Cabinet—the Earl of Carnarvon, Lord Cranborne, and General Peel. Their reluctance had already induced the government to sketch out a less bold scheme than their colleagues had been prepared to propose; and their retirement, otherwise a source of weakness, now enabled the Cabinet to agree upon a more extended measure.

At length, on the 18th March, the bill, which had caused so much expectation, was introduced. The franchise was granted in boroughs to every householder paying rates, who had resided for two years: in counties to every occupier rated at 15*l.*; and there were added various franchises, based upon education and the payment of taxes. As a counterpoise to the extended occupation suffrage, a scheme of dual voting was proposed for voters of a higher qualification. There was to be a redistribution of thirty seats.

Earl of Derby's Reform Bill.

The scheme was founded throughout upon the principle of securities and compensations, the conception of which was due to the peculiar relations of the Government to different parties. Household suffrage in boroughs, the distinc-

Its securities and compensations.

tive principle of Mr. Bright and the radicals, had also found favour with Mr. Henley, Mr. Walpole, Sir Roundell Palmer, and a certain section of the Conservatives; and could not be opposed by the Whigs, without an open breach with advanced reformers. On the other hand, it was qualified by a two years' residence, by the personal payment of rates, by voting papers, by education and tax-paying franchises, and by dual voting. These securities, as they were called, against a democratic franchise, commended the measure to the Conservative party; but their futility had been apparent to the seceding ministers, and was soon to be proved by their successive rejection or abandonment. The measure embraced proposals calculated to please all parties; and ministers were prepared to assent to any amendments by which its ultimate character should be determined by the majority. The results may be briefly told. Household suffrage in boroughs was maintained, with one year's residence instead of two; the county franchise was reduced to 12*l.*; a lodger franchise was added; the higher class franchises, the dual votes, and voting papers disappeared from the bill; and the disqualification of large numbers of compound householders was averted. *Its ultimate form.*

The scheme for the redistribution of seats was also enlarged. Every provision which had reconciled Conservatives to the measure was struck out: every amendment urged by the liberal party was grafted upon the bill. And thus the House of Commons found itself assenting, inch by inch, to an extended scheme of reform, which neither Conservatives nor Whigs wholly approved. Parties had been played off against one another, until a measure which gratified none but advanced reformers,—probably not more than a sixth of the House of Commons,—was accepted, as a necessity, by all.

While the bill was under discussion in the House of Commons, the public excitement gave an impulse to the Liberal party, in passing every amendment favourable to extended franchises. And one remarkable episode illustrated at once the strength of popular sentiment, and the impotence of the executive Government to resist it. A great demonstration in favour of reform was announced to take place on the 6th May, in Hyde Park, when Mr. Walpole, the Home Secretary, not profiting by his sore experience of the previous year, issued a proclamation, stating that the use of the park for the holding of such meeting was not permitted, and warning and admonishing all persons to refrain from attending it. But, in spite of this proclamation, the meeting was held, and large assemblages of people occupied the park, without disorder or disturbance.

Meeting in Hyde Park, May 6, 1867.

The right of the Government to prohibit the meeting was contested not only by Mr. Beales and the Reform League, but by Mr. Bright and many other members of the Liberal party. On the other hand, the conduct of the Government in first prohibiting the meeting, and then allowing it to take place, in defiance of their authority, was censured as bringing the executive into contempt. In deference to the strong opinions expressed upon this subject, Mr. Walpole resigned the seals of the

Home Department, but retained his seat in the Cabinet.

Meanwhile, the state of the law in reference to the use of the parks for public meetings was so unsatisfactory, that the Government had brought in a bill to prohibit, under the penalties of a misdemeanour, the holding of any meeting in the royal parks, without the consent of the crown. This bill being violently opposed, was overtaken by the close of the session, and abandoned; and the law has still been left uncertain, and incapable of enforcement. It cannot be questioned that the meetings of 1866, and 1867, should either have been allowed, or effectually prevented. The latter course could only be taken at the risk of bloody collisions with the people; and accordingly such meetings have since been permitted, and have signally failed as popular demonstrations.[1]

Unsatisfactory state of the law.

In the House of Lords, several amendments were made to the Reform Bill; but the only one of importance agreed to by the Commons was a clause of Lord Cairns, providing, with a view to the representation of minorities, that in places returning three members, no elector should vote for more than two candidates.[1]

Proceedings in the Lords upon the Reform Bill.

The scheme of enfranchisement, however, was not yet complete. The settlement of the boundaries of boroughs and the divisions of counties was referred to a commission, and the consideration of the reform bills for Scotland and Ireland was postponed until the next session.

Boundaries of boroughs and counties.

[1] Such meetings were regulated by Act in 1872.

Before these measures were introduced, in 1868, the Earl of Derby was obliged by ill-health to retire, and was succeeded as Premier by Mr. Disraeli, to whose extraordinary tact, judgment, and address the passing of the English Reform Act was acknowledged to be due. Many difficult questions remained to be settled, which needed the exercise of all his abilities. The Scotch Reform Bill, founded generally upon the same principles as the English bill, proposed an increase of seven members to represent Scotland. This provision contemplated an addition to the number of the House of Commons, which was resisted; and justice to the claims of Scotland was eventually met by the disfranchisement of seven English boroughs having less than 5,000 inhabitants; and in this form the bill for the representation of Scotland was passed.

Resignation of Earl of Derby.
Mr. Disraeli Premier.
The Scotch Reform Act, 1868.

The Reform Bill for Ireland left the county franchise unaltered, reduced the borough franchise, and proposed a partial redistribution of seats, which was shortly abandoned. The measure, avowedly incomplete, and unequal to the English and Scotch schemes, was nevertheless assented to, as at least a present settlement of a question beset with exceptional difficulties.

The Irish Reform Act, 1868.

The boundaries of the English boroughs and the new divisions of counties were still to be settled; and, after an inquiry by a select committee, the boundaries, as defined by the commissioners, were, with several modifications, agreed to.

Boundaries of boroughs and counties.

The series of measures affecting the electoral system was not even yet concluded. A measure was, after long discussions, agreed to, for transferring the cherished jurisdiction of the Commons, in matters of election, to judges of the superior courts, and for amending the laws in restraint of corrupt practices. And, lastly, a bill was passed to facilitate the registration of the year, so as to insure the election of a Parliament during the autumn, by the new electors. *Election Petitions and Corrupt Practices Act, 1868.*

These measures for extending the representation of the people were little less important than the great Reform Acts of 1832. The new franchises embraced large numbers of the working classes, and greatly enlarged the basis of electoral power. At the same time, a certain counterpoise to household suffrage was found in the addition of twenty-five members to the English counties, which their population fully justified, and the withdrawal of thirty-three members from English boroughs. *Constitutional importance of these measures.*

Considering how this great constitutional change had been accomplished,—not by the deliberate judgment of statesmen, but by the force of circumstances,—its results were, not unnaturally, viewed with grave misgivings. The Earl of Derby himself had said, 'No doubt we are making a great experiment, and taking a leap in the dark;'[1] and many thoughtful men believed the state to be approaching the very verge of democracy. Nor can there be any reasonable doubt that the popular element of the

[1] August 6th 1867; upon the question 'that this bill do pass.'

constitution acquired a decided preponderance. Even with a limited franchise, popular influences had prevailed; and an extended representation necessarily invested them with greater force, and clothed them with more authority. Yet, the sound principles of these measures have since been generally acknowledged. If the settlement of 1832 was to be disturbed,—and no one contended for its perpetuity,—household suffrage was an ancient franchise known to the constitution: it had been advocated in 1797 by Mr. Fox and Mr. Grey: it found favour with men of widely different political sentiments; and its basis was broad and rational. The redistribution of seats was unquestionably judicious and moderate.

It may be too soon yet to estimate the results of the new constitution. Rank, property, the employment of labour, and other social influences, have apparently retained their ascendency; but however the popular will may be pronounced, no constitutional means are left for resisting it. At once to lead, to satisfy, and to control this vast power, and to hold it in harmony with other authorities, will demand the highest statesmanship. A Government resting upon the confidence of an enfranchised people will indeed be strong: but its policy must be that of the community, which is the source of power.

Whatever may be our institutions, public opinion has become the ultimate ruler of our political destinies. However formed,—whether by statesmen, or demagogues,—whether by society at large, or by the press,—or by all of them combined —it dominates over ministers and parliaments. Under a more restricted representation, it dictated the policy of the state; and under our present constitution, it will exercise its influence more promptly and decisively. In public opinion, therefore, rests at once our safety, and our danger. If rational and well ordered, like the society of this great country, whose judgment it should express, we may rely upon it with confidence. If it should become perverted and degenerate, who shall save us from ourselves?

While the discussions upon the later measures of Parliamentary reform were still proceeding, the condition of Ireland, its discontents, and disaffection, the outrages of the Fenians, and the continued suspension of the Habeas Corpus Act, demanded the attention of Parliament; and the policy of the Government in relation to that country was explained. Ministers promised an inquiry into the relations of landlord and tenant, proposed to create a new Catholic university by royal charter, and intimated that when the Commission already inquiring into the condition of the Irish Church should report, they might review that establishment. Hints were also given of promoting religious equality, by an increase of the *regium donum*, and by the endowment of the Catholic clergy,— a policy, as it was described by Lord Mayo, of levelling upwards, and not downwards. On the other side, Mr. Gladstone declared the policy by which he was prepared to redress the grievances of Ireland, and to bring peace and contentment to that country.

In 1865, and again in 1867,[1] Mr. Gladstone had disclosed a growing conviction that a review of the church establishment in Ireland would soon be necessary; and he now announced that, in his opinion, the time had come when the Protestant Church, 'as a state church, must cease to exist.' It was in this form that he would secure religious equality in Ireland. He also urged the necessity of an early settlement of the land question.

Irish Church.

The disestablishment of the Irish Church henceforth became the primary question of the time, and was accepted by the entire Liberal party, as its watchword. Parliamentary reform was being settled by the united action of all parties: but this was a question by which Conservatives and Liberals were again divided into hostile ranks. Mr. Gladstone soon carried resolutions, in opposition to the Government, by which it was sought to prevent the creation of new public interests in the church, until Parliament had settled the future position of that establishment. Ministers, defeated upon so momentous a policy, tendered their resignation, but obtained from the Queen a power of dissolving Parliament, whenever the state of public business would permit it. A dissolution at that time would have involved an appeal to the old constituencies, instead of to the new electoral bodies, which were to be called into being by the measures still pending in Parliament; and eventually ministers allowed the Suspensory Bill, founded upon Mr. Gladstone's resolutions,

Mr. Gladstone's resolutions.

May, 1868.

His suspensory bill.

---

[1] March 28th, 1865; May 7th, 1867.

to be passed through the House of Commons, while the reform bills were being completed in view of a dissolution in the autumn. The exceptional position of ministers during this interval could not fail to elicit criticism. They had suffered a grave defeat upon a vital question of state policy: a measure which they denounced was being carried through the House of Commons, in defiance of them: they had advised Her Majesty not to withhold her consent from the Suspensory Bill, which otherwise could not have been passed by the Commons: they had received authority to appeal from the Commons to the country, and yet deferred the exercise of that authority, and continued to hold office, and to pass important measures, in presence of a hostile majority. Yet it cannot be denied that the peculiar circumstances of the occasion naturally led to such a position, on the part of ministers. They could not be expected to resign without an appeal to the people; and a sudden dissolution, while the great measures of enfranchisement were still incomplete, would have been an idle and mischievous disturbance of the country, involving a second dissolution a few months later. The Irish Church question had come athwart Parliamentary reform, and was left to await its further progress. The Suspensory Bill was rejected by the House of Lords: the supplementary measures of reform were completed; and at length an appeal was made to the people. The main issue was the policy of disestablishing the Irish Church; the second was the confidence to be reposed, by the majority of the electors, in one or other of the great political parties, whose policy, character, and conduct had recently been displayed in the contentions of the three last eventful years.

The result of the elections was decisive of these issues. All the conditions of success were on the side of the Liberal party. The policy of disestablishing the Irish Church united English Dissenters, Scottish Presbyterians, and Irish Roman Catholics with Liberal politicians of every shade, who had long regarded that institution as theoretically indefensible. The wide extension of the suffrage had also increased their power. Many Conservatives had persuaded themselves that the lower class of electors would be on their side; but generally it was found that the sympathies of the new constituencies were with the Liberal party.[1] There were, indeed, some remarkable exceptions. Mr. Gladstone himself was defeated in South-West Lancashire,—a new division of that county which came within the Conservative influence of Liverpool. Other parts of that great manufacturing county, and its boroughs, also showed a strong preference for Conservative candidates. On the whole, however, the Liberal party, throughout the country, sent to Parliament a majority of about 120, pledged to support Mr. Gladstone, and to vote for the disestablishment of the Irish Church. So decided and incontestable was the national verdict, that Mr. Disraeli, without waiting for the meeting of Parliament, placed in Her Majesty's hands the resigna-

Its decisive results.

Resignation of ministers, 2nd Dec., 1869.

[1] In the United Kingdom 1,408,239 electors voted for Liberal candidates, and 883,530 for Conservative candidates, thus showing a majority of 524,709 in favour of the former.

tion of ministers; and Mr. Gladstone (who had been returned for Greenwich) was at once charged with the formation of a new administration. It united Peelites, Whigs, and advanced Liberals: it embraced Mr. Bright and Mr. Lowe.

Mr. Gladstone Premier.

And now was witnessed the extraordinary power of a Government representing the popular will, under an extended franchise. Mr. Gladstone had committed himself to the boldest measure of modern times. Thirty years before, the House of Lords and the Conservative party had successfully resisted the theoretical assertion of the right of the state to appropriate the surplus revenues of the Irish Church; and now it was proposed to disestablish and disendow that church, and, after the satisfaction of existing interests, to apply the bulk of its revenues to secular purposes. Founded upon the principle of religious equality, it was a masterly measure,—thorough in its application of that principle,—and complete in all its details. Given the principle,—which public opinion had now fully accepted,—its legislative workmanship was consummate. The church was severed from the state, and its bishops deprived of their seats in Parliament. At the same time, the annual grants to Presbyterian ministers, in the form of *regium donum*, and to the Roman Catholic college of Maynooth, were commuted.

The Irish Church Bill, 1869.

This great ecclesiastical measure,—by far the greatest since the Reformation,—was supported by arguments of rare ability, and by overwhelming majorities. The Lords secured somewhat better terms for the church, but all their amendments which otherwise affected the principle, or main conditions of the bill were disagreed to; and the bill, unchanged in every essential point, was passed in a single session.

When the disestablishment of the Church in Ireland had been accomplished, Mr. Gladstone immediately undertook to redress another Irish grievance. For nearly forty years the relations between landlords and tenants in Ireland had been discussed in Parliament, and especially the system of evictions, and the rights of tenants to compensation for unexhausted improvements. This difficult question, so nearly affecting the rights of property, was grappled with by Mr. Gladstone in 1870, and carried to a successful conclusion, like the Irish Church bill, in the same session.

Irish Land Bill, 1870.

This period also witnessed the settlement of another important question affecting the Church, which had been under the consideration of Parliament for thirty-five years. In 1866, a compromise in regard to church rates, first suggested by Mr. Waldegrave-Leslie, had been viewed favourably by Mr. Gladstone. It was to abolish compulsory church rates, and to facilitate the raising of voluntary church rates. In 1867, Mr. Hardcastle succeeded in passing a bill through the Commons to give effect to this arrangement: but it was rejected by the Lords, upon the second reading.

Church rates, 1866-68.

And, at length, in 1868, Mr. Gladstone introduced a bill founded upon the same principle. It commended itself to dissenters as giving up the principle of compulsion; and to churchmen as affording a legal recognition of voluntary church rates, and providing machinery for their assessment and collection. The church had already been practically reduced to a voluntary system of church rates; and this bill, if it surrendered her theoretical claims, at least saved her from further litigation and obloquy. It was approved by the Commons, and was even accepted by the Lords, after consideration by a select committee, and the addition of several amendments. And thus, at length, this long-standing controversy between churchmen and dissenters was brought to a close. If the church failed in securing all her legal rights, the present settlement was founded upon the practical result of a long contention in the courts and in Parliament, and was a compromise which all parties were contented to accept. *Church rates, 1868.*

Other questions affecting the interests of churchmen, dissenters, and Roman Catholics were also pressing for a settlement, at this time. Foremost of these was that of religious tests at the universities, by which dissenters were denied their share in the privileges and endowments of those national seats of learning, for which churchmen alone were qualified. *University Tests.*

The injustice of this exclusion had been repeatedly discussed: but it was not until 1866 that the entire Liberal party were determined to redress it. In that year a bill, introduced by Mr. Coleridge, was passed by the Commons, and rejected by the Lords. Again, in 1868, the second reading of a bill with the same objects, introduced by Mr. Coleridge, was agreed to after full discussion, and by a large majority:[1] but was prevented, by the pressure of other measures, from being further proceeded with in that session.

In 1869, a similar bill was passed by the Commons and again rejected by the Lords. Again, in 1870, the University Tests Bill was passed by the Commons; and referred by the Lords to a select committee, whose deliberations deferred the bill to another session. But, at length, in 1871, the same bill, having again been sent up to the Lords, was ultimately agreed to.

<small>University Tests Bill, 1869.
University Tests Bill, 1870.
University Tests Act, 1871.</small>

This Act, stating that the benefits of these universities 'shall be freely accessible to the nation,' enacted that persons taking lay academical degrees, or holding lay academical or collegiate offices in the universities of Oxford, Cambridge, or Durham, shall not be required to subscribe any religious test or formulary. But as it did not open to dissenters the headships of colleges, or professorships of divinity, or offices required to be held by persons in holy orders or by churchmen, some dissatisfaction was still expressed at this settlement. Otherwise another controversy was, at length, closed; and one of the last grievances of dissenters redressed.

Another religious controversy was also settled by Parliament. The celebrated Ecclesiastical Titles Act was an offence to Roman Catholics, while it was wholly inoperative as a protection

<small>Ecclesiastical Titles Act, 1871.</small>

---

[1] By 198 against 140.

against the Church of Rome. After an inquiry into its operation by a committee of the House of Lords, in 1868, and discussions in both Houses concerning the form in which the law should be expressed, rather than its policy, the Act was eventually repealed in 1871, with the general acquiescence of all parties. The law and the Queen's prerogative in regard to ecclesiastical titles and jurisdiction were again asserted by Parliament, but the original Act with its penalties, which had never been enforced, was removed from the statute book.

Of all social questions none can be compared in importance with that of the education of the people. Not only is it essential to their moral, intellectual, and material welfare, but at a time when large masses of the community had recently been invested with political power, it was obviously the duty of the state to apply itself earnestly to the task of popular enlightenment; and this task was undertaken immediately after the new scheme of representation had been completed.

In 1869, an important measure was passed in the interests of education, for the reform and regulation of endowed schools.

In the same year a comprehensive scheme for the improvement of education in Scotland was passed by the Lords; but was unfortunately lost, partly by reason of amendments made to the bill by the Commons, and partly in consequence of the late period at which these amendments were communicated to the Lords.

In England great advances had been made, since

1834, in popular education, aided by the state. But as the system was entirely founded upon local and voluntary efforts, it too often happened that the places which most needed the civilising agency of the schoolmaster were left destitute. All parties admitted the necessity of providing more effectual means for the general education of the people; but the old 'religious difficulty' caused the widest divergence of opinions concerning the principles upon which education should be conducted. The church party naturally desired to retain the teaching of the church catechism, with a liberal conscience clause for the satisfaction of dissenters. Another party, known as Secularists, advocated secular education only in the schools, leaving religious instruction to be sought elsewhere. Another party, again, insisted upon religious instruction in the schools, while they objected to the church catechism and formularies.

Elementary Education Act, 1870.

In 1870, Mr. Gladstone's government were prepared with a scheme for the settlement of this great social question. The country was divided into school districts under the government of elected school boards, and provision was made for the support of schools out of local rates. The voluntary system, which had already accomplished so much good, was retained: but a more complete organisation and extended means were provided. This wise and statesmanlike measure—which was carried through the House of Commons, with great ability, by Mr. Forster, —was nearly lost by the intractable differences of the several parties, upon the religious question. It was at length settled, however, upon the principle of a conscience clause exempting every child from any religious instruction or observance to which his parents should object, and of excluding from schools, provided by a school-board, every denominational catechism or formulary.

No measure in which religious jealousies are concerned, can be settled to the satisfaction of all parties; and this scheme, accepted by the church and by a very large proportion of nonconformists, was naturally obnoxious to the secular party. But already its general acceptance by all religious denominations in the country, and the earnest spirit in which it is being carried into effect, promise well for its practical success.

The last question of constitutional policy which need be referred to, is that of the ballot. <small>The Ballot.</small> This question had long divided the Liberal party. It had been the distinctive principle of advanced Liberals: but had been opposed by Lord Palmerston, and by most of his Whig followers. In 1869, however, the recent extension of the representative system, disclosures at the late general election, and the altered relations of the leaders of the Liberal party to that section of their followers who favoured secret voting, brought about a change of policy in regard to that question. Ministers accordingly proposed an inquiry into the mode of conducting Parliamentary and municipal elections, with a view to limit expense, and to restrain bribery and intimidation; and it was generally understood that this inquiry was designed to prepare the way for the general adhesion of ministers and the Liberal party to the principle of secret voting.

This committee continued its investigations throughout the session; and being reappointed, in 1870, presented a report, recommending several changes in the mode of conducting elections, and the adoption of secret voting. The government introduced a bill founded upon this report: but the education bill and other important measures interfered with its further progress. Ministers, however, and the Liberal party now stood committed to the principle of the ballot; and this most important constitutional question, which for nearly forty years had been discussed rather as a political theory than as a practical measure, was accepted by a powerful Government, and a large majority of the House of Commons, as the policy of the state.

Ballot Bill, 1870.

In 1871, another bill was brought in and passed, after protracted discussions, by the Commons: but it was received by the Lords at so late a period of the session that they declined to consider it; and this complement to an extended franchise still awaits the final judgment of Parliament.[1]

Ballot Bill, 1871.

Such have been the constitutional measures of the last ten years. In all, we recognise the development of those liberal principles which had characterised the policy of a previous generation. In politics, more power has been given to the people: in religion, more freedom and equality.

Conclusion.

[1] The ballot was, at length, adopted in 1872.

INDEX.

ABBOT, Mr. Speaker, opposes Catholic relief, iii. 141, 142; his speech at the Bar of the Lords, 143, *n*.

Abercorn, Earl of, his rights as peer of Great Britain and of Scotland, i. 288

Abercromby, Mr., his motion on Scotch representation, i. 359

Abercromby, Sir R., his opinion of the Irish soldiery, iii. 326; retires from command, *ib.*

Aberdeen, Earl of, the Reform Bill of his ministry, i. 452; his ministry, ii. 217; its fall, 218; his efforts to reconcile differences in the Church of Scotland, iii. 244, 253

A'Court, Colonel, deprived of his command for votes in parliament, i. 28

Addington, Mr., mediated between George III. and Pitt on the Catholic question, i. 95; formed an administration, 97; official difficulties caused by the King's illness at this juncture, 195–199; his relations with the King, 98; resigned office, 99; led the 'King's friends,' 100; took office under Pitt, 101; made a peer, *ib.*; permitted debate on notice of motion, 402, *n*. *See also* Sidmouth, Viscount

Additional Curates Society, sums expended by, iii. 218, *n*.

Addresses to the crown, from parliament, respecting peace and war, or the dissolution of parliament, ii. 86, 90; and from the people, 89; Lord Camden's opinion, 90

Admiralty Court, the, judge of, disqualified from sitting in parliament, i. 375

Adullam, Cave of,—a party so named, 1866, iii. 431

Advertisement duty, first imposed, ii. 245; increased, 327; abolished, 381

Affirmations. *See* Quakers

Agitation, political. *See* Opinion, Liberty of; Political Associations; Public Meetings

Aliens, protection of, iii. 49–56; Alien Acts, 50, 52; Traitorous Correspondence Act, 52; Napoleon's demands refused, 54; the Conspiracy to Murder Bill, 58; Extradition Treaties, 59

Almon, bookseller, proceeded against, ii. 252

Althorp, Lord, the Melbourne ministry dismissed, on his elevation to the House of Lords, i. 146; brings forward cases of imprisonment for debt, iii. 28; his church-rates measure, 1834, 203; his plans for tithe commutation, 219; commenced the modern financial policy, 418

American colonies, the war with, stopped by the Commons, i. 56, ii. 87; pledge exacted by George III. of his ministers to maintain the war, i. 49; the war with, a test of party principles, ii. 147, 150; first proposals to tax them, iii. 343; Mr. Grenville's Stamp Act, 347; repealed, 349; Mr. Townshend's scheme, 350; repealed, except the tea duties, 351; attack on the tea ships, 352; the port of Boston closed, 353; the constitution of Massachusetts superseded, *ib.*; attempts at conciliation, 354; the tea duty repealed, 355; independence of colonies recognised, 356; its effect on Ireland, 309

Anne, Queen, the land revenues at her accession, i. 229; their alienation restrained, *ib.*; her civil list and debts, 233; increase of peerage, during her reign, 274; created twelve peers in one day, *ib.*; holders of offices disqualified by the Act of Settlement of her reign, 370; popular addresses to, praying a dissolution, ii. 90; the press in the reign of, ii. 243; her bounty to poor clergy, iii. 216

Anti-Corn Law League, the, ii. 413–417

Anti-Slavery Association, the, ii. 277–404

Appellate jurisdiction of the House of Lords bill, i. 298

Appropriation of grants by parliament, the resolution against issue of unappropriated money, i. 76; the commencement of the system, 231, ii. 98; misappropriation of grants by Charles II., i. 232

Appropriation question, the, of Irish Church revenue, iii. 260–268

Arcot, Nabob of, represented in parliament by several members, i. 396

Army, the, duty of muster-masters, 30, *n.*; their abolition in 1818, *ib.*; interference of military in absence of a magistrate, ii. 276; Orange lodges in, 402; impressment for, iii. 20; freedom of worship in, 127, 134; the defence of colonies, 375; flogging in, abated, 405

Army and Navy Service Bill opposed by George III., i. 105; withdrawn, 107

Army and Navy Service Bill, the, iii. 126

Arrest, on mesne process, iii. 29; abolished, 30

Articles, the Thirty-nine, subscription to, by clergy, and on admission to the universities, iii. 78, 91, 198; by dissenting schoolmasters, abolished, 93, 94

Assizes, the, a commission for holding, issued during George III.'s incapacity, i. 188

Associations. *See* Political Associations

Auchterarder Cases, the, iii. 242, 244

Australian colonies, the settlement and constitutions of, iii. 358, 370

BAKER, Mr., his motion against the use of the king's name, i. 69

Ballot, vote by, motions for adoption of, i. 416, 445; one of the points of the Charter, ii. 408; in the Colonies, 371; its adoption in England recommended by a committee, 1870, iii. 454; a bill brought in for that purpose, but dropped, *ib.*; another bill passed by the Commons in 1871, but rejected by the Lords, *ib.*

Baptists, the number and places of worship of, iii. 223, 224 *n.*

Baronetage, past and present numbers of, i. 323

Barré, Colonel, deprived of his command for votes in parliament, i. 28; resigned his commission, 47; passed over in a brevet, *ib.*

Beaufoy, Mr., his efforts for the relief of dissenters, iii. 100-102
'Bedchamber Question, the,' i. 155
Bedford, Duke of, remonstrated against Lord Bute's influence, i. 32; attacked by the silk-weavers, ii. 267
Berkeley, Mr. H., his motions for the ballot, i. 447
Birmingham, public meetings at, ii. 352-385; election of a legislatorial attorney, 352; political union of, 384, 386
Births, bills for registration of, iii. 151, 192
Bishops, their number in the house, i. 299; attempts to exclude them, 300; their present position, 302; their votes upon the Reform Bill, 309, 310; Irish representative bishops, 281; deprived of their seats by Irish Church Act, iii. 441
Blandford, Marquess of, his schemes of reform, i. 412
Boards. *See* Local Government
Bolingbroke, Lord, his theory of 'a patriot king,' i. 12
Boroughs, different rights of election in, i. 331, 355; number, &c. of English nomination boroughs, 330, 332; of Scotch, 355; of Irish, 359; total number in the representation of the United Kingdom, 361; seats for, bought or rented, 335, 343, 345; advertised for sale, 337; prices of, 337, 344, 367; 'borough-brokers,' 339; law passed against the sale of boroughs, 346; government boroughs, 347; changes effected by the Reform Acts, 1867, 1868, iii. 441
Boston, Lord, assaulted, ii. 273
Boston, the port of, closed by Act, iii. 353
Bourne, Mr. S., his Vestry Act, iii. 277
Boyer, an early reporter of debates in parliament, ii. 36
Braintree Cases, the, iii. 205

Brandreth, execution of, ii. 345
Brand, Mr., his motion against the pledge required of the Grenville ministry, i. 109
Bribery at elections, prior to parliamentary reform, i. 333; commenced in reign of Charles II., *ib.*; supported by George III., 341, 344; acts to restrain, 334, 336, 346; bribery since the Reform Act, 431; later bribery acts, 435; proof of agency, 435; inquiry by commission, 436; gross cases, 437; travelling expenses, 438; policy of legislation, 439, iii. 441
Bribery of members of parliament. *See* Members of the House of Commons
Briellat, T., tried for sedition, ii. 289
Bristol, reform riots at, ii. 387
Brougham, Lord, his motion against the influence of the crown, i. 134; opinion on life peerages, 294; advised, as chancellor, the creation of new peers, 311; his motion for reform, 420; on the duration of parliament, 442; defends Leigh Hunt, ii. 335; describes the license of the press, 338, *n.*; promotes popular education, 377, iii. 412; his law reforms, 389
Brownists, the, iii. 67
Buckingham, Marquess of, his refusal to transmit the address of the Irish parliament to the Prince of Wales, i. 194
Bunbury, Sir C., attempts amendment of the criminal code, iii. 395
Burdett, Sir F., his schemes of reform, i. 406, 407; committed for contempt, ii. 60; resists the warrant, 76; apprehended by force, 77; his actions for redress, *ib.*; his Catholic Relief Bills, iii. 155, 162
Burgage tenure, the franchise, i. 331
Burghs (Scotland), reformed, iii. 287

Burial, the, of dissenters with Church of England rites, iii. 188, 193; bills to enable dissenters to bury in churchyards, 194; permitted in Ireland, *ib.*

Burke, Mr., his scheme of economic reform, i. 52, 239, 258; drew up the prince's reply to Pitt's scheme of a regency, 184; his proposal for sale of the crown lands, 254; for reduction of pension list, 258; opposed parliamentary reform, 403; his ideal of representation, 458; opposed Wilkes's expulsion, ii. 11; his remark on the opposition made to the punishment of the reporters, 41; on pledges to constituents, 70; the character of his oratory, 115; separates from the Whigs, 163; his alarm at the French Revolution, *ib.* 286; among the first to advocate Catholic relief, iii. 95; his opposition to relief of dissenters, 105, 109

Bute, county, the franchise of, prior to reform, i. 358

Bute, Earl of, his unconstitutional instructions to George III., i. 11; aids his personal interference in government, 18; his rapid rise, 21; becomes premier, 22; arbitrary conduct, *ib.*; and parliamentary bribery, 378, 379; his fall, 25; secret influence over the King, 25, 31, 34; retired from court, 27; driven from office, ii. 247, 266

CABINET, the, admission of a judge to seat in, i. 103; temporary tenure of the offices in, by the Duke of Wellington, 148; Minute of, 1832, 315. *See* also Ministers of the Crown

Calcraft, Mr., deprived of office for opposition to court policy, i. 30

Cambridge University, admission of dissenters to degrees at, iii. 92, 198; the petition for admission of dissenters, 1834, 196; state of feeling at, on Catholic relief, in 1812, 137

Camden, Lord, disapproved the Middlesex election proceedings, ii. 16, 22; defended his conduct in the cabinet, 19; opinion on popular addresses to the crown, 90; supports the right of juries in libel cases, ii. 257, 262, 263; his decisions condemning the practice of general warrants, iii. 2-8; protects a Catholic lady by a private Act of Parliament, 96; opposes taxation of the American colonies; 349, 351; a friend to liberty, 392

Campbell, Lord, his opinion on life peerages, i. 294; his Act to protect publishers in libel cases, ii. 253

Canada, a crown colony, iii. 357; free constitution granted, *ib.*; the insurrection, and re-union of the provinces, 365; responsible government in, 366; establishes a protective tariff, 369; popular franchise in, 370

Canning, Mr., his conduct regarding the Catholic question, i. 95, 112; in office, 112, 136; overtures to, from the court, 125; declined to support George IV. against his Queen, 129, 133, *n.*; character of his oratory, 118; his influence on parties, ii. 175; in office, 189; secession of Tories from, *ib.*; supported by the Whigs, 190; advocates Catholic relief, 189, iii. 115, 136, 139, 146; brought in the Catholic Peers' Bill, 147; his death, ii. 191, iii. 156

Capital punishments, multiplication of, since the Revolution, iii. 393; since restricted to murder and treason, 398

Caricatures, influence of, ii. 265

Carlton House, the cost of, i. 251

Carmarthen, Marquess of, proscribed for opposition to court policy, i. 54

Caroline, Queen (of George IV.), the proceedings against her, i. 129; the Divorce Bill, 131; withdrawn, 132; effect of proceedings against, upon parties, ii. 186

Catholic Association, the, proceedings of, ii. 368–375, iii. 164, 167

Catholic Emancipation opposed by George III., i. 93, 108; by George IV., 136; the measure carried, 137; a plea for parliamentary reform, 412. *See also* Roman Catholics

Castle, the government spy, iii. 41

Cato Street Conspiracy, the, ii. 362; discovered by spies, iii. 43

Cave, the. *See* Adullam, Cave of

Cavendish, Lord J., his motion on the American war, i. 57

Cavendish, Sir H., reported the Commons' debates (1768–1774), ii. 30, *n*

Censorship of the press, ii. 239–243

Chalmers, Dr., heads the Free Kirk movement, iii. 240; moved deposition of the Strathbogie presbytery, 247

Chancery, Court of, reformed, iii. 388, 389

Chancellor, Lord. *See* Great Seal, the

Charlemont, Earl of, heads Irish volunteers, iii. 314; opposes claims of Catholics to the franchise, 320

Charles I., alienated the crown lands, i. 228

Charles II., wasted crown revenues recovered at his accession, i. 228; misappropriated army grants, 232; bribery at elections, and of members, commenced under, 333, 376

Charlotte, Princess, question as to the guardianship of, i. 271

Charlotte, Queen (of George III.), accepted the resolutions for a regency, 185, 213

Chartists, the, torch-light meetings, ii. 407; the national petition, *ib.*; meetings and riots, 408; proposed election of popular representatives by, 409; the meeting and petition of 1848, 410–413

Chatham, Earl of, in office at accession of George III., i. 13; his retirement, 20; refusal to resume office, 26, 31; his demeanour as a courtier, 39; formed an administration, 40; endeavoured to break up parties, *ib.*; ill health, 42; retired from office, 43; his statement as to the influence of the crown, 44; receives overtures from Lord North, 47; approved the Grenville Act, 366; advocated parliamentary reform, 393; favoured triennial parliaments, 441; his opposition to the proceedings against Wilkes, ii. 4, 16; his bill to reverse the proceedings, 22; his resolution, 11; moved addresses to dissolve parliament, 22, 23, 90; condemned the King's answer to the city address, 21; strangers excluded during his speeches, *ib.*, 30; supported popular addresses to the crown, 90; his opinion on the exclusive rights of the Commons over taxation, 104; his position as an orator, 113, 125; effect of his leaving office on parties, ii. 142; his protest against colonial taxation, iii. 348; that measure adopted by his ministry during his illness, 350; his conciliatory propositions, 354; proposed to claim India for the Crown, 377

Chippenham election petition, Walpole displaced from office by vote upon, i, 365

Church of England, the relations of the Church to political history, iii. 60; the Church before the Reformation, *ib.*; the Reformation, 61; under Queen Elizabeth, 68; relations of the Reformed Church with the State, 67; Church policy from James I. to Charles II., 71-74; attempts at comprehension, 76, 79; the Church at the Revolution, 77; under William III., *ib.*; state of, at accession of George III., 82; Wesley and Whitefield, 85; motion for relief from subscription to the Articles, 91; surrender by the Church of the fees on dissenters' marriages, &c., 192; the Church-rate question, 201; state of Church to end of last century, 209; hold of the Church over society, 211; church building and extension, 215; Queen Anne's bounty, 216; ecclesiastical revenues, *ib.*; sums expended by charitable societies, 218, *n.*; tithe commutation, 218; activity by the clergy, 220; Church statistics, 223; relations of the Church to dissent, 224; to Parliament, 226

Church in Ireland, the establishment of, iii. 70, 71; state of, at accession of Geo. III., 82; at the Union, 255; the tithes question, 256, 269; advances to the clergy, 258; Church reform, 259; the Temporalities Act, 260; the appropriation question, *ib.*; the Irish Church commission, 263; the report, 268; power monopolised by churchmen, 302; Irish Church question, 1865-1868; Mr. Gladstone's resolutions and suspensory bill, 1868, 444; result of the elections upon the Irish Church, 446; the Irish Church disestablished and disendowed, 1869, 447

Church of Scotland, the presbyterian form of, iii., 68; legislative origin of, 69; Church policy from James I. to Geo. III., 74, 77, 79, 87; motion for relief from the Test Act, 107; the patronage question, 236-247; earlier schisms, 239; the Free Kirk secession, 251

Church rates, the law of, iii. 201; the question first raised, 203; the Braintree cases, 205; number of parishes refusing the rate, 206; bills for abolition of, 207; final settlement of the question, 1868, 448

Civil Disabilities. *See* Dissenters; Jews; Quakers; Roman Catholics

Civil list, the, of the crown, i. 232; settlement of, on accession of Geo. III., 234; charges, debts, and pensions thereon, 233-261; charges removed therefrom, 243, 244; Civil List Acts, of 1782, 242; of 1816, 244; regulation of the civil list, 242-246; no debts upon, during the last three reigns, 247. *See also* Pensions from the Crown

Clerke, Sir P. J., his Contractors' Bill, i. 388

Coalition Ministry, the, the formation of, i. 63; coalition ministries favoured by Geo. III., ii. 143, 157; the Coalition, 1783, 153-155; attempted coalitions between Pitt and Fox, 165, 177; coalition of the Whigs and Lord Sidmouth's party, 177; Lord Aberdeen's ministry, 217

Cobbett, W., trials of, for libel, ii. 334; withdraws from England, 349; prosecuted by Whig government, 379

Cockburn, Lord, his description of Scotch elections, i. 357

Coke, Lady Mary, admired by the Duke of York, i. 264

Coke, Lord, an authority for life peerages, i. 293

Coke, Mr., moved a resolution hostile to the Pitt ministry, i. 78

Colliers and salters, in Scotland,

slavery of, iii. 38; emancipated, 39
Colonies, British, colonists retain the freedom of British subjects, iii. 338; colonial constitutions, 339, 356, 360, 365; democratic form of, 369, 371; the sovereignty of England, 340; colonial expenditure, 341, 375; and commercial policy, 341, 363, 369; taxes common to dependencies, 342; arguments touching imperial taxation, 343; taxation of American colonies, 347-354; the crown colonies, 356; colonial administration, 360; first appointment of Secretary of State for, *ib.*; patronage surrendered to the colonies, 362; responsible government, 366; conflicting interests of England and colonies, 369; dependencies unfitted for self-government, 376; India, 377
Commerce, restrictions on Irish, iii. 305; removed, 310, 312, 332; Pitt's propositions, 320; restrictions on colonial commerce, 341; the protective system abandoned, 363, 415; the Canadian tariff, 369
Commission, the, for opening parliament during incapacity of George III., questions arising thereupon, 186, 191, 213; the form of such commission, 213; his inability to sign a commission for prorogation, 207: and for holding assizes, 188
Commissions to inquire into bribery at elections, 436
Common Law, Courts of, reformed, iii. 389
Commons, House of, position of, at accession of George III., i. 329; instances of his personal interference with, 28, 36, 45, 66, 107; debate thereon, 51, 69, 76; resistance of the house to Pitt's first ministry, 72; resolutions against a dissolution, 74, ii. 90; against the issue of money unappropriated by parliament, i. 76; against the recent changes in the ministry, 77; resolutions to be laid before George III., 79; resolution against interference by the Lords, 80; comments on this contest, 83; debates on the pledge required of the Grenville ministry, 109; action of the Commons as regards a regency, 171-224; doubts respecting the issue of new writs during George III.'s incapacity, 177; the election of a speaker during the King's incapacity, 183; the vote to authorise the use of the great seal, 186, 213; the address on the King's recovery, 190; the relations between the two houses of Parliament, 304; the composition of the house since the Revolution, 327; its dependence and corruption, *ib.*; defects in the representation, 328; nomination boroughs, 330-360; ill-defined rights of election, 331; number of small boroughs, 332; influence of peers in the house, 333, 360; bribery at elections, 333; since reform, 431; at the general elections of 1761, 335; of 1768, 337; sale of boroughs, 336-346; gross cases of bribery, 340; bribery supported by George III., 341, 344; crown and government influence over boroughs, 17, 347; revenue officers disfranchised, 348; majority of members nominated, 361; trial of election petitions, 362; by committee of privileges, 363; at the bar of the house, 364; the Grenville Act, 365; corruption of members, 369-389; by places and pensions, 369; measures to disqualify placemen and pensioners, 372; number of, in parliament, 373; judges disquali-

fied, 375; bribes to members, 376–385; under Lord Bute, 378; the shop at the pay-office, 379; apology for refusing a bribe, 380; bribes by loans and lotteries, 382; by contracts, 387; parliamentary corruption considered, 389; the reform movement, 393–431; efforts to repeal the Septennial Act, 441; vote by ballot, 445; qualification Acts, 448; proceedings at elections improved, 449; later measures of reform, 450; relation of the Commons to crown, law, and people, ii. 1–112; contests on questions of privilege, 1; the proceedings against Wilkes, 2; his expulsion, 5; his expulsion for libel on Lord Weymouth, 10; his re-elections declared void, 13, 14; Luttrell seated by the house, 14; motions upon the Middlesex election proceedings, 16; the house address the King condemning the city address, 21; the resolution against Wilkes expunged, 25; exclusion of strangers from debates, 27, 51; the exclusion of ladies, 52, *n.*; the lords excluded from the Commons, 32; contest with the printers, touching the publication of debates (1771), 33, 38; and with the city authorities, 43; report of debates permitted, 49; reporters' and strangers' galleries, 55; publication of division lists, *ib.*; strangers present at divisions, 57; publicity given to committee proceedings, 58; to parliamentary papers, *ib.*; freedom of comment upon parliament, 59; early petitions to parliament, 60; commencement of the modern system of petitioning, 63; debates on, restrained, 69; pledges of members to their constituents, 70; discontinuance of certain privileges, 73; to servants, *ib.*; of prisoners kneeling at the bar, 74; privilege and the courts of law, 75–83; case of Sir F. Burdett, 76; Stockdale and Howard's actions, 79; commit Stockdale and his agents, 81; commit the sheriffs, *ib.*; right of the Commons to publish papers affecting character, 78; increased power of the Commons, 83; the proceedings regarding Jewish disabilities, 84; control of the Commons over the government, 85; over peace and war, and over dissolutions of parliament, i. 56, 73, ii. 86; votes of want of confidence, i. 57, 76, 81, ii. 90; and of confidence, i. 142, 425, ii. 91; impeachments, 92; relations between the Commons and ministers since the Reform Act, i. 152, ii. 95; their control over the national expenditure, i. 229, ii. 98; liberality to the crown, ii. 99; stopping the supplies, 423, *n.*, ii. 102; supplies delayed, 80, ii. 102; restraints upon the liberality of the house, ii. 103; exclusive rights over taxation, ii. 104; the rejection by the Lords of a money bill, 105; relative rights of the two houses, 108; conduct of the house in debate, 125; increased authority of the chair, 128; oath of supremacy imposed on the Commons, iii. 63; O'Connell refused his seat for Clare, 174; number of Catholic members in, 176; Quakers and others admitted on affirmation, 177; a new form of oath established for Jews, 187, *n.*; a resolution of the House not in force after a prorogation, 187, *n.*; refusal to receive the petitions of the American colonists, 348. *See also* Members of the House of

COM

Commons; Parliament; Petitions
Commons, House of, Ireland, the composition of, iii. 300; conflicts with the executive, 307; claim to originate money bills, *ib.*; bought over by the government, 314, 317, 330
Commonwealth, the destruction of crown revenues under, i. 228
Conservative Party, the. *See* Parties
Constitutional Information Society, ii. 282; Pitt and other leading statesmen, members of, *ib.*, 283; reported on by secret committee, 302, 303; trial of members of, for high treason, 306
Constitutional Association, the, ii. 367
Contempt of court, imprisonment for, iii. 26
Contracts with Government, a means of bribing members, i. 387; contractors disqualified from sitting in parliament, 389
Conventicle Act, the, iii. 75
Convention, National, of France, correspondence with, of English societies, ii. 283, 329
Conventions. *See* Delegates, Political Associations
Conway, General, proscribed for votes in parliament, i. 28, 29; took office under Lord Rockingham, 33; disclaimed the influence of the 'King's friends,' 35; his motion condemning the American war, 56
Copenhagen House, meetings at, ii. 315, 324
Corn Bill (1815), the, ii. 341, iii. 416
Corn laws. repeal of, ii. 212, 413, iii. 418
Cornwallis, Marquess, his policy as Lord-lieutenant of Ireland regarding Catholic relief, iii. 116, 326; concerts the Union, 327

COU

Cornwall, Duchy of, the revenues of, the inheritance of Prince of Wales, i. 248; their present amount, *ib.*
Cornwall, Mr. Speaker, his death during George III.'s incapacity, i. 183
Corporations, the passing of the Corporation and Test Acts, iii. 75, 77; extortion practised on dissenters under the Corporation Act, 90; motions for repeal of Corporation and Test Acts, 100–104, 107; their repeal, ii. 192, iii. 157; the consent of the bishops, 159; the bill amended in the Lords, 160; admission of Catholics to, 168, 302, 322; and Jews, 182.——(England), the ancient system of Corporations, 278; loss of popular rights, 279; corporations from the Revolution to George III., 280; corporate abuses, *ib.*; monopoly of electoral rights, 280, 282; corporate reform, 283; the bill amended by the Lords, 284; self-government restored, 285; the corporation of London excepted from the bill, 286.——(Ireland), apparent recognition of popular rights in, 94, 290; exclusion of Catholics, 292; the first municipal reform Bill, *ib.*; opposition of the Lords, 294; the municipal reform Act, 295. ——(Scotland), close system in, 288; municipal abuses, 289; reform, *ib.*
Corresponding societies, proceedings of, ii. 269, 282, 291, 328; trials of members of, 292, 307; bill to repress, 329
County elections, territorial influence over, i. 353; expenses of contests at, 354, 355
Courier newspaper, trial of, for libel, ii. 331
Courts of law, the, and parliamentary privilege, ii. 74–84; deci-

sions in Burdett's case, 76; in the Stockdale cases, 79
Crawfurd, Mr. S., his motion as to duration of parliament, i. 442
Crewe, Mr., his Revenue Officers' Bill, i. 348
Cricklade, bribery at, i. 340; disfranchised, *ib.*
Criminal code, improvement of, iii. 393, 396; counsel allowed in cases of felony, 399; summary jurisdiction of magistrates, 404; the transportation question, 400
Crosby, Brass, Lord Mayor, proceeded against for committing the messenger of the house, ii. 44, 47
Crown, the, constitutional position of, since the Revolution, i. 1; paramount authority of, 2; sources of its influence, 2-6; by government boroughs, 347; by places, peerages, and pensions, 134, 237, 369; by bribes, 376; by loans and lotteries, 382; by contracts, 387; measures for the diminution of its influence, by disqualification of placemen, &c., 61, 348, 369, 374, 388; by the powers of the Commons over the civil list expenditure, 229, 257; and over supplies, ii. 98; constitutional relations between the crown and ministers, i. 6, 14, 104, 145, 154, 159, ii. 95; the influence of the crown over the government during Lord Bute's ministry, i. 22; Mr. Grenville's, 27; Lord Rockingham's, 36, 60; Lord North's, 44; Lord Shelburne's, 62; 'the coalition ministry,' 65; Mr. Pitt's, 87, 90; Mr. Addington's, 98; Lord Grenville's, 103; the influence of the crown during the regency, 119; during the reigns of William IV. and her Majesty, 138-166; debates upon the influence of the crown, 35, 51, 69, 76, 134, 135; violation of parliamentary privileges by the crown, 28, 36, 45, 54, 66, 76; bribery at elections, and of members supported by the crown, 341, 344, 381; influence of the crown exerted against its ministers at elections, 16, 17; in parliament, 28, 36, 66, 90, 104, 136; the attitude of parties a proof of the paramount influence of the crown, 92, 124; its influence exerted in favour of reform, 138, 143; wise exertion of crown influence in the present reign, 163; its general influence increased, 164; parliament kept in harmony by influence of the crown, 307; the prerogatives of the crown in abeyance, 167-224; the Regency Bills of George III., 168-213; of William IV., 219; of Queen Victoria, 223; powers of the crown exercised by parliament, 181-188, 212, 215; the Royal Sign Manual Bill, 216; questions as to the rights of an infant king, 219; of a king's posthumous child, 222; the ancient revenues of the crown, 225; the constitutional results of the improvidence of kings, 230; the parliamentary settlement of crown revenues, 231; the civil list, 232-248; private property of the crown, 249; provision for the royal family, *ib.*; land revenues, 248; the pension list, 256; rights of crown over the Royal Family, 262; over grandchildren, 264, 271; over royal marriages, 264; the Royal Marriage Act, *ib.*; the question submitted to the judges, 266; opinion of law officers on the marriage of Duke of Sussex, 270; the attempt to limit the rights of crown in the creation of peers, 275; numerous applications to the crown for peerages, 283; the advice of par-

liament tendered to the crown as to peace and war, a dissolution, and the conduct of ministers, 56, 73, ii. 83-91; addressed by the people on the subject of a dissolution, 89; improved relations between the crown and Commons, 95-99; the delay or refusal of the supplies, i. 80, ii. 102; the recommendation of the crown required to motions for grant of public money, 103. *See also* Ministers of the Crown

Crown colonies, the. *See* Colonies

Crown debtors, position of, iii. 25

Crown lands. *See* Revenues of the Crown

Cumberland, Duke of, conducted ministerial negotiations for the King, i. 31, 33; protested against resolutions for a regency bill, 185; his name omitted from the commission to open parliament, 188; married Mrs. Horton, 262; (*Ernest*) grand master of the Orange Society, ii. 400; dissolves it, 403

Curwen, Mr., his Act to restrain the sale of boroughs, i. 346

Cust, Sir John, chosen speaker, i. 18; altercations with, when in the chair, ii. 128

Customs and excise officers disfranchised, i. 348; numbers of, 349

D ANBY, Earl, his case cited with reference to ministerial responsibility, i. 115

Daviot Case, the, iii. 245

Deaths, Act for registration of, iii. 192

Debates in parliament, the publication of, prohibited, ii. 34; sanctioned by the Long Parliament, 34; early publications of debates, 36; abuses of reporting, 37, 38; the contest with the printers, 40; opposed in twenty-three divisions, 41; reporting permitted, 49; late instance of complaints against persons taking notes, 51; reporting interrupted by the exclusion of strangers, i. 82. *n.*, ii. 51; political results of reporting, 53; still a breach of privilege, 54; galleries for reporters, 55; freedom of comment on debates, 59; improved taste in debate, 127; personalities of former times, 125

Debt, imprisonment for, iii. 31; debtors' prisons, 32; exertions of the Thatched House Society, 33; insolvent debtors, 34; later measures of relief, 35

Delegates of political associations, the practice of, adopted, ii. 269, 328, 388, 400, 408; assembled at Edinburgh, 293; law against, 344; in Ireland, 368

Democracy, associations promoted in 1792, ii. 279, 281; alarm excited by, 284; proclamation against, 287; in Scotland, 292; in the Colonies, iii. 370; discouraged by good government, 419. *See also* Party.

Denman, Lord, his decision in Stockdale v. Hansard, ii. 78

Dering, Sir E., expelled for publishing his speeches, ii. 34

Derby, Earl of, the reform bill of his ministry, 1859, i. 453; the rejection of the bill, 456; his first ministry defeated on the house tax, ii. 102; his ministries, ii. 216, 221, 229, iii. 433; persuades the Lords to agree to Jewish relief, iii. 186; his reform bill, 1867, 436; his resignation, 1869, iii. 1

Derbyshire insurrection, the, ii. 345

D'Este, Sir A., his claim to the dukedom of Sussex, i. 270

Devonshire, Duke of, disgraced for

opposition to the treaty with France, i. 23 ; resigned his lord-lieutenancy, *ib.*

Diplomatic relations with the Papal Court Bill, iii. 230, *n.*

Disraeli, Mr., his reform bill, 1859, i. 453; his reform resolutions, 1867, iii. 435; his reform bill in the same year, 436; how amended, and its ultimate form, 437; succeeds Lord Derby as premier, 440; his Scotch reform bill, *ib.*; and other supplementary measures of reform, 441; his resignation, 446

Dissenters, origin of dissent, iii. 65–77; the penal code of Elizabeth, 63, 65; dissent from James I. to Chas. II., 71–77; attempts at comprehension, 76, 79; Corporation and Test Acts, 75, 77; conduct of dissenters at the Revolution, 77; the Toleration Act, 78; dissenters in reigns of Anne and Geo. I. and II., 81; the Occasional Conformity Act, 82; annual Acts of Indemnity, *ib.*, *n.*; their numbers at accession of Geo. III., 83, *n.*; impulse given by Wesley and Whitefield, 85; relaxation of penal code commenced, 88; general character of the penal code, 89; extortion practised on dissenters by the City of London under the Corporation Act, 90; debate on subscription to the Articles by dissenters, 91; and admission to universities, 92; subscription by dissenting schoolmasters abolished, 93, 94; offices in Ireland thrown open, *ib.*; first motions for repeal of the Corporation and Test Acts, 100–105; motions for relief of Unitarians, 109; and of Quakers, 112; Lord Sidmouth's Dissenting Ministers' Bill, 134; relief from requirements of the Toleration Act, 136; the army thrown open, 143; bills for relief of dissenters in respect of births, marriages, and burials, 151, 152, 188–192; repeal of the Corporation and Test Acts, ii. 192, iii. 157; dissenters admitted to the Commons on making an affirmation, 177; admitted to universities and endowed schools, 195, 200; the London University, 198; the Dissenters' Chapels Bill, 199; final repeal of penal code, 200; the church-rate question, 201; progress of dissent, 212, 222; numbers of different sects, &c., 222, 223; in Scotland, 255, *n.*, in Ireland, 268; relations of the Church and dissent, 226; and of dissent to political liberty, *ib.*

Dissolutions of Parliament. *See* Addresses to the Crown; Parliament

Divisions, instance of a stranger counted in a Commons' division, ii. 28; twenty-three divisions on one question, 41; the lists of, published by both houses, 57; presence of strangers at, *ib.*

Donoughmore, Lord, his motions for Catholic Relief, iii. 131, 136, 138

Douglas, Neil, trial of, for sedition, ii. 351

Dowdeswell, Mr., opposed the expulsion of Wilkes, ii. 11, 18

Downie, D., trial of, for high treason, ii. 304

Drakard, J., trial of, for libel, ii. 336

'Droit le Roi,' the book burnt by order of the Lords, ii. 7

Droits of the Crown and Admiralty, the, vested in the crown till accession of William IV., i. 235, 245

Dundas, Mr., his amendment to Mr. Dunning's resolutions, i. 52

Dundas, Mr., leader of the Tories in Scotland, ii. 172

Dundas, Mr. R., his influence in Scotland, ii. 181

Dungannon, convention of volunteers at, iii. 314

Dunning, Mr., his resolutions against the influence of the crown, i. 52; denied the right of the house to incapacitate Wilkes, ii. 18

Dyer, cudgelled by Lord Mohun for a libel, ii. 244

Dyson, Mr., soubriquet given him by the reporters, ii. 40

EARL MARSHAL'S Office Act, the, iii. 154

East Retford, the disfranchisement bill of, i. 414

East India, the Company allowed a drawback on tea shipped to America, iii. 352; first parliamentary recognition and regulation of, 377; Mr. Fox's India Bill, 378; Mr. Pitt's, 381; the Bill of 1853, 382; India transferred to the crown, 383; subsequent administration, ib.

Eaton, D. I., trial of, for sedition, ii. 302

Ebrington, Lord, his motions in support of the reform ministry, i. 425, 426

Ecclesiastical Commission, the, iii. 217

Ecclesiastical Titles Act, the, 1851, iii. 232; its repeal, 1871, 451

Economic reform, Mr. Burke's, i. 52, 239, 258

Edinburgh, the defective representation of, i. 356; bill to amend it, 359

Edinburgh Review, the influence of, ii. 181

Education, proposals for a national system in England, iii. 412; the Endowed Schools Act, 1869, 451; the Scotch Education Bill, 1869, ib.; the Elementary Education Act, 1870, 452; in Ireland, 270,

413; address of the House of Lords on the subject, 415; the system continued, ib.

Edwards, the government spy, iii. 43

Edward II., the revenues of his crown, i. 226

Edward VI., his sign manual affixed by a stamp, i. 217

Effingham, Earl of, his motion condemning the Commons' opposition to Mr. Pitt, i. 79

Eldon, Lord, the suspected adviser of George III. against the Grenville ministry, 1807, i. 111; at first disliked by the Regent, 121; condoled with George IV. on the Catholic emancipation, 137; scandalised when the crown supported reform, 140; chancellor to the Addington ministry, 198; his declaration as to George III.'s competency to transact business, 204; obtained the royal assent to bills, ib.; his interview with the King, 202; negotiated Pitt's return to office, 203; his conduct impugned, 204; motions to omit his name from Council of Regency, 205; his opinion as to the accession of an infant king, 220; his position as a statesman, ii. 119; retired from office on promotion of Canning, ii. 189; opposes the repeal of the Corporation and Test Acts, 192, iii. 160; and Catholic relief, 171; assisted poor suitors to put in answers, 27; favours authority, 392; resists amendment of the penal code, 397

Election petitions, the trial of prior to the Grenville Act, i. 362; under that Act, 365; later election petition Acts, 367; their transfer to judges of superior courts, 369, n.; iii. 441

Elections, expensive contests at, i. 333, 338, 354; vexatious contests, 350; Acts to amend election proceedings, 449; writs for, addressed to returning officers, 450. See also Reform of Parliament

Elective franchise, Ireland, the regulation of, iii. 155, 172; admission of Catholics to, 168, 335

Elizabeth, Queen, her church policy, iii. 63

Ellenborough, Lord, his admission to the cabinet, when Lord Chief Justice, i. 103; his conduct on the trials of Hone, ii. 350, n.; a cabinet minister, iii. 392; resists amendment of the criminal code, 397

Entinck, Mr., his papers seized under a general warrant, iii. 7; brings an action, ib.

Erskine, Lord, his motions against a dissolution, i. 70, 74; his speech on the pledge required from the Grenville ministry, 113; his support of reform, 402, 404, 407; the character of his oratory, 117; a leading member of the Whig party, ii. 161; supports the rights of juries in libel cases, 258; case of Dean of St. Asaph, ib.; of Stockdale, 259; promotes the libel Act, 260, 263; defends Paine, 280; and Hardy and Horne Tooke, 307

Erskine, E., seceded from the Church of Scotland, iii. 229

Erskine, Mr. H., the leader of the Whigs in Scotland, ii. 172

Establishment Bill, the, brought in by Burke, i. 241

Ewart, Mr., his efforts to reform the criminal code, iii. 398

Exchequer chamber, court of, reverse the decision in Howard v. Gosset, ii. 82

Excise Bill, its withdrawal in deference to popular clamour, ii. 266

Ex-officio information filed by government for libels, ii. 248, 336, 378; bills to restrain, 251, 255

Expenditure, national, vast increase in, since 1850, iii. 420

Extradition treaties, iii. 59

FACTORIES, labour of children, &c., regulated in, iii. 411

Families, great, the state influence of, i. 8, 353; opposed by George III., 11, 40: their influence at the present day, 165

Financial policy, the present system of, iii. 418

Fitzgerald, Mr. V., defeated in the Clare election, iii. 163

Fitzherbert, Mr., proscribed for opposition to court policy, i. 29

Fitzherbert, Mrs., married the Prince of Wales, i. 269

Fitzwilliam, Earl, dismissed from his lord-lieutenancy for attending a public meeting, ii. 356; his conduct as Lord-lieutenant of Ireland, iii. 114, 324; his motion on the state of Ireland, 136

Five Mile Act, the, iii. 75

Flogging, articles on military flogging punished as libels, iii. 335; in army and navy abated, 405

Flood, Mr., his reform bill, i. 401; his efforts for independence of Ireland, iii. 315; for reform, 319

Foreigners. See Aliens

Four and a half per cent. duties, the, sources of the revenue to crown, i. 235, 245; charged with pensions, 257; surrendered by William IV., 261

Fox, Mr. C. J., his remarks on the policy of George III., i. 49, 51, 55, 60; coalesced with Lord North, 63; in the coalition ministry, 65; brought in the India Bill, 67; dismissed from office, 71; heads the opposition to Pitt, 74; his name struck off the list of privy councillors by the King, 89; and proscribed from office, 100; admitted to office, 103; again dismissed, 108; his death loosened the tie between the Regent and the Whigs, 120; his conduct regarding the Regency Bill, 177, 181; comments thereon, 193; his disapproval of the Royal Marriage Act, 265; the Westminster election, 351; cost of the scrutiny, 352; received unfair treatment from Mr. Pitt, *ib.*; denounced parliamentary corruption by loans, 385; supported the proceedings against Wilkes, ii. 26; his wise remark on unrestrained reporting, 51; his position as an orator, 114; opposes the repressive policy of 1792, ii. 165, 288; and of 1794-6, 149, 320-327, iii. 12; his advice to the Whigs to take office rejected, ii. 150; refuses office under Lord Shelburne, 151; in office with Lord North, 153; his policy contrasted with Mr. Pitt's, *ib.*, *n.*, 159; sympathises with the French Revolution, 163; attempted coalitions with Mr. Pitt, 165, 176; deserted by his party, 166; secedes from Parliament, 173; in office with Lord Sidmouth, 177, iii. 125; effect of his death on parties, ii. 178; his remark on the rights of juries in libel cases, 256; his libel bills, 260; takes the chair at a reform meeting, 1779, 269; advocates the relief of Catholics, iii. 95, 122; and of Dissenters and Unitarians, 103, 104, 108; his India Bill, 378

Fox, Mr. Henry, Sir R. Walpole's agent in bribery, i. 378

Fox Maule, Mr., presents petition of the General Assembly, iii. 250

France, the treaty of peace with, proscription of the Whigs for disapproval of, i. 23; members bribed to support, 379

Franchise, the, of England, at the accession of George III., i. 331; —— of Scotland, 355; —— of Ireland, 359; under the Reform Act, 427-430; later measures of reform, 450; the fancy franchises of the Whigs, 451; of the Tories, 454; franchises proposed in 1866, iii. 435; granted in 1867-68, 437-440. *See also* Reform in Parliament

Free Church of Scotland, the, iii. 252

Freedom of opinion. *See* Opinion, Freedom of

Free trade, the policy of, adopted, ii. 210, 416, iii. 412; effect of, on colonial policy, 363

French Revolution, effect of, on parties, ii. 163; sympathy with, of English democrats, 279, 281, 283; alarm excited by, 284, 360, 365

'Friends of the People,' the society of, statements by, as to the composition of the House of Commons, i. 332, 361; leading Whigs members of, ii. 64; discountenances democracy, 283

Frost, J., tried for sedition, ii. 289

Fuller, Mr. R., bribed by a pension from the crown, i. 371

GASCOYNE, General, his anti-reform motion, i. 423

Gatton, the number of voters in, prior to reform, i. 332; the price of the borough, 367

Gazetteer, the, complained against for publishing debates, ii. 39

General Assembly, the (Church of Scotland), petitions for relief from the Test Act, iii. 107; passes the Veto Act, 240; rejects Lord Aberdeen's compromise, 244; addresses Her Majesty, 248; admits the *quoad sacra* ministers, 249; petitions Parliament, 250; the secession, 251; the Veto Act rescinded, 252

General warrants, issued in the case of the 'North Briton,' iii. 2; against Mr. Entinck, 7; actions brought in consequence, 4; condemned in Parliament, 9

Gentleman's Magazine, the, one of the first to report parliamentary debates, ii. 36

George I., his civil list, i. 233; the powers he claimed over his grandchildren, 264; consented to the Peerage Bill, 275

George II., his Regency Act, i. 168; his civil list, 233; the great seal affixed to two commissions during his illness, 186; his savings, 236

George III., the accession of, i. 9; his education, 10; determination to govern, 11-17; his jealousy of the Whig families, 11; his secret counsellors, 12; his arbitrary conduct and violation of parliamentary privileges during Lord Bute's ministry, 22; during Mr. Grenville's, 28; his differences with that ministry, 27, 31, 33; his active interference in affairs during that ministry, 31; pledged himself not to be influenced by Lord Bute, *ib.*; consented to dismiss Mr. S. Mackenzie, 32; the conditions of the Rockingham ministry, 34; exerted his influence against them, 36, 39; attempted, with Chatham, to destroy parties, 40; his influence during Chatham's ministry, 41, 43; tried to retain him in office, 43; the king's ascendency during Lord North's ministry, 44, 49, 58; his irritation at opposition, 45, 48; exerted his will in favour of the Royal Marriage Bill, 45; took notice of proceedings in parliament, 46; proscribed officers in opposition, 47; exacted a pledge of his ministers to maintain the American war, 49; his overtures to the Whigs, 49, 50; debates on his personal interference in parliament, 51-55, 69; sought to intimidate the opposition peers, 54; the defeat of his American policy, 56; his approval of Lord North's conduct, 58; the results of the king's policy, 59; the second Rockingham ministry, 60; their measures to repress his influence, 61, 258, 349, 373; Lord Shelburne's ministry, 62; the king's resistance to the 'coalition,' 66-70; his negotiations with Pitt, 63, 64; use of his name against the India Bill, 67; his support of Pitt against the Commons, 78-82; his position during this contest, 83; its result upon his policy, 87; his relations with Pitt, *ib.*; his general influence augmented, 89, 92; prepared to use it against Pitt, 90; the king's opposition to the Catholic question, 93; his illness from agitation on this subject, 98; his relations with Addington, 96, 98; Pitt reinstated, 99; the king's refusal to admit Fox to office, 100; the admission of Lord Grenville and Mr. Fox to office, 103; his opposition to changes in army administration, 104; unconstitutional use of his influence against the Army and Navy Service Bill, 105; the pledge he required of his ministers, 107; his anti-Catholic appeal on the dissolution (1807), 116; his influence prior to his last illness, 117; his character compared to that of the Prince Regent, 119; the king's illnesses, 167-216; the first illness, 167; his scheme for a regency, 169; modified by ministers, 170; speech and addresses on this subject, 170; consented to the withdrawal of his mother's name from Regency Bill, 173; his second illness, 175; recovery, 189; anxiety to provide for a regency, 195; his third illness, in the interval between the Pitt and Addington ministries, *ib.*; recovery, 197; fourth illness, 199; questions arising as to his competency to transact business, 201-206; gave his assent to bills, 202; anecdote as to his reading the bills, 202; Pitt's interview with the king, 203; his last illness, 206; the passing the Regency Bill, 208-213; his civil list, 234; other sources of his revenue, 235; the purchase of Buckingham House, 236; his domestic economy, *ib.*; debts on his civil list, 237; profusion in his household, 240; his message on the public expenditure, 241; his pension list, 257; his annoyance at his brothers' marriages, 262; his attachment to Lady S. Lennox, 263; the Royal Marriage Act, 264; claimed the guardianship of Princess Charlotte, 271; profuse in creation of peers, 277; his expenditure at elections, 342; supported bribery at elections, and of members, 341, 344, 381; his opposition to reform, 91, 399; his answer to the city address on the proceedings against Wilkes, ii. 20; his objection to political agitation by petitions, 65; his party tactics on accession, ii. 142; influence of his friends, 143; overcomes the Coalition, 155; influenced by Lord Thurlow, 160; his repugnance to the Whigs, 161, 178; to Fox, 176; directs the suppression of the Gordon riots, 275; his speech and message respecting seditious practices 1792 and 1794, 287, 302; attacked by the mob, 316; opposes Catholic relief, iii. 117, 118; and the Army and Navy Service Bill, 128; his message to Parliament touching affairs in Ireland, 316; seeks to tax the American colonies, 344, 347

George IV., the ascendency of the Tory party under, i. 129; the proceedings against his Queen, *ib.*; his aversion to Lord Grey and the Whigs, 133; his popularity, 134; his opposition to Catholic claims, 136; yielded, but showed his dislike to his ministers, 137; the Act to authorise him to affix his sign manual by a stamp, 216; his civil list and other revenues, 244, 245; his conduct on the passing of the Catholic Relief Bill, iii. 168, 172

Germaine, Lord G., his statement respecting George III.'s personal influence, i. 49

German Legion, the, Cobbett's libel on, ii. 335

Gerrald, J., tried for sedition, ii. 298

Gibson, Mr. Milner, heads movement against taxes on knowledge, ii. 382; his proposal to establish county financial boards, iii. 297

Gillray, his caricatures, ii. 265

Gladstone, Mr., separates from Lord Palmerston's ministry, ii. 219; his financial policy, iii. 418; rejected by Oxford University, 1865, 429; introduces a reform bill, 1866, 431; becomes premier in 1868, 447; his Irish Church Bill, 1869, *ib.*; his Irish Land Bill, 448; and other measures, 449 *et seq.*

Glasgow, the defective representation of, i. 356

Gloucester, bribery at, i. 437

GLO

Gloucester, Duke of, married Lady Waldegrave, i. 262

Goderich, Lord, his administration, ii. 191

Goldsmiths' Hall Association, the, ii. 293, 298

Good Hope, Cape of, a constitution granted to, iii. 372

Gordon, Lord G., the petitions that he presented to Parliament, ii. 64; heads the Protestant Association, ii. 272, iii. 98; presents their petition, ii. 273; committed to Newgate, 276

Gosset, Sir W., sued by Howard for trespass, ii. 82

Government, executive, control of Parliament over, ii. 85; strong and weak governments since the Reform Act, 95. See also Ministers of the Crown

Gower, Earl of, his amendment to resolutions for a regency, i. 212; cleared the house, ii. 31

Gower, Lord F. L., his resolution for the state endowment of Irish priests, iii. 156

Grafton, Duke of, dismissed from lord-lieutenancy for opposing the court policy, i. 23; accepted office under Lord Chatham, 40; complained of the bad results of Chatham's ill-health, 42; consequent weakness of the ministry, 43; his resignation, *ib.*; his ministry broken up by debates upon Wilkes, ii. 18

Graham, Sir J., separates from Lord Palmerston's ministry, ii. 219; case of opening letters by, iii. 46; his answer to the claim, &c., of the Church of Scotland, 248

Grampound, the disfranchisement bills of, i. 409

Grant, Mr. R., his motions for Jewish relief, iii. 198, 181

Grattan, Mr., the character of his oratory, ii. 118; advocates Catholic relief, iii. 123, 131, 136–141;

GRE

the independence of Ireland, 313, 315, 332; his death, 145

Great seal, the, use of, under authority of parliament, during George III.'s illness, i. 182, 186, 209; questions arising thereupon, 191; affixed by Lord Hardwicke to two commissions during illness of George II., 186

Grenville Act, trial of election petitions under, i. 365; made perpetual, 366

Grenville, Lord, the proposal that he should take office with Pitt, i. 100; formed an administration on his death, 103; differed with the King on the army administration, 104; the Army Service Bill, 105; cabinet minute reserving liberty of action on the Catholic question, 107; pledge required by the King on that subject, 108; dismissed, *ib.*; his advice neglected by the Regent, 121; attempted reconciliation, 122; failure of negotiations on the 'household question,' 126; his difficulty in issuing public money during George III.'s incapacity, 214; the tactics of his party, ii. 176, 186; in office, 176, iii. 125; introduces the Treasonable Practices Bill, ii. 317; advocates Catholic relief, iii. 120; his Army and Navy Service Bill, 126; fall of his ministry, 128

Grenville, Mr. George, succeeded Lord Bute as premier, i. 25; did not defer to George III., 26; remonstrated against Lord Bute's influence, *ib.*, 31; supported the king's arbitrary measures, 28; differences between them, 31; his Election Petitions Act, 365; his statement of amount of secret service money; 379; the bribery under his ministry, 380; opposed Wilkes's expulsion, ii. 12; his motion for reduction of land tax, 101; attacked by Wilkes, ii. 103; his schemes for taxation of American colonies, iii. 347.

Grey, Earl, his advice neglected by the Regent, i. 121; declined office on the 'household question,' 126; advocated reform, and led the reform ministry, 139, 310, 402, 407, 420; lost the confidence of William IV., 145; accused Lord Eldon of using George III.'s name without due authority, 201, 205; the regulation of the civil list by his ministry, 246; his views on the present state of the House of Lords, 308, n.; advised the creation of new peers, 311, 315; favoured a shorter duration of parliament, 441; the character of his oratory, ii. 119; the separation of his party from the Radicals, ii. 182, 199; carries Parliamentary Reform, 196; his ministry, 198–204; his Army and Navy Service Bill, iii. 127; advocates Catholic claims, 130; and relief from declaration against transubstantiation, 144

Grey, Mr. (1667), an early reporter of the debates, ii. 35

Grosvenor, General, his hostile motion against Mr. Pitt's ministry, i. 78

Grote, Mr., advocated vote by ballot, i. 446

HABEAS CORPUS SUSPENSION ACTS, the,—of 1774, ii. 302, 313, iii. 12; of 1817, ii. 343, iii. 16; of 1860 and 1871, 19; cases of, between the Revolution and 1794, iii. 11; the Acts of Indemnity, 12–19;—— in Ireland, 19, 147

Halifax, Earl of, issue of general warrants by, iii. 2, 7; action brought against him by Wilkes, 6; obtained the consent of George III. to exclude his mother from the Regency, i. 173

Hamilton, Duke of, a Scottish peer, not allowed the rights of an English peer, i. 288

Hamilton, Lord A., advocated reform in the representation of Scotland, i. 358

Hanover, House of, the character of the first two kings of, favourable to constitutional government, i. 76

Hanover, kingdom of, the revenues attached to the crown till her Majesty's accession, 247

Hansard, Messrs., sued by Stockdale for libel, ii. 78

Harcourt, Lord, supported the influence of the crown over parliament, i. 37

Hardwicke, Lord, affixed the great seal to commissions during illness of George II., i. 186

Hardwicke, Lord, changes caused by his Marriage Act, iii. 151

Hardy, T., tried for treason, ii. 307

Harrowby, Earl of, supported George IV. on the Catholic question, i. 114

Hastings, Mr. Warren, impeachments not abated by dissolution, established in his case, ii. 93

Hastings, the sale of the seat for this borough, i. 346

Hawkesbury, Lord, the supposed adviser of George III. against the Grenville ministry, i. 111; his declaration as to the King's competency to transact business, 201; his refusal of Napoleon's demands against the press and foreigners, ii. 332, iii. 54

Heberden, Dr., his evidence regarding the King's illnesses, i. 204, 205

Henley, Mr., seceded from the Derby ministry on the question of reform, i. 455

Henry III., V., VI., and VII., the

revenues of their crowns, i. 226, 227

Henry VIII., his sign manual affixed by a stamp, i. 217; his crown revenues, 227

Herbert, Mr., his bill as to the expulsion of members, ii. 19

Heron, Sir R., his bill for shortening the duration of parliament, i. 442

Hewley, Lady, the case of her charities, iii. 199

Hindon, bribery at, i. 340

Hobhouse, Mr., committed for libelling the house of commons, ii. 60

Hobhouse, Sir J., his vestry Act, iii. 277

Hoghton, Sir H., his Dissenters Relief Bills, iii. 93

Holdernesse, Lord, retired from office in favour of Lord Bute, i. 19

Holland, Lord, his amendment for an address to the Prince of Wales, i. 210

Hone, W., trials of, for libel, ii. 349

Horner, Mr. F., his speech against a regency bill, i. 210

Horsley, Bishop, his opinion on the rights of the people, ii. 319; amends the Protestant Catholic Dissenters Bill, iii. 106

Household, the. See Royal Household

House tax, the, Lord Derby's ministry defeated on, ii. 102

Howard, Messrs., reprimanded for conducting Stockdale's action, ii. 80; committed, 81; sued the sergeant-at-arms, 82

Howick, Lord, denounced secret advice to crown, i. 111, 112. See also Grey, Earl

Hudson, Dr., tried for sedition, ii. 290

Hudson's Bay Company, the, ii. 615

Hume, Mr., his motion against Orange lodges in the army, ii. 402; his scheme for voluntary enlistment, iii. 24; his proposed reform of county administration, 297; his exertions in revision of official salaries, 386

Hunt, Leigh, tried for libel, ii. 335

Hunt, Mr., headed the Manchester meeting, ii. 354; tried for sedition, 363

Huskisson, Mr., his prophecy as to reform in Parliament, i. 416; his commercial policy, ii. 187, iii. 417

Hyde Park, meeting in, prohibited 1866, iii. 434; park railings pulled down, and riots in the park, *ib.*; another meeting prohibited in 1867, but held in defiance of government, 437; failure of a bill to give additional powers to government, 439; unsettled state of the law, *ib.*

IMPEACHMENT of ministers by parliament, ii. 92; rare in later times, 93; not abated by a dissolution, *ib.*

Impressment, for the army, iii. 20; for the navy, 21

Imprisonment, for debts to the crown, iii. 25; contempt of court, 26; on mesne process, 29; for debt, 31. See also Prisons

Indemnity Acts, the, on expiration of the Habeas Corpus Suspension Acts, iii. 15, 16;——Annual, the first passed, 82, *n.*

Independents, the, their tenets, iii. 67; their toleration, 73; numbers, &c., 222, 224, *n.*

India Bill, the (1783), thrown out by influence of the crown, i. 71

India. See East India

Informers. See Spies

Insolvent debtors, laws for the relief of, iii. 34

Ireland, the position of the Church in, caused alarm to William IV.,

i. 145; number of archbishops and bishops of, 281; lost their seats in Parliament by Act of 1869, *ib. n.*; representative bishops of, *ib.*; —— civil list of, 245; pensions on the crown revenues of, 257, 258; consolidated with English pension list, 261; —— the parliament of, their proceedings on the regency, 194; address the Prince, *ib.*; Irish office-holders disqualified for parliament, 373; —— the representative peers of, 280; restriction upon the number of the Irish peerage, *ib.*; its absorption into the peerage of the United Kingdom, 289; Irish peers sit in the Commons, 281; —— representation of, prior to the Reform Bill, 359, 361; nomination boroughs abolished at the Union, 360; Irish judges disqualified, 375; —— the Reform Act of, 430; amended (1850), *ib.*; the Reformation in, iii. 70; dangerous state of, 1823–25, 154; and in 1828, 163; burial grounds in, open to all persuasions, 194; the tithe question, 256, 263–268; national education, 270, 413; Maynooth and Queen's Colleges, 270; Government of Ireland prior to the Union, 299; the parliament, 300; the executive, 302; power monopolised by churchmen, *ib.*; supremacy of English Government, 303; commercial restrictions, 305; partially removed, 310, 312; residence of lord-lieutenant enforced, 302, 306; conflicts between the Commons and the Executive, 307; state of Ireland, 1776, 308; the volunteers, 311; they agitate for independence and parliamentary reform, 312–315, 318; the convention at Dungannon, 314; independence granted, 316; admission of Catholics to the elective franchise, 110, 322; the United Irishmen, ii. 329, iii. 322; feuds between Protestants and Catholics, 324; the rebellion of 1798, 325; Union with England concerted, 327; opposition bought off, 330; the Union effected, 333; its results, *ib.*; effect of Catholic relief and reform in the representation, 172, 335; present position of Ireland, *ib.*; and of its Catholic inhabitants, 336; the number of Irishmen on the English bench, 337, *n.*; —— corporate reform, 290; new poor law introduced into, 408; disestablishment of the Irish Church, 1869, 447; the Irish land bill, 1870, 448

Irnham, Lord, his daughter married to the Duke of Cumberland, i. 262

JAMAICA, colonial institutions in, iii. 340, 356; contumacy of assembly repressed, 364

James I., his crown revenues, i. 227

James II., expelled by union of church and dissenters, iii. 77; his proposal to tax colony of Massachusetts, 343

Jews, the admission of, to parliament, ii. 84; naturalisation Act of, 1754, repealed, 266; tolerated by Cromwell, iii. 73; excepted from Lord Hardwicke's Marriage Act, 151; the first motions for their relief, 178; Mr. Grant's motions, *ib.*, 181; Jews admitted to corporations, 182; returns of Baron Rothschild and Mr. Salomons, 183, 184; attempt to admit Jews under declaration, 185; the Relief Acts, 186, 187; number of, returned, *ib.*

Johnson, Dr., a compiler of parlia-

mentary reports, ii. 36, 37, 50, 113, *n*.
Jones, Mr. Gale, committed for libel on the House of Commons, ii. 60
Judges, the introduction of a judge into the Grenville cabinet, i. 103; disqualified from parliament, 375; except the Master of the Rolls, *ib.*; their conduct in libel cases, ii. 348, 349; number of Irishmen on the English bench, iii. 337, *n.*; spirit and temper of the judges, 391; their tenure of office assured, 392
Junius, the letter of, to the king, ii. 252
Juries, rights of, in libel cases, ii. 253–263

KENNINGTON COMMON, Chartist meeting at, ii. 410
Kent, Duchess of, appointed Regent (1830), i. 221
Kentish petitioners imprisoned by the Commons, ii. 62
Kenyon, Lord, his opinion on the coronation oath, i. 93
Kersal Moor, Chartist meeting at, ii. 409; election of popular representative at, *ib.*
King, Lord, moved to omit Lord Eldon's name from the council of regency, i. 205
King, questions as to accession of an infant king, i. 219; as to the rights of a king's posthumous child, 222; rights of a king over the royal family, 262. *See also* Crown, the.
'King's Friends, the,' the party so called, i. 13; their influence, 35; led by Addington, 100, 103; their activity against the Army Service Bill, 106; the 'nabobs' rank themselves among them, 335; a section of the Tory party, ii. 143; estranged from Pitt, 176; coalesce with the Whigs, 177; estranged from them, 179
Knight's (a negro) case, iii. 37
Knighthood, the orders of, i. 324

LADIES, debates in the Commons attended by, ii. 29; their exclusion, 52, *n.*
Lambton, Mr., his motion for reform, i. 361, 410
Lancaster, Duchy of, the revenues of, attached to the crown, i. 227, 235, 248; present amount, *ib.*
Land bill (Ireland) 1870, iii. 448
Land revenues of the crown. *See* Revenues of the Crown
Land tax, the, allowed twice over to crown tenantry, i. 253; reduced by vote of the Commons, ii. 101; third reading of a land tax bill delayed, i. 74; ii. 108
Lansdowne, Marquess of, his amendment to resolutions for a regency, i. 212; his motions respecting the marriages of Catholics and Dissenters, iii. 152; for relief of English Catholics, *ib.*
Lauderdale, Earl of, condemned the King's conduct to the Grenville ministry, i. 115
Law, the, improvement in the spirit and administration of, iii. 389; legal sinecures abolished, 390
Legislatorial attorneys, election of, at public meetings, ii. 351; practice of, imitated by the Chartists, 408
Leicester, case of bribery from corporate funds of the borough of, i. 413
Lennox, Lady S., admired by George III., i. 263
Lethendy case, the, iii. 245
Letters, opened at the Post-office, by government, iii. 44; the former practice, 45, and *n.*; case of, in 1844, 46
Libel, the Libel Act, ii. 260–264; Lord Sidmouth's circular to the

lord-lieutenants respecting seditious libels, ii. 345; conduct of judges in libel cases, 348, 349. See also Sedition, &c.

Liberal Party, the. See Party

Liberty of opinion. See Opinion, Liberty of

Liberty of the subject. See Subject, Liberty of

Licensing Act, the, ii. 242; not renewed, 243

Life peerages, i. 290; to women, 292; the Wensleydale peerage case, 295

Liverpool, Earl of, his ministry, i. 128; conducted the proceedings against Queen Caroline, 130; his administration, ii. 182, 187; disunion of the Tories on his death, 189; his ministry and the Catholic question, iii. 140

Loans to government, members bribed by shares in, i. 382; cessation of the system, 386

Local government, the basis of constitutional freedom, iii. 275; vestries, open and select, 276; Vestry Acts, ib., 277; municipal corporations before and after reform, 278-294; local boards, 296; courts of quarter sessions, 297

Logan, the Rev., his defence of Warren Hastings, ii. 259

London, city of, address George III. condemning the proceedings against Wilkes, ii. 20

London, Corporation of, extortion practised by, on dissenters, iii. 90; address of the Common Council on the Manchester massacre, ii. 356; schemes for its reform, iii. 286

London Corresponding Society, the, ii. 282, 283; reported on by a secret committee, 302; trial of members of, for high treason, 307; inflames public discontent, 315; calls a meeting at Copenhagen House, ib.; address on an attack on George III., 324; increased activity of, 328; suppressed by Act, 329

London Magazine, the, one of the first to report parliamentary debates, ii. 36

London University, founded, iii. 198

Lord-lieutenant of Ireland, the residence of, enforced, iii. 306

Lords, House of, relations of, with the crown, i. 2, 307; the influence of the crown exerted over the Lords, 23, 54, 66, 143, 312; debates on the influence of the crown, 52; rejection of the India Bill by the Lords, 71; they condemn the Commons' opposition to Mr. Pitt, 79; their proceedings on the reform bills, 142, 308, 424; the proposed creation of peers, 143, 312, 426; position of the house in the state, 273, 302; increase of its numbers, 274-282; such enlargement a source of strength, 303; twelve peers created in one day by Queen Anne, 274; the representative peers of Scotland and Ireland, ib., 280; proposed restrictions upon the power of the crown, and the regent, in the creation of peers, 275, 278; profuse creations by George III., 277; composition of the house in 1860, 282; its representative character, 285; the rights of peers of Scotland, 286; the appellate jurisdiction of the Lords, 290; bill to improve it, 298; the life-peerage question, 291; Lords spiritual, 299; their past and present number, ib.; attempts to exclude them, 300; the political position of the house, 302; the influence of parties, 305; collisions between the two houses, 306; the danger now increased, 307; the creation of sixteen peers by William IV., 309; creation of new peers equivalent to a dissolution, 315;

position of the house since reform, 316; their independence, 317; the scanty attendance in the house, 320; smallness of the quorum, 321; indifference to business, *ib.*; deference to leaders, *ib.*; influence of peers over the Commons through nomination boroughs, 333; and through territorial influence, 353, 362; refusal of the Lords to indemnify the witnesses against Walpole, 378; the proceedings against Wilkes, ii. 5, 10; the book 'Droit le Roi' burnt, 7; their address to condemn the city address on the Middlesex election proceedings, 21; debates on those proceedings, 16, 22; strangers and members excluded from debates, 30, 52; scene on one occasion, 31; report of debates permitted, 49, 54; presence of strangers at divisions, 57; publicity given to committee proceedings, 58; to parliamentary papers, *ib.*; the privilege to servants discontinued, 73; and of prisoners kneeling at the bar, 74; the control of the Lords over the executive government, 85; they advise the crown on questions of peace and war, and of a dissolution, 86; their rejection of a money bill, 105; relative rights of the two houses, 108; conduct of the house in debate, 125; the Catholic peers take their seats, iii. 174. *See also* Parliament; Peerage; Peers.

Lords, House of (Ireland), composition of, iii. 300

Lords spiritual. *See* Bishops

Lottery tickets (government), members bribed by, i. 384

Lowe, Mr., his opposition to the reform bill, 1866, 431; a member of Mr. Gladstone's cabinet, 1868, 447

Loughborough, Lord, joins the Tories, ii. 166; prompts the repressive policy of the government, 286

Luddites, the, outrages of, ii. 340

Ludgershall, price of seat, i. 339

Lunatics, a state provision for, iii. 409

Lushington, Dr., a life peerage offered to, i. 294; disqualified from parliament, 317

Luttrell, Colonel, his sister married to the Duke of Cumberland, i. 262; opposed Wilkes for Middlesex, ii. 14; enforced the exclusion of reporters, 51

Lyndhurst, Lord, his motion on the life-peerage case, i. 295; brought in the Dissenters' Chapels Bill, iii. 200

Lyttelton, Lord, his address respecting the regency, i. 172; his complaint against the book called 'Droit le Roi,' ii. 7

Lyttleton, Mr., his motion on the dismissal of the Grenville ministry, i. 115

MACCLESFIELD, Lord, his decision touching the rights of the king over his grandchildren, i. 264

Mackenzie, Mr. S., dismissed from office, i. 34

Mackintosh, Sir J., his defence of Peltier, ii. 333; his efforts to reform the criminal code, iii. 397

M'Laren and Baird, trial of, for sedition, ii. 351

Magistrates, military interference in absence of, ii. 276; the summary jurisdiction of, iii. 404

Manchester, Duke of, strangers excluded on his motion relative to war with Spain, ii. 31

Manchester, public meeting at, ii. 353; the massacre, 354; debates thereon in Parliament, 355-358

Mansfield, Lord, exhorted George III. to exert his influence over parliament, i. 37; the precedent of his admission to the cabinet cited, 104; his opinion on the right of the Commons to incapacitate Wilkes, ii. 16, 22; accused by Wilkes of altering a record, 9; his decisions touching the rights of juries in libel cases, ii. 253, 258; produced the judgment in Woodfall's case to the House of Lords, 256; his house burnt by the Protestant rioters, 275; his opinion on military interference in absence of a magistrate, 276; his decision in the negro case, iii. 36; and recognising toleration, 91; his tolerant acquittal of a priest, 96; a cabinet minister, 392

Manufacturing districts, state of the, ii. 352, iii. 211

Marchmont, Lord, his motion on the Middlesex election proceedings, ii. 19

Margarot, M., trial of, for sedition, ii. 298

Marriages, laws affecting the, of Dissenters and Catholics, iii. 151–153, 188–192; effect of Lord Hardwicke's Act, 151

Martin, Mr., his duel with Wilkes, ii. 5

Mary (Queen of England), her sign manual affixed by a stamp, i. 217

Marvell, A., reported proceedings in the Commons, ii. 35

Massachusetts, proposal of James II. to tax, iii. 343; constitution of, suspended, 353

Maynooth College, founded, iii. 270; Peel's endowment of, 271; popular opposition to, *ib.*

Mazzini, J., his letters opened by government, iii. 46

Meetings. *See* Public Meetings

Melbourne, Viscount, in office, i. 145; his sudden dismissal, 146; reinstated, 153; in office at the accession of her Majesty, 154; organised her household, *ib.*; kept in office by the 'bedchamber question,' 155; retired from office, 158; his ministries, ii. 205, 206; receives a deputation of working men, 389; reception of delegates from trades' unions, 405; framed the Tithe Commutation Act, iii. 219; and the first Irish Corporations Bill, 292

Melville, Lord, his impeachment, ii. 93; impeachment of, a blow to the Scotch Tories, ii. 180

Members of the House of Commons, number of nominee members prior to reform, i. 361; members bribed by pensions, 369; bribery under Charles II., 376; under William III., 377; George II., 378; and George III., *ib.*, 381; bribed by loans and lotteries, 382; by contracts, 387; wages to, provided for in Lord Blandford's reform bill, 412; the abolition of property qualifications, 448; their exclusion from the House of Lords, ii. 31; the system of pledges to constituents considered, 70; certain privileges of, discontinued, 73. *See also* Commons, House of

Meredith, Sir W., his speech against capital punishments, iii. 395

Middle classes, the, strength given to Whigs by adhesion of, ii. 186, 196, 365; a combination of the working and middle classes necessary to successful agitation, 384, 416

Middlesex, electors of, cause of, supported by public meetings, ii. 268

Middlesex Journal, the, complaint against, for misrepresenting debates, ii. 39

Middlesex, sheriffs of, committed by the House in the Stockdale actions, ii. 80

Military officers, deprived of command for opposition to the policy of George III., i. 28, 47; this practice condemned under the Rockingham ministry, 34

Military and Naval Officers Oaths Bill, the, iii. 143

Militia, the Catholics in, ii. 114

Miller, proceeded against for publishing debates, ii. 41; interposition of the city authorities, *ib.*; tried for publication of a libel, 254

Mines, labour of children, &c., regulated in, iii. 411

Ministers of the crown, the responsibility of, i. 6, 108; regarded with jealousy by George III., 9; constitutional relations between the crown and ministers, 14, 108, 145, 154, 159, 205; the influence of the crown exerted against its ministers, 36, 66, 90, 106; appeals by ministers from the House of Commons to the people, by dissolutions of parliament, 86, *n*., 141, 150, 158, 308, 424, ii. 90; the pledge exacted by George III. of his ministers, i. 107; ministers supported by the crown and the Commons in reform, 142, 310, 424; the influence of great families over ministries, 165; numerous applications to, for peerages, 283; votes of want of confidence, 57, 77, 81, ii. 90; and of confidence, 141, 425, ii. 91; ministers impeached by the Commons, 92; the stability of recent ministries considered, 95; ministers defeated on financial measures, 101; increasing influence of public opinion over, 144, 186, 264, 364; the principles of coalition between, 157, 217; responsibility of ministers to their supporters, 192, 214; the premiership rarely held by the head of a great family, 229; revision of salaries of, iii. 387

Minorities, proposed representation of, at elections, in reform bill (1854), i. 452; Lord Cairns's clause, 1867, iii. 439

Mohun, Lord, cudgelled Dyer for a libel, ii. 244

Moira, Earl, his mission to the Whig leaders, i. 125; the 'household question,' 126

Moravians. *See* Quakers

Morton, Mr., moved the insertion of the Princess of Wales's name into the Regency Bill, i. 174

Muir, T., trial of, at Edinburgh, for sedition, ii. 292; comments thereon in Parliament, 299

Municipal Corporations. *See* Corporations

Murray, Lady A., married to the Duke of Sussex, i. 270

Murray, Mr., his refusal to kneel at the bar of the Commons, ii. 74

Mutiny bill, the passing of, postponed, i. 82

Mutiny Act (Ireland) made permanent, iii. 313; repealed, 316

'NABOBS,' the, their bribery at elections, i. 335, 338; rank themselves among the 'King's friends,' 335

Napoleon, First Consul of France, demands the repression of the press, ii. 332; the dismissal of refugees, iii. 54; trial of Peltier for libel on, ii. 333

Naturalisation Act, passing of, iii. 53

Navy, impressment for, iii. 21; flogging in, abated, 405

Negroes freed by landing in England, iii. 35; in Scotland, 37; the slave trade and slavery abolished, ii. 277, 404, iii. 39

New Brunswick, the constitution of, iii. 358

Newcastle, Duke of, in office at accession of George III., i. 12; his resignation, 21; dismissed from his lord-lieutenancy, 23

Newenham, Mr., his motion respecting the debts of Prince of Wales, i. 251

New Shoreham, voters for the borough of, disfranchised for bribery, i. 339

Newfoundland, the constitution of, iii. 358

Newport, the Chartist attack on, ii. 409

New South Wales, a legislature granted to, iii. 359; transportation to, abolished, *ib.*; democratic constitution of, 370

Newspapers, the first, ii. 240, 243; stamp and advertisement duties first imposed, 245; increased, 327; removed, 380–383; improvement in newspapers, 264, 337; commencement of 'The Times' and other papers, 265, *n.*; measures of repression, 330, 358

New Zealand, constitution granted to, iii. 372

Nomination boroughs. *See* Boroughs

Nonconformists. *See* Dissenters

Norfolk, Duke of, his eldest son abjured the Catholic faith, 1780, iii. 99, *n.*; his Catholic Officers Relief Bill, 143; enabled by Act to serve as Earl Marshal, 154

' North Briton,' the, proceedings against, ii. 248, 250, iii. 2

North, Lord, his relations, as premier, with George III., i. 44; his complete submission to the King, 44, 49, 58; his overtures to Chatham, 48; to the Whigs, 49; his ministry overthrown, 56; his conduct in office approved by the King, 57; joined the 'coalition ministry,' 63; dismissed from office, 71; liberal in creation of peers, 277; in the bribery of members, 381; with money sent by George III., *ib.*; by shares in a loan, 384; his second loan, 386; approved the Middlesex election proceedings, ii. 18, 24; his carriage broken by mob, 47; his personalities in debate, 126; in office, 142, 145; driven from office, 150; the Coalition, 153; his measure to conciliate the American colonies, iii. 355

Northampton borough, cost of electoral contest for (1768), i. 339; case of bribery from the corporate funds of, 413

'North Briton' (No. 45), the publication of, ii. 3; riot at the burning of, 8

Northumberland, Duke of, supported in bribery at elections by George III., i. 341

Norton, Sir F. (the speaker), supported Dunning's resolutions, i. 53; his speech to George III. touching the civil list, 238, 239; altercations with, when in the chair, ii. 128

Nottingham Castle, burnt by mob, ii. 387

Nova Scotia, responsible government in, iii. 368

Nugent, Lord, his bill for Catholic relief, iii. 151; obtained relaxation to Irish commerce, 310

OCCASIONAL CONFORMITY ACT, the, iii. 82

O'Connell, Mr., advocated universal suffrage, &c., i. 416; reprimanded for libelling the house, ii. 60; his position as an orator, 121; leads the Irish party, ii. 201; heads the Catholic Association, 369; agitates for repeal of the Union, 393; trials of, 394, 397; released on writ of error, 399; returned for Clare, iii. 163; his re-election required, 174; his motions on Irish tithes and Church, 260–267

O'Connor, F., presents the Chartist petition, ii. 412, 413

Octennial Act, the (Ireland), iii. 306

OFF

Official salaries, revision of, since the Reform Act, iii. 386

Officers under the crown, disqualified from sitting in parliament, i. 348, 372; number of, in parliament, 135, 374

Oldfield, Dr., his statistics of parliamentary patronage, i. 361

Oliver, Mr. Alderman, proceeded against by the Commons for committing their messenger, ii. 44, 46

Oliver, the government spy, iii. 41

Onslow, Mr. G., ordered the house to be cleared, to exclude the peers, ii. 32; to hinder the reporting the debates, 33; complained of the publication of debates, 39; the soubriquet given him by the reporters, 38

Opinion, liberty of, the last liberty to be acquired, ii. 238; the press, from James I. till the accession of George III., 240; the 'North Briton' prosecutions, 247; the law of libel, 252; political agitation by public meetings, 265; by associations, 269; democratic associations, 279; repressive measures, 1792–99, 285; Napoleon and the English press, 332; the press, before the Regency, 336; repressive measures under the Regency, 340; the contest between authority and public opinion reviewed, 363; the Catholic Association, 368; the press under George IV., 376; its freedom established, 379; the Reform agitation, 383; for repeal of the Union, 393; Orange lodges, 400; trades' unions, 404; the Chartists, 407; the Anti-Corn Law League, 413; political agitation reviewed, 417. *See also* Press; Political Associations; Public Meetings

Orange societies, suppressed by Act, ii. 371; revived, 373; organisation of, 400; in the army,

PAR

402; dissolved, 403; peculiar working of Orange societies, *ib.*

Orators and oratory. *See* Parliamentary Oratory

Orsini conspiracy, the, plotted in England, iii. 57

Oxford University, state of feeling at, on Catholic relief, iii. 137; admission of dissenters to degrees at, 198

Oxford borough, the seat for, sold by the corporation, i. 338

PAINE, T., tried for seditious writings, ii. 280

Pains and penalties, bill of, against Queen Caroline, i. 131

Palmer, the Rev. T. F., trial of, for sedition, ii. 296; comments thereon in Parliament, 299

Palmerston, Viscount, his removal from office, 1851, i. 160; the reform bill of his ministry, 456; his resolutions on the Lords' rejection of the Paper Duties Bill, ii. 110; adhered to Mr. Canning, ii. 189; in the Duke of Wellington's ministry, 192; in office, 216; secession of the Peelites, 219; his overthrow in 1857 and 1858, 220, 221, iii. 58; his second ministry, ii. 222; political tranquillity under his rule, iii. 426; his death, 429; change of policy which ensued, 430

Papal aggression, 1850, the, iii. 227.——Court, diplomatic relations with, Bill, 230, *n.*

Paper duty, the, abolished, ii. 382

Paper Duties Repeal Bill (1860), rejected by the Lords, i. 318, ii. 108

Parish, the, local affairs of, administered by vestries, iii. 276

Parke, Sir J. *See* Wensleydale, Baron

Parliament, government by, established at the Revolution, i. 1; constitutional position of, at the accession of George III., 2, 16; violation of parliamentary privileges by the crown, 23, 28, 36, 45, 54, 143; the reform of parliament, 138, 308, 393; the dissolution of, of 1784, 86; of 1807, 116; of 1830, 417; of 1831, 141, 424; of 1834, 150; of 1841, 158; influence of families over parliament, 165; the meeting of parliament during George III.'s illnesses, 175, 207; commissions for opening parliament during his illness, 186, 213; second opening after King's recovery (1789), 189; adjournments caused by King's inability to sign the commission for prorogation, 175, 207: parliament and the revenues of the crown, and the civil list, 229–260; the duration of parliament, 440; motions for triennial parliaments, 441; time between summons and meeting of, shortened, 449; relations of parliament to the crown, the law, and the people, ii. 1–112; the unreported parliament, 30, n.; publication of the debates and division lists, 34, 53, 55; petitions to parliament, 60; the publication of parliamentary papers, 58; the relinquishment of certain parliamentary privileges, 73; privilege and the courts of law, 75; the publication of papers affecting character, 78; control of parliament over the executive government, 85; over supplies to the crown, 108; sketch of parliamentary oratory, 112; group of parliamentary orators of the age of Chatham and Pitt, 113; of later times, 118; character of modern oratory, 123; the personalities of former times, 125; increased authority of the chair, 128. Secessions of the Whigs from, 148, 173, 321; repression of the press by Parliament, 244; attempted intimidation of, by the silk-weavers, 266; by the Protestant Associations, 272; relations of the Church and Parliament, iii. 226; supremacy of, over the Irish Parliament, 305; Parliament since the Reform Act, 385; vast amount of public business, 422. *See also* Commons, House of; Lords, House of

Parliament (Ireland), state of, before the Union, iii. 299; exclusion of Catholics, *ib.*, 303; expired only on demise of the Crown, 301; Poynings' Act, 303; supremacy of the English Parliament, 305; agitation for independence, 312, 315; submits to the permanent Mutiny Bill, 313; independence granted, 316; corrupt influence of the government, 317; motions for Parliamentary Reform, 319; the Union carried, 329

Parnell, Sir H., his views of financial policy, iii. 419

Party, influence of, in party government, ii. 131; origin of parties, 133; parties under the Stuarts, and after the Revolution, 134, 136; Whigs and Tories, 135; their distinctive principles, 138, 144, 223; parties on the accession of George III., 140, 145; the American war a test of party principles, 147; secessions of the Whigs from Parliament, 148, 173, 321; overtures to the Whigs, 150; commencement of a democratic party, 151; crisis on death of Lord Rockingham, *ib.*; the Coalition, 153–155; ruin of the Whigs, 156; principles of coalition, 157; the Tories under Mr. Pitt, 158, 168; the Whigs and the Prince of Wales, 161, 178, 182; effect of the French Revolution upon parties, 163, 166;

PAR

position of the Whigs, 164, 167, 171; the Tories in Scotland, 171; schism among the Tories, 174; parties on Pitt's retirement from office, 175; the Whigs in office, 1806, 177–179, iii. 124; coalesce with Lord Sidmouth's party, ii. 177; the Tories reinstated, 179; position of the Whigs, 180; the strength they derived from the adhesion of the middle classes, 181, 365; the Tories under Lord Liverpool, 182–189; under Canning, 189; influence of national distress, and of proceedings against Queen Caroline, upon parties, 185, 186; increase of liberal feeling, 107; effect of the Catholic question upon parties, 190, 192, iii. 129, 140, 168; party divisions after Mr. Canning's death, ii. 191; the Duke of Wellington's ministry, *ib.*; secession of liberal members from his cabinet, 192; the Whigs restored to office, 195; supported by the democratic party, 196; Whig ascendency after the Reform Acts, 198; state of parties, *ib.*; the Radicals, *ib.*; the Irish party, 201; the Tories become 'Conservatives,' 203; increase in power, *ib.*; breaking up of Earl Grey's ministry, 204; dismissal of Lord Melbourne's ministry, 205; Liberals reunited against Sir R. Peel, *ib.*; his liberal policy alarms the Tories, *ib.*; parties under Lord Melbourne, 206; a conservative reaction, 208; effect of Peel's free-trade policy upon the Conservatives, 211, 212; the obligations of a party leader, 214; the Whigs in office, 216; Lord Derby's first ministry, *ib.*; coalition of Whigs and Peelites under Lord Aberdeen, 217; fall of his ministry, 218; the Peelites retire from Lord Palmer-

PEE

ston's first administration, 219; his overthrows, in 1857 and 1858, 220; Lord Derby's second ministry, 221; passed the Jewish Relief Act, iii. 186; Lord Palmerston's second administration, ii. 222; fusion of parties, 223; essential difference between Conservatives and Liberals, *ib.*; party sections, 224; changes in the character, &c., of parties, 225; politics formerly a profession, 227; effects of Parliamentary Reform on parties, 230; the conservatism of age, 232; statesmen under old and new systems, *ib.*; patronage, an instrument of party, 234; review of the merits and evils of party, 236; the press an instrument of party, 244, 264, 265; opposition of the Whigs to a repressive policy, 288, 357; to the Six Acts, 358; the Habeas Corpus Suspension Bills, 311, iii. 12–19; the Treasonable Practices, &c. Bills, ii. 317–323; the Irish Church appropriation question adopted by the Whigs, iii. 266; abandoned by them, 268

Patronage, an instrument of party, ii. 234; the effect of competition, 235; abuses of colonial patronage, iii. 362; surrendered to the colonies, 363

Patronage Act (Scotland), iii. 253. *See also* Church of Scotland

Pease, Mr., his case cited regarding Jewish disabilities, i. 85

Peel, Mr. *See* Peel, Sir R.

Peel, Sir R., the first, his Factory Children Act, iii. 411

Peel, Sir R., obtained the consent of George IV. to Catholic emancipation, i. 137; his first administration, 148; his absence abroad, *ib.*; his ministerial efforts, 150; advised a dissolution, *ib.*; resignation,

153; declines to take office on the 'bedchamber question,' 155; his second administration, 158; his anti-reform declaration, 416; the character of his oratory, ii. 120; his commercial policy, ii. 187, iii. 418; seceded from Canning on the Catholic question, 189; opposes that measure, iii. 141, 149; brings in the Relief Act, ii. 192, iii. 168; his first ministry, ii. 205; his policy and fall, *ib.*, iii. 267; his relation to the Conservatives, ii. 209, 212; his second ministry, 209; his free-trade policy, 210; repeal of corn laws, 212, 413, 416; his obligations as a party leader, 214; obtains the bishops' consent to the repeal of the Corporation and Test Acts, iii. 159; proposes to retire from the Wellington ministry, 166; loses his seat at Oxford, 168; the Irish Franchise Act, 172; his Dissenters' Marriage Bills, 190; plan for commutation of Irish Tithes, 266; resists the appropriation question, *ib.*; proposes endowment to Maynooth and the Queen's Colleges, 270; his scheme for Irish corporate reform, 294; the first minister to revise the criminal code, 398

Peerage, the number of, i. 73; of the United Kingdom, 281 and *n.*; antiquity of, 282; claims to, 283; changes in its composition, 284; the Scottish peerage, 286; fusion of peerages of the three kingdoms, 290; life peerages, 291; to women, 292; peerages with remainders over, 293; authorities favouring life peerages, *ib.*; the Wensleydale peerage case, 295; the peerage in its social relations, 322. *See also* Lords, House of; Ireland, Peerage of; Scotland, Peerage of

Peerage Bill (1720), rejected by the Commons, i. 275

Peers, scanty attendance of, at the house, affecting their political weight, i. 320; their influence over borough and county elections, 333, 353; their exclusion from debates in the House of Commons, ii. 32; the Catholic, restored to the privilege of advising the Crown, iii. 107, 148; exempted from the oath of supremacy, 146; the Catholic Peers Bill, 147; take seats in the House of Lords, 174; creation of, to carry the Union with Ireland, 331. *See also* Lords, House of

Pelham, Mr., bribery to members, a system under, i. 378

Peltier, J., trial of, for libel, ii. 333

Pembroke, Earl of, proscribed for opposition to court policy, i. 54

Penryn, the disfranchisement bill, i. 414; the proposal to transfer the franchise to Manchester, *ib.*

Pensions from the crown, charged on civil list, i. 256; on crown revenues, *ib.*; restrained by parliament, *ib.*, 258; consolidation of pension list, 261; the regulation of (1837), *ib.*; bribery by pensions, 369; holders of, disqualified from sitting in parliament, *ib.*

Perceval, Mr., formed an administration, i. 108; denied giving secret advice to George III., 110; the dissolution during his ministry, 116; his relations with the King, 117; his position at commencement of regency, 120; obnoxious to the Regent as adviser of Princess Caroline, 121; ministerial negotiations at his death, 125; in office, ii. 179, 182, iii. 129

Peto, Sir M., his Dissenters Burial Bills, iii. 193

Petitions to parliament, the right

of petitioning endangered by George III.'s answer to the city address touching Wilkes, ii. 20; the commencement of the practice, 60; of political petitions, 61; forbidden under Charles II., *ib.*; petitions rejected and petitioners imprisoned by the Commons, 62; commencement of the modern system, 63; objected to by George III., 65; progress of the system, *ib.*; the numbers presented of late years, 66, *n.*; abuses of petitioning, 68; debates on presentation of, restrained, 69; for grant of public money to be recommended by the crown, 103

Phillimore, Dr., his Catholic Marriages Bill, iii. 153

Pillory, punishment of, abolished, iii. 400

Pitt, Mr. *See* Chatham, Earl of

Pitt, Mr. William, Chancellor of the Exchequer under Lord Shelburne, i. 62; his first refusals to assume the government, 63, 65; is premier, 71; his contest with the Commons, 72–83; his final triumph, 83; reflections on this contest, 83–89; his relations with George III., 87; in opposition to the King on reform, 90; quitted office on the Catholic question, 97; his mismanagement of that question, *ib.*; his pledge to the King not to revive it, 98; again in office, 99; with Addington, 101; evaded the Catholic question, 102; his opinion on the rights of Prince of Wales as Regent, 177–181; his letter to him respecting the regency, 180; moved resolutions for a bill, *ib.*, 185; proposition as to use of the great seal, 181, 186; introduced the bill, 189; his conduct in these proceedings considered, 193; confirmed the King's confidence in him, 194; embarrassment caused by the King's illness on his leaving office, 196; brought forward the budget after his resignation, *ib.*; his doubts as to the King's sanity, on his return to office, 204; profuse in the creation of peers, 277, 279; his unfair conduct as to the Westminster scrutiny, 351; abolished some of the Irish nomination boroughs, 360; discontinued bribes to members, 382; by loans and lotteries, 386; advocated reform, 396, 397; his reform bill, 399; afterwards opposed reform, 402; his position as an orator, ii. 113; Tory principles never completely adopted by, ii. 146, 153 *n.*. 158; entered Parliament as a Whig, 152, 156; the leader of the Tories, 158; his first ministry a coalition, 157; his policy contrasted with Mr. Fox's, 153 *n.*, 159; his feelings towards the French Revolution, 163, 286; attempted coalitions with Fox, 165, 176; joined by portion of the Whigs, 166; the consolidation of his power, 168, 286; dangerous to liberty, 173; his liberal views on Catholic question, 174, iii. 115–123, 333; his retirement from office, ii. 175; his return, 176; the Tory party after his death, 179; member of the Constitutional Information Society, 270, 282; commences a repressive policy, 226; brings in the Seditious Meetings Bill. 319; opposes relief to dissenters, iii. 102–105, 109; his proposal for commutation of Irish tithes, 256; his Irish commercial propositions, 320; carried the Union with Ireland, 330; his India Bill, 381

Pitt, Mr. Thomas, moved to delay the grant of supplies, ii. 102

Pius IX., his brief appointing

bishops in England, iii. 228; and against the Queen's Colleges, 274
Placemen. *See* Officers under the Crown
Pledges, by members to constituents, considered, ii. 70
Plunket, Lord, the character of his oratory, ii. 120; his advocacy of Catholic relief, iii. 146, 150
Police, modern system of, iii. 403
Political associations, commencement of, ii. 265, 268, 270; for Parliamentary Reform, 269, 383; Protestant associations, 272-277, iii. 96; anti-slave trade, ii. 277, 404; democratic, 279, 281, 315, 324, 328; proceeded against, 292, 304; suppressed, 329, 343, 359; associations for suppressing sedition, 290, 367; for Catholic relief, 368; finally suppressed, 375; for repeal of the Union with Ireland, 393; Orange lodges, 400; trades' unions, 404; the Chartists, 407; the Anti-Corn Law League, 413
Ponsonby, Mr., chosen leader of the Whigs, ii. 182
Poole, borough, electoral corruption at, i. 338
Poor laws, the old and new systems, iii. 405; in Scotland and Ireland, 408
Population, great increase of, in the manufacturing districts, ii. 352; its effect on the position of the Church, iii. 211
Portland, Earl of (1696), the enormous grant to, by William III., recalled, i. 229
Portland, Duke of, headed the 'coalition,' i. 65; assisted George III. in opposing the Army Service Bill, 106; in office, 108
Post Office. *See* Letters, Opening at
Potwallers, the electoral rights of, i. 331
Poynings' Act, the, iii. 303

Pratt, Lord Chief Justice. *See* Camden, Lord
Presbyterians, in England, iii. 67; in Scotland, 68, 74; in Ireland, 70, 268. *See* Church of Scotland
Press, the, under censorship, ii. 239; from the Stuarts to accession of George III., 240-246; the attacks on Lord Bute, 247; general warrants, 249; the prosecutions of, 1763-1770, 250; publishers liable for acts of servants, 252; the rights of juries in libel cases, 253-263; the progress of free discussion, 264, 337, 364, 376, 383; caricatures, 265; laws for repression of the press, 318, 327, 330, 348, 358; the press and foreign powers, 332; the press not purified by rigour, 366; complete freedom of the press, 379; fiscal laws affecting, 380; public jealousies of, 382. *See also* Opinion, liberty of
Prince Regent. *See* Wales, Prince of
Printers, contest of the Commons with, ii. 33, 39. *See also* Debates in Parliament
Prisons, debtors', iii. 32; improved state of, 401
Privileges and elections committee, trial of election petitions before, i. 363
Privileges of parliament. *See* Parliament; Crown, the
Protection, &c., against Republicans' Society, the, ii. 291
Protestant associations, the, ii. 272, iii. 97; the petition, and riots, ii. 273, iii. 97. *See also* Orange Societies
Protestant Dissenters Ministers Bill, iii. 134
Protestant Catholic Dissenters, bill for relief of, iii. 106
Public meetings, commencement of political agitation by, ii. 265, 268; riotous meetings of the silk-weavers, 226; meetings to

support the Middlesex electors, 268; for Parliamentary reform, 1799, *ib.*; in 1795, 315; in 1831, 386; of the Protestant Association, 273, iii. 97; to oppose the Sedition and Treason Acts, ii. 324; in the manufacturing districts, 1819, 351; for Catholic relief, 373; for repeal (Ireland), 393; of the trades' unions, 405; the Chartists, 407, 410; the Anti-Corn Law League, 413; laws to restrain public meetings, 319, 343, 359

Public money, difficulties in the issue of, caused by George III.'s incapacity, i. 214; motions for, to be recommended by the crown, ii. 103

Public Opinion. *See* Opinion, Liberty of; Press, the; Political Associations; Public Meetings

Public Works Commission, the, separated from Woods and Forests, i. 255

Publishers, criminally liable for acts of servants, ii. 252

Puritans, the, under Queen Elizabeth, iii. 65; under James I. and Charles II., 71, 75; numbers imprisoned, 76. *See also* Dissenters

QUAKERS, number of, imprisoned, temp. Chas. II., iii. 76; motions for relief of, 112; excepted from Lord Hardwicke's Marriage Act, 151; admitted to the Commons on making an affirmation, 177. *See also* Dissenters

Qualification of members, the Acts repealed, i. 448

Quarter Sessions, courts of, county rates administered by, iii. 297; efforts to introduce the representative system into, *ib.*

Queen's Bench, Court of, the decision in favour of Stockdale, ii. 79, 80; compelled the sheriffs to pay over the damages, 80

Queensberry, Duke of, his rights as a peer of Great Britain and of Scotland, i. 286, 288

Queen's Colleges, Ireland, founded, iii. 273; opposition from Catholic clergy, 274

Quoad sacra ministers, the, in the Church of Scotland, iii. 249

RADICAL PARTY. *See* Party

Rawdon, Lord, moved an address to the Prince of Wales to assume the regency, i. 182

Reeves, Mr., his pamphlet condemned, ii. 325

Reform in parliament, arguments for, i. 393; advocated by Chatham, *ib.*; Wilkes, 394; the Duke of Richmond, *ib.*; the Gordon riots unfavourable to, 395; Pitt's motions, 396; discouraging effect of the French Revolution, 402; Earl Grey's first reform motions, 403; Sir F. Burdett's, 406, 407; Lord John Russell's, 408–413; Mr. Lambton's, 410; Lord Blandford's, 412; disfranchisement bills for bribery, *ib.*; O'Connell's motion for universal suffrage, 416; the dissolution of 1830, 417; impulse given by French Revolution, *ib.*; storm raised by Duke of Wellington's declaration, 418; Lord Brougham's motion, 420; Lord Grey's reform ministry, *ib.*; the first reform bill, 421; ministers defeated by the Commons, 141, 423; supported by the crown, *ib.*, 424; the dissolution of 1831, *ib.*; the second reform bill, 142, 424; the bill thrown out by the Lords, 142, 308, 424; proposed creation of peers, 143, 312, 425; resignation of the reform ministry, 143, 312, 426; they are supported by the Commons and recalled to office, 143, 312, 426; the third bill passed, 142, 312, 427; the act considered, 427; Scotch and Irish reform acts, 429, 430; the Irish franchise extended, 430; the political results of reform, 153, 431, ii. 96; bribery and bribery acts since reform, i. 431, 439; triennial parliaments, 441; vote by ballot, 445; reform, later measures for, 450; obstacles to parliamentary reform, 458; carried by the Whigs as leaders of the people, ii. 196; influence of, on parties, 230; on official emoluments, iii. 386; on law reform, and amendment of the criminal code, 387, 393; on the spirit and temper of the judges, 392; on the condition of the people, 404; on commercial and financial policy, 415; on Parliament, 422; the first reform meetings, 268; and in Ireland, iii. 318; reform discouraged from the example of the French Revolution, 284, 360, 364; repressed as seditious, 292–299, 313, 351; cause of, promoted by political agitation and unions, 383; review of reform agitation, 392; in abeyance during the last years of Lord Palmerston, iii. 428; revived by Earl Russell in 1866, 430; his reform bill, 431; its disastrous issue, 433; position of Earl of Derby's ministry in regard to reform, 435; their reform bill 1867, 436; how amended, 436; its ultimate form, 437; the Scotch Reform Act, 1868, 440; other supplementary measures of reform, 441; constitutional importance of these measures, *ib.*

Reformation, the, effect of, upon England, iii. 61; doctrinal moderation of, ii. 64; in Scotland, 68; in Ireland, 70

Reformatories instituted, iii. 403

Refugees. *See* Aliens

Regent, the Prince. *See* Wales, Prince of

Regency Act, the, of 1751, i. 168; of 1765, 171–174; the Princess of Wales excluded by Lords, and included by Commons in the Act, 173; the resolutions for a Regency Bill (1788–9), 180; proposed restrictions over the Regent's power to create peers, 278; the resolutions accepted by Prince of Wales, 185; the bill brought in, 189; its progress interrupted by George III.'s recovery, *ib.*; comments on these proceedings, 190; comparison of them to the proceedings at the Revolution, 192; the Regency Act of 1810, debates thereon, 208; resolutions for a bill agreed to, 210; laid before the Prince, 213; the act passed, *ib.*; the Regency Act of 1830, 221; the Regency Acts of Her Majesty, 223

Regent, the office of, the legal definition of, i. 183 and *n*. *See also* Wales, Prince of

Registration of births, marriages, and deaths, Act for, iii. 192

Religious liberty, from the Reformation to George III., iii. 60–82; commencement of relaxation of the penal code, 88; Corporation and Test Acts repealed, 157; Catholic emancipation carried, 168; admission of Quakers to the Commons by affirmation, 177; Jewish disabilities, 186; registration of births, marriages, and deaths, 192; the Dissenters' Marriage Bill, *ib.*; admission of dissenters to the universities, 195; dissenters' chapels, 199; church rates, 201. *See* also Church of England; Church in Ireland; Church of Scotland; Dissenters; Jews; Quakers; Roman Catholics

Reporters. *See* Debates in Parliament

Representation in Parliament, defects in, i. 328. *See also* Reform in Parliament

Revenues of the crown, its ancient possessions, i. 225; forfeitures, 226; grants and alienations, *ib.*; increase of revenues by Henry VII. and VIII., 227; destruction of the revenues under the Commonwealth, 228; recovery and subsequent waste, *ib.*; restraints on alienation of crown property, 229; constitutional result of the improvidence of kings, 230; settlement of crown revenues by parliament, 231; the revenues prior to the Revolution, *ib.*; the civil list from William III. to George III., 232; settlement of the civil list at the accession of George III., 234; charges thereon, 236; the surplus of hereditary revenues, 243; regulation of civil list, 244; other crown revenues, 235, 245; the loss of the Hanover revenues, 247; the Duchies of Lancaster and Cornwall, 248; private property of the crown, 249; provision for the royal family, *ib.*; mismanagement of the land revenues, 253; proposal for sale of crown lands, 254; appropriation of the proceeds, 255; pensions charged on lands and revenues, 256

Revenue commissioners, disqualified from sitting in parliament, i. 370;
—— Officers' Disfranchisement Bill carried by the Rockingham ministry, 61, 348

Revenue laws, restraints of, on personal liberty, iii. 25;—— offices thrown open to dissenters and Catholics, 111, 157, 168

Revolution, the, parliamentary government established at, i. 1; position of the crown since the Revolution, 2; revenues of the crown prior to, 231; the system of appropriation of grants to the crown commenced at, ii. 99; and of permanent taxation, 106; effect of on the press, 243; the church policy after, iii. 77

Revolutions in France, the effect of, on reform in England, i. 402, 405

Revolution Society, the, ii. 281

Rialton, Lady, case of, cited on the 'Bedchamber Question,' i. 157

Richard II., the revenues of his crown, i. 226

Richmond, Duke of, his motion respecting the regency, i. 172; for reduction of civil list, 239; statement as to the nominee members, 361; advocated parliamentary reform, 394; his motion on the Middlesex election proceedings, ii. 23

Roache, Mr., opposed Mr. Wilkes for Middlesex, ii. 14

Rockingham, Marquess, dismissed from his lord-lieutenancy for opposing the crown, i. 23; made premier, 33; his ministerial conditions, 34; influence of the crown in parliament exerted in opposition to him, 36, 39; dismissed from office, 40; his second administration, 60; carried the contractors, the civil list, and the revenue officers bills, 61, 241, 258, 348, 373, 389; and the reversal of the Middlesex election proceedings, ii. 26; denounced parliamentary corruption by loans, i. 385; his motion condemning the resolution against Wilkes, ii. 19; moved to delay the third reading of a land-tax bill, ii. 102; Whigs restored to power under, 151, 229; his death, 151; his administration consent to the independence of Ireland, iii. 315

Rolls, Master of the, sole judge not disqualified from parliament, i. 375

Roman Catholics, the first Relief Act, 1778, ii. 272, iii. 96; the riots in Scotland and London, 97, 98; the Scotch Catholics withdraw their claims for relief, ii. 272, iii. 98; the penal code of Elizabeth, iii. 63; Catholics under James I., Chas. I., and Cromwell, 71-74; the passing of the Test Act, 77; repressive measures, William III.-Geo. I., 79-81; the Catholics at accession of Geo. III., 82, 89, 94; their numbers, 83, n.; later instances of the enforcement of the penal laws, 96; bill to restrain education of Protestants by Catholics, 99; the case of the Protestant Catholic Dissenters, 106; another measure of relief to English Catholics, 1791, 106; first measures of relief to Catholics in Ireland and Scotland, 110, 111, 322; the Catholics and the militia, 114; effect of union with Ireland on Catholic relief, ii. 174, iii. 115; Catholic claims, 1801-1810, 118-132; the Army and Navy Service Bill, 126; the Regency not favourable to Catholic claims, 133; freedom of worship to Catholic soldiers, 134; the Catholic Question, 1811-1823, 136-150; treated as an open question, 140, 149; Acts for relief of Naval and Military Officers, 143; the Catholic Peers Bill, 147; the Catholic Question in 1823, 149; efforts for relief of English Catholics, 151; the laws affecting Catholic marriages, 152, 153; Office of Earl Marshal Bill, 154; Sir F. Burdett's motion, 155; State provision for Catholic clergy carried in the Commons, 156; the Duke of Wellington's ministry, ii. 191, iii. 156; repeal of the Corporation and Test Acts, 157; Catholic relief in 1828, 162; the Act, ii. 192-195, iii. 168, 335; the Catholic peers take their seats, 174; Catholic emancipation too long deferred, 175; number of Catholic members in House of Commons, 176; Bills for relief in respect of Catholic births, marriages, and deaths, 188-193; final repeal of penalties against Roman Catholics, 200; numbers, &c. of, in England, 222, 223; in Ireland, 268; the papal aggression, 227; the Maynooth and Queen's Colleges, 270; exclusion of Irish Catholics from the Corporations, 293; from the Parliament, 299, 303; number on Irish bench, 336. See also Corporations

Roman Catholic Officers Relief Bill, the, iii. 143

Romilly, Sir S., his opinion on the pledge required from the Grenville ministry, i. 110; his justification of the purchase of seats, 344; his efforts to reform the penal code, iii. 396

Ross, General, his complaint to the house, of court intimidation, i. 75

Rothschild, Baron L. N. de, the admission of, to Parliament, ii. 84; returned for London, iii. 182; claims to be sworn, 183

Rous, Sir J., his hostile motion against Lord North's ministry, i. 57

Royal family, the provision for, i. 249-253; power of the crown over, 262; exempted from Lord Hardwicke's Marriage Act, 263

Royal household, the, a question between the Whig leaders and the Regent, i. 126; the 'bedchamber question,' 155; profusion in George III.'s, 236; proposed reduction in William IV.'s household, 246

Royal Marriage Act (1772), i. 45, 264; arbitrary principles of this act, 267

Royal Sign-Manual Bill, the, to authorise George IV. to sign documents by a stamp, i. 216

Russell, Lord John (now Earl Russell), his first motions for reform, i. 408–416; his disfranchisement bills, 414; advocated the enfranchisement of Leeds, Birmingham, and Manchester, 415; moved the first reform bill, 422; his later reform measures, 450, 452, 456; attempts to form a free-trade ministry, ii. 212; in office, 216; retires from Lord Palmerston's ministry, 219; carries the repeal of Corporation and Test Acts, iii. 157; his efforts to obtain the admission of Jews to Parliament, 186; his Dissenters' Marriage Bills, 190, 192; his Registration Act, 192; his letter on the papal aggression, 230; overthrows the Peel ministry upon the Appropriation Question, 267; carries Municipal Reform, 283; and amendments of the criminal code, 398; succeeds Lord Palmerston as premier, 1865, 429; revives the question of reform, 430; his Reform Bill, 1866, 431; its disastrous issue, 432; his resignation, 433

ST. ALBANS disfranchised, i. 433

St. Asaph, Dean of, the case of, ii. 258

Salomons, Mr., the admission of, to parliament, ii. 84; returned for Greenwich, iii. 184; claims to be sworn, *ib.*

Salters (Scotland). *See* Colliers

Sandwich, Earl of, denounced Wilkes for the 'Essay on Woman,' ii. 6; 'Jemmy Twitcher,' 7 *n.*

Savile, Sir G., condemned the resolution against Wilkes, ii. 17; his bills to secure the rights of electors, 24; among the first to advocate Catholic relief, iii. 96; his bill to restrain Catholics from teaching Protestants, 99

Sawbridge, Mr., his motions for reform, i. 399; for shortening duration of parliament, 441

Say and Sole, Lord, his apology to Mr. Grenville for refusing a bribe, i. 380

Schism Act, the, iii. 82

Scot and lot, a franchise, i. 331

Scotland, the hereditary crown revenues of, i. 245; the pensions charged thereon, 257, 260; the consolidation of Scotch and English civil lists, 261;——the peerage of, 274; the representative peers of, *ib.*; Scottish peers created peers of Great Britain, 286; their rights, *ib.*; the probable absorption of the Scottish peerage into that of the United Kingdom, 289;——Scottish judges disqualified, 375;——the defective representation of Scotland prior to reform, 355; the Reform Act of, 429; the Tory party in, ii. 171, 180; literary influence of the Scotch Whigs, 181; alarm of democracy in, 292; trials for sedition and high treason, 293, 304, 351; the slavery of colliers and salters abolished, iii. 39; the reformamation in, 68; intimidation of parliament by the mob, ii. 271, iii. 97; motion for repeal of the Test Act (Scotland), 107; relief to Scotch Episcopalians, 108; to Scotch Catholics, 111; religious disunion in, 254; statistics of places of worship in, *ib.*, *n.*; municipal reform in, 287; new poor laws introduced into, 408; Reform Act, 1868, iii. 440

Scott, Sir John, the ministerial adviser during the regency proceedings, i. 192

Secret service money, issue of, restrained, i. 242; a statement of the amount of, 379

Secretary of State, the powers given to, in repression of libel, ii. 249, 347, iii. 2, 8; of opening letters, 44;——for the Colonies, date of formation of office, 360

Sedition and seditious libels, trials for, Wilkes and his publishers, ii. 248; the publishers of Junius's Letters, 252; the Dean of St. Asaph, 258; of Stockdale, 259; Paine, 280; Frost, Winterbotham, Briellat, and Hudson, 289; Muir and Palmer, 292, 296; Skirving, Margarot, and Gerrald, 297; Eaton, 301; Yorke, 313; Mr. Reeves, 325; Gilbert Wakefield and the 'Courier,' 331; of Cobbett, 334, 379; J. and L. Hunt and Drakard, 335; Hunt and Wolseley, 363; O'Connell and others, 394, 397; measures for repression of sedition in 1792, 285; 1794, 302; 1795, 317; 1799, 329; 1817, 342; 1819, 358; societies for the repression of, 290, 367. *See* also Treason, High, Trials for

Seditious Meetings Bills, the, ii. 319, 361; Libels Bill, 361

Selkirk, Earl of, supports the King on the Catholic question, i. 114

Septennial Act, efforts to repeal, i. 441; arguments against, 443; in favour, 444

Session, Court of (Scotland), proceedings of, in the patronage cases, iii. 242-247

Shaftesbury, bribery at, i. 340

Sheil, Mr., the character of his oratory, ii. 122

Shelburne, Earl of, dismissed from command for opposition to the crown, i. 28; his motion on the public expenditure, 53; on the intimidation of peers, 54; his administration, 62; supported by the royal influence, *ib.*; in office, ii. 151, 229; his concessions to America, 154

Sheridan, Mr., the character of his oratory, ii. 115; one of the Whig associates of the Prince of Wales, 161; adhered to Fox, 167; his motion on the state of the nation, 1793, 288; brought Palmer's case before the Commons, 299; urged repeal of the Habeas Corpus Suspension Act, 311, 312; his opposition to the Seditious Meetings Bill, 322

Shrewsbury, Duke of, his precedent cited as to the temporary concentration of offices in the Duke of Wellington, i. 148

Sidmouth, Viscount, withdrew from Pitt's administration, i. 101; took office under Lord Grenville, 103; joined George III. in opposing the Army Service Bill, 105; resigned office, 106; supported the King, *ib.*, 114; as premier, ii. 175; in office with the Whigs, 177; his repressive policy, 340, iii. 19: his circular to the lord-lieutenants, ii. 345; his employment of spies, iii. 41; his Dissenting Ministers Bill, 134. *See also* Addington, Mr.

Silk-weavers, riots by, ii. 266; bill passed for protection of their trade, 267

Sinecures, official and legal, abolished, iii. 386, 389

Six Acts, the, passed, ii. 358

Skirving, W., trial of, for sedition, ii. 297

Slavery, in England, ii. 35; in Scotland, 37; in the Colonies, 39

Slave Trade, the abolition of, advocated by petitions to parliament, ii. 64

Slave-trade Association, the, ii. 277. iii. 39

Smith, Mr. W., his anecdote as to bribery of members by Lord North, i. 382, *n.*; his Unitarian Marriages Bills, iii. 151, 154

Smith O'Brien, abortive insurrection by, ii. 400

Sommersett's (the negro) case, iii. 36

Spa Fields, meeting at, ii. 345

Speaker of the House of Commons, the, election of, during George III.'s incapacity, i. 183; altercations of members with, ii. 127; the increased authority of the chair, 128

Spencer, Earl, election expenses of, i. 337

Spies, employment of, by government, iii. 39; under Lord Sidmouth, 41; their employment considered, 42; the Cato Street conspiracy discovered by, 43

Spring Rice, Mr., his scheme for settling church rates, iii. 204; his speech on the state of Ireland, 334, *n.*

Stafford, Marquess of, his motion on the pledge exacted from the Grenville ministry, i. 112, 113

Stamp Act, the American, the influence of the crown exerted against its repeal, i. 36; iii. 346, 347

Stamp duty. *See* Newspapers

State trials. *See* Treason, High, Trials for

Steele, Sir R., opposed the Peerage Bill, i. 276

Stockdale, Mr., his actions against Messrs. Hansard for libel, ii. 78; committed for contempt, 80; the case of, ii. 259

Strangers, the exclusion of, from debates in parliament, ii. 27, 29; the attendance of ladies, 29; their exclusion, 52, *n.*; their presence permitted, 55

Strathbogie cases, the, ii. 245

Subject, liberty of, the earliest of political privileges, iii. 1; general warrants, 2; suspension of the Habeas Corpus Act, 10, 19, *n.*; impressment, 20; the restraints caused by the revenue laws, 25; imprisonment for debt, *ib.*, 31; for contempt of court, 26; arrest on mesne process, 29; debtors' prisons, 32; insolvent debtors, 34; negroes in Great Britain, 35; colliers and salters in Scotland, 38; spies and informers, 39; opening letters, 44; protection of aliens, 49; extradition treaties, 59

Sudbury, the seat for, advertised for sale, i. 337; disfranchised, 433

Sunderland, Lady, case of, cited on the 'Bedchamber Question,' i. 157

Supplies to the crown delayed, i. 80, 103, *n.*, 423; refused, 101; granted, 99

Supremacy, oath of, imposed by Queen Elizabeth, iii. 63; on the House of Commons, *ib.*; Catholic peers exempted from, 107, 147; altered by the Catholic Relief Act, 167, 168

Surrey, Earl of, his motion on the dismissal of the 'coalition' ministry, i. 76

Sussex, Duke of, voted against a Regency Bill, i. 211; his marriages, 270

TAXATION and expenditure, the control of the Commons over, i. 230, ii. 98, 104; temporary and permanent taxation, ii. 106

Temple, Earl, proscribed by the King for intimacy with Wilkes, i. 28; his agent in the exertion of the crown influence against the India Bill, 68; employed to dismiss the 'coalition,' 71; accepted and resigned office, 72

Tennyson, Mr., his motions to shorten the duration of parliament, i. 442

Thatched House Society, the, iii. 33

Thelwall, J., tried for high treason, ii. 306

Thistlewood, A., tried for high treason, ii. 345; for the Cato Street plot, 362

Thompson, proceeded against, for publishing debates, ii. 39; brought before Alderman Oliver, 42

Thurles, Synod of, opposition of, to the Queen's Colleges, iii. 274

Thurlow, Lord, the character of, ii. 160, iii. 392; his negotiations for George III. with the Whigs, i. 50; his advice to the King on his proposed retreat to Hanover, 64; co-operated in his opposition to the India Bill, 68; is made Lord Chancellor, 72; supported the resolutions for a Regency, 182; affixed the great seal to commissions under the authority of parliament, 188; announced the King's recovery, 189; resisted the Cricklade Disfranchisement Act, 340

Tierney, Mr., joins the Whigs, ii. 167; their leader, 174, 186

Tindal, Chief Justice, his opinion respecting the law of church rates, iii. 205

Tithes, the commutation of, iii. 218; in Ireland, 256, 269; associated with the question of appropriation, 264

Toleration Act, the, iii. 78; dissenters relieved from its requirements, 94, 135

Tooke, Horne, trial of, for high treason, ii. 305

Tory party, the, supplied the greater number of the 'King's friends,' i. 13; the ascendency of, under George IV., 129; the period of their ascendency in the House of Lords, 305. *See also* Party

Townshend, Mr., his manœuvre to secure a share in a loan, i. 384; his proposed land tax reduced by the Commons, ii. 101; his scheme for colonial taxation, iii. 350

Trades' unions, ii. 404; procession of, through London, 405; reception of their petition by Lord Melbourne, 406

Traitorous Correspondence Act, passing of, iii. 52

Transportation, commencement of the punishment, iii. 358; establishment of the Australian penal settlements, *ib.*; discontinued, 359, 400

Transubstantiation, Lord Grey's motion for relief from declaration against, iii. 144

Treasonable Practices Bill, the passing of the, ii. 317

Treason, High, trials for, of Walker, ii. 301; of Watt and Downie, 304; of Hardy and others, 307; of Watson, Thistlewood, and others, 345

Treasury warrants, the form of, for issue of public money during George III.'s incapacity, i. 214

Tutchin, beaten to death for a libel, ii. 244

UNDERWOOD, Lady C., married the Duke of Sussex, i. 270

Uniformity, Act of, of Queen Elizabeth, iii. 63; of Charles II., 75

Union, the, of England and Ireland, agitation for repeal of, ii. 393; effect of, on Catholic relief, iii. 115; the means by which it was accomplished, 330

Unions, political, established, ii. 383; their proceedings, 385; organise delegates, 388; proclamation against, 389; threatening attitude of, 390

Unitarians, the, toleration withheld from, iii. 78; further penalties against, 79; first motion for relief of, 109; relief granted, 136; laws affecting their marriages, 151–153

United Englishmen, Irishmen, and Scotsmen, the proceedings of, ii. 328, iii. 322, 323; suppressed by Act, ii. 329

United Presbyterian Church, the, iii. 236, n., 239

Universal suffrage, motions for, i. 395, 407, 416; agitation for, ii. 283, 316, 351, 408; in the colonies, iii. 371

Universities, the, of Oxford and Cambridge, admission of dissenters to, iii. 92; settlement of the question in 1871, 449; —— of London, 198

VAN DIEMEN'S LAND, a legislature granted to, iii. 359, 371; transportation to, discontinued, 359

Vestries, the common law relating to, iii. 276; Mr. S. Bourne's and Sir J. Hobhouse's Vestry Acts, 277

Veto Act, the (Church of Scotland) iii. 240; rescinded, 252

Victoria, Queen, her Majesty, her accession, i. 154; the ministry then in office, ib.; her household, ib.; the 'bedchamber question,' 155, 159; her memorandum concerning acts of government, 160; judicious exercise of her authority, 163; the Regency Acts of her reign, 223; her civil list, 246; her pension list, 261

Volunteers, the (Ireland), iii. 311; demand independence of Ireland, 312, 314; and Parliamentary Reform, 318

WAKEFIELD, bribery at (1860), i. 437

Wakefield, Mr. G., tried for libel, ii. 331

Waldegrave, Dowager Countess of, married to the Duke of Gloucester, i. 262

Waldegrave, Earl of, his opinion on the education of George III., i. 10

Wales, Prince of (George IV.), his character, i. 119; subject to court influence, 120; indifferent to politics, ib.; his separation from the Whigs, 123, 127; raised and disappointed their hopes, 121; proposals for their union with the Tories, 123, 125; the 'household question' between him and the Whigs, 126; debates as to his rights as Regent (1788), 178–181; disclaimed his right, 179; his reply to the Regency scheme, 184; accepted the resolutions, 185; his name omitted from the commission to open parliament, 188; the address from the Irish parliament, 194; accepted resolutions for Regency Bill (1810), 213; his civil list, 244; his debts, 250; his marriage with Mrs. Fitzherbert, 269; the guardianship over Princess Charlotte, 271; a member of the Whig party, ii. 161; deserts them, 167, 182; alleged effect of Mr. Fox's death upon his conduct, 178; attack on, when Regent, 342; unfavourable to Catholic claims, iii. 133

Wales, Princess Dowager of, her influence over George III., i. 10; advocated the exercise of his personal authority, 24; the insertion of her name into the Regency Bill, 174

Wales, the Princes of, the Duchy of Cornwall their inheritance, i. 248

Wales, progress of dissent in, iii. 213

Walker, T., tried for high treason, ii. 301

Walpole, Horace, cited in proof of parliamentary corruption, i. 335, n., 378, 383; appointment offered to his nephew, 369

Walpole, Mr., seceded from Lord Derby's ministry on question of reform, i. 455

Walpole, Sir R., opposed the Peerage Bill, i. 276; displaced from office by vote on an election petition, 364; bribery of members a system under, 377; the charges of bribery not proved, ib.; his remark on misrepresentations by reporters, ii. 38; his indifference to newspaper attacks, ii. 246; withdrew the Excise Bill, 266; his refusal to levy taxes on our colonies, iii. 343

Warburton, Bishop, his name affixed to notes on the 'Essay on Woman,' ii. 6

Ward, Mr., advocated vote by ballot, i. 447

Warrants. *See* General Warrants

Watson, J., tried for high treason, ii. 345

Watt, R., tried for high treason, ii. 304

Wellesley, Marquess, commissioned to form a ministry, i. 125; his ministry and the Catholic claims, iii. 139; his motion, ib.

Wellington, Duke of, obtained the consent of George IV. to Catholic emancipation, i. 137; anti-reform character of his ministry, 415; his anti-reform declaration, 418; failed to form an anti-reform ministry, 143, 312; formed a ministry with Peel, 146; his assumption of different cabinet offices during Peel's absence, 148; his opinion on the proposed creation of new peers, 313; his position as an orator, ii. 121; seceded from Canning on the Catholic question, 189; in office, 191, 196; secession of Liberal members from his cabinet, 192; beaten on repeal of the Test, &c. Acts, 192, iii. 157; his ministry and Catholic claims, ii. 192, iii. 156, 164; prosecutes the Tory press, ii. 378

Wensleydale, Baron, the life-peerage case (1856), i. 295

Wesley, the Rev. J., effect of his labours, iii. 85; number, &c. of Wesleyans, 222, 223

Westminster election (1784), Fox's vexatious contest at, i. 351; the scrutiny, and his return withheld, ib.; act passed in consequence, 353

Westminster Hall, public meetings prohibited within one mile of, ii. 344

West India duties, the, vested in the crown till the accession of William IV., i. 245

Westmoreland county, expense of a contested election for, i. 354

Weymouth, Lord, overtures to, from George III., i. 49; libelled by Wilkes, ii. 9; proposal that the Whigs should take office under him, ii. 150

Wharncliffe, Lord, his motion against the dissolution (1831), i. 141, ii. 88

Wheble, proceeded against for publishing debates, ii. 39; discharged from custody by Wilkes 41

Whig Club, the, meeting of, to oppose the Treason and Sedition Bills, ii. 323

Whig party, the, period of ascendency of, i. 8; regarded with jealousy by George III., 11; proscription of, under Lord Bute, 23; separation between them and Prince Regent, 120, 123; decline office on the 'household question,' 126; unsuccessful against

VOL. III.   K K

WHI

the ministry, 128; espouse the Queen's cause, 133; lose the confidence of William IV., 145; the period of their ascendency in the House of Lords, 305

Whitaker, Mr., opposed Wilkes for Middlesex, ii. 14

Whitbread, Mr., his remarks on the Perceval ministry, i. 111; moved to omit Lord Eldon's name from the council of regency, 206; his party estranged from Earl Grey's, ii. 182

White Conduit House, threatened meeting at, ii. 389

Whittam, a messenger of the house, committed by the Lord Mayor for apprehending a printer, ii. 42; his recognisance erased, 45; saved from prosecution, *ib.*

Wilberforce, Mr., promoter of the abolition of slavery, ii. 277; endeavours to obtain admission of Catholics to the militia, iii. 114

Wilkes, Mr., advocated parliamentary reform, i. 394; is denied his parliamentary privilege, ii. 3; proceeded against for libel in the 'North Briton,' 4; absconded and is expelled, 5; proceeded against in the Lords, 6; returned for Middlesex, 8; committed, *ib.*; his accusations against Lord Mansfield, 9; the question he raised at the bar of the house, *ib.*; expelled for libel on Lord Weymouth, *ib.*; re-elected, 13; again elected, but Luttrell seated by the house, 14; elected alderman, 15; efforts to reverse the proceedings against him, 16; his complaint against the deputy-clerk of the crown, 24; again returned for Middlesex, and takes his seat, 25; lord mayor, *ib.*; the resolution against him expunged, i. 61, ii. 26; instigated the publication of debates, 37; interposed to protect printers, 41; is

WIN

proceeded against by the Commons, 43; advocated pledges to constituents by members, 70; attacks Lord Bute and Mr. Grenville in the 'North Briton,' 247; proceeded against, 249, 267, iii. 3; brings actions against Mr. Wood and Lord Halifax, 4, 6; dogged by spies, 40

Williams, Sir Hugh, passed over in a brevet, for opposition to the court policy, i. 47

William III., his personal share in the government, i. 6; his sign manual affixed by a stamp, 218; the revenues of his crown, 228; grants to his followers, *ib.*; his civil list, 232; tried to influence parliament by the multiplication of offices, 369; the bribery of members during his reign, 377; popular addresses to, praying a dissolution of parliament, ii. 88; his church policy, iii. 78–80; towards the church of Scotland, 80; towards Catholics, 81

William IV., supported parliamentary reform, i. 138, 312, 424; dissolved parliament (1831), 114, 424; created sixteen peers in favour of reform, 309; exerted his influence over the peers, 143, 427; withdrew his confidence from the reform ministry, 145; suddenly dismissed the Melbourne ministry, 146; the Wellington and Peel ministry, 148; the Melbourne ministry reinstated, 153; regency questions on his accession, 219; his civil list, 245; opposed the reduction of his household, 246; surrendered the four and a half per cent. duties, 260; his declaration against the Appropriation Question, iii. 263

Williams, a printer, sentenced to the pillory, ii. 251

Windham, Mr., his position as an orator, ii. 117

Wines and Cider Duties Bill (1763),

the first money bill divided upon by the Lords, ii. 107
Winterbotham, Mr., tried for sedition, ii. 289
Wolseley, Sir C., elected popular representative of Birmingham, ii. 352; tried for sedition, 203
Wood, Mr. G., his Universities Bill, iii. 196
Woodfall, his trial for publishing Junius's Letter, ii. 253; the judgment laid before the Lords, 256
Woods, Forests, and Land Revenues Commission, i. 255; separated from the Public Works, 256
"Woman, Essay on," Wilkes prosecuted for publishing, ii. 6
Working classes, measures for the improvement of the, iii. 411. *See* also Middle Classes
Wortley, Mr. S., his motion for address to Regent to form an efficient ministry, i. 125

Wray, Sir C., opposed Fox at the Westminster election, i. 351
Writs for new members, doubt respecting issue of, during King's illness, i. 177; writs of summons for elections, addressed to returning officers, 450

YARMOUTH, freemen of, disfranchised, i. 434
York, Duke of, opposed the regency proceedings, i. 185, 211; his name omitted from the commission to open parliament, 187, 213; attached to Lady Mary Coke, 264
Yorke, Mr., enforced the exclusion of strangers from debates, ii. 52
Yorke, H. R., tried for sedition, ii. 313
Yorkshire, petition, the, for parliamentary reform, i. 398, ii. 63

THE END.

LONDON: PRINTED BY
SPOTTISWOODE AND CO., NEW-STREET SQUARE
AND PARLIAMENT STREET

Made in the USA
San Bernardino, CA
28 October 2017